Hegel and Whitehead

SUNY Series in Philosophy
ROBERT C. NEVILLE, Editor

and

SUNY Series in Hegelian Studies
QUENTIN LAUER, S.J., Editor

Hegel and Whitehead

CONTEMPORARY PERSPECTIVES ON SYSTEMATIC PHILOSOPHY

Edited by
George R. Lucas, Jr.
UNIVERSITY OF SANTA CLARA

State University of New York Press

DEDICATION

For Sam E. Dunnam IV

whose commitment to open philosophical inquiry
helped make these studies possible

ACKNOWLEDGEMENTS

Earlier versions of these essays were presented at an international symposium on Hegel and Whitehead, held at Fordham University from June 2 through June 6, 1984.

Support for this project was provided through a Research Conference grant from the Division of Research of the National Endowment for the Humanities (Washington, D. C.) and the Deutsche Forschungsgemeinschaft (Bonn, West Germany) as well as through the generosity of the Center for Process Studies (Claremont, CA), the Office of the Academic Vice President of the University of Santa Clara (Santa Clara, CA), the Wells Fargo National Bank, and numerous private donors.

Published by
State University of New York Press, Albany

© 1986 State University of New York

All rights reserved

Printed in the United States of America

No part of this book may be used or reproduced
in any manner whatsoever without written permission
except in the case of brief quotations embodied in
critical articles and reviews.

For information, address State University of New York
Press, State University Plaza, Albany, N.Y., 12246

Library of Congress Cataloging in Publication Data

Main entry under title:
Hegel and Whitehead.

(SUNY series in Hegelian studies) (SUNY series in philosophy)
Earlier versions of these essays were presented at an international symposium on Hegel and Whitehead, held at Fordham University, June 2-6, 1984.
Includes index.
1. Hegel, Georg Wilhelm Friedrich, 1770-1831—Congresses. 2. Whitehead, Alfred North, 1861-1947—Congresses. I. Lucas, George R. II. Series.
III. Series: SUNY series in philosophy.
B2948.H318 1986   192   85-9745
ISBN 0-88706-144-3
ISBN 0-88706-143-5 (pbk.)

Contents

Introduction

Hegel, Whitehead, and the Status of Systematic Philosophy   3
George R. Lucas, Jr.

I. *Historical Perspectives*

The Contemporary Significance of Hegel and Whitehead   17
Errol E. Harris

Realism, Idealism, and Speculative Philosophy   29
Tom Rockmore

Spinoza, Hegel, Whitehead: Substance, Subject, and Superject   39
Hans-Christian Lucas

II. *Metaphysics and Systematic Philosophy*

Types of Explanation in Hegel and Whitehead   61
Klaus Hartmann

Hegel and Whitehead on Totality: the Failure of a Conception of System   86
Robert C. Neville

A Plea for an Open, Humble Hegelianism   109
Jan Van der Veken

Hegel and Whitehead: Why Develop a Universal Theory?   121
Michael Welker

Concept and Concrescence: An Essay in Hegelian-Whiteheadian Ontology   133
George L. Kline

III. *Nature and Mind*

Hegel and Whitehead on Nature   155
J. N. Findlay

Whitehead and the Problem of the Knowledge of Nature 167
Ivor Leclerc

"The Life of Consciousness and the World Come Alive":
Nature and Self-Consciousness in Hegel's
Phenomenology 186
Quentin Lauer, S. J.

Negation and Contrast: The Origins of Self-Consciousness
in Hegel and Whitehead 207
Ernest Wolf-Gazo

IV. Moral, Aesthetic, and Religious Experience

The Process of Morality 219
Thomas Auxter

Hegel and Whitehead on Aesthetic Symbols 239
Curtis L. Carter

God and the World in Hegel and Whitehead 257
Brian Leftow

Narrative, Story, and the Interpretation of Metaphysics 268
David A. Pailin

The Meaning of Religious Experience in Hegel and
Whitehead 285
John E. Smith

Conclusion

The "Conning" of History 313
George Allan

Index 323

Introduction

George R. Lucas, Jr.
UNIVERSITY OF SANTA CLARA

Hegel, Whitehead, and the Status of Systematic Philosophy

Hegel and Whitehead rank alongside Aristotle and St. Thomas Aquinas among the foremost synoptic thinkers in the tradition of Western philosophy. The broad systematic scope of their respective philosophical enterprises has long suggested to critical observers a certain fundamental similarity of outlook between Hegel and Whitehead, both on the vocation and on the content of philosophy proper. Such observations have continually prompted an interest in critical comparative studies and evaluations of their respective philosophical systems. A tradition of critical Hegel-Whitehead scholarship can in fact be dated back some fifty years, beginning with comparative studies by Gregory Vlastos and R. G. Collingwood and continuing well into the present decade.[1]

While Hegel-Whitehead study thus represents an enduring and important tradition of secondary philosophical scholarship in its own right, the broader significance of the essays collected here transcends the boundaries of a narrow scholastic inquiry. In an important sense, Hegel and Whitehead symbolize (even as their critical comparative study recapitulates) the deep divisions between European and Anglo-American intellectual and cultural life, as well as the equally deep division in philosophy itself between practitioners of an analytic or critical method on the one hand and advocates of a more synoptic or speculative mode of inquiry on the other.

Hegelianism, in a variety of manifestations, continues as the dominant motif in continental European intellectual life. Moreover, the transformation of Hegelianism through Marxism now shapes the dominant political and cultural ethos in many sectors of the modern world. Thus, it is accurate to say that, for better or worse, one is denied a full appreciation of modern European intellectual and cultural life, as well as denied an adequate grasp of contemporary political and ideological conflict, in the absence of a critical appreciation of the Hegelian synthesis.

In Great Britain and America, however, the kind of synoptic or speculative pursuits of which Hegel is the principal modern example have long been out of fashion, and "appreciation" (or even "critical appreciation") is hardly the appropriate term to describe the reception of Hegel's thought in the contemporary Anglo-American tradition. G. E. Moore's refutation of idealism in 1903, for example, virtually insured the minority status of Hegel scholarship in Britain until quite recently. In America, the realist antagonism toward idealism, subsequently echoed by proponents of logical and linguistic analysis, caused Hegel scholarship to all but disappear in this country by World War II.

For much of his professional career, Whitehead reflected this Anglo-American milieu. His early work on the conceptual foundations of algebra, his pioneering collaboration with Bertrand Russell on the logical foundations of mathematics, and his subsequent interests in the conceptual foundations of modern science and relativity theory all reflect a thorough, and (for that period) thoroughly orthodox grounding in the philosophy of logical empiricism.

Yet Whitehead subsequently turned toward more speculative philosophical pursuits coincident with his arrival at Harvard University in the fall of 1924. For many critics, this "speculative turn," culminating in the publication of his seminal work in cosmology, *Process and Reality* (1929), appears both inexplicable and entirely out of line with his earlier philosophical and scientific interests.

Whitehead himself, however, explained his later speculative bent as stemming from a desire to explore in greater detail certain fundamental conceptual problems which his earlier studies in the philosophy of mathematics and natural science had raised in his own mind—a desire, as it were, to systematically rethink the logical, conceptual, and finally the necessary metaphysical foundations undergirding the revolutionary developments in early twentieth-century physical science. As Whitehead's biographer Victor Lowe reminds us, it is these sustained interests, rather than any presumed "existential crises" arising from the tragic aftermath of World War I, which must finally be understood as the basis for Whitehead's controversial "speculative turn."[2]

It is first and foremost, however, this speculative turn which has come to link Whitehead with Hegel in the minds of many of the former's disciples and critics. For, having attempted to delineate a broad spectrum of general and inclusive cosmological categories, Whitehead proceeded to explore the application (as well as the further refinement) of his metaphysical-conceptual scheme to virtually every area of human experience and inquiry. Excepting any detailed treatment of ethics and political philosophy, Whitehead addressed his interest and attention to the natural and the social sciences and their history, to aesthetics and the role of creative imagination in the logic of scientific discovery (long before Karl Popper addressed such issues), to the impact of science on society, to the dialectical interplay of order and creativity (or, as Whitehead termed it, freedom and discipline) in the evolution of human culture, as well as to the role of education in the shaping of culture. All of this "culminates" (as Whitehead's disciples would characterize the matter) in the formulation of a particularly unique and imaginative mode of philosophical theism which, in its own right, has proved to be a major impetus to twentieth-century theological speculation. These features of Whitehead's later speculative period thus invite apparently obvious comparisons with the scope and impact of Hegel's philosophical synthesis, which addresses many of the same issues and had similar historical consequences in the nineteenth century.

While he willingly confessed a modest indebtedness to F. H. Bradley, Whitehead repeatedly denied any direct acquaintance with Hegel's thought and consistently eschewed any interest in Hegel's philosophy, which he once characterized as "complete nonsense."[3] Notwithstanding, the perceived aura of "speculative Hegelianism" cast a certain shadow over Whitehead's later "American" period. Whitehead's later thought, for example, has never been particularly well-known or influential in his homeland, where it has historically been regarded as something of an anomaly. While a broad-based and lively interest in Whitehead's later philosophy has developed in the United States from the 1930s to the present, Whiteheadian scholarship remains a distinctive and vigorous but decidedly minority tradition in American philosophy, largely owing to its speculative and highly technical character. Indeed, Whitehead's philosophy has come to exert a far more pervasive influence in the disciplines of religious studies, philosophy of religion, and American theology than in philosophy proper. It is not unusual for scholars in comparative literature, history, and the fine arts to have a greater command and appreciation of Whitehead's work than professional philosophers. Perhaps the greatest irony is that, despite its apparent "Hegelian" undertones, Whitehead's philosophy has until recently enjoyed only a scattered following in Europe.

* * *

The relative status and perceived significance of Hegel in Great Britain and America and of Whitehead in Europe have shifted dramatically in recent years in a manner which essentially prompted the studies of their thought which follow in this volume. J. N. Findlay's radical re-assessment of Hegel in 1958[4] sparked a renewed interest in Hegel studies in Great Britain and especially in America— as attested by the founding of active and vigorous Hegel Societies in the U.S. in 1969 and in Great Britain at Oxford University during the 1970s. Charles Taylor's recent masterly survey of Hegel's thought has completed the process of re-assimilation of Hegel studies as a recognized and significant area of Anglo-American philosophical inquiry.[5]

In 1978, Prof. Charles Hartshorne was invited to inaugurate, through a visiting professorship, a new European Center for Process Studies at the University of Leuven in Belgium, under the direction of Prof. Dr. Jan Van der Veken. Since that time, a number of European and American scholars have taught and studied at this center, and several doctoral dissertations have been completed interpreting the significance of Whitehead's philosophy in the context of contemporary European intellectual trends. Verlag Karl Alber in Freiburg and Munich has recently undertaken an ambitious publication program in Whitehead studies, encompassing a number of recent studies of his philosophy by Swiss and German scholars,[6] while several of Whitehead's own works have recently been translated into German.[7] These recent activities complement the earlier efforts of established European Whitehead scholars, such as Reiner Wiehl in Germany and Alix Parmentier in France.[8]

The need for a thorough international exchange among Hegel and Whitehead scholars, incorporating these new developments in the scholarship of both fields, emerged with a sense of urgency in 1981. In August of that year, the Deutsche Forschungsgemeinschaft and the Allgemeine Gesellschaft für Philosophie in West Germany sponsored an international conference on Whitehead's philosophy in Bonn, involving the participation of a significant number of prominent European, British, and American scholars. A follow-up conference took place at Bad Homburg in October, 1983. The present collection of essays intends both to continue this European-American dialogue and to focus discussion and scholarly investigation precisely at the point of greatest present concern to the participants in that exchange thus far: *viz.*, the need for a critical comparative assessment of the philosophies of Whitehead and Hegel, combined with a greater critical awareness of Whiteheadian scholarship among European scholars knowledgeable about Hegel and a greater critical awareness of contemporary Hegel scholarship among Anglo-American Whiteheadians.

The pertinent issues emergent thus far in this dialogue can be summarized as follows. European scholars, on the basis of a customary familiarity with Hegel's thought, have been quick to notice more than a casual resemblance between Hegel and Whitehead. Some of these scholars perceive in Whitehead, moreover, a possible stimulus toward a broader and more favorable assessment of the diverse pluralism of philosophical pursuits actually achievable within the Anglo-American tradition, even as they perceive among Whitehead scholars a more sympathetic assessment of Continental traditions than is generally customary among English-language philosophers. It is worth noting that more customary assessments of the Anglo-American tradition by many Continental philosophers rival the smug and unflattering characterizations of Hegel and the contemporary Continental tradition by British and American intellectuals. The Whitehead-Hegel exchange thus holds promise of a welcome avenue around this obstacle of mutual insularity and often profound ignorance.

Even more significantly, Whitehead is perceived as having developed a systematic perspective which appears "Hegelian" in many respects, but in which the natural sciences are *not* portrayed as discontinuous with other areas of human inquiry. Thus, his philosophy presents European scholars whith a challenging alternative to the dominance of the older *Geisteswissenschaft* tradition of Whilhelm Dilthey and other neo-Kantians, as well as to the more recent hermeneutic philosophers of the critical circle (including Hans-Georg Gadamer and Paul Ricoeur)—all of whom insist upon an unbridgable distinction in both method and content between the disciplines of the natural and the "human" sciences.[9]

* * *

So elaborate and intimidating are the major works of Hegel and Whitehead separately considered, however, that mastery of both simultaneously to a degree sufficient for adequate scholarly comparison and criticism of both is considered difficult to attain. So different are the respective methodological approaches and literary styles employed by these two philosophers that serious doubts have been raised regarding the legitimacy of some of the critical comparisons which *have* been attempted in the past.¹⁰ Indeed, it often appears that the sole common characteristic of Hegel and Whitehead is the penchant of both for obscure and highly idiosyncratic philosophical vocabulary which, as George L. Kline subsequently observed, "has been more often deplored than analyzed."¹¹

I have already noted that Whitehead himself denied any genuine knowledge of or interest in Hegel, and for much of his professional career he allied himself with the early analytic traditions of logical empiricism, and later critical realism, from which perspectives Hegel's particular version of "absolute" idealism was regarded as anathema. Furthermore, Whitehead's principal sources of inspiration and perceived strengths as a philosopher derived in large degree from his training and achievements in mathematics and the physical sciences. Hegel's *Naturphilosophie*, by contrast, is generally perceived as derivative and obscure, the least significant component of his larger philosophical system.

The principal substance of the Hegelian synthesis lies in the realm of what Hegel himself termed *objektiver Geist:* social ethics, political philosophy, and the philosophy of history. To be sure, Whitehead in *The Function of Reason* (1929) and *Adventures of Ideas* (1933) sketches both a theory of cultural development and a philosophy of history of sorts. But he is generally faulted for subordinating ethics to aesthetics (in a manner consonant with the prevailing fashion in Anglo-American philosophy during the early decades of the twentieth century) as well as for largely ignoring the importance of social and political philosophy in his overall synthesis. Once again, the only apparent area of real similarity lies in the widely shared view that both philosophers, in distinctive fashions, exemplified the kind of comprehensive "system-building" and speculative pursuits which are less in professional vogue at present than at any other period in the history of Western philosophy.

Critical comparisons of Hegel with Whitehead, however, invite attention to recent reassessments of the neglected or heretofore misinterpreted aspects of each. The foregoing account of the relative unimportance of an understanding of the natural sciences in Hegel's thought has been challenged by recent attempts to reinvigorate and reinterpret Hegel's philosophy of science and concept of nature.¹² Likewise, the conventional view of the unimportance and incongruity of moral and political philosophy within the framework of Whitehead's aesthetically oriented cosmology has been challenged by comparatively recent explorations of the nascent implications of that cosmology for ethics and political thought.[13]

These recent reinterpretations of Hegel and Whitehead invite response to the question regarding the extent to which the two philosophical systems might be interpreted as mutual correctives. That is, to what extent is it plausible to regard Whitehead as having provided a systematic explication of the kind of empirical and logical foundations necessary for any metaphysical system stressing an historically oriented "event-ontology," with Hegel supplying the more complete account of the moral, social, and political ramifications of any such ontology? Given the implicit role of cosmology or "worldviews" in shaping moral and political ideologies, especially in the case of Hegel and Marx, the investigation of this question promises to be much more than a mere exercise in abstract academic esoterica.

Finally, Hegel and Whitehead, as noted, provide the two most important modern and widely influential illustrations of post-Kantian synoptic philosophy—what is often referred to less generously as "mere speculative system-building." Thus, this volume responds directly to a major issue which currently divides the profession of philosophy: *viz.*, whether the synoptic or "speculative" tradition which both philosophers so clearly exemplify still offers anything of value to the discipline of philosophy. That tradition and both the philosophers here considered have frequently been the focus of unprecedented hostility, principally within the tradition of twentieth-century Anglo-American thought. Such hostility has had the beneficial effect of generating substantive and useful criticisms of the obvious inherent limitations of systematic thought generally, and of the philosophical systems of Whitehead and Hegel in particular. Such attitudes have the unfortunate effect, however, of driving a wedge between the philosophical traditions of different cultures and languages—one which often appears as much a function of mere prejudice and avoidable ignorance as it does a function of authentic and thorough critical evaluation.

The vocation of philosophy has neither been enriched nor been well served by this deplorable state of affairs.[14] The vocation of philosophy in particular and the cause of fruitful cross-cultural intellectual exchange in general are very much enhanced, by contrast, in the careful and scholarly comparative and critical studies in this volume. The issues raised in these essays bear in a significant way upon the future development of the discipline of philosophy itself, whatever the individual differences of opinion or purely subjective preferences for or against the synoptic tradition, or for or against the particular philosophers here discussed.

As a result, this collection should prove interesting not only to scholars specializing in either Hegel or Whitehead, but also to philosophers of the natural and social sciences, and to scientists interested in the Whiteheadian and/or Hegelian influences on the work of distinguished colleagues such as Ilya Prigogine, David Bohm, and the late Rene Dubos and Werner Heisenberg. These essays will hold obvious importance for contemporary theologians on both sides of the Atlantic, as well as for those interested in fostering a more fruitful "ecumenical" dialogue between proponents of analytic and Continental philosophy. And finally, this collection addresses the needs and interests of those who perhaps respect Richard Rorty's rejection of system-building, but hold, notwithstanding, that the quest for an inclusive or "synoptic" view of things is not therefore without genuine value.[15]

In thus recounting the manner in which past and present research has revealed striking anticipation and contributions from both Hegel and Whitehead toward contemporary perspectives in a variety of fields (even among those professionals who might themselves be unaware of, or even vehemently deny such influence and such modernity to these philosophers) I have established a strong case for the importance of the essays which follow—essays which effectively transcend, even as they collectively address, the current deep divisions within the profession of philosophy itself.

Notes

1. Cf. G. R. Lucas, *The Genesis of Modern Process Thought* (London and Metuchen, N.J.: Scarecrow Press, 1983), pp. 99–135.

2. Cf. Victor Lowe, "Alfred North Whitehead: A Biographical Perspective," *Process Studies*, 12, no. 3 (Fall, 1982), pp. 137–147. Thus Lowe has consistently denied any radical division in Whitehead's thought, preferring to see the various different "periods" as in fact representing a sustained and orderly development of Whitehead's systematic philosophical interests. See Lowe's *Understanding Whitehead* (Baltimore: The Johns Hopkins University Press, 1962) and the first volume of Lowe's detailed intellectual biography of Whitehead (Johns Hopkins Press, 1985).

3. *Essays in Science and Philosophy* (New York: Philosophical Library, 1948), p. 10. The absence of any direct influence of Hegel on Whitehead is

documented more fully in G. R. Lucas, *Two Views of Freedom in Process Thought: A Study of Hegel and Whitehead* (Chico, CA: Scholars Press, 1979), ch. I, sec. 2.

4. J. N. Findlay, *Hegel: A Re-examination* (Oxford: Oxford University Press, 1958).

5. Charles Taylor, *Hegel* (Cambridge: Cambridge University Press, 1975).

6. E.g.: Reto Luzius Fetz, *Whitehead: Prozessdenken und Substanzmetaphysik* (Freiburg and Munich: Verlag Karl Alber, 1981); Ernest Wolf-Gazo, *Whitehead: Einführung in seine Kosmologie* (Verlag Karl Alber, 1980); *Whitehead und der Prozessbegriff*, eds. Wolf-Gazo and Harald Holz (Karl Alber, 1984); *Prozessphilosophie: Eine Einführung* (forthcoming, 1985).

7. *The Function of Reason* was translated by Eberhard Bubser, *Funktion der Vernunft* (Stuttgart: Reclam, 1976); *Process and Reality* has been recently translated by Hans-Guenter Holl, *Prozess und Realität: Entwurf einer Kosmologie* (Frankfurt: Suhrkamp Verlag, 1979).

8. Wolf-Gazo provides a detailed history of the influence of Whitehead in German-language philosophy in "Die Whitehead-Rezeption im deutschen sprachraum seit 1945," in *Whitehead und der Prozessbegriff*, pp. 53–70, updating an important earlier study of the broader reception of Whitehead in Europe by George L. Kline, "Whitehead in the Non-English-Speaking World," *Process and Divinity—The Hartshorne Festschrift*, eds. Reese and Freeman (LaSalle, IL: Open Court, 1964), pp. 235–268.

9. It is interesting to note that contemporary European interest in Whitehead already has provided in advance a substantive parallel to the rhetorical challenge which Prof. Adolph Grünbaum issued to the dominance and perceived inadequacies of the "Geisteswissenschaft-hermeneuticist" approach of Continental thought in his 1982 Presidential Address to the Eastern Division of the American Philosophical Association in Baltimore: *Proceedings and Addresses of the American Philosophical Association*, 57, no. 1 (September, 1983), pp. 5–31. This is, however, hardly an approach which Prof. Grünbaum himself would find congenial as an alternative—although it *is* an approach now being recommended by scholars who are somewhat more knowledgeable about the "Geisteswissenschaft-hermeneuticist" tradition than Prof. Grünbaum himself.

10. Klaus Hartmann, for example, challenges the adequacy of earlier comparative studies in his essay for this volume on "Types of Explanation in Hegel and Whitehead."

11. George L. Kline, "Some Recent Reinterpretations of Hegel's Philosophy," *The Monist*, 47, no. 1 (January 1964), p. 34.

12. Cf. my essay, "A Re-interpretation of Hegel's Philosophy of Nature," *Journal of the History of Philosophy*, 22, no. 1 (January, 1984), pp. 103–113, as contrasted with Milic Capek's recent study of Hegel's *Naturphilosophie* which sharply criticizes Hegel's technical competence in science while offering a more sympathetic assessment of the substantive *philosophical* issues raised there: "Hegel and the Organic View of Nature," *Hegel and the Sciences*, eds. R. S. Cohen and M. W. Wartofsky (Amsterdam: D. Reidel, 1984), pp. 109–121. Prof. Michael J. Petry's extensive three-volume commentary with English translation of Part II of Hegel's *Encyclopedia* helped refocus attention on this neglected dimension of Hegel's thought. Cf. *Hegel's Philosophy of Nature*, 3 vols. (Oxford: Oxford University Press, 1970). See also Errol E. Harris, "Hegel and the Natural Sciences," *Beyond Epistemology: New Studies in the Philosophy of Hegel*, ed. Frederick G. Weiss (The Hague: Martinus Nijhoff, 1974), pp. 129–153. See also Dietrich V. Englehardt, "Das chemische System der Stoffe, Krafte und Prozesses in Hegel's Naturphilosophie und der Wissenschaft seiner Zeit," and Hans Querner, "Die Stufenfolge der Organismen in Hegels Philosophie der Natur," both in *Hegel-Studien*, 11 (1974), pp. 125–139 and 153–163, respectively.

13. A pioneering dissertation on this topic written by Lynn Belaief at Columbia University in 1963 under the supervision of Justus Buchler and John Herman Randall has just been revised for publication: *Toward a Whiteheadian Ethics* (Landham, MD: University Press of America, 1984). See also Richard S. Davis, "Whitehead's Moral Philosophy," *Process Studies*, 3 (Summer, 1973), pp. 75–90, which includes a critique of Belaief's dissertation. Prof. Douglas Sturm of Bucknell University assesses the structure and probable classification of a Whiteheadian political philosophy in "Process Thought and Political Theory," *Review of Politics*, 41 (July, 1979), pp. 375–401, while John B. Cobb, Jr. explores the implications of Whitehead's thought as the basis for a political theology in his recent book, *Process Theology as Political Theology* (Philadelphia: Westminster Press, 1982). See also Cobb and W. Widick Schroeder, eds., *Process Philosophy and Social Thought* (Chicago: Center for the Scientific Study of Religion, 1981).

14. Prof. John E. Smith of Yale University, in a recent Presidential Address for the Eastern Division of the American Philosophical Association, assessed the extent of the damage which this state of mutual prejudice and uninformed a priori bias has done to the profession of philosophy. In particular, he marvels at the novel tactic which this deep ideological division has produced, in which one's intellectual opponents are no longer simply themselves critically evaluated or refuted, but both they and their particular philosophical interests are simultaneously denied a legitimate standing in

the field! Cf. John E. Smith, "The New Need for a Recovery of Philosophy in America," *Proceedings and Addresses of the American Philosophical Association,* 56 (September, 1982), pp. 5-18.

15. Cf. *Philosophy and the Mirror of Nature* (Princeton: Princeton University Press, 1979). Robert C. Neville, writing in this volume, shares Rorty's suspicion of the quest for completeness, wholeness, or totality—but nonetheless finds it urgent to continue the systematic enterprise in a more limited and pluralistic fashion.

I
Historical Perspectives

Errol E. Harris
CUMBRIA, ENGLAND

The Contemporary Significance of Hegel and Whitehead

The most common reason we are given for the impossibility of returning to a system like Hegel's is its incompatibility with the outlook and attitude established by contemporary science. The advance of modern science and technology, Professor Charles Taylor has told us, has burst the bounds of the Hegelian system and has shattered the ideals and illusions of nineteenth-century Romanticism. Nobody could make similar allegations about Whitehead, whose metaphysic is intimately and intricately bound up with contemporary scientific and mathematical concepts. If a close parallel can be found between the thought of Whitehead and that of Hegel, Professor Taylor's strictures will seem rather less formidable. That there is such a parallel, I am firmly convinced and long ago tried to demonstrate.[1]

But Whitehead's metaphysic is today, no less than Hegel's, discredited in many quarters, not only as obscure and fanciful, but also as a thoroughly outdated and old-fashioned attempt at comprehensive system-building. In this respect, at least, it is generally admitted that Whitehead and Hegel are alike: they are both notorious system builders. And metaphysical systems are nowadays regarded as disreputable—each such system representing both an arrogant claim to omniscience and a pontifical pretence of finality.

In the light of contemporary scientific theory, however, any such criticism is perverse. The theories of modern physics and biology tend in different but complementary ways toward a holism which provides actual empirical evidence in favour of metaphysical systems like those of Hegel and Whitehead, and which further affords a foundation and even a demand for just such system-building embodying principles and types of explanation as first clearly set out by R. G. Collingwood in his *Essay on Philosophical Method*. I have tried elsewhere to demonstrate all this at length, not only theoretically, but in practice.[2] It would not be appropriate now to repeat the details of those attempts, and the more stubborn opponents of systematization will have to refer to them directly. Meanwhile, let us recall that Hegel castigated any unsystematic philosophizing as the mere expression of whimsical opinion, unworthy of the name of *Wissenschaft.* (Cf. *Enzyclopädie,* Sect. 14).

Thomas Kuhn, whose work has been taken seriously and has been widely discussed in recent years by both philosophers and scientists, contends that all science operates under the aegis of what he calls a 'paradigm', which essentially includes a conception of the overall nature of things and their fundamental characteristics. This clearly implies that all science presupposes a metaphysical system of some sort, the explicit formulation of which, one would have thought, is the appointed task of the philosopher. If any such is to be sought today it is hardly likely to be forthcoming from analysts or existentialists, and if guidance and inspiration is to be found in recent philosophy at all we shall have little alternative but to go back to Whitehead. A comparison of Whitehead with Hegel should, for these reasons, repay close study; and when it is made it discloses an outstanding example of two great minds, almost a century apart, independently thinking astonishingly alike.

Whitehead is known and widely revered today as the father of process philosophy, as opposed to the more traditional metaphysics of substance. In one of his earlier works, *The Concept of Nature,* he protests emphatically against the idea of substance, maintaining that the primary reality consists of events.[3] He develops this notion into a conception of reality, the fundamental principles of which are creativity and process. These concepts are not commonly associated with Hegel, yet they are as essential and as fundamental to Hegel's position as they are to Whitehead's and in much the same way.

Hegel asserts, in the introduction to his *Enzyklopädie,*[4] that dialectic "is the principle of all life, all movement and all activity in the actual world *(in der Werklichkeit).*" For Hegel, dialectic is the fundamental principle of all reality. Its basic character and category is Becoming, the ubiquitous and fundamental movement of thought, of Nature and of Spirit, which issues in the absolute Idea, as well as in absolute Spirit. Hegel frequently describes Spirit and the Idea as "eternal restlessness," and in the *Enzyclopädia* he says, "The Idea is essentially process insofar as it is absolute negativity and therefore dialectical" (Sect. 215).

Objection might be raised that process and creativity in Whitehead are not the same kind of movement as dialectic in the Hegelian system, because they do not involve negativity and contradiction in the same way; but any such objection would be a misconception of either or both theories. For Whitehead the process is one of concrescence, as it also is for Hegel, the coming into being of the concrete. In both cases, the concrete is a systematic ordered whole; and it is with reference to this alone that the significance and function of negativity can be properly understood. For both thinkers it is in fact the same, though stressed rather differently by each.

To give an adequate account of the role of negativity in either of these two philosophies would require at least a paper to itself. Here I shall have to be brief and selective. For Hegel, "the truth is the whole," and at every stage of the dialectic the whole is being developed (or is developing itself) out of partial and abstract elements, the true natures of which are solely determined by their place in the whole. Taken in isolation, therefore, the whole immanent in each of them demands their supplementation by what they omit, their "other," which, because it is what they exclude, negates them. Negation is the principle of distinction and differentiation, essential equally to the precise discrimination of parts and the integrative concrescence of the whole; for no undifferentiated whole is more than an abstraction, and the true and ultimate whole, "the true form in which the truth exists," is always and only a fully differentiated system.[5] The dialectical function of negativity, in consequence, is nothing other than the nisus towards the whole, the immanence of which in the part demands its other, defines its limits, and unites it with its opposite in a systematically differentiated totality. It is precisely this unity of opposites in their mutual distinction (the unity of being and nothing) which is becoming.

For Whitehead, concrescence is primarily the grasping into the unity of the actual entity of the multiplicity of nature (in fact, of the whole universe) by each and every actual occasion; and negativity appears in negative prehensions. "A negative prehension," Whitehead tells us, "is the definite exclusion of that item from positive contribution to the subjects's [i.e., the actual entity's] own real internal constitution." It nevertheless "expresses a bond."[6] That negative prehensions serve the same function for Whitehead as for Hegel is illustrated by the following passage from *Process and Reality:*

The importance of negative prehensions arises from the fact, that (i) actual entities form a system, in the sense of entering into each other's constitutions, (ii) that by the ontological principle every entity is felt by some actual entity, (iii) that, as a consequence of (i) and (ii), every entity in the actual world of a concrescent actuality has some gradation of real relevance to that concrescence, (iv) that, in consequence of (iii), the negative prehension of an entity is a positive fact with its emotional subjective form, (v) there is a mutual sensitivity of the subjective forms of prehensions, so that they are not indifferent to each other, (vi) the concrescence issues in one concrete feeling, the satisfaction.[7]

From this it is evident that negative prehensions are necessary to the grasping into unity of the entire universe by each actual occasion, and the systematic character of that unity determines their relevance. For this reason, in Whitehead's thought as in Hegel's, negativity always has a positive aspect and is always significant negation. And the negative prehension with its emotional subjective form is an element in that "lure for feeling" which appetitively urges on the concrescent process toward satisfaction. Thus the unity of the actual entity is an expression and a reflection of the ultimate unity of the universe. This is as true for Whitehead as it is for Hegel, as will presently appear.

Although both of these philosophers are eminently and unquestionably process philosophers, neither of them abandons the concept of substance absolutely. What they do is to reinterpret it, transforming it from that of a solid and static substrate to a fluid and dynamic activity of self-differentiation by the universal whole. That they are alike in this respect is evident from their respective attitudes to Spinoza's doctrine. "In the analogy with Spinoza," Whitehead writes, "his one substance is for me the one underlying activity of realisation individualising itself in an interlocked plurality of modes. Thus the concrete fact is process."[8] The process is that of self-individualization by the totality which is the universe, and which is constituted in and by the mutual prehension of its modal differentiations. This is precisely what Hegel's dialectical becoming effects.

Hegel criticizes Spinoza's conception of substance (I think unjustifiably) as lacking any principle of self-differentiation which can explain the diversity of its attributes and modes, so that substance remains the only genuine reality, in which all differences are absorbed and obliterated.[9] Although I think this misrepresents Spinoza, it makes Hegel's intention clear to recast the conception of substance as a concrete universal, the immanent principle of self-particularization, or as he puts it, the universal which has its particulars in itself. In the final outcome, Hegel insists that this universal is the absolute Idea, which is infinite restlessness, and its ceaseless activity is that of self-differentiation and self-unification in one—the essential drive and nature of dialectic.

That Whitehead's process of concrescence is always and essentially one of integration, uniting into a whole a multiplicity of differences, is beyond question; and that every such whole is the expression of the universal whole is not difficult to demonstrate. Likewise, in every such whole the principle of order and unification is always immanent. About the first of these assertions Whitehead leaves us in no doubt when he writes:

'Creativity' is the universal of universals characterizing ultimate matter of fact. It is that ultimate principle by which the many, which are the universe disjunctively, become the one actual occasion, which is the universe conjunctively. It lies in the nature of things that the many enter into complex unity.[10]

The universe disjunctively is the multiplicity of actual entities, each of which prehends into unity all the rest, and so becomes the universe conjunctively. The universe is the macrocosm of which each occasion is the microcosm. Both, therefore, are different versions, or expressions, of the same whole; and the principle of unity in the former is immanent equally in the latter.

The role played by "eternal objects" in the process of concrescence reinforces this immanence of the whole in each and all of the parts. Just what Whitehead means by "eternal objects" is a matter for debate, but some statements about them can be made without undue hesitation. In *Science and the Modern World* he lists as examples, "colours, sounds, scents, geometrical characters" (p. 151), and he also says that they are "transcendent entities," that have in the past been called "universals," and "are thus, in their nature, abstract" (p. 228). It is only in their nature or "essence" that they are abstract, however, not in their ingression into actual occasions. He defines them further, in *Process and Reality*, as "potentialities of definiteness" which function as a "lure for feeling." *How* something is felt is the mode of ingression of an eternal object into the actual entity concerned (PR 131). Further, they are the objects of conceptual prehensions, the "only operations of 'pure' mentality," and are identified with Platonic forms (PR 49, 70). It seems fairly clear from all this that Whitehead intends eternal objects to be concepts, abstract if taken in their essential nature, but, in their ingression into actual entities, principles of structure determining the way in which prehensions are felt and ordered.

In Whitehead's theory every actual entity prehends every other, and the subjective form of its prehensions is regulated by eternal objects. As so formed it achieves satisfaction and becomes a superject which is objective to subsequent occasions. Thus eternal objects, the prehensions of which constitute the mental pole of every actual entity, are implicit in every prehension, physical or mental; in other words, concepts are "at work" in all reality. And this is what Hegel tells us in the introduction to his *Wissenschaft der Logik*.

The immanence of concepts in all reality is emphasized in Whitehead's account of the primordial nature of God, which, he tells us, is "the unconditioned conceptual valuation of the entire multiplicity of eternal objects," their togetherness, determining the relevance to each and every actual entity of all eternal objects (PR 46–47). This too, he says, is abstract and "deficiently actual" apart from God's physical prehension of the actual entities of the evolving universe (PR 134, 521). The primordial nature of God is thus the ordering principle of the entire universe determining the relevance of each eternal object to every actual entity. Thus the principle of wholeness and concrescence is immanent in every finite entity and is, in God's primordial nature, the conceptual logical totality.

There can be little doubt that God's primordial nature is Whitehead's counterpart of the Idea in Hegel's Logic. Hegel asserts that the Idea is "God in his eternal essence, prior to the creation of Nature and finite spirit," and Whitehead says of God in his primordial nature, "he is not *before* all creation, but *with* all creation" (almost as if he had Hegel in mind).[11] Hegel says of the logical Idea that it is abstract apart from its dialectical unfolding, its embodiment in Nature and its self-knowledge in spirit, just as Whitehead's God is deficiently actual in his primordial nature but fully actual in his consequent nature. For Hegel, every category of the Logic is a provisional definition of the Absolute and the whole range of categories *aufgehoben* in the absolute Idea is what the Logic is—the doctrine of the Concept. This is just what, for Whitehead, God is in his primordial nature.

Equally it will be true to say that, as for Hegel, Nature is the Idea in the form of otherbeing or externality, so for Whitehead Nature is the exposition or embodiment of God's primordial nature. As for Hegel, the Idea returns to itself out of Nature as spirit and comes to know itself as absolute, so for Whitehead God's consequent nature is the prehension of the total evolving scheme of things which he explicitly says is conscious: "the realization of the actual world in the unity of his nature, and through the transformation of his wisdom." The subjective aim of every actual entity is to achieve concrete unity, and God, in prehending all superjects realizes all subjective aims. His consequent nature is thus the final realization in full self-consciousness of all striving—the ultimate unity of all subjects with all objects. It is, in short, Hegel's absolute Spirit.

But what of creativity and the dialectic? Although we may admit that Hegel is essentially a process philosopher and that negativity is as important for Whitehead as it is for Hegel, is the Whiteheadian process really dialectical, and is God, in his consequent nature, really absolute? These are the points, perhaps, which will be most hotly disputed by the stauncher Whiteheadians.

Hegel has told us that dialectic is the principle of all movement and all activity. It is so because it is the process of self-differentiation of the whole which is immanent in all its moments and in all reality. Each partial and provisional element, therefore, fails to maintain itself in isolation, because its true and only nature is as a moment in the whole, so that it demands and goes over into its other to unite with it and to constitute a more complete and adequate exemplification of the ultimate universal principle of wholeness. This is, in the last resort, absolute Spirit, which, throughout the dialectical movement, is realizing itself as subject. Characteristic of this process throughout is *Aufhebung:* the absorption, preservation, and elevation of what has been superseded.

Whitehead nowhere gives as explicit an account of the method of process as does Hegel, but in what he does say about it we can recognize most of the important features of dialectic. In his anxiety to preserve realism, Whitehead avoids a purely logical or conceptual account of process and traces the stages of concrescence at the level of organism, which, for Hegel is the level of *Geistesphilosophie* rather than *Logik,* so that we find the closest parallel between Hegel and Whitehead in what Hegel calls "Anthropology," "Phenomenology," and "Psychology."

But for both of them the process is one of self-realization of subjective unity. The category of subjective unity, Whitehead says, "has to do with self-realization," which is "the ultimate fact of facts."[12] The unity of the subject establishes a sort of pre-established harmony making the many feelings which belong to an incomplete phase compatible for synthesis.[13] This, in effect is Kant's unity of apperception, which Hegel identifies with the Concept. Actualization in this unity, Whitehead tells us, involves "objective definition at the hands of other entities," apart from which truth and falsity are meaningless.[14] Here we have the *determinatio* which is *negatio* as Hegel takes it over from Spinoza. And the result is unity—the unity of the subject-superject which "is the purpose of the process originating the feelings."

The subject, as it prehends the multiplicity of other entities in the world, has the whole immanent in it. Its subjective aim results from its prehension of the primordial nature of God. "Each temporal entity," Whitehead writes, "in one sense, originates from its mental pole, analogously to God himself. It derives from God its basic conceptual aim, relevant to its actual world. . . ."[15] And the unity which is the purpose of the process is, as we have seen, ultimately gathered up into the unity of God's consequent nature.

That the process is *aufhebend* the following passage gives testimony:

Each stage carries in itself the promise of its successor, and each succeeding stage carries in itself the antecedent out of which it arose. For example the complexity of the datum carries in itself the transition from the conformal feelings to supplementary feelings in which contrasts, latent in the datum, achieve real unity between the components.[16]

The main account which Whitehead gives of process is of concrescence within the individual actual entity; but as the transition from one "epoch" or "duration" to the next is simply the prehension by the subsequent generation of actual occasions of the preceding objectified superjects, the principles involved are the same throughout. The phases are those of dative ingression, conformal physical feeling, conceptual feeling, and comparative feeling. The first two are virtually one, for the conformal feelings are simply the veridical prehensions of the data. So we have an Hegelian triad: first immediacy, then distinction and differentiation, and finally articulated synthesis.

The latter two stages of feeling are constituted by the realization of specific modes of diversity and identity, the realization also involving an adjustment of intensities of relevance.[17]

Whitehead concludes the section with the remark:

In place of the Hegelian hierarchy of categories of thought, the philosophy of organism finds a hierarchy of feelings.[18]

CONTEMPORARY SIGNIFICANCE 25

Feelings, for Hegel, are on the level of spirit; so what we are dealing with here is *Empfindung*, and the dialectic which is being traced is that from sentience to feeling *(Gefuhl)* and the unity of the subject. Feeling, for Hegel, is the inwardizing *(Erinnerung)* of the natural effects on the organism as "soul" and its process (as with Whitehead) brings us to the unity of the subject: "Die Seele ist zum *individuellen Subjecte* vereinzelt."[19] It is, for Hegel, the first stage of the process which finally culminates in Spirit and becomes absolute in its ultimate self-knowledge; and this is, of course, a recapitulation at a higher stage of the logical dialectic. Interestingly we find Whitehead asserting of his own version of the development of process:

But *what* becomes is always a *res vera*, and the concrescence of a *res vera* is the development of a subjective aim. This development is nothing else than the Hegelian development of an idea.[20]

The reiteration or retention of a pattern of prehensions along an historic route of actual occasions constitutes an enduring object; and an animal body involves the intersection of numerous such objects in a complex structure. The final node of such a body is the presiding occasion of the complex social nexus. This presiding occasion inherits a wealth of superjective material including prehensions of diverse types, which in it are synthesized and united into a harmony of contrasts issuing, Whitehead says, into intensity of experience, so that the human body is conscious of its bodily inheritance. Consciousness, accordingly, is a late phase in the process of concrescence in a highly complex society of actual occasions.

Such an account is entirely consonant with and runs closely parallel to Hegel's view on *Empfindung*, or soul, as the *Errinerung* of the processes in the organic body registering the widespread influences of the natural world. And just as, for Hegel, Spirit is the truth of Nature, and each successive phase of spirit is subject to which the preceding phase is object, so for Whitehead "conscious intellectuality" as a

higher grade of mental activity is the intellectual self-analysis of the entity in an earlier stage of incompletion, effected by intellectual feelings produced at a later stage of concrescence.[21]

The final outcome of this development in Hegel's *Geistesphilosophie* is absolute Spirit, which he identifies in the *Religionsphilosophie* with the Holy Spirit. It is the ultimate self-knowledge of the whole, Aristotle's *noesis noeseos*, what God is. So also Whitehead brings the process to culmination in God's consequent nature. God, for Whitehead, is both primordial and consequent. He is the beginning and the end. So likewise for Hegel. Whitehead tells us that the completion of God's nature is the objectification in him of the world. By such objectification the mere potentiality of eternal objects acquires physical reality, so that God's consequent nature is the complete totality of the universe. God is thus at once eternal and everlasting—the eternal structural principle of all reality everlastingly actualizing itself in the prehension of its own creation. In the same way, Hegel tells us that the absolute idea is eternally realized as the infinite restlessness that ceaselessly differentiates itself through self-diremption, to create a world of nature—itself in the form of otherbeing—which it draws back into itself and with which it unites in absolute Spirit.

When Whitehead wrote, the current philosophical opposition was between Idealism and Realism: the first was represented in Britain by the Oxford school of T. H. Green and F. H. Bradley, and in America by thinkers such as Royce and Hocking; the second was represented by writers like Bertrand Russell and the American Critical Realists. Whitehead was anxious to retain an "objectivist" position, while doing justice to the insights of the idealists. As he himself says in the preface to *Process and Reality*, if his cosmology is to be deemed successful, "it becomes natural to ask . . . whether the type of thought involved be not a transformation of some main doctrines of Absolute Idealism onto a realistic basis" (PR viii). In some respects, therefore, he leaned strongly in the realist direction, insisting on the indispensability of "physical data" for knowledge and the "conformal phase" of feeling, while at the same time repudiating what he called "vacuous actuality" (that is, actuality devoid of subjectivity or mind), and emphasizing the formative role in concrescence of the mental pole. Nature, he declared in an early work, is closed to mind.[22] But then almost immediately he protests against and rejects any tendency to bifurcate Nature into what is purely physical and what is mind-dependent. In his mature thought, as we have seen, Nature is the process of concrescence throughout which principles of definiteness, the objects of conceptual prehensions, which are the germ of mind, are everywhere immanent, so that no actuality is "vacuous"; and this mentality develops until it emerges as consciousness, which attains its ultimate and complete realization in the consequent nature of God. So Whitehead's philosophy reconciles the Realism and the Idealism of his day.

Hegel, at that time, was misunderstood by his own idealistic followers equally with his materialistic Marxist critics as wishing to reduce the world to pure subjectivity; whereas in truth, as contemporary scholars have come to realize, Hegel is emphatically realist in his conception of Nature, out of which, he teaches, spirit is dialectically generated, so that in the self-consciousness of spirit, Nature becomes aware of itself *(an und für sich)*, and, because what anything truly *is* is what it dialectically *becomes*, Spirit is the truth of Nature. But this is not to overlook the concomitant fact that "The external world is the truth implicitly *(an sich)*, for the truth is actual and must exist."[23] Hegel also, therefore, reconciles Idealism and Realism with an insight which was not again recovered before Whitehead.

Notes

1. *Nature, Mind and Modern Science* (London: Allen & Unwin, 1954).

2. *Foundations of Metaphysics in Science* (London: Allen & Unwin, 1965); *Hypothesis and Perception: the Roots of Scientific Method* (London: Allen & Unwin, 1972).

3. *The Concept of Nature* (Cambridge: Cambridge University Press, 1920), pp. 15ff.

4. Section 81.

5. Cf. *Phänomenologie des Geistes*, Preface.

6. *Process and Reality* (New York: Macmillan, 1929), p. 66.

7. *Ibid.*

8. *Science and the Modern World* (New York: Macmillan, 1925), pp. 102f.

9. Cf. *Wissenschaft der Logik*, Pt.I, Bk.I. sect. III, Introd.; Bk.II, sect. III, Ch. III, Anm.; *Enzyklopädie*, Sect. 50.

10. *Process and Reality*, p. 31.

11. PR 521.

12. PR 340.

13. PR 341.

14. *Ibid.*

15. PR 343.

16. PR 250.

17. PR 251.

18. PR 252.

19. *Enzyklopädie,* Sect. 359.

20. PR 254.

21. PR 88, 167.

22. *The Concept of Nature,* p. 4.

23. *Enzyklopädie,* Section 38, *Zusatz.*

Tom Rockmore
UNIVERSITÉ LAVAL

Realism, Idealism, and Speculative Philosophy

It is frequently the case that philosophers understand their own positions, especially in relation to others, in terms of metaphors of inversion, reversal, or transformation. The point of this kind of self-description is to suggest that one's later view acknowledges, on occasion builds upon, and certainly avoids the weaknesses of its predecessors. Examples of such claims, formulated in terms of metaphors of inversion or its conceptual analogues, include Kant's "Copernican revolution," Marx's suggestion that his own theory "sets Hegel's on its feet," and Heidegger's appeal to the figure of chiasmus to describe the evolution of his own thought. Although useful, such metaphors on occasion conceal more than they reveal and should not be accepted without scrutiny.

Whitehead appeals to notions of inversion or transformation in a fairly traditional manner in order to define the relation of his own position to forms of idealism. One such passage occurs in *Process and Reality* as an account of the "Order of Nature." On the topic of his concept of the actual entity, he writes: "The philosophy of organism is the inversion of Kant's philosophy." The reason is that whereas for the critical philosophy "subjective data pass into the appearance of an objective world," on the contrary, in Whitehead's view, "objective data pass into subjective satisfaction."[1] In another passage from the preface of that book, concerning the relation of his position to F. H. Bradley's, Whitehead remarks in part that "it becomes natural at this point to ask whether the type of thought involved be not a transformation of some main doctrines of Absolute Idealism onto a realistic basis" (PR viii).

The discussion to follow will rely upon the relation between systematic thought and a reading of the history of philosophy. This distinction is usually invoked invidiously in order to dismiss the relevance of historical considerations. This is not the place to discuss this distinction, although it can be noted that it has its own history, which accordingly tends to undermine its claim to absolute status. Kant, who drew it clearly[2] in order to buttress his claim to a merely systematic approach, just as clearly relied for the formulation of his own position upon a reading of a number of earlier views, especially including those of Plato and Descartes, Leibniz and Hume.

That the relation between Whitehead and Hegel is mainly studied through systematic comparison, and not through their reading of the history of philosophy, is due to a significant difference in the origin of their respective positions. It is indeed well known that Hegel is explicit in his concern to develop his own thought as the conscious attempt to include all that is of positive value in the preceding history of philosophy. For Hegel, then, systematic and historical concerns cannot fairly be isolated. Where this is done in the Hegel discussion (and the attempt has frequently been made) it is accordingly mistaken.

Whitehead does give credit to some philosophers (such as Bradley and Locke) and is known to have been deeply interested in the positions of Plato and Leibniz among others. Nonetheless, it seems probable that his philosophical views are largely the result (in any event more so than for Hegel) of reflection about problems in the philosophy of mathematics and the philosophy of science. The point is not merely to deprecate Hegel's ignorance in these areas, which has been overestimated, nor is it to stigmatize unfairly the later growth of Whitehead's interest in the history of philosophy, since this is in some ways a help rather than a hindrance. Rather, the intention is to point to the difference in the relation of the views of Hegel and Whitehead to the history of philosophy.

It is important to note that the difference in genesis does not suggest a difference in criteria for the evaluation of the two positions. Hegel clearly invited an assessment of his own thought in terms of the history of the philosophical tradition. That this has not more often been attempted is more a reflection on the quality of Hegel scholarship than of the position it concerns. Now Whitehead at least suggests such an evaluative approach since his own self-understanding obviously rests in part upon his reading of others' views. In this way, Whitehead at least seems aware that whatever the genesis of his own thought, its philosophical merit can only be measured against other philosophical positions. Indeed, it could not be otherwise. For whatever the origin of, or the claims made for a given theory, its philosophical merit can never be evaluated on an abstract basis, but only in relation to other views.

I

In the passages just cited, Whitehead refers to Kant and to "Absolute Idealism." The latter term is usually employed loosely to refer to Hegel and certain of his British disciples. In the German tradition, Kant, Fichte, and Hegel all distinguished forms of idealism. In Hegel's often tendentious interpretation of his predecessors, he designated Kant and Fichte as "subjective idealists," or theoreticians of consciousness, to distinguish their views from Schelling's so-called "objective idealism," which supplements transcendental philosophy *(Transzendental philosophie)* through a philosophy of nature *(Naturphilosophie)*. While Hegel himself never employs the term "absolute idealism" to refer to his own position, his position has since been routinely identified as "absolute idealism," as the result of his stress (after the break with Schelling) on a structured form of the absolute. The term is further employed to link Hegel's position and British idealism.

While even so biased an observer as Friedrich Engels refers to Hegel as "the Aristotle of modern times," there is no reason to think that Whitehead himself had even this cursory a knowledge of Hegel's doctrines. For instance, in the magisterial discussion of the *Adventures of Ideas*, Hegel is characteristically never mentioned. And he does not fare much better in Whitehead's other writings. When Whitehead refers to "absolute idealism," in the first instance he has in mind Bradley's view, but beyond it he refers as well to the idealist approach to knowledge in general as distinguished from realism.

Interestingly, in view of the credit Whitehead extends to Bradley's formative influence on his own thought, there is little direct discussion of the latter's view. The most detailed discussion of which I am aware is in the *Adventures of Ideas*, significantly in the chapter devoted to "Philosophic Method."[3] Here Whitehead in short succession accepts Bradley's view of relation as requiring an "inclusive whole," and further accepts a concept of feeling at the base of experience, specifically including both subjective form and the apprehension of an object. For a better understanding of what Whitehead does *not* accept—what indeed, as he notes, led him to expound his position in independence of Bradley's—one must look to scattered remarks in *Process and Reality*. Here Bradley is criticized *inter alia* (in terms that apply to German idealism as Whitehead understands it) for an espousal of mere appearance (PR 85), a repudiation of Hume's insistence on the objectivity of the world

(PR 237), and for the fact that his doctrine of appearance is merely a consequence of Kant's subjectivism (PR 289).

Like Sartre, whose thought Whitehead did not know, Whitehead is a rigorously consistent thinker. These scattered remarks about Bradley agree closely with the claim, noted above, that the realism of the Philosophy of Organism inverts Kant's idealism. Even on this cursory account, it is obvious that Whitehead regards Bradley's view, and indeed idealism as well, as a repudiation of objectivity, in terms of a putative contrast between realism and idealism. More precisely, Whitehead's own insistence on realism is understood by him as a visible alternative to later idealism, in fact as a qualified return to that doctrine of *realitas objectiva* which is inconsistently present and insufficiently elaborated in the views of such prior thinkers as Descartes and Locke.

To a greater extent than Hegel, Whitehead understands epistemology as the attempt to overcome the problem of skepticism. Whitehead's reading of modern philosophy in terms of the relation of epistemology and skepticism can be summarized briefly as follows.

Descartes' position is inconsistent in its insistence on doctrines of a *realitas objectiva* and of the subjectivist principle—that is, the view that the datum can be adequately analyzed in terms of universals. The latter principle leads to what Santayana calls the "solipsism of the present moment," a consequence accepted by Whitehead, in which we can neither prove the reality of the external world nor that the ideas in our mind correspond to something distinguished from our mind. The problem introduced by the adherence to the subjectivist principle is continued in Hume's position, which combines it with a sensationalist principle—that the primary activity of experience is the entertainment of the datum. This same problem further reappears in German idealism as a consequence of Kant's acceptance of Hume's analysis of the datum and replacement of objectivity by apparent objectivity (see PR 231, 236). According to Whitehead's reading of the critical philosophy, Kant has claimed that we can know only concepts (PR 236). By inference, then, Kant's position ends in skepticism and solipsism. And by further inference, to the extent that Hegel's thought builds on Kant's, it must also be subject to the same defects.

Whitehead's position is obviously intended by him to remedy the skepticism and solipsism to which idealism is allegedly subject— both of which he believes to follow from the subjectivist principle. From an historical perspective, he is concerned to stress the concept of *realitas objectiva*, already noted. On his own account, Whitehead's causal theory of perception comprises an inversion of Kant's since the correct account must reveal that (as he writes) "the datum includes its own interconnections" (PR 173). In a word, by putting forward a novel view of the object as an actual entity which cannot even be misdescribed in terms of universals (PR 76), the new form of realism is intended to resolve the problems that idealism inherits from rationalism and empiricism by traversing the distinction between universals and particulars.

If we distinguish between Whitehead's positive doctrine and his reading of modern philosophpy, the claim for the philosophical importance of his own view can be seen to depend upon his analysis of the related problems of solipsism and skepticism in German idealism. If we now *bracket* the intrinsic nature of Whitehead's own doctrine, we can concentrate on the claims made for it in relation to German idealism. Here two points can be distinguished. On the one hand, Whitehead seems to be suggesting that realism and idealism are exclusive alternatives, whose difference concerns objectivity versus apparent objectivity. On the other hand, Whitehead wants to suggest, as noted, the presence of the pre-idealist problems of solipsism and skepticism in German idealism.

An examination of the views of Kant and Hegel reveals, however, that idealism and realism are *not* exclusive alternatives, that in any case idealism does *not* substitute apparent objectivity for objectivity, and that the problems of solipsism and skepticism present in pre-idealistic thought do *not* persist in German idealism.

II

Whitehead's reintroduction of realism is understood by him as an alternative to the idealist view of apparent objectivity: for instance, Kant's doctrine that apart from concepts there is nothing to know. As concerns the critical philosophy, both criticisms are misleading. According to Kant, concepts cannot indeed be known, since knowledge must begin with experience. Nor is objectivity "merely apparent," unless by "objectivity" is meant "what is given in appearance." Kant's point is not to deny objectivity in favor of subjectivity, it is rather to argue that what we experience is in fact constituted by us on the basis of a sensory input whose content is given from "without." It seems difficult to deny that the mind does in fact have a role in constituting what it perceives. It is very doubtful that there are pure, uninterpreted data given on the plane of consciousness, and perhaps not even on the unconscious plane either.

Whitehead often implies that idealism and realism are exclusive alternatives. While a claim of this kind *might* perhaps be ventured with respect to Berkeley, such a sweeping claim is simply inaccurate with respect to the entire tradition of German idealism. Here the concern is not to substitute idealism for realism, if by the latter is understood a "denial of empirical objectivity," even if in some of Fichte's popular writings that might seem to be the case. Rather, the concern is *precisely* to *synthesize* realist and idealist perspectives. Kant's critical philosophy is explicitly understood by him as neither empiricist nor rationalist, but rather as representing a true middle way, a *tertium non datur* as some have held, which combines the positive virtues of both in order to avoid dogmatism and skepticism.

The problem of solipsism arises in Kant's position in several places within the *Critique of Pure Reason*, most notably in the celebrated "Refutation of Idealism." It is well known that for Kant, it was a scandal that philosophy was unable to prove the existence of the external world. In the "Refutation of Idealism," Kant concentrates on the dogmatic form of idealism associated by him with Berkeley, which is interpreted as denying the existence of the external world. Kant's argument is that inner experience presupposes for its possibility outer experience. Stated in this way, the argument is problematic to be sure, since on Kant's own account things cannot be given apart from the subject. But since Kant also holds that an appearance relates to something which appears as its required precondition (that is, a necessary noumenon) his view avoids the problem of solipsism present in either Berkeley or Descartes as Kant reads them. And as concerns Hegel, suffice it to say that he neither discusses this problem, nor does it seem to arise, in his own position.

From the epistemological perspective, the point of Kant's "Refutation of Idealism" is that it refutes the claim that, in knowing, the subject "knows" only itself. Since that result does not follow from the form of idealism represented by Kant or later German idealists, one cannot reasonably argue that realism needs to be reintroduced for that reason. The deeper problem is whether epistemology requires a return to realism in order to avoid skepticism. I hold that Whitehead's affirmative answer to this question rests on a failure to grasp the sense in which German idealism constitutes an advance on the pre-idealist forms of epistemology subject to this problem. Accordingly, I shall now outline the novel divergence of German idealism from pre-idealist epistemology.

Whitehead suggests that idealism results in skepticism, which can only be remedied through a return to realism. Kant on the contrary holds that realism must lead to skepticism. Common to the various representative theories of perception prior to Kant, whether rationalist or empiricist, is the distinction (which can be formulated here in Cartesian language) between the idea as the *image* of the thing in contrast to the thing itself. Kant's insight is that if the object is produced by the subject, on the basis of a given sensory content, according to rules of its own, then the possibility of knowledge can be demonstrated.

In order to appreciate Kant's view of epistemology, it is important to recognize at least two points. In the first place, Kant clearly breaks with earlier forms of epistemology in at least two senses. On the one hand, he raises the problem of the possibility of knowledge in general, whereas earlier writers were concerned with how one can know one or another object. On the other hand, he denies the independence of the object by making objectivity dependent on subjectivity as a condition of knowledge. Secondly, it must be stressed that the result is not a merely apparent form of objectivity, since the object which we in fact experience and which is studied in natural science is an *appearance* shaped by the mind. Indeed, as Hegel helpfully observes, in the critical philosophy the appearance is "objective" in at least three senses: (i) as an external existent; (ii) as universal and necessary; (iii) and as the knowable essence of the existent thing, as distinguished from mere thought.[4]

Nor is the assertion of skepticism accurate as concerns Hegel's position. Although he is indeed critical of Kant's critical philosophy (which he regards as *uncritical* at crucial points) Hegel never denies—and in fact amplifies—Kant's claim that subject and object must correspond if knowledge is to be possible. This is not the place to rehearse Hegel's interesting, but insufficiently studied views of skepticism. It is sufficient to note that he does not regard Kant's position as prey to this problem because of an alleged dissolution of the object in a bath of universals. Hegel's point in this regard, which Whitehead does not answer, is that beyond mere ostensive designation, all experiential knowledge ultimately must take the form of this analysis in terms of universals. Hegel objects rather to Kant's *limitation* of knowledge merely to appearance in terms of a putatively untenable distinction between phenomena and noumena. Hegel suggests that this distinction is untenable, since to draw it is to go beyond it, and there is nothing that we can so easily know as a mere object of thought.[5]

Hegel interprets Kant's insistence on the correspondence of subjectivity and objectivity as merely the most recent form of the frequently asserted (but entirely undemonstrated) identity of thought and being, with which the entire history of philosophy is concerned. In his own position, Hegel argues for an epistemological unity of thought and being in terms of a presupposed ontological disunity. It follows that Hegel declines the Cartesian view in which the subject can know only itself. But Hegel neither denies the reality of objectivity, nor does he deny the real in favor of the ideal, since his view of knowledge *presupposes* an ontological distinction between subject and object.

III

The argument so far has been that Whitehead's grasp of German idealism is inadequate to diagnose the presence of the difficulty for which his own view is an alternative. I suggest that the source of Whitehead's failure to grasp the specificity of German idealism lies in part in an exaggeration of the degree of continuity within the Platonic philosophical tradition. Perhaps in reaction to rival interpretations that exaggerate discontinuity, Whitehead is overly concerned to show the persistence of broad methodological principles thoughout the history of philosophy. But if, as Whitehead suggests, the western philosophical tradition is in the main a series of footnotes to Plato, it should not be overlooked that the footnotes are varied and present often genuine alternatives and indeed on occasion incompatible perspectives. For if (as Whitehead also suggests) philosophy is never the same after the shock of a great philosopher, then this is even more the case for the movement of German idealism, arguably one of the two richest strands in the entire philosophical tradition. Later thought cannot, then, legitimately take up again a pre-idealist perspective as if idealism had never existed.

The point about Whitehead's failure to grasp the specificity of German idealism is related to an important difference in the concepts of speculative philosophy espoused by Hegel and Whitehead. On a superficial plane, the similarity between their respective concepts of speculative thought is certainly striking. Both Hegel and Whitehead seek to provide general categorial frameworks, adequate for the interpretation of any and all items of experience. Both, then, regard speculative philosophy as the attempt to construe particulars given in experience against the wider conceptual background. Both further suggest that the frameworks must be coherent and necessary—and both also avoid for that purpose any reliance upon mathematical deduction.

But subtending these similarities are a number of differences, of which I shall mention merely one here. Science in all its forms has often been held to require for its possibility universality and necessity. A central aim of post-Kantian German idealism is in fact to attain this scientific status by the reconstruction of the critical philosophy in fully systematic form. Hegel's position continues this task. But, following Fichte, he rejects Reinhold's model of a grounded system in favor of what has recently come to be called "antifoundationalism." For although Hegel holds that the categorial framework requires the kind of rigorous justification attempted in its behalf beginning with Kant, he also holds that in the final analysis the claim to know must be tested against experience.

The relation of this point to Whitehead's view of speculation can be seen as follows. Despite the genuine interest of Whitehead's speculative view, what it lacks is a self-conscious (or "reflexive") moment so prominent in German idealism—above all in Hegel's thought. In fact, it would seem that the Philosophy of Organism is dogmatic in the Kantian sense of the term. For although Whitehead claims "necessity" for his philosophic scheme (that is, that it contain "in itself its own warrant of universality throughout all experience, provided that we confine ourselves to that which communicates with immediate matter of fact" [PR 5]) a rigorous justification of this claim is not provided, nor is the question ever posed in a genuinely critical manner.

There is a moral to this discussion. The fact that Whitehead elaborated his philosophical thought in apparent independence of a reading of the history of philosophy is both a help and a hindrance. The advantage is that he was able to avoid a certain narrowness—steming from undue concentration merely on the philosophic tradition itself—by casting his net more widely to include such sources as contemporary mathematics and natural science. These sources are often attended to mainly in the breach—and, at least with respect to this agenda, Whitehead invites comparison with Kant. But this kind of approach has an attendant disadvantage, which should be noted. For in consciously seeking his inspiration outside philosophy, Whitehead is less well placed than is Hegel to profit from the genuine flashes of insight to be found within the preceding history of philosophy. Accordingly, this particular source of novel insight in Whitehead's thought is also a cause for concern.

Whitehead's misinterpretation of the relation of his own position to German idealism thus conceals an uncertain grasp of the genuinely *critical* nature of the latter movement, which mistakenly prompts, even as it is reflected in, his recurrence to an allegedly "pre-critical mode" of thought.

Notes

1. These passages occur at p. 135 of *Process and Reality* (New York: Macmillan, 1929). Following accepted custom, all subsequent references to this work will appear in parentheses in the body of this essay, utilizing the pagination of this edition.

2. *Kritik der reinen Vernunft* (2nd edition, 1787), p. 864.

3. *Adventures of Ideas* (New York: Macmillan, 1933), ch. XV, sec. 11.

4. Cf. Hegel's *Encyclopedia of the Philosophical Sciences*, sec. 41.

5. *Encyclopedia*, sec. 44.

Hans-Christian Lucas
RUHR UNIVERSITÄT—BOCHUM

Spinoza, Hegel, Whitehead: Substance, Subject, and Superject

The possibility of a fundamental comparison between the thought of Hegel and of Whitehead emerges from the essential character of reality as it is presented in the most mature expositions of their systems. For Hegel, as for Whitehead, reality is the total coherence of all entities, determined essentially as motivity or becoming. Hegel, within the scope of his philosophy of subjectivity, develops a multi-level theory of history[1] which is at the same time an ontology of historicity.[2] Whitehead elaborates a cosmology in which process is the pre-eminent determination of reality—a connection well known from the title of his major work.[3] Both thinkers moreover felt compelled to secure their own philosophic positions by counter-arguments against the position of substance-metaphysics. The thesis to be defended here in brief outline can be stated thus: In undertaking a critical evaluation of the history of philosophy, neither Hegel nor Whitehead pursued an interest which was primarily historico-theoretical. On the contrary, both thinkers attained from this critical evaluation the decisive motives for elaborating their own systems.[4]

In the following reflections, particular emphasis is placed on Hegel's and Whitehead's respective confrontations with Spinoza's philosophy of the One Substance. This accentuation, however, by no means implies that the fundamental importance of Plato and Aristotle for both thinkers is to be called into question, especially in view of Whitehead's now virtually proverbial dictum that the entire European philosophical tradition can be characterized as a series of footnotes to Plato.[5] Nor is the estimation of Kant by both thinkers to be overlooked here. To be sure, when Whitehead asserts that his organic philosophy should be understood primarily as a recurrence to pre-Kantian modes of thought,[6] he openly embraces a theoretical position for which Hegel was frequently criticized. But surely the selected focus of this investigation on the critique of Spinoza may find its justification in the words of Whitehead himself: "The philosophy of organism is closely allied to Spinoza's scheme of thought."[7] And further: "The organic doctrine is closer to Descartes than to Newton. Also it is close to Spinoza; but Spinoza bases his philosophy upon the monistic substance, of which the actual occasions are inferior modes. The philosophy of organism inverts this point of view."[8]

At issue for Whitehead is, therefore, as he says, the inversion of Spinoza's philosophy. With respect to Hegel, Ernest Cassirer trenchantly summarizes just such an inversion in regard to history: "The true life of the idea, of the divine, begins in history. In Hegel's philosophy, the formula of Spinoza, *Deus sive Natura*, is transformed into *Deus sive Historia*. Yet the apotheosis is not concerned with particular historical events, but rather with the historical process as a whole."[9]

To put it tersely, the following will be a comparison between the movement "from substance to subject"[10]—a formula with which Rothenstreich characterizes Hegel's turning away from substance-metaphysics—and the movement "from subject to superject"—which Gernot Böhme presents as one of three ways to make Whitehead's rejection of substance-metaphysics understandable.[11]

I

In Hegel's reception and critique of Spinoza fairly diverse phases can be distinguished, but we can, without further ado, admit the continual and fundamental significance which Hegel's relationship to Spinoza's philosophy had for the development of his thought. Although some question still remains as to precisely when Hegel first occupied himself with Spinoza's own writings, it can be documented that Hegel, together with his friends Hölderlin and Schelling at the seminary in Tübingen, read and discussed with great interest the consequential *Letters on Spinoza* by Jacobi. The formula, ἓν καὶ πᾶν, pronounced by Lessing as the shibboleth of pantheism or Spinozism and subsequently published and discussed by Jacobi, was written by Hölderlin in Hegel's literary album[12] and taken up in earnest by Schelling as the program of his early writings.

Schelling's Fichte-oriented reinterpretation of Spinoza's One Substance as absolute Ego is scarcely intelligible apart from the reinterpretation of Spinoza prefigured by Jacobi.[13] Despite documentation that Schelling studied Spinoza's own writings, however, his occupation with Spinoza during this period can be ascribed to that ambiguous "Spinozism" prevalent in Germany at the close of the eighteenth century which was often only indirectly concerned with

Spinoza himself. The situation is similar with the Hen-Panta doctrine, i.e., the metaphysical monism which, construed along the lines of Spinoza's immanent One Substance, maintained the existence of the One Being as the unifying presupposition of difference in the finite. The doctrine was elaborated within Hegel and Hölderlin's circle of friends[14] after Hegel, in 1797, had met up again with Hölderlin in Frankfurt. There are indications from this period that Hegel had already occupied himself with Spinoza's writings in Frankfurt,[15] perhaps even in Bern. At any rate, we may take it that Hegel, by the time he began his sojourn in Jena, was already seen as a Spinoza scholar.[16]

At the time, however, that Hegel joined Schelling in Jena, where the two philosophers developed an idealistic metaphysics of substance, they had already had divergent experiences in their encounters with Spinoza's philosophy. Hegel especially is critical of appearances of Spinozism during this time, e.g., in *Faith and Knowledge*. From about 1801, Hegel and Schelling begin to develop a philosophical program which, like Fichte's, is designed to transcend the dualism not overcome by Kant, but which is nonetheless averse to Fichte's own solution through a philosophy of subjectivity, inasmuch as this option seemed to both thinkers to leave subject and object disunited. For Hegel, the history of modern philosophy presents a succession of diverse oppositions. In his view, the most recent philosophy only transformed this polarity into "the oppositional form of reason and sensibility, intelligence and nature, or, [expressed] according to the universal concept, of absolute subjectivity and absolute objectivity."[17] These oppositions, experienced as bifurcations, refer (on Hegel's view) beyond themselves to the very unity with respect to which they can appear as self-autonomizing separations. The understanding endeavors to fasten und stabilize these oppositions, while for reason the experience of bifurcation becomes the "source of *the need of philosophy*," ("Quell des Bedürfnisses der Philosophie")[18] the task of which Hegel represents as the "construction of the Absolute in consciousness."[19]

For both Schelling and Hegel, the Absolute can be known, although to be sure reason must purify itself of its fixation with the finitudes which the philosophy of subjectivity in its medium, reflection, has brought forth. The paradigm which both thinkers share during this period is Spinoza's substance, which, however, they already interpret along manifestly different lines. While for Schelling the Absolute is to be conceived as the "total indifference of the subjective and the objective,"[20] Hegel emphasizes that Spinoza's substance, which is determined as "cause and effect, concept and Being simultaneously," ceases to be mere concept, "because the oppositions are unified in a contradiction."[21] Hegel praises Spinoza for beginning philosophy with an antinomy, and for doing so without falling into the error of wanting to base philosophy on a single proposition or first principle. Hegel's own concept of the Absolute corresponds exactly with this interpretation of Spinoza's substance: "The Absolute is the identity of identity and non-identity, opposition and unity (Einsseyn) are in it simultaneously."[22] Thus, even though Schelling and Hegel at this point already conceive differently of the absolute identity, they are nevertheless in agreement that the Absolute does not proceed beyond itself.[23]

But just this point compels Hegel to abandon substance as the most basic idea and highest concept of metaphysics. Indeed, Hegel's conception, dating from 1803/04, of a theory of consciousness as *history of consciousness,* in connection with the introduction of a philosophy of spirit, leads Hegel to problems of foundation which cannot be solved from the standpoint of a substance construed, to be sure, as *causa sui,* but all the same, persisting within itself.[24] In the *Logic, Metaphysics* and *Philosophy of Nature* of 1804/05 the Absolute appears as substance under the designation of "highest being" at the end of the "Metaphysics of Objectivity," but this does not constitute the apex of metaphysics. Not until the "Metaphysics of Subjectivity" is substance translated into Ego, which is at once singular und universal and for itself in its very relation to the other.[25]

Hegel's famous dictum in the Preface ("Vorrede") to the *Phenomenology of Spirit* terminates this development and determines quite clearly the path he will have to take in his later criticism of Spinoza, but at the same time it demonstrates the broad extent to which Spinoza's substance is incorporated in Hegel's absolute and in-itself historical subjectivity. Hegel avers there that everything depends on "conceiving and expressing the True, not only as *substance,* but [equally] as *subject.*"[26] It is surely not a coincidence that in 1805/06 Hegel's marked interest for Aristotle is in evidence,[27] nor that in that same winter he makes significant use of an objective teleology, which previously he had, like Spinoza, always rejected. Indeed, in the *Phenomenology* he lauds Aristotle for having "defined nature as purposive activity," and purpose as "the immediate, the quiescent, which is self-moving, which is subject."[28] But the realized purpose, or, as Hegel expresses it, "the finitely existing *Real*," (das daseiende Wirkliche) is on his view "the *movement and the unfolded Becoming.*"[29]

Let us bear in mind that a substance-metaphysics such as Spinoza's determines the relationship of the One to the many in such a way that the many are in and through the One. The inevitable question in this context is how the One can release from itself the other, the many, how the Absolute can differentiate itself within itself and how we are to construe the difference which thus emerges. In particular, the question about the foundation for this self-differentiation seems to Hegel insolvable without recourse to a teleology of the Absolute. Thus, Schelling's position of the indifference of the Absolute equally falls prey to Hegel's express criticism, and, indeed, subsequently Schelling is frequently even identified with Spinoza in Hegel's criticism.[30]

The Spinoza-critique of the mature Hegel is especially prominent in the *Science of Logic* and the *Lectures on the History of Philosophy.* When considering the arguments of these two parts of the system, one must bear clearly in mind that Hegel is postulating there— above and beyond a mere parallelism—an inherent connection between logical sequence and the sequence of the history of philosophy.[31] This stands out with special clarity when Hegel brings the categories of Being and Becoming from the first pages of the *Logic* in close relation to the thought of Parmenides and Heraclitus: "That which is *first* in *Science* necessarily showed itself historically as *first.* And we must regard the Eleatic *One* or *Being* as the first beginning in the knowledge of Thought."[32]

The commencement of the history of philosophy is thus referred to Parmenides' Being and coupled conceptually with the commencement of the logical progression; yet this association obtains only for the sake of overcoming the very immediacy of Being and Nothingness by means of Heraclitus' Flux of Becoming: "The profound *Heraclitus,* in contradistinction to that simple and one-sided abstraction, set forth the higher, total concept of Becoming, saying that *Being exists just as little as Nothing,* or that everything *flows,* which means, everything is *Becoming.*"[33] The history of philosophy therefore does not represent to Hegel a tangle of diverse systems, but rather an inherently logical sequence, possessing ultimately the character of a teleologically directed development. Those systems which truly have accomplished an advance in knowledge[34] signify, in essence, "levels of the determination of the Idea itself in its logical Conception."[35] Therefore, just as Hegel's logic, and thus indeed his entire system, is to be construed as the coming to be of ever more concrete configurations, so also his history of philosophy. All the same, however, subsequent philosophizing represents a critical overcoming of earlier systems only in as much as the preceding systems are refuted through an *immanent* critique.[36] Only in this fashion, i.e., by establishing itself as the verity of the antecedent systems, does the subsequent system evince itself as richer, deeper, more developed and concrete.[37]

This entails that Hegel, in his critique of Spinoza's One-Substance metaphysics, consciously opposes this system as a stratified and multi-faceted philosophical scheme, being the resultant of diverse formative strains and at the same time representing their synthesis. On the one hand, Spinoza's basic conception bears for Hegel the same import as the Eleatic One,[38] but on the other, Hegel stresses, Spinoza brought European thought closer to "the Oriental intuition of identity."[39] From the standpoint of the history of philosophy, however, Hegel declares Spinoza's philosophy to be at one and the same time the annulment of Cartesian dualism *and* the consistent execution of Descartes' philosophical program.[40] Accordingly, the Spinozistic Substance is in Hegel's eyes true, but not without some restriction. Indeed, it is, as Hegel proclaims, "not the whole truth," since substance need also be conceived as "active in itself and alive, and hence as determining itself as spirit." The deficiency of Spinoza's substance is therefore crystalized in the determination of its principle as "merely rigid substance which is not yet spirit."[41]

Hegel proceeds to a critique of Spinoza's methodology, objecting vehemently to the exposition for beginning with definitions, although in content his remarks concern primarily the first definition of the *Ethics* alone. But the identity of existence and essence which is expressed there meets with Hegel's full approval. It is, after all, to be understood in the very Hegelian sense of the identity of non-identicals. "The unity," Hegel says, "of thought and existence is maintained from the very start (the essence is the universal, the Thought); and it is just this unity which will always be at issue."[42] In Hegel's own system this identity presents itself in the *Logic* as *Reality* (Wirklichkeit). The entire section entitled "Reality" is in fact a critical confrontation with Spinoza's conception of substance,[43] even though reference is made to Spinoza *expressis verbis* only in the explanatory remarks. Hegel's critique of the hiatus between substance and its attributes and Spinoza's failure to show how substance could release the attributes out of itself, now becomes for Hegel the decisive issue. The consistent elaboration of this critique, however, is for Hegel tantamount to "the *unveiling* of substance, and this is the *genesis of the Concept*."[44]

Reality must establish itself through this process as a mesh of interrelations, as a field wherein reality, possibility, contingency, necessity, and freedom are all mutually referential. The law of motion in this relational field will prove to be reciprocal action (Wechselwirkung). Hegel finds in Spinoza's own definition of the *causa sui* an incipient effort towards the overcoming of the rigid understanding of substance: "Had Spinoza explicated more thoroughly what is contained in the concept of the *causa sui*, his substance would not have been the static thing it was."[45]

According to the coincidence of logical development and the progress of the history of philosophy, as set forth above, Hegel would be obliged to exhibit the overcoming of Spinoza through Leibniz and finally through Kant. This assignment, however, compels him ultimately to have recourse to Aristotle. Although the relational field of reality is initially explicated in terms of the paradigm of 'ενϕνεσα and δύναμ, it is, in the final analysis, Leibniz's[46] explication of the created monads as entelechies which is meant to serve as the departure-point for a movement beyond Spinoza's in-itself-persisting Substance. Thus, the monad, construed as an entelechy, supplements Spinoza's deficient representation of substance *qua causa sui* with the (decisive) elements of self-reflection, self-manifestation, and self-revelation (des Sich-selbst-offenbarens): "The monad . . . has no *passivity*, although it is finite; rather, the alterations and determinations in it are manifestations of itself in itself. It is *entelechy;* revelation is its own doing."[47]

To be sure, Hegel succeeds in taking this step with Leibniz beyond Spinoza only insofar as he annuls Leibniz's transformation of the concept of entelechy and reverts to its original, Aristotelian meaning; that is, insofar as he reads Leibniz's use of entelechy as the unreconstructed Aristotelian concept of 'εντελέχεια: "They are the *entelechies* of Aristotle, conceived as pure actualities (Thätigkeiten); they are forms in themselves."[48] While Leibniz reads entelechy according to the etymological model 'εντελεσ + έχεσν, meaning "possessing completion"[49] and so once again suggesting the quiescent persistence of an entity within itself, Hegel construes the concept ostensibly in the sense of 'possessing within itself the aspired end (Zweck),' as would be suggested by the etymological model 'εν + τελοσ + 'έχειν. This understanding of entelechy is evidenced, for example, in Hegel's discussion of Aristotle's *Metaphysics*: "That which is usually called energy in Aristotle is also called entelechy. The latter is the same conceptual determination as energy, but more specific insofar as it [namely, entelechy] is free activity (Thätigkeit) and possesses the goal (Zweck) within itself, sets the goal for itself and is active in setting it—[it is] determination as determination of the end (Zweck), realisation of the end."[50]

The translation (Überführen) of Spinoza's rigidly-understood substance into the "*actuality* of substance *as the calm emergence* of itself (*Actuosität* der Substanz, *als ruhiges Hervorgehen* ihrer selbst)"[51] was possible for Hegel only through a recurrence to Aristotle, which was more or less only formally mediated by Leibniz. Substantiality, according to the already cited principle of the *Phenomenology*, is developed into subjectivity once the standpoint of absolute substance is achieved, and this is defined in terms of entelechy: "But the highest point is rather where δύναμ, 'ενέργεια and 'ενιελέχεια are unified. The *absolute substance*, the true (das Wahrhafte), that which exists in and for itself (das Anundfürsichseiende), is more closely determined by Aristotle in this passage [*Metaphysics* XII, 6 and 7] as the '*unmoved*,' the immobile, 'and eternal,' but what is simultaneously 'moving,' pure 'activity (Thätigkeit),' *actus purus*."[52])

II.

With respect to Whitehead a comparable historical exposition (entwicklungsgeschichtlicher Aufweis) of the development of his changing relationship to Spinoza cannot be undertaken here. In the following an effort will be made only to clarify the reasons for Whitehead's emphatic assertion in *Process and Reality* that "the philosophy of organism is closely allied to Spinoza's scheme of thought."[53] Spinoza's attraction for Whitehead lies ostensibly in the higher coherence he brought to Cartesianism by beginning with only *one* substance.[54] Among the background motifs relevant here is Whitehead's critique of Newton's mechanistic world-view, to which he admittedly prefers Descartes' philosophy. When summarizing the points of agreement and disagreement between his organic philosophy and the views of the founders of modern philosophy and science, Whitehead states the matter thus: "The organic doctrine is closer to Descartes than to Newton. Also it is close to Spinoza; but Spinoza bases his philosophy upon the monistic substance, of which the actual occasions are inferior modes. The philosophy of organism inverts this point of view."[55]

Such an inversion (which incidentally, Whitehead also claims to undertake in regard to Kant's philosophy) can be meaningful only if its aim is the inauguration of a speculative enterprise, as was the case with Hegel and Schelling in Hegel's early Jena period. While for Schelling and Hegel the decisive questions of theory-construction turn in this period on the relationship of reflection and speculation,[56] *Process and Reality*, as is well known, begins at once with the chapter on "Speculative Philosophy."[57] Of course, one must bear in mind that an inversion may well represent nothing more than the other side of the same coin and thus remain in a sense bound to the very position it purports to reject, as occurs, albeit in a more differentiated fashion, with Hegel's concept of "Aufhebung" in its triple connotation of *negare, tollere,* and *conservare.*

Whitehead aims his critique of the substance concept against the tradition founded ultimately on Aristotle's logic, which derives a substance-quality metaphysics from the subject-predicate form of the proposition. This tradition finds its culmination in the philosophy of Descartes, and yet at the same time it is in Cartesian dualism that the fatal effect of this tradition forcefully emerges, namely, the bifurcation (Aufspaltung) of the sciences, or—to speak with Hegel—the *Entzweiung* of modern thought.[58] Significant in this context is Whitehead's emphatic claim that Aristotle does not, in his metaphysical reflections, flatly take over the relation which dominates his logic.[59] Indeed, Whitehead stresses in this regard almost hyperbolically that "probably Aristotle was not an Aristotelian."[60] Whitehead contraposes the tradition from Aristotle to Descartes, which grants the category of 'quality' precedence over that of 'relatedness', with the inversion of this order: "In these lectures 'relatedness' is dominant over 'quality.' "[61]

It is in precisely this context that Whitehead's estimation of Spinoza in relation to Descartes proves ambivalent. The idea that an individual substance, together with its predicates, instantiates reality in its highest form, does allow for *both* a monistic *and* a pluralistic philosophy; but since relations among a plurality of such substances have no place in this system, the only *consistent* philosophy which proceeds from the subject-predicate model is, for Whitehead, monistic.[62] It becomes clear in this setting why Whitehead on the one hand praises Spinoza for undertaking the logical systematization of Descartes' philosophy, purging it of inconsistencies, but on the other hand deplores the outcome: Spinoza could achieve his ends only by re-inforcing and intensifying those very tendencies of Cartesianism which Whitehead condemns. In this respect Whitehead stands closer to Descartes, since organic philosophy is conceived, in contradistinction to the monism of Spinoza, as pluralistic.[63]

Whitehead's plurality is, however, not a plurality of substances or subjects construed ultimately in terms of traditional, substance-oriented philosophy—that is, according to the paradigm of 'υποκείενον as that which underlies every process.[64] On the contrary: in place of the Real, which substance-philosophy interprets as presence in the dual sense of *Anwesenheit* and *Vorliegen,* Whitehead allows a reality to emerge which is construed as *event.*[65] The basic characteristic of an event, as Whitehead depicts it, is *concrescence,* and each event represents an actual entity in the act of self-completion. Thus, for Whitehead, as for Hegel, Spinoza's conception of the *causa sui* becomes fruitful for developing a central conceptual scheme: "An actual entity is at once the product of the efficient past, and is also, in Spinoza's phrase, *causa sui.*"[66] Whitehead had emphasized before the universal significance of self-causation in Spinoza's sense for the concept of concrescence: "To be *causa sui* means that the process of concrescence is its own reason for the decision in respect to the qualitative clothing of feeling. It is finally responsible for the decision by which any lure for feeling is admitted to efficiency. The freedom inherent in the universe is constituted by this element of self-causation."[67]

The theory of the "superject" now becomes intelligible in the context of Whitehead's delimitation of his theory over and against the Cartesian position. According to Whitehead, Descartes understood the thinking subject as the creator of occasional thoughts, while the philosophy of organism inverts the order of priority: thought is construed as the constitutive operation in the creation of that which occasionally thinks. Whitehead thus says: "In this inversion we have the final contrast between a philosophy of substance and a philosophy of organism. The operations of an organism are directed towards the organism as a 'superject,' and are not directed from the organism as a 'subject.' "[68] The subject-object dichotomy, which Spinoza sought to overcome by recourse to his monism, is now raised (aufgehoben) to another level, namely, that of time: object is the past; subject is the present. "The operations are directed *from* antecedent organisms and *to* the immediate organism. They are 'vectors,' in that they convey the many things into the constitution of the single superject."[69]

One may summarize as follows: Actual entities at once direct the process of their concrescence and represent the object of this process itself; they are therefore at one and the same time subject and superject, whereby the superject is that which determines.

The central task which now arises for Whitehead is the grounding of the plurality of actual entities and their relatedness. The basic operation utilized for this purpose may be understood as the transformation of the Spinozistic modi into actual entities, whereby these are conceived as Aristotelian ουσίαι[70]: "Spinoza's 'modes' now become the sheer actualities. . . . The coherence, which the system seeks to preserve, is the discovery that the process, or concrescence, of any one actual entity involves the other actual entities among its components. In this way the obvious solidarity of the world receives its explanation."[71] Reality presents itself for Whitehead as the relational field of actual entities, i.e., reality is to be understood as a process of processes. It seems convincing, therefore, that Whitehead's metaphysics, which sets as its goal the destruction of the philosophical tradition based on the substance concept of Aristotle, is to be understood simultaneously as the reconstruction of a more complex and thus more adequate concept of an entity (Wesensbegriff), the pedigree of which is equally Aristotelian.[72] As we have already seen with respect to Hegel, so also for Whitehead the guiding principle becomes the conception of reality, elaborated in Aristotle's *Metaphysics*, as the synergism of δύναμισ, 'ενέργεια and 'εντελέχεια.

III

These brief remarks on Hegel and Whitehead could by no means offer a presentation, much less an analysis, of their respective systems as elaborations of process thought. Certainly considerations regarding the basic problem could be proffered, from which it might have become clear in what manner both thinkers criticized the philosophical tradition and yet at the same time rendered certain traditional positions fruitful for the elaboration of their own systems by a transformation of meaning. And certain (possibly surprising) parallels have thus been uncovered, although they do not, to be sure, imply any direct derivation.

One could perhaps give the following reasons for the unmistakable parallels in the basic thematic of their metaphysical systems. While for the one, philosophy is to be understood as a "system in development"[74] and the history of philosophy is thus to be interpreted teleologically as the process of self-unfolding of the Absolute, for the other at least this much stands without question, that, namely, the history of philosophy must be understood as an irreversible process: "Philosophy never reverts to its old position after the shock of a great philosopher."⁷⁵ The conviction that philosophy plays a leading role in the construction of those theories which preside in each epoch allows both thinkers to seek from within a situation of "Entzweiung" or of bifurcation the possibility of reconciling the divergent spiritual currents by revising the prevailing set of basic metaphysical premises.

The contemporary relevance of these remarks manifests itself in the crude fact that the critical situation has not attenuated but rather is so exacerbated that the self-annihilation of the human race is a technological possibility. The principle task designated by both thinkers is the critical mediation of traditional, particularly modern (neuzeitlich) philosophy with contemporary thought, and, advancing from there, the mediation of scientific and philosophical thinking. Even if we have let go that self-confident optimism which could trust in the unbroken progress of spirit, there remains the hope that the metaphor yet retains its strength when it declares: Dwarfs on the shoulders of giants do see more than they.⁷⁶

Notes

I would like to thank Anderson Weekes for translating the German text.

1. K. R. Meist: "Zur Role der Geschichte in Hegels System der Philosophie." In *Kunsterfahrung und Kulturpolitik im Berlin Hegels*. Ed. by O. Pöggeler and A. Gethmann-Siefert. *Hegel-Studien*, Beiheft 22. (Bonn, 1983), pp. 49–82. Especially p. 64ff. In my opinion the differentiation of Hegel's concept of history takes place during his Heidelberg period in connection with his effort to elucidate philosophically the problematic relationship of power and right in history, cf. my "Die Weltgeschichte als das Weltgericht. Zur Modifikation von Hegels Geschichtsbegriff in Heidelberg." (To be published.)

2. H. Marcuse: *Hegels Ontologie und die Grundlage einer Theorie der Geschichtlichkeit*. Frankfurt/M. 1932.

3. A. N. Whitehead: *Process and Reality*. Corrected Edition. Ed. by D. R. Griffin and D. W. Sherburne. New York/London, 1978. (In the following cited as PR according to this edition; parenthetical pagination refers to the Macmillan edition of 1929.) German translation: *Prozess und Realität*, tr. with critical annotations by H.-G. Holl. Frankfurt/M., 1979.

4. Concerning Hegel cf. in this regard the very compact but nonetheless comprehensive presentation of this influence by K. Düsing: *Hegel und die*

Geschichte der Philosophie. Ontologie und Dialektik in Antike und Neuzeit. "Erträge der Forschung, Band 206" (Darmstadt, 1983).

5. PR p. 39 (63).

6. PR p. XI (VI).

7. PR p. 7 (10).

8. PR p. 81 (125).

9. E. Cassirer: *Vom Mythus des Staates.* (Orig. *The Myth of the State.*) German translation by F. Stoessl. Zürich, 1949. P. 341.

10. Cf. the title of N. Rothenstreich's book: *From Substance to Subject.* Studies in Hegel. The Hague 1974.

11. G. Böhme: "Whiteheads Abkehr von der Substanzmetaphysik.—Substanz und Relation." In *Whitehead. Einführung in seine Kosmologie.* Ed. by E. Wolf-Gazo. Freiburg/München, 1980, p. 45.

12. A more thorough presentation of these relationships can be found in my: "Causa sive ratio." In *Cahiers Spinoza 4.* Paris, 1983, pp. 171–204; especially p. 183ff.

13. Cf. my "Moi absolu et Substance Unique. Remarques sur le spinozisme du jeune Schelling." (To be published.)

14. Cf. D. Henrich: "Jacob Zwillings Nachlass. Gedanken, Nachrichten und Dokumente aus Anlass seines Verlustes." In *Homburg v.d. Höhe in der deutschen Geistesqeschichte.* Studien zum Freundeskreis um Hegel und Hölderlin. Ed. by Ch. Jamme A. O. Pöggeler. Stuttgart, 1981. Pp. 245–266.

15. Cf. my "Sehnsucht nach einem reineran, freieran Zustande. Hegel und der württembergische Verfassungsstreit." In *Frankfurt aber ist der Nabel dieser Erde.* Schicksal einer Generation der Goethezeit. Ed. by Ch. Jamme A. O. Pöggeler. Stuttgart, 1983. Pp. 73–103. Especially p. 100f.

16. The fact that Hegel was called by Paulus to help work—albeit to a modest extent—on the first complete edition of Spinoza's works speaks well for my claim here. Cf. my "Hegel et l'edition de Spinoza par Paulus." In: *Cahiers Spinoza 4.* Paris, 1983. Pp. 127–138.

17. G. W. F. Hegel: *Differenz des Fichte'schen und Schellingschen Systems der Philosophie*. Cited according to G. W. F. Hegel: *Gesammelte Werke*. Vol. 4. Hamburg 1968, p. 13. (In the following this edition is cited with the abbreviation GW.) Cf. in this context my: "Spinoza in Hegels Logik." In *Mededelingen 45 vanwege het Spinozahuis*. Leiden, 1982. Especially p. 7ff.

18. GW 4, p. 12.

19. GW 4, p. 11.

20. Thus the first section of *Darstellung meines Systems der Philosophie*. (1801); vd. *F. W. J. Schellings sämmtliche Werke*. Erste Abtheilung. Vol. 4. Stuttgart/Augsburg, 1859, p. 114.

21. GW 4, p. 24.

22. GW 4, p. 64. Hegel can here refer back to his so-called "Systemfragment of 1800" where a conception of life is developed as "die Verbindung der Verbindung und der Nichtverbindung." *Hegels theologische Jugendschriften*. Ed. by H. Nohl. Tübingen, 1907, p. 348.

23. Cf. *F. W. J. Schellings sämmtliche Werke*. Erste Abtheilung. Vol. 4. *loc. cit.* p. 120.: "So besteht also die wahre Philosophie in dem Beweis, dab die absolute Identität (das Unendliche) nicht aus sich selbst herausgetreten, und alles, was ist, insofern es ist, die Unendlichkeit selbst sey, ein Satz welchen von allen bisherigen Philosophien nur Spinoza erkannt hat." The Absolute acquires cosmological dimensions understood as "universe." Cf. Schelling *ibid.* p. 125.

24. Cf. K. Düsing: "Idealistische Substanzmetaphysik. Probleme der Systementwicklung bei Shelling und Hegel in Jena." In *Hegel Studien*. Beiheft 20. *Hegel in Jena*. Ed. by D. Henrich and K. Düsing. Bonn, 1980. Pp. 25-44. Concerning the problem that a fundamental critique of the substance concept would have to mean a similar critique of metaphysics, yet if it is undertaken for the sake of revising this concept thus remains within the scope of substance-metaphysics, cf. W. Stegmaier: *Substanz. Grundbegriff der Metaphysik*. Stuttgart-Bad Cannstatt 1977. Pp. 19ff. W. Cramer (*Das Absolute und das Kontingente. Untersuchungen zum Substanzbegriff*. Frankfurt/Main, 1976.) understands Hegel's philosophy—one ought to supplement his "mature" philosophy—in this sense: "Hegels System kann als ausgeführter Spinozismus bezeichnet werden, als ein Spinozismus, der sich dessen bewusst geworden ist, dass die Differenzierung des Einen in das Viele in der Philosophie ausgeführt werden muss. Die Differenz zwischen Moment und Anderem aber ist im Systeme Hegels letztlich so untergegangen wie im Spinozismus." An altogether different question, which

however cannot be discussed here, is whether Spinoza's philosophy ever needed such an emendation. Cf. e.g. P. Macherey: *Hegel ou Spinoza.* Paris 1971.

25. GW 7, p. 150ff. Cf. in this regard K. Düsing: *Hegel und die Geschichte* . . . p. 176.

26. GW 9, p. 18.

27. Cf. the "Bericht Gablers über Hegel." In H. Kimmerle: "Dokumente zu Hegels Jenaer Dozententätigkeit (1801–1807)", in *Hegel-Studien.* Vol. 4. Bonn, 1967. Pp. 70–71.

28. GW 9, p. 20.

29. *Ibid.* Italics mine; cf. in this regard K. Düsing: *Hegel und die Geschichte* . . . p. 110f.

30. Cf. especially Hegel's famous, ironical formulation: "sein *Absolutes* für die Nacht auszugeben, worin, wie man zu sagen pflegt, alle Kühe schwarz sind, ist die Naivität der Leere an Erkenntniss", in the "Vorrede" of the *Phänomenologie des Geistes.* GW 9, p. 17; cf. also the detailed annotations on p. 485.

31. Cf. my *Wirklichkeit und Methode in der Philosophie Hegels.* Untersuchungen zur Logik. Der Einfluss Spinozas. Diss. Köln, 1974. Especially the section "Logik und Geschichte der Philosophie", pp. 67ff.

32. G. W. F. Hegel: *Wissenschaft der Logik.* Erster Band. Die objective Logik. Ed. by G. Lasson, 1934. Unchanged reprint Hamburg, 1963 (in the following cited as L I) p. 74. Lasson used as the basis for his edition the second, revised version of the "Seinslogik." In the 1812 edition the connectedness of the history of philosophy and conceptual-logical development was in this passage not as sharply formulated: "Das Denken oder vielmehr Vorstellen, dem nur ein bestimmtes Seyn, oder das Daseyn vorschwebt, worein die *reale* Verschiedenheit des Seyns und Nichts fllt, ist zu dem Anfang der reinen Wissenschaft zurück zu weisen, welchen Parmenides gemacht hat, der unter den Menschen der erste gewesen zu seyn scheint, welcher sein Vorstellen und damit auch das Vorstellen der Folgezeit zu dem reinen Gedanken des Seyns geläutert und erhoben, und damit das Element der Wissenschaft erschaffen hat." GW 11, p. 48; cf. *ibid.* p. 45.

33. GW 11, p. 45; L I p. 68. A conspectus of the divergencies of the two editions of the *Logik* is to be expected in volume 20 of the *Gesammelte Werke,* which will note the differences with a comparative apparatus.

34. "In Ansehung der Philosophie sind überhaupt aber nur diejenigen namhaft zu machen, deren Principe einen Ruck gethan und durch welche die Wissenschaft eine Erweiterung erlangt hat." G. W. F. Hegel: *Werke*. Vollständige Ausgabe durch einen Verein von Freunden des Verewigten. (In the following shortly cited as *Werke* and vol. nr.) Vol. 13, Berlin, 1833, p. 133.

35. *Werke* 13, p. 53, Cf. *ibid.* p. 42: "So ist die Philosophie *System in der Entwicklung;* so ist es auch die Geschichte der Philosophie." Further *ibid.* p. 53: "In der Reihe der Philosophien muss darauf hingewiesen werden, wie sie die Systematisierung der philosophischen Wissenschaft selber ist. Man kann meinen, dass die Philosophie in den *Stufen der Idee* eine andere Ordnung haben müsse als die Ordnung, in welcher *in der Zeit* diese Bestimmungen hervorgegangen sind. *Im Ganzen ist die Ordnung dieselbe.*" (Italics mine.)

36. GW 12, p. 15: "Die wahrhafte Widerlegung muss in die Kraft des Gegners eingehen und sich in den Umkreis seiner Stärke stellen." Hegel objects that the critique of Fichte and Schelling remained external, whereby their refutation of Spinoza had to fail. (*Ibid.* p. 14f.)

37. *Werke* 13, p. 55.

38. *Werke* 15 (Berlin, 1836), p. 378.

39. *Werke* 15, p. 368; cf. *ibid.* p. 376. Cf. also *Werke* 10 vol. 2 (*Ästhetik*), p. 171, where Hegel speaks of "Morgenland" as the "erste Expansion des sich zur Befreiung vom Endlichen aufschliessenden Bewusstseins".

40. *Werke* 15, p. 368.

41. *Ibid.* p. 377, p. 382; cf. GW 12, p. 14f.

42. *Werke* 15, p. 379.

43. Cf. E. Fleischmann: "Die Wirklichkeit in Hegels Logik. Ideengeschichtliche Beziehungen zu Spinoza." In *Zeitschrift für philosophische Forschung*, 18, 1964, pp. 3–29. Cf. further my *Wirklichkeit und Mathode . . .* pp. 160ff.; concerning Hegel's occupation with Spinoza cf. also G. Maluschke: *Kritik und absolute Methode in Hegels Dialektik.* In *Hegel-Studien,* Beiheft 13. Bonn, 1974. Especially pp. 55–81.

44. GW 12, p. 15.

45. *Werke* 15, p. 379.

46. The principle of individuality, as the other component of the overcoming of Spinozism, which Hegel interprets as pushing towards acosmism, cannot be discussed within the limited scope of this paper. Cf. in this regard my: "Das Eine und/als das Andere. Zur systematischen Bedeutung von Hegels Leibniz-Rezeption." In *Leibniz. Werk und Wirkung IV.* "Internationaler Leibniz-Kongress Vorträge." Hannover, 1983. Pp. 433–441.

47. GW 11, p. 378.

48. *Werke* 15, p. 456.

49. G. W. Leibniz: *Monadologie.* § 18: "On pourroit donner le nom d'Entelechies à toutes les substances simples, on Monades creées, car elles ont en elles une certaine perfection ('εχουσιτὸ 'ατελέσ), il y a une suffisance ('αυτάρκεια) qui les rend sources de leurs actions internes et pour ainsi dire, des Automates incorporels." Leibniz himself refers to his *Theodizee*, § 86. The *Monadologie* is cited according to the bilingual (French-German) edition Hamburg, 1956, pp. 32ff. (Auf Grund der kritischen Ausgabe von Andre Robinet (1954) und der Übersetzung von Arthur Buchenau mit Einführung und Anmerkungen herausgegeben von Herbert Herring.)

50. *Werke* 14 (Berlin, 1833) p. 325. Similarly, Kant's conception of life as an end (Zweck) in itself, in contrast to the mechanistic understanding of rationalism, reminds Hegel of Aristotle: "Das Leben ist die Energie, als Entelechie sich erhaltend. . . . In diesem Ausdruck des Aristoteles ist der Begriff des Lebens enthalten; aber dieser aristotelische Begriff der Natur, der Lebendigkeit, ist verloren gegangen, ist abwesend in neuerer Betrachtungsweise der Natur des Lebens, wo man Druck, Stoss, chemische Verhältnisse, überhaupt äusserliche Verhältnisse zum Grunde legt. Erst in der Kantischen Philosophie tritt jener Begriff wieder hervor: Das Lebendige ist sich selbst Zweck, muss als Selbstzweck beurtheilt werden." *Ibid.* p. 346.

51. GW 12, p. 394.

52. *Werke* 14, p. 326.

53. PR p. 7 (10). D. Bidney also begins his interpretation with this citation. ("The Problem of Substance in Spinoza and Whitehead." In *The Philosophical Review.* Vol. XLV New York/Menaska, 1936. Pp. 574–592.) Bidney's main thesis is, however, the following: "There is a conflict of philosophical traditions at the basis of the metaphysics of Spinoza and Whitehead, and all the problems of Spinoza's metaphysics recur in Whitehead's works in a more acute form" (p. 574).

54. PR p. 6 (10); cf. PR p. 73 (114): "Spinoza is practically a logical systematization of Descartes, purging him of inconsistencies."

55. PR p. 81 (125).

56. It is difficult to judge the relationship of Schelling and Hegel during this period. But precisely in regard to these two conceptions Hegel, as the less experienced professor, proved not to be the less experienced philosopher. Cf. K. Düsing: "Spekulation und Reflexion. Zur Zusammenarbeit Schellings und Hegels in Jena. In *Hegel-Studien*. Vol. 5 (1969), pp. 95–128; cf. further the same: "Idealistische Substanzmetaphysik," *loc. cit.* pp. 30f.

57. Cf. the "Preface" of PR p. xiii (viii); Whitehead names there as the first habit of thought which is to be rejected: "The distrust of speculative philosophy."

58. PR pp. 158f. (240ff.) Cf. concerning the whole context of this issue the very instructive book, to be mentioned here again, by R. L. Fetz: *Whitehead: Prozessdenken und Substanzmetaphysik*. Freiburg/München, 1981, here especially p. 34 ff.; cf. as well the already cited study by G. Böhme: "Whiteheads Abkehr von der Substanzmetaphysik. Substanz und Relation," *loc. cit.*

59. PR p. 30 (45).

60. PR p. 51 (81).

61. PR p. xiii (ix). It must be surprising, in view of the almost congruent basic thematic, that Whitehead makes no direct references to the virtually classic work of E. Cassirer: *Substanzbegriff und Funktionsbegriff: Untersuchungen über die Fragen der Erkenntniskritik* (Berlin, 1910). Cf. in this context e.g. p. 10: "Vor allem aber ist es die Kategorie der *Relation*, die durch diese metaphysische Grundlehre des Aristoteles zu einer abhängigen und untergeordneten Stellung herabgedrückt wird. . . . Das kategoriale Grundverhältnis des *Dinges* zu seinen *Eigenschaften* bleibt fortan der leitende Gesichtspunkt, während alle relativen Bestimmungen nur insofern in Betracht gezogen werden, als sie sich . . . in Zustände an einem Subjekt oder an einer Mehrheit von Subjekten umdeuten lassen."

62. PR p. 137 (208f).

63. PR pp. 73f. (114).

64. I come very close here to the—in my opinion very convincing—argumentation of R. L. Fetz; cf. his *Whitehead: Prozessdenken und Substanzmetaphysik* pp. 124f.

65. In this regard it ought to be investigated thoroughly how Whitehead's critique of the metaphysical tradition stands in relation to Heidegger's critique of the ontological tradition. (As far as I can see, Whitehead himself takes no position in this regard.) Cf. in this context regarding Heidegger e.g. O. Pöggeler: "Sein als Ereignis." In *Zeitschrift für philosophische Forschung.* Vol. 13, 1959, pp. 597–632.

66. PR p. 150 (228).

67. PR p. 88 (135).

68. PR p. 151 (228).

69. PR p. 151 (228f.). Cf. in this context G. L. Kline: "Life as Ontological Category: A Whiteheadian Note on Hegel." In W. E. Steinkrauss/K. I. Schmitz: *Art and Logic in Hegel's Philosophy.* New Jersey: Humanities Press, 1980. Pp. 158–162. Kline's thesis that Whitehead's primarily temporal distinction between subject and object has no correlate in Hegel's thought ought to provide incentive to further reflections. I will mention here only the concept of "positivity" in Hegel's early writings as an impetus.

70. Concerning this interpretative model cf. I. Leclerc: "Being and Becoming in Whitehead's Philosophy." In *Kant-Studien.* Vol. 51. (1959/60) pp. 427–437; here especially pp. 429ff.

71. PR p. 7 (10).

72. Cf. R. L. Fetz, *loc. cit.* p. 209.

73. Cf. R. L. Fetz, *loc. cit.* p. 219, p. 263.

74. See above footnote 35.

75. PR p. 11 (16).

76. Concerning the history of this metaphor cf. R. K. Merton: *On the Shoulders of Giants.* A Shandean Postscript. New York, 1965. (German translation: *Auf den Schultern von Riesen.* Ein Leitfaden durch das Labyrinth der Gelehrsamkeit. Frankfurt/M., 1983.)

II

Metaphysics and Systematic Philosophy

Klaus Hartmann
UNIVERSITY OF TÜBINGEN

Types of Explanation in Hegel and Whitehead

If we are to trust a minority tradition in the secondary philosophical literature,[1] there is a growing awareness that Whitehead's philosophy bears a likeness to the philosophy of Hegel, and that a renewed effort to explore this proximity could be rewarding. It is possible that certain central elements of Hegel's system may be read into Whitehead's cosmology so that Whitehead's system can stand as an updated and corrected version of Hegel's speculative position. On the other hand, it is equally possible that certain of Hegel's most valuable insights might be lost in the process. In what follows I try to deal with the philosophical task posed by these alternative possibilities. In particular, I argue that an assimilation of their respective positions will not be meaningful unless the types of explanation adopted by each prove compatible.

I. Points of Coincidence

At a certain level of inspection which it would be unkind to call superficial there appear significant areas of coincidence between Whitehead and Hegel. Three such areas stand out among several: both philosophers are concerned with *organic wholes* (indeed, Whitehead adopts the term "philosophy of organism" to denote his position in *Process and Reality*[2]); they both consider *process* crucial; they both defend a *teleological scheme* ordering levels of items of the universe. We may, in addition, note that both philosophers object to the substance/accident schema, Hegel considering it penultimate, Whitehead rejecting it out of hand. Finally mention should be made of the fact that both philosophers effect a return from the characteristic epistemological focus on the cognizing subject in late modern thought, to a broader focus upon the nature of "objectivity" in general. Hegel deals with the subject as an entity of a certain level of determinacy within a catalogue of determinations in which all manner of entities and their conceptual features find their places.[3] Whitehead, in turn, expressly opts for "pre-

Kantian modes of thought" (PR vi). Subsequent passages in *Process and Reality* suggest that what is meant by this phrase is a realistic account of the world that allows for the concurrence of bodies to explain their powers or, indeed, their interconnectedness as found in Locke (cf. PR 28, 37).[4] The subject as we know it will appear as incorporated in the context of the universe, related to it in ways not fundamentally different from the ways in which any entity of the universe is related to any other.

While in Whitehead's case confirmation of what has been said can be easily obtained from *Process and Reality*, verification of Hegel's position is somewhat more cumbersome, so a brief orientation may be in order. Hegel's concern for organic wholes is apparent in all his systematic writings, including the *Phenomenology of Spirit*, the *Science of Logic*, and the *Encyclopedia*. In the *Logic*, he develops concepts like "Being-for-Self," "Subjectivity," and "Idea," as well as other concepts which he views as basic to organic systems, such as mechanism, chemism, and teleology. The latter concepts receive more concrete treatment in the philosophies of "Nature" and of "Spirit" (the second and third parts of the *Encyclopedia*) in order to cover cosmological features such as space and time and the union of subjectivity and embodiment in what Hegel calls "spirit." In the Philosophy of Spirit we also find a treatment of social systems under the heading of "objective spirit," of which the *Philosophy of Right* presents a more detailed account.

Hegel's concern for *process* is most clearly indicated through his emphasis on historical development in the political domain (discussed in the final portion of the *Philosophy of Right* and in the *Lectures on the Philosophy of History*) as well as in the domains of thought—the arts and religion (the subject-matter of the *Lectures on the History of Philosophy*, the *Lectures on Aesthetics*, and the *Lectures on the Philosophy of Religion*). But apart from historical development, there is process proper in nature: physical, chemical, and organic process, and "process of the genus" (all in the Philosophy of Nature). Natural process by itself is viewed as a concrete form of time, which for Hegel is itself prior to process. This concept of time in turn has its model in the concept of coming-to-be and passing-away discussed in the *Logic* as the index of finite beings. Yet another meaning of process can be associated with what Hegel calls "the movement of the Concept,"[5] a theoretical progression without commitment to a real time process.

Abundant material to illustrate Hegel's *teleological ordering* of levels of entities (or of "Being") is available in the systematic works mentioned above. A glance at the table of contents of any of these works shows that they are modeled on a system of tiers, levels, or stages of concept development, terminating in a stage where thought has come full circle. The "movement of the Concept" is Hegel's way of moving from stage to stage.

Finally, to document in Hegel what was said about the substance/accident schema, we can refer to his statements concerning "substance versus subject" in connection with his critique of Spinoza in the *Phenomenology*,[6] his critique of Kant in the *Logic*[7] (expressing dissatisfaction with a rationalization of objects only) or the drift, in the *Logic*, from Being in Part I through substance in Part II to Subjectivity and Idea in Part III. Hegel's "objective" view is understood as the converse of this customary drift, in that he offers instead an "objective logic" as the *antecedent* of the then conventional hierarchy of metaphysics, within which Subjectivity and the Concept are treated.[8]

The foregoing may suffice to back up the claim that Whitehead and Hegel have much in common—namely, the basic themes of organicity and process, together with related morphological aspects. However, the mere mention of Hegelian complexities (*Science of Logic* versus *Encyclopedia;* historical or natural process versus "the movement of the Concept;" the rationalization of stages by way of this movement of the Concept) is enough to indicate problems affecting any attempt to assimilate the two philosophers to each other. To press the point from Whitehead's angle, we may refer to the fact that his philosophy of organism is, at the same time, a plea for *atomism*—this feature of ontology constituting the "ultimate metaphysical truth" (PR 53). Consequently, plural organic wholes will require a complex interpretation in terms of real constituents and supervening novelty. Accordingly, what Whitehead calls a "scheme of ideas" (PR vii–x; *passim*) or a "system of general ideas," or a "general scheme" (PR 4) will have to be investigated as to its implications regarding this commitment to atomism before we can determine Whitehead's proximity to Hegel. In a parallel undertaking, we will have to clarify Hegel's meaning with a view to an evaluation of what we may call the Whitehead-Hegel interface.

I contend that the aims of the two philosophers differ in point of the *type of philosophical explanation* favoured by each. The respective types of explanation correlate with the distinction between *metaphysics* (as exemplified in Whitehead's cosmology) and *ontology* (as exemplified in Hegel's categorial theory). We will approach the two philosophers in light of this distinction and then conclude with some comments regarding the scope and compatibility of philosophical explanation generally.

II. Whitehead the Metaphysician

When we look at Whitehead's methodological reflections in the Preface and in Part I of *Process and Reality,* we find that his professed aim is to provide a "scheme" accommodating everything there is in the universe. He thinks that the world is not made up of macroscopic substances but should be construed in terms of microscopic entities called "actual entities" (PR 27) or (as he prefers in *Science and the Modern World*) "actual occasions." These are described as little organisms featuring a period of self-centered, or teleological, formation to the point of satisfaction and termination. Actual entities "feed" on predecessor entities whose "concrescence" they are (much like instances of a Hegelian Being-for-Self which is what it is through reference to its Other). After termination, successor entities will arise which in turn are heirs to the panorama of predecessors, each successor entity constituting a concrescence of that panorama. It is in this relationship of inheritance (PR 167, 183 and *passim*) or "prehension" (Part III of PR), which replaces the traditional causal relation, that an entity in the present exerts and develops its organic and (what seems the same) subjective function. In addition, Whitehead conceives of an ideal factor conditioning actual entities: for him, these prehend so-called "eternal objects" which provide guidance for what the entity in question aspires to become.

Now Whitehead is certainly interested in determining the nature of an actual entity, bound up as it is with its relatedness to its predecessors. In absorbing and (in the case of "negative prehensions") excluding contributions from its predecessors, an actual entity presides over itself and so features a proto-psychic or, to use Leibniz's term, a "monadic" character. If ontology is that discipline of philosophy which studies the real with a view to finding appropriate concepts for its items, we can say that Whitehead offers an *ontology* alternative to the Aristotelian one, an ontology committed to a single category of what there is, that of monad or actual entity.[9]

But over and above such a conceptual undertaking which belongs to a "scheme of ideas" in the sense of ontology, Whitehead's philosophy can also be construed as *metaphysical*. Much depends here, of course, on a more precise meaning of the term, "metaphysics."

Whitehead himself uses the terms "metaphysics" and "metaphysical" quite frequently to characterize his project in *Process and Reality*, but he offers only a very vague and imprecise definition of the term as essentially synonymous with "speculative philosophy" (e.g., PR 4, 6, and 16). We zero in on his meaning, however, when we take note of his claim that "the potentiality for being an element in a real concrescence of many entities into one actuality, is the one general metaphysical character attaching to all entities, actual and non-actual; and that every item in its universe is involved in each concrescence" (PR 33). If we understand this approach as constituting a *strategy* for explaining *why* the universe is the way it is, then the metaphysical bent of Whitehead's philosophy turns out to lie inherently in his so-called "ontological principle" (misleadingly termed a "category of explanation"): "Every condition to which the process of becoming conforms in any particular instance, has its reason *either* in the character of some actual entity in the actual world of that concrescence, *or* in the character of the subject which is in the process of concrescence" (PR 36). Such terminology itself indicates that Whitehead himself made no clear distinction between metaphysics and ontology. If my distinction is upheld, the ontological principle turns out to be the fulcrum of a metaphysical project.

To locate Whitehead's position and his claim to metaphysics in a critical context, let us inspect briefly some of the more important traditional notions of metaphysics. There is, first, the projection of the term back onto Aristotle in the phrases "metaphysica generalis" (= ontology) and "metaphysica specialis." In Aristotle proper, First Philosophy covers the doctrine of Being qua Being as well as God, so that an external agent like God is not yet seen as posing a metaphysical problem as opposed to ontological topics. Later scholasticism, by contrast, put theology alongside psychology and cosmology, leaving us wondering whether, in special metaphysics, we are dealing with claims about certain existences which differ from ontological legislation about Being as such. Passing to the Kantian understanding of metaphysics (leaving Locke and Leibniz to find their places in connection with Whitehead's own position) we note the guiding idea that metaphysics deals with entities about which we can know nothing since they are not given in experience. Metaphysics is said to claim entities, and a knowledge of entities such as a first cause or God that go to explain what appears to us. The hiddenness of the explanatory entity is, for Kant, sufficient to discount it, except as a topic for thought.

It is significant that emphasis centers on the existential posits of metaphysics. While Kant would seem to go along with the existential posit of an unknowable thing in itself (as the hidden cause of our impressions), his critique of the ontological argument makes it clear that what cannot be defended is the existential posit of God, deriving from Reason's claim that existence can be a matter of knowledge by way of argument. In subsequent notions of metaphysics, the emphasis on existence versus essence is even more pronounced, as when Schelling thinks that so-called "Positive Philosophy" should start from an existential posit of Being as prior to its essence,[10] or when Sartre distinguishes ontology from metaphysics by claiming that the latter deals with occurrences and disappearances as opposed to essences and structures.[11]

Now if we try to locate Whitehead in the context of comparative understandings of metaphysics, we find that his is a position involving indebtedness to several ideas incidental to metaphysics. There is a sense in which Whitehead (like Locke) claims *hidden entities* as the true reality: they are monads featuring the temporal and spatial make-up of actual entities. They are, however, not hidden or unknown in the sense that we could not give an ontological account of them; to call them "actual entities" means, on the contrary, that we claim to know what they are. There is also a sense in which Whitehead, prompted by his relational view of actual entities, rests his case on *existential posits*. Every actual entity, in order to be, implies reference to the sum-total of predecessor entities in the universe (an implication which, for conscious subjects, shades over into givenness). Consequently, the ontological principle can be both a principle accounting for the structure of each entity, and a principle linking the existence of an entity and its "whatness" to a universal existential posit. Thus there is also a sense in which Whitehead echoes another Kantian inspiration in defining metaphysics: namely, that it involves an *unconditioned*—not now, however, in the sense of the sufficient reason for a cosmic series, but in the sense rather of this sum-total of actual entities required for the concrescence of any one entity. Thus on both counts (the existential posits implied *by* concrescence and the sum-total of predecessors required *for* concrescence) Whitehead's philosophical perspective can be considered metaphysical.

To pass on to what distinguishes Whitehead's position from the metaphysical tradition—including Locke whom he apostrophizes quite often and Leibniz to whom he is in fact close—let us examine his position on the problem of *time,* an essential ingredient in his unique variant of metaphysics. On his view, each actual occasion encompasses a quantum of time (made up of the epoch of its self-formation), which upon expiring is subject to prehensive inheritance by a universe of successor entities. Or, as the phrase goes, each actual entity is a "subject-superject" (PR 43, 129); i.e., both a subject guiding its self-formation by prehending its predecessors, and the result of its self-formation left for others to prehend. These two aspects together afford each entity the discontinuous continuation of what its predecessors were.

This Whiteheadian view of time or, better, this account of how the real can be temporal, will seem rather odd unless we go beyond a merely doxographic statement and try to see it as an answer to age-old problems. The traditional view was that time, regarded as an objective feature of the real, presents itself in two forms: as duration or permanence, and as change. Change was seen as alteration with respect to an unchanging, identical substratum, persistent substance—locomotion, or change of place, serving as a key phenomenon to back up the claim. The difficulty—apart from the epistemological problem of whether permanence can be said to be temporal at all unless contrasted with subjective change in the stream of consciousness[12]—was how to rationalize change (other than locomotion) ontologically. Would it be all right to put it down to law-governed causal impact and restrict it to qualitative change due to qualitative causes? Or could there also be "existence-change" (as Jonathan Bennett calls it[13])? The traditional scheme denies the latter in view of its need for persistent substance. But supposing we denied substance: could not ways then be found to explain change, including existence-change?

Whitehead opts for this solution and offers a far-reaching recasting of time theory. His suggestion is that, rather than putting up with two modes of time (permanence and change), we may make change the unique mode so that, with the permanent substratum abandoned, every change would constitute an existence-change. Along this line, every actual entity stands for an epoch preceding an existence-change into a new actual entity and its epoch. Or, more correctly, since there is no single-file relationship between predecessor and successor entities: all actual entities contemporary for a spectator (in presentational immediacy) stand for an epoch preceding existence-changes of all of them into a new sum-total to be given in presentational immediacy. (We neglect here relativistic qualifications such as Whitehead made in *Principles of Natural Knowledge*).

By and large, time is thus a uniform structure of existence-changes, and what has to be accounted for now is what was "understood" in classical theory, namely persistence. This has to be rationalized by various devices of content transmission (prehension, subjective aim, eternal objects) which are ramifications of Whitehead's basic inspiration in time theory. Clearly, though, a mainstay of the tradition, namely that locomotion, or mechanical movement, requires persistence of that which moves, has to be given up in favor of unconvincing contortions.[14]

To return to our review of Whitehead as metaphysician, let us focus on the metaphysical implications of his theory of time. It would seem that an *agency* is required to *insure* the enactment of ever new actual entities. Mysterious though this may be, a general principle called "Creativity" is credited with this feat. What adds to our wonderment is that Whitehead sees in it a mere reformulation of Aristotelian "matter" as well as of the more modern notion of "neutral stuff" (PR 31). However, rather than being passive and receptive, Creativity is said to be "the pure notion of the activity conditioned by the objective immortality of the actual world" (PR 46f.)—i.e., creativity is the activity needed for the fresh emergence of actual entities in light of predecessor entities, and thus is itself the "principle of novelty" (PR 31).

We may well wonder whether creativity is a "real principle" inherent in something that is, or an "ideal principle," an explanatory subterfuge of the philosopher. Whichever way we see it, the required efficacy of creativity will justify its description as a metaphysical tenet. By the same token, the assumption that predecessor entities will suffer their eclipse in step with the creation and self-formation of the new set of actual entities (although there must be no continuous ideal time in terms of which this synchrony can legitimately be depicted) must count as a metaphysical tenet. It is a temporal version of Leibniz's pre-established harmony.

Yet another metaphysical stance is available in Whitehead's adoption of *eternal objects* (or essences of actual entities) which, as we noted before, serve as paradigms for the actual entities' choice of what they mean to become. To propose an external ground for the determinateness in actual entities is surely a metaphysical subterfuge, since one means through this to hypostatize universals and make them a ground for the real, much the way the exoteric Plato did.

A final metaphysical element in Whitehead can be seen in the introduction of *God* into his scheme. In keeping with traditional views, God is both an *agent* of pure knowledge who knows all essences [in this context, Whitehead speaks of the "primordial nature" of God (PR 47–50, 523)] and a *respondent* to the world, much in line with Leibniz's central monad or with idealistic theorems, including Hegel's, about God [in this connection, Whitehead speaks of the "consequent nature" of God (PR 523f.)]. The detail of Whitehead's views on God is somewhat involved so that we may be allowed to refrain from attempting to clarify what he has in mind.[15] It may be sufficient here to register the fact that God's function in Whitehead's scheme is a metaphysical one.

To return to general reflections on the nature of Whitehead's project, let us sharpen the *methodological* issue. To the extent that what Whitehead has in mind is an *ontological* account of what is in a world pattern, he offers no more than an "interpretation" (PR 4), an "imaginative generalization" (PR 7), indeed a "descriptive generalization" (PR 15f.), although he also speaks in the same breath of "constructive thought" (PR x) and "imaginative construction" (PR 7) which must needs feature a hypothetical element. His constructive thought is meant to serve purposes of explanation: there are 27 "categories of explanation" (PR 33–39) and, beyond that, ultimates like "creativity," "many," "one," and "togetherness" (PR 31f.) which figure prominently in the desired explanation. Needless to say, God, too, has an explanatory role to play. Thus, on a number of counts, Whitehead's aim can be said to be *metaphysical explanation* of the real or of the universe. However, in view of his epochal theory of time, his explanatory desire does not, as in classical metaphysics, cover the metaphysical origin of the world. His theory has an open end towards the past (it is impossible, indeed, to think of a first set of actual entities) and avoids the assertion of an existential and primordial Absolute accounting for the cosmos (unless, that is, his views on God are pressed in this direction). To that extent, then, Whitehead's position appears as quasi-descriptive (in a sense somehow compatible with hidden entities).

III. Hegel the Ontologist

In turning to Hegel for parallels with respect to Whitehead, we should bear in mind that his manner of doing philosophy is governed by an attempt to develop a presuppositionless method—an agenda far removed from any realistic, immediate, or predominantly thematic treatment of some given subject-matter. As a consequence, it is not very instructive simply to catalogue his pronouncements on a number of select topics shared with Whitehead. Rather, we must focus first on his general philosophical approach.

In my view, Hegel's philosophy constitutes a developed form of *ontology* or a *theory of categories*.[16] We could, to use Whitehead's phrase, call it a "scheme of ideas," although everything would then turn upon what we *meant* by "scheme" and "ideas." A major concern of Hegel is to propose concepts whose pertinence with reference to Being can be assumed and, in the course of the argument, demonstrated. In the case of demonstrably pertinent concepts, we may, as Hegel himself does for part of his *Science of Logic*, speak of "categories,"[17] and further label the extent or degree of their pertinence (i.e., the extent to which they "hold true" of Being) their "categoriality."

Recourse to categories is, of course, a time-honored position to adopt, occurring as early as Aristotle's *Categories* or even in the early Academy. But while Aristotle claimed a categorial scheme centering on substance and a complementary group of accidents to articulate the world and make judgments about it possible, Hegel follows a different tack. He distinguishes categories in terms of relational types. There are categories whose referents are atomic, non-relational, or self-relational only: categories of Being belonging to a "Logic of Being," such as Being as the zero case of categoriality, quality, Being-for-Self, quantity, and measure. Next there are categories which feature a built-in relation: categories of Essence belonging to a "Logic of Essence," such as "thing" and appearance, substance and accident, substance as cause and effect. And finally, there are categories (Hegel does not here use the term) featuring the inclusion of any opposite: categories of the Concept, belonging to a "Logic of the Concept," such as Subjectivity, Concept, Objectivity, and Idea. We must bear in mind, of course, that the concepts referred to by Hegel are not essences in the sense of paradigmatic or generic universals. Rather, they are concepts marking the comparative ingredience of Thought in Being. Thus Hegel's Essence could be seen as a concept diagnosing the comparative pertinence of generic essences with respect to their substrates.

Let us explore the rationale of such a scheme. First, we note that the scheme allows for a variety of "addresses" of Being; there is no commitment to only one basic concept of Being (such as "actual entity") or to categorial monism (monadism). We can address the real in abstract terms, as Determinate Being (Dasein), or we can indicate its complexity as we do when we interpret the world in terms of substance and accident. Or we may favor still more concrete accounts of the real in terms of Subjectivity and Objectivity, including concepts of system, such as mechanism, teleology, or organicity.

Hegel's scheme in fact constitutes a *systematic hermeneutic* of possible categories or "addresses of Being," which is not merely limited to Hegel's own ontological system, but which also serves as a matrix to diagnose the categorial commitments of the various philosophies that have been proposed (a diagnosis worked out in detail in Hegel's *Lectures on the History of Philosophy*). It suggests a wide area of choice for philosophical theory—building by way of emphasis on certain categorial commitments to the exclusion of others. Indeed, a diagnosis to fit Whitehead could be adapted from Hegel's treatment of Leibniz.[18]

By itself, Hegel's scheme exhibits an ordered pluralism of categorization and a plea for the higher reaches of mental, cultural, and social categories. The idea is clearly not to condone ad lib categorization. On the contrary, Hegel runs through an ordered progression of categories (identified earlier as "the movement of the Concept") which, in the interest of the truth, cannot stop until categories of ontological perfection have been reached. The claim is, of course, not that a most perfect category figures as the universal (monistic) category "applying" to everything, but that there are various thematic realms, or regions, answering to the various categories in question. The end of the progression is reached in the self-reflection of the Absolute Idea which stands for thought assured of its categoriality or truth. This is not to say that anything short of that stage is simply untrue. Early or middle-level categories are "true" in their comparative untruth: if there were nothing more than these, the world would fail to feature perfection. Moreover, the ontological problem of a position committed to atomism (such as Whitehead's) would be, to what extent higher categories are considered genuine pledges for novel ontological realms or merely predicates qualifying monadic individuals.

In view of Hegel's orientation towards concept and categoriality, it could be said that his (systematic) philosophy engages in *no metaphysical commitment* in the senses dealt with earlier. All that categories (i.e., defensible addresses of Being) require is that their non-emptiness be assumed so that an identity of content of Being and Concept can be claimed. We are not making a metaphysical commitment to cows, for example, when we claim substance as a category. But if there were neither cows nor trees nor artifacts nor anything of the sort, then the category might be mistaken. The establishment of a given category is not itself, however, an existence-proof. Instantiation is assumed. Similarly, no metaphysical commitment is required for the identity commitment of a given category.[19]

A corollary to the categorial make-up of Hegel's philosophy is that a move from one category to the next is *not* to be construed *genetically* or in such a way that, in time, and with mounting complexity, items take on a novel determination. Such a mutation may in fact take place, but what we can understand about it is only the relationship between one categorial level and another which has to be diagnosed intraconceptually, rather than in terms of genetic process. Or, read backwards, we are offered a genealogy providing understanding through linear antecedents. This is indeed the core of Hegel's type of explanation, an explanation not of why the world came to be the way it is, or why things happen the way they do, but of what it means for the world to be the way it is.

In this context, a word on Hegel's *dialectic*, the procedure affording moves from category to category, may be in order. The dialectic should be viewed in three ways: 1) as a tenet about conceptual determinateness, maintaining that a concept is not definite without taking account of its opposite; 2) as a theory to bear out this tenet by assimilating the opposite of a given concept, or its Other, to its negation, so that on pain of contradiction we have to move toward a synthesis of preceding opposing determinations in a novel concept; and 3) as a demonstration of categorial pertinence in the case of those concepts which can be reconstructed by means of Being and negation. If negation accounts for determinateness and if it is Being which is qualified by negation, then the categorial pertinence of the reconstructed concepts, or their categoriality, can be regarded as demonstrated.

Mention should also be made of the built-in *architectonic* of Hegel's dialectic (i.e., of its principal ordering) easily overlooked when attention focuses exclusively on linear moves and transitions. In Hegel's dialectic, early and very abstract concepts of qualitative Being (such as Being-in-Itself, Difference, Being-for-Self) can be seen to "govern" richer concepts, thus affording them principal or fundamental explanation in terms of their prototypes. Principal explanation qualifies what would otherwise be merely linear genealogy. Resuming the above analysis, we can say that in view of its three methodological features—categorial scheme, dialectic and architectonic—Hegel's *Logic* implements the idea of a self-grounding ontology, as opposed to a merely hypothetical scheme.

In our survey of Hegel's general philosophical approach, let us broach a complication. I have in mind the fact, noted before, that his categorial scheme is run through twice, on two different levels, namely in the *Science of Logic* and in the *Encyclopedia*. One may certainly say that the *Logic* is more abstract over against the more concrete Philosophies of Nature and of Spirit, but the two levels do not compare generically as the more general to the more specific. What Hegel means is that, in the *Logic*, we refrain from presupposing space and time as dimensions of the multiple occurrence of categorized items, thus excluding further categorial distinctions to which such multiplicity may give rise. It makes good sense to think that Hegel intended the *Logic* as an extended *metaphysica generalis* (= ontology) which the *Encyclopedia* was meant as a *metaphysica specialis*.[20] Admittedly, Hegel sometimes oversteps this self-imposed boundary, but basically the *Logic* can be read as a general ontology, albeit one geared to a division of Being into several realms. If it is argued that, by contrast, the *Encyclopedia* is full of metaphysical commitments concerning our spatio-temporal world, we can answer that Hegel indeed assumes a fair number of regional categories to be non-empty, but does not therefore make metaphysical commitments in the senses described earlier. To illustrate from the *Encyclopedia*: plurality or multiplicity, as occasioned by space and time, gives rise to the basic concepts of physics and biology, as well as on a higher plane, to concepts of the social and political spheres and, lastly, to concepts coming under the rubric of Absolute Spirit such as Art, Religion and Philosophy (concepts which suggest a "return" from multiplicity to oneness).

However, the suspicion of a metaphysical commitment of the *Encyclopedia* lingers on. While we may indeed claim for it a categorial makeup, however much disputed by a critic like Schelling,[21] there seems to be an exception in the case of God, brought on in connection with Absolute Spirit. God is the one example where a category has *unique instantiation*, such that the category is tantamount to an existence-proof.[22]

Methodology aside, let us turn to a select thematic point: Hegel's views on *time* and *process* (as distinct from "the movement of the Concept"). Hegel distinguishes, as we noted before, coming-to-be and passing-away, time, process and development, and historical development. (1) Hegel holds, as an ontological thesis stated in the

Logic,[23] that finite things, featuring a separation of Being and their Concept, are perishable. *Passing-away* serves, as it were, as an ontological qualifier of anything for which his ontology registers a lack of ultimacy, perfection or "closure." One may of course argue that Hegel here illicitly draws upon physical entities, or confuses passing-away with the giving way of an imperfect category to a higher one in terms of the movement of the Concept.

(2) *Time*, discussed in the Philosophy of Nature,[24] resembles coming-to-be and passing-away, but differs from them in that its lack of closure is not adventitious but rather integral to its Concept. For Hegel, time is a determination of nature such that the side-by-sideness of space repeats itself in another side-by-sideness such that anything spatial (point, plane or cube) has an extension, an ecstasis beyond itself. It is a self-direction, a structure featuring the outstandingness of closure. According to this ecstatic notion of time (a phrase normally associated with Heidegger), the "given" present, our seat in the time of the inner sense, is taken to point beyond itself, to our future. The dynamic, or metaphysical, aspect of time concerning the termination of the present and its renewal is not part of Hegel's categorial account of time. His rationalization of time is, if we like, formal in the manner of an ontological qualifier: time is a structure according to which something lacks self-coincidence and has itself for an opposite. To reach it would mark the self-coincidence, or closure, reserved for non-temporal entities. In a way, a temporal being always aspires to full Being but never achieves it.[25] By implication, this structure cannot serve to introduce categorial novelty.

(3) *Process* is seen as an enrichment of time in the sense that, over and above temporal ecstasis as a formal qualifier of entities, it denotes a content-laden directedness of an entity, or set of entities, towards subsequent content-laden phases (which it is for empirical observation or science to fill in). All that remains for the philosopher is to articulate process in terms of the various regions in which it occurs.[26] For Hegel, these belong to the realm of Nature. For the realm of Spirit, he speaks of *development*,[27] covering transitions from soul through consciousness, self-consciousness and other stages to, lastly, Objective and Absolute Spirit. In this context, in view of the apparent identity of the "carrier" of Spirit (man) the trajectory through the various categorial stages assumes the semblance of a learning process of humanity.[28]

The notion of development leads us on to 4) *historical development*. This is said to occur in the realm of thought (or Absolute Spirit), covering philosophy, art, and religion, but more strictly, as historical development proper, on the level of the State (in the realm of Objective Spirit). Here Hegel proposed a real progression to a goal of perfection envisioned by philosophy. The problem is, of course, whether such development can be claimed on the strength of Hegel's systematic philosophy. Can history be rationalized dialectically? Hegel seems to think so, although it is a foregone conclusion that his historical development does not lead to categorial novelty. All it leads to in Hegel's optimistic view is improvement on a given categorial (social and political) plane—as Hegel himself says, from "one is free" to "all are free." In keeping with this, the goal of historical development is different from the Absolute of Hegel's systematic philosophy: it is the rallying point of an objective (social and political) dimension, so-called "World-Spirit," a kind of regulative idea for peoples with varying constitutions vying for supremacy. But what is more important is that the idea of an historical dialectic, even in its weakened form of historical *progression,* implies a *metaphysical commitment* that such and such will happen. This Hegel's dialectic can never show.

Hegel's dubious proposal for theorizing real (albeit regionally restricted) development has served as the prototype for subsequent theories devoted to the task of *rationalizing future progress,* Whitehead not excepted. It is significant that there has been a growing tendency to extrapolate the notion of development in human affairs to processes in nature. Cases in point are Engels, in his *Dialectic of Nature,*[29] and however differently, C. Lloyd Morgan, Samuel Alexander, and Whitehead himself. Whitehead thinks, for example, that "our present cosmic epoch is formed by an 'electromagnetic' society" whose antecedent was a "geometric society" (PR 149). He is also committed to progress in civilization[30] and to social progress.[31] Such views certainly require analysis in view of the commitments made and the vague notion of novelty adopted.

IV. Comparative Success in Explanation

We are now prepared to reach an evaluation of the two types of philosophical explanation exemplified by Whitehead and Hegel, respectively. Supposing we are right in distinguishing ontological from metaphysical explanation, can we go on maintaining that the two philosophers share important persuasions such that differences of explanation prove comparatively unimportant? Alternatively, does Whitehead improve upon Hegel by adopting a metaphysical type of explanation, or is he subject to Hegelian criticism to the effect that he falls back behind critical ontology, embracing pre-critical metaphysics?

1) Whitehead

Turning to Whitehead first, it is comparatively easy to voice criticism of his *metaphysics,* particularly when we concern ourselves not so much with a spirited idea like the epochal theory of time, so much as with the concealed system constructed on its basis. Let us look at that system first, and then venture a comment concerning Whitehead's underlying inspiration.

First, Whitehead's theory appears paradoxical in that (according to his system) predecessor entities which serve as referents for present actual entities in the stage of formation have reached their eclipse.[32] Admittedly, we must not bring a linear notion of time to bear on the problem, mapping eclipse and fresh emergence on a continuous line—but the paradox persists nonetheless. It might be said that predecessor entities terminate only in so far as they have been prehended, or revived, by their successor entities. But this extraordinary explanation happens not to be Whitehead's thesis. A kind of pre-established harmony (beyond that already bound up with the plurality of constituents of an organism; PR 342) seems required, with an external agency (creativity) responsible for new entities and their proper epochal adjacency. Accordingly, creativity as an explanatory principle for the existence of new entities is, as we suspected before, a metaphysical miracle. It is as miraculous as the occasionalist function of God entertained by Geulincx.

Another point of criticism concerns *concrescence.* Granting diversity to start from, actual entities will suffer from qualitative *entropy* as they establish, each for itself, concrescence. There is no reason why they should not gradually even out their diversities. It has, of course, been argued that they protect themselves by negative prehensions, warding off any levelling process, and further, that they can themselves prehend the eternal objects paradigmatic for their form. In fact, this complex explanation explains nothing: negative prehensions compromise the ontological principle so that stability as well as change of form can equally count as explained. Reference to eternal objects does not fare any better. Clearly, the argument of Plato's *Meno,* or of the hermeneutic circle, applies: how shall an entity find a paradigmatic essence unless it knows what to look for—and if it does, such essence is redundant. Nor will reference to eternal objects be strict since in that case utter stability would result. Rather, the degree of reference must be left to the discretion of the entity in question. It seems that the very multiplicity of explanations (ontological principle, negative prehensions, prehensions of eternal objects) causes a problem, the one weakening the other to the point of redundancy or leaving qualitative development to the individual entity and its preference of sameness or change. Entropy will be a statistical probability, with less deviation in the lower reaches to oblige induction and greater prominence of subjective willfulness in the upper reaches of the universe (a Hegelian or even Aristotelian echo).

Whitehead's theory of content transmission from epochal generation to generation constitutes what would normally be called a *genetic* account (excepting ultimate genesis from an absolute origin). As the argument from entropy qualified by idiosyncratic deviation would suggest, Whitehead has no rational way of accounting for, or explaining, *categorial levels of organism,* be they levels of individual (actual entities with developed psychic poles or minds) or plural organisms (societies). He does call for a teleological development, but "emergent evolution," regarded as a sequence of events with mutations, remains something irrational.[33] The achievement of novelty is a crucial requirement and yet, novelty as such is no more than a blanket term covering fortuitous changes as well as moves to new categorial levels, nor can the one or the other be explained as for their contingent, but probable occurrence. Hegel, the rationalist, is trivially right in considering genetic explanation unsatisfactory: we do not understand the occurrence of change except in terms of the categorial levels bounding the move in question. It is only this *relationship* which can be rationalized, however, *not* the contingent arrival at a consequent on the basis of an antecedent. Of course, Whitehead had a greater ambition, namely to offer a philosophical theory of contingent cosmological processes.

Another problem confronts us when we turn to *plural organic unities* and their atomic constituents. Whitehead makes it clear that actual entities remain primary, in that in a society or nexus the character sustained is to be understood as an element of form exemplified in each member of that society or nexus (PR 51f.). Thus novelty through multiplicity in plural organisms is not comprehensible: the organism is simply a class of members with a certain characteristic, and the question is as before, how a novel characteristic emerges in a single actual entity or in a sufficient number of them severally. In order to accommodate *mind* in particular, Whitehead has to speak of a "final subject" (PR 385, 410) which, with the help of a "transmutation" of diverse physical feelings into one (PR 384) can function as what, in Leibniz's *Monadology*, is the apperceptive monad of many bodily monads. It is for such subjective unity that Whitehead introduces the notion of "pre-established harmony." To remedy the situation, it seems we would need the notion of a *Concrete Universal* designed to offer a rational account of novel unity.[34] Whitehead wants novelty, categorial and otherwise—as is shown by his concern for consciousness and higher mental phenomena—but a rational account of how this can be is replaced by the assumption of peculiar happenings, such as "transmutations" and the emergence of novel feelings.

Little need be added by way of criticism of Whitehead's notion of *teleology*, microscopic as well as macroscopic. It has become sufficiently apparent that his is an optimistic assessment of process which, when we ask for an explanation, sends us on to a vision in which God figures as an agent of the desired teleology. Indeed, Whitehead's position takes on a Schellingian (or Neoplatonic) tinge when he credits God with a primordial nature in terms of which God contemplates eternal objects which somehow condition the world's teleology, while in terms of the consequent nature, God forms a prehensive unity of, and with, the world, constituting the world's self. In a sense, God is needed to gather up loose ends of the various strains of explanation in Whitehead's cosmology without there being a rigorous argument for his inclusion in the system.

It remains to comment on what may be Whitehead's central inspiration and the guiding idea for his metaphysical system, namely his *epochal theory of time*. Earlier on, we suggested that this theory constitutes an option for change as something which cannot be explained in a theory accepting substance, the result being that existence-change becomes the unique mode of time to the exclusion of the other mode, permanence. Now we can grant that the tradition, wishing to understand change with reference to something stable (qualitative change as well as locomotion) encounters severe difficulties. But our question must be whether Whitehead's move—to preempt permanence by epochal existence-changes—is worth the price: namely, to incur a host of metaphysical problems. Proximity to science may be an important consideration in espousing atomism. But on the other hand, science does not seem to require the epochal theory of time, even if the notion of substance with its "life-world" character causes difficulties. Beyond a certain point, one suspects that metaphysical explanation in Whitehead is not compelling, requiring as it seems more explanatory devices than states of affairs to be explained. Precisely its most spectacular single topic, process, is a case in point.

But there is a more fundamental way of looking at Whitehead's central inspiration—an attempt, if we like, to give it a "transcendental deduction." One may safely say that Whitehead's model of an actual entity establishing itself through prehensions of its Other (i.e., its predecessors) is a dialectical model. (We noted its proximity to Hegel's Being-for-Self.) However, the dialectical relation inherent in the actual entity's prehensions is not a logical one (a relation between a conceptual posit and its opposite as part of a "homogeneous dialectic"[35]) but one which is directed towards a "heterogeneous" object and designed to transmit content as selectively assimilable to the new entity. The sum-total of prehensive assimilation replaces double negation in the sense of sublation and survival of content. In the limiting case, the prehensive relation is one between indiscernibles which are nevertheless Others of each other.

The novel position adopted by Whitehead now is that the dialectical relation inherent in prehension is meant to account not simply (structurally, logically) for selfhood over against an Other (in the sense of a return to itself), but for gradual take-over, for self-formation—i.e., for subjective *genesis*. It takes time to become. Whitehead thus proclaims a link between dialectical structure and temporally articulate existence. The difficulty is, of course, that we do not understand the inception of genesis (induced by whom?) or of its phases (prior to subjecthood which might govern a process). An account of self-genesis is necessarily paradoxical, except in structural terms as categorial levels bounding the distance bridged by genesis.[36]

Nor do we understand the entity's *termination* on completion or satisfaction as belonging to genesis. But here it may be a structurally dialectical consideration again which comes into play: without termination, it looks as if, by the time of completion or satisfaction, the relations between a fully existent actual entity and its Others would be undialectical (or non-constitutive). The existent entity would no more "require" the "Others," since it exists and could continue to exist in its own right. Dialectical explanation of systemic unity in atomism would have failed. So Whitehead draws on both the genetic and the structural understandings of the dialectic: the genetic one to account for self-formation, the structural one to argue for termination which, genetically, is unconvincing. The two together result in the epochal theory of time.

The difficulty is to understand the relationship between, or the fusion of, structure and existence (genesis up to completion or satisfaction). The two aspects are telescoped into one compound assumption—self-formation of an actual entity by dialectical prehension of its predecessors, and termination—in order to assuage the conflicting claims of genetic or metaphysical and categorial explanations. The compound assumption cannot be defended by only one ambiguous theory—it rests on mere conviction.

2) Hegel

To be fair, we will do well to contrast the above criticism of Whitehead with a few observations on Hegel's difficulties and limitations. I focus in particular upon three points. One is the *theoretical status of Hegel's dialectic*. We can grant that it affords welcome solutions in connection with categorial posits like Qualitative Being, Essence, and Concept, or with an understanding of unity in terms of the Concrete Universal. But the logical foundations of the dialectic—typified by the introduction of negation and double negation—may continue to pose problems.[37]

Another point concerns the type of philosophy bound up with *dialectical concept analysis or categorial ontology*. For Hegel, rationality as afforded by the dialectic is the supreme concern and delimits what can and should be handled in philosophy—namely, "what-is" questions together with genealogical explanation. Hegel may hope to offer a self-founding ontology, the very opposite of a hypothetical "scheme of ideas" such as Whitehead's, but the limitation is apparent. Criticism of this limitation has accordingly prompted existentially-oriented philosophies as diverse as those of Schelling, Kierkegaard, Marx, Samuel Alexander, C. Lloyd Morgan and Whitehead (who has gone farthest in finding a solution in his basic conceptions of actual entity, prehension, and concrescence). In our context, it may be sufficient to register a philosophical intention at loggerheads with Hegel's.

For a third point, let us concentrate on a charge which Whitehead brought against the tradition, though not explicitly against Hegel. We mean the criticism inherent in the "fallacy of misplaced concreteness." Whitehead discusses this idea briefly in *Process and Reality*. Speaking of generalization in philosophy, he writes: "This fallacy consists in neglecting the degree of abstraction involved when an actual entity is considered merely so far as it exemplifies certain categories of thought. There are aspects of actualities which are simply ignored so long as we restrict thought to these categories" (PR 11). In his earlier statement in *Science and the Modern World* to which he refers in *Process and Reality*, the idea is related to "simple location of instantaneous material configurations" (SMW 74).[38] While in Whitehead's view actual entities (in the language of physics: "bits of matter") have no simple location, related as they are to ever so many other entities, abstraction can make a difference. "By a process of constructive abstraction we can arrive at abstractions which are the simply-located bits of material," a procedure which for Whitehead counts as an example of the fallacy of misplaced concreteness (SMW 85).

There seem to be two points, or aspects, which Whitehead takes as bound up with one another: the point of *illicit generality* of philosophical statement, and the misleading result of thought when it pinpoints *items as unrelated*, irrespective of their interconnections. As for the latter aspect of the fallacy, what it boils down to is the assertion of the (contrary) metaphysical truth of the universal interconnectedness of entities, and thus an averral of Whitehead's cosmological persuasion. It is not a methodological fallacy as such, but can count as a fallacy only if Whitehead's metaphysic is correct.

As for the former aspect to Whitehead's fallacy (illicit generality or abstraction) it is clear that Whitehead, too, indulges in it when he proposes his "scheme." But what about Hegel? Is he guilty of this fallacy in view of the fact that he engages in abstract discourse about Being and all manner of determinations? The question concerns the capacity of the Concept to pinpoint something in its terms, to identify and characterize a referent qua conformal to the conceptual content or meaning. This much must be granted also for Whitehead. Whitehead, however, thinks that actual entities set the standard for abstraction (except for subsidiary notions used to reflect on them, such as the "categories of explanation" or his "categorial obligations"). Hegel, by contrast, thinks that he can propose concepts undercutting such determinate beings. In view of the principial ordering of his philosophy (i.e., ascending from abstractions to concrete concepts) he has no reason not to accept the abstract notions of the tradition. But at the same time, Hegel provides them with a new rationale (a conceptual genealogy) and sees the imperfection of abstract concepts.

Hegel's solution is not to resort to referents exhibiting concreteness or determinateness in accordance with the ontological principle, and to legislate about concepts accordingly, but to locate *the remedy for abstraction in the Concept itself* (i.e., in concepts of relational or other-inclusive character such as Essence, Nature and Spirit). So we might say that Hegel himself agrees that abstract concepts are untrue, but that his way out is non-metaphysical concreteness. These are, if we like, two different ways of avoiding an impasse. Whitehead takes the line of representationalism (*vorstellendes Denken*—"picture thinking" in terms of patterns, or of multiple location). Hegel engages in strictly conceptual or categorial philosophy. Hegel's limitation on this level is that the impact that the co-existence of categorized items and levels makes on items and levels of *another* category cannot be determined with strictness. The social domain, as discussed in the *Philosophy of Right*, is a telling example. We do not know, for example, *how* society will be different simply because of the fact that the state exists.

A last question remains: namely, whether Whitehead's philosophy could be read as an updated version of Hegel in light of problems of existence and contingency, including problems occasioned by the atomism of science. It certainly makes good sense to see in Whitehead's cosmology a realistic, indeed atomistic, reductionist, and representational version of Hegel's philosophy, at least to the extent that this deals thematically with topics like organism, subjectivity, process and teleology, and so offers morphological blueprints. In a resourceful way, Whitehead devises a *metaphysical analogue* to Hegel's categorial position. It is an analogue, though, which commits us to a conflation of categorial (structurally-dialectical) and metaphysical inspirations which cannot be rationally defended.

It seems that we have a choice between stressing thematic and morphological similarities on the one hand, and emphasizing differences in foundational matters on the other.

Notes

1. For example, see Gregory Vlastos, "Organic Categories in Whitehead," *Journal of Philosophy* 34 (May 1937), pp. 253–263. More recently, see Darrel E. Christensen, "Whitehead's 'Prehension' and Hegel's 'Mediation': Parallel Concepts at the Service of Different Methodologies," *Review of Metaphysics*, forthcoming.

2. Alfred North Whitehead, *Process and Reality* (New York: Macmillan, 1929), p. vi *et. seq.* Following a convention of Whiteheadian scholars, references to this text will hereafter appear in parentheses in the body of the paper as "PR," followed by the pagination of the 1929 Macmillan edition.

TYPES OF EXPLANATION   83

3. This assessment is based on the view that Hegel's mature position is that of the *Science of Logic* and the *Encyclopedia*. I thus differ from Christensen's approach to Hegel via the *Phenomenology of Spirit.*

4. Cf. J. Locke, *Essay Concerning Human Understanding*, ed. by P. H. Nidditch, Bk. II, ch. XXIII, sec. 7; also Bk. IV, ch. VI, sec. 11.

5. *Hegel's Science of Logic*, trans. A. V. Miller (London: George Allen & Unwin, 1969) pp. 55f., 826, substituting "Concept" for Miller's "Notion."

6. *Hegel's Phenomenology of Spirit*, trans. A. V. Miller (Oxford: Oxford University Press, 1977), pp. 9f.

7. *Hegel's Science of Logic*, pp. 45–47.

8. *Ibid.*, pp. 63f.

9. Cf. Ivor Leclerc, *Whitehead's Metaphysics* (London: Allen & Unwin, 1958) ch. IV.

10. See F. W. J. Schelling, *Philosophie der Offenbarung* (Paulus-Machshrift), ed. by M. Frank (Frankfurt am Main, 1977), pp. 154ff.

11. See Jean-Paul Sartre, *L'être et le néant* (Paris, 1950), p. 257, and p. 713 at which point metaphysics is defined. Cf. also Klaus Hartmann, *Sartre's Ontology* (Evanston, IL: Northwestern University Press, 1966), pp. 142–145.

12. Kant argues the other way round whether there could be an ordered time sequence in the inner sense without substance as a permanent point of reference: *Critique of Pure Reason*, trans. N. Kemp Smith (New York: St. Martin's Press, 1965) "First Analogy," pp. 212–217.

13. J. Bennett, *Kant's Analytic* (Cambridge, 1966), pp. 187ff.

14. A similar problem arises for Leibniz, in whose monadology it is hard to account for locomotion. Monads move on their own accord, as ordained by God, suffering only by recoil, not by push exerted by another monad. See *Neues System*, in C. J. Gerhardt, *Die philosophischen Schriften von G. W. Leibniz*, vol. IV (Berlin, 1880), p. 486.

15. A detailed analysis is available in Michael Welker, *Universalität Gottes und Relativität der Welt* (Neukirchen-Vluyn: Neukirchener Verlag, 1981).

84 *Klaus Hartmann*

16. For a brief statement of my views on Hegel's philosophy, see "Hegel: A Non-Metaphysical View," in *Hegel: A Collection of Critical Essays*, ed. Alisdair MacIntyre (New York: Anchor Books, 1972), pp. 101-124.

17. *Science of Logic*, pp. 34f., 41 [WdL I:13, 20].

18. *Science of Logic*, pp. 539f [WdL II:167-68].

19. Hegel's view in this matter is complex. He thinks that there is a difference between concepts that carry an explicit identity presumption with respect to their referents (like categories of Essence and Concept) and those which, for lack of determinacy, do not. On an existential reading, we might therefore conceive of existence-changes of referents restricted to determinations of qualitative Being.

20. Cf. K. Brinkmann, *Aristoteles' allgemeine und spezielle Metaphysik* (Berlin, 1979), pp. 218-237.

21. See F. W. J. Schelling, *Zur Gesichte der neueren Philosophie*, "Schriften von 1813-1830," in *Ausgewählte Werke* (Darmstadt, 1968), pp. 408-446; esp. 438-443. The stumbling block is Hegel's phrase that the Idea "resolves to let the 'moment' of its particularity . . . go forth freely as Nature" (*Encyclopedia* sec. 244, trans. William Wallace (1873), *The Logic of Hegel* (Oxford: The Clarendon Press, 1973) p. 296.

22. In his own way, Schelling once again took exception to Hegel's including the Christian God into his philosophy. See *Philosophie der Offenbarung* (Paulus-Nachschrift), pp. 127-134, esp. 134.

23. *Science of Logic*, p. 89.

24. *Encyclopedia* secs. 257-259.

25. Sartre has set great store by this ontological feature of time. See *L'être et le néant* (Paris 1943), pp. 187f.

26. See *Encyclopedia* secs. 286ff. (Process of the Elements), secs. 326 (The Chemical Process), sec. 367 (Process of the Genus). In the course of this progression, causal process gives way to teleological process.

27. See *Encyclopedia* sec. 380.

28. This semblance is particularly strong in Hegel's *Phenomenology of Spirit*. A commentator reading this work as an account of man's "learning process"

is J. Loewenberg, *Hegel's Phenomenology: Dialogues on the Life of Mind* (LaSalle, IL, 1965).

29. Engels tries, in his *Dialektik der Natur* [Marx-Engels-Werke, vol. 20 (Berlin, 1962), pp. 305–570] to account for novelty by the change-over of quantity into quality (and vice versa), applicable to all manner of cases and states of affairs. Hegel himself speaks of such change-overs (*Science of Logic*, pp. 366–371), but in terms of a *reflection* on change-overs, not as a claim that causal antecedents lead to novel consequents.

30. See *Adventures of Ideas*, Part IV.

31. See *Science and the Modern World*, ch. XIII.

32. Cf. P. Weiss's criticism in *Reality* (New York, 1949), Book II, ch. 5, on "persistence," pp. 203–217. His position is that everything persists but is incomplete, requiring entities which are future with respect to it to achieve the future.

33. Cf. R. G. Collingwood's criticism in *The Idea of Nature* (Oxford: The Clarendon Press, 1976), pp. 165–174.

34. Whitehead's insistence on objective diversity, and thus his criticism of the class concept as insufficient to account for plural unity (PR 348) does not constitute a suitable equivalent of the Concrete Universal.

35. This description of Hegel's dialectic originates with Gregory Vlastos, "Organic Categories in Whitehead," *Journal of Philosophy* 34 (1937), pp. 253–263, esp. 253f., who speaks of Hegel's three terms of the dialectic as "ontologically homogeneous," i.e., as being of "the nature of the Idea," or of Thought. [Reprinted in *Alfred North Whitehead: Essays on his Philosophy*, ed. George L. Kline (Prentice-Hall, 1963), pp. 158–167.]

36. A remotely similar problem arises in Sartre's attempt, in *L'être et le néant* (Paris, 1943), p. 121, to picture the genesis of a Being-for-Self as coming about by an "ontological act."

37. We need only list names like A. Trendelenburg, H. Rickert, K. R. Popper, W. Becker, D. Henrich, and B. Puntel.

38. *Science and the Modern World* (New York: Macmillan, 1925).

Robert C. Neville
STATE UNIVERSITY OF NEW YORK AT STONY BROOK

Hegel and Whitehead on Totality: The Failure of a Conception of System

The concept of totality seems to be central to systematic philosophy. It marks the scale or domain of things to be understood, and is thus related to the problem of reality. It suggests an order disposing the things to be understood, and hence is intimately bound up with the problem of the one and the many. Because the form of philosophic understanding in some sense or other needs to be adequate to the subject matter, the concept of totality bears upon the notion of philosophic system. But the concept of totality is problematic in the extreme. Kant knew the concept was in trouble when he asked whether a totality of things is finite or infinite and recognized that coherent justifications could be offered for *each* of the opposing answers.[1] In the twentieth century we have recognized another grave difficulty, namely, that the claim that such and such constitutes a totality is often just a fiction, an unsupported assumption that if there are fragments there must be a whole.[2]

In this essay I want to examine the use that two major systematic philosophers, Hegel and Whitehead, made of the concept of totality. Since in a brief compass it is impossible to do a thorough study, my selective principle will be to focus on those elements of the discussion that bear particularly on our own possibilities regarding systematic philosophy. My conclusion will be that neither is able to articulate a conception of totality adequate to the use to which he would put it. As a result, we can sustain conceptions of world and system only if they do not require conceptions of totality, at least so far as Hegel's and Whitehead's suggestions go.

Although every philosopher has a selective focus when writing about other philosophers (sometimes unwittingly), the selective focus in this essay warrants an introductory remark. My own agenda is to develop a practice of systematic thinking which does not presuppose totality in either reality or in a system representing it. Neither this agenda nor its negation, the assertion that reality or a representative system is totalized, was the agenda of Hegel or Whitehead. My concern about totality is one they did not share directly. Hence the questions I put to their philosophies are ones they themselves did not exactly ask, and the responses I represent them as making are to some degree uncharacteristic of their thought. Hegel and Whitehead scholars may see my arguments as perversions of the way their respective masters saw things. Yet scholarship of that sort is inimical to philosophic conversation. Conversation requires responding to alien questions legitimated by the questioner, not the responder. The texts of Hegel and Whitehead—even more the arguments within their own agendas—set strict controls on what we can represent as their side of the conversation. Nevertheless, their thought must have a new look, speak in a new voice, when brought into conversation with new concerns. One element in the greatness of both of these thinkers is that their philosophies increase in interest as they are reshaped in ongoing dialogue.

Hegel

The concept of totality and its thematic use pervade Hegel's philosophy. Hegel's *thematic* use of the concept of totality takes its rise, I believe, from Kant's Table of Categories. For Kant, totality is the synthesis of unity and plurality, the categories of quantity. Hence for Hegel any issue concerning the one and the many brings a use of the concept of totality. In a more general sense, totality is the analogue of the synthesis or reconciliation of any positive element with what denies or extends out from that element. Following Kant's Table, totality is allied with limitation, which is the synthesis of the qualitative categories of reality and negation, with community, which is the synthesis of the relational categories of substance and causation, and with necessity, which is the synthesis of the modal categories of possibility and existence. Thus for Hegel, totality is determinate or limited, inclusive or a matter of interrelatedness, and necessary, a function of infinite spirit.[3] I will limit my analysis to two roles for the concept, that involving the infinite-finite relation, and that involved in the movement of negative dialectic. Despite the fact that much that is important will be left unsaid, those two roles complement and correct one another. I apologize for the dissonance of discussing Hegel's concrete notions so abstractly.

One commonly recognized aspect of Hegel's genius is his claim that if one can set limits to a thing or domain, in some sense the setting of limits takes place from a position transcending those limits. Hence Hegel could reject Kant's critical limitation of reason as disingenuous: the faculty exercising the critique is, if not reason, then as much like reason as the true author of the *Iliad* and *Odyssey* is like the mythical Homer, being blind himself and also called Homer. Hegel's principle is that if a thing is determinate it is determinate with respect to something outside itself. Therefore the determinateness of one thing requires those other things with respect to which it is determinate, which also being determinate implicate others until all possibly related things are involved in what Quentin Lauer calls a totality of interrelatedness.[4]

Lauer also points out that, because of the above argument, for Hegel it is the infinite which is the primary bearer of determinateness. No finite thing is determinate by itself, and only the infinite contains all determinations. Hegel's concept of the infinite is extraordinarily complex and problematic. I don't want to gloss over the issues here, but will limit my discussion to one issue concerning the infinite and determinateness. Whereas finite things are determinate in reference to external things which bound them, by virtue of what is the infinite itself determinate? There are two main ways of responding to this question.

The first is to stress the difference between finite and infinite reason. Although it is the character of finite reason to grasp determinateness in terms of contrast—and finite objects are so to be grasped—infinite reason constitutes its own determinateness by its very movement of totalling up the finite determinations. The infinite's determinateness consists in its determinate contents. In making this point Hegel stressed in many contexts the necessity of actual knowledge of the determinate steps of spirit, not a romantic absolute like the night in which all cows are black. Denying a wholly transcendent infinite, Hegel asserted the necessary and actual character of spirit which is infinite because it is determinately finite, and finite only because it is an infinite totality of finite interrelatedness.

Now let me ask a stupid question. Is the infinite a finite or infinite totality? Put another way, noting the difference between bad and good infinites, is there a finite set of categories constituting the infinite *Geist*?[5] Is the chart of the Hegelian system from the back of Walter Stace's *Philosophy of Hegel*, which adorned my graduate school room like a mandala, a possible enterprise? Is there a highest order of orders, the inclusive absolute order, which is the final totality? The question these many formulations ask is stupid, of course, because it misunderstands Hegel's idea of the notion, the infinite philosophical category or category of *Geist*. An infinite category is determinate because of what it integrates or interrelates, not because of what it relates to externally. In fact, as Hegel's dialectic shows, an infinite category that still has an external neighbor is not yet fully determinate, and reason moves on to the more inclusive whole.

Stupid or not, the question seems inevitable if one is interested in totality. What if things are not fully interrelated, but only fragmentarily related, with little necessity, no inclusive order, with partial and idiosyncratic determinateness? Fragmentary relatedness, however, does not appear viable for Hegel, for whom the higher notion always functions as a "third term" to integrate and transcend its relatively finite contents.

Let us examine more closely this third term, for it is at the heart of the claim that the infinite is a totality.[6] Suppose by hypothesis that the third term has no character of its own by virtue of which it integrates its contents. Suppose instead that the contents simply fit together by virtue of their own natures. In this case there really is no third term, no higher infinite notion, only the good luck of a perfect fit of otherwise independent contents. But if this is so, philosophy suddenly becomes narrowly empirical, because it would have to look at each case to see whether the contents fit together. And since we know, for Hegel, that the diversity comes through the process of contradiction, the contents are highly unlikely to "just fit" together. The point of the third term, of the notion, in many instances is to reconcile what is otherwise incompatible. So we must reject this hypothesis and suppose that the third term has a determinate character of its own by virtue of which it interrelates or totals up its contents.

Consider how the character of the third term is determinate. Although its determinateness arises genetically from its function of interrelating and thereby determining its relatively finite contents, the logical status of its determinate character cannot be reduced to the aggregate determinations of its contents. Rather, the aggregate determinations of its contents call for something new, for some originary work to be done, for a new determination that will bring them truly into an infinite whole and fulfill their own full determinate natures. To say that the determinateness of this new element in the third term arises from its determinate contents is empty. As Hegel would argue, something actual has to happen, something particular as well as universal. If nothing happens there is no totality, only an aggregate; and even an aggregate may be impossible. Then with respect to what is the new element in the third term determinate? There seem to be two possibilities: the contents that it interrelates, or something yet external and on its own logical or ontological level.

Can the new element in the third term be determinate with respect to its interrelated contents alone? I think not, for two reasons. First, it cannot determinately be itself over against its contents precisely because its nature comes from making them its contents. Its very function is to transform the contents into a new whole which is its own self. We are in this case referred back to the previous dilemma: the whole is either a mere aggregate or a seamless new thing, with the determinateness of the whole explained in neither case. The second reason the new element in the third term cannot be determinate with respect to its contents is that if it were it would have to be related to its contents by yet another third term. That is, the very dialectic urging that an infinite is required for the finite to be fully finite, would interpose a mediation between the determinate contents and the determinate third term that integrates them, and then mediations between all those joints, ad infinitum. Yet we know that for Hegel such a bad infinite regress is just the consequence that is supposed to be ruled out by absolute infinite reason.

It must be the case, then, that the determinateness in the new element in the third term consists in a contrast with something still external, on its own logical or ontological level. This gives determinateness to the totality of the infinite, even though it admits that the totality is only relative, not inclusive of that external thing with respect to which the third term, now the infinite absolute notion, is determinate. Hegel would embrace this solution, if reluctantly, because it acknowledges his stress on actuality. The actual achievement of the notion is determinate because it stands in contrast to the possibilities it excludes. There are two unsettling consequences of the solution, however. One is that the contrast between the actual and the merely possible is a meagre finite notion: the infinite is not supposed to have a possible alternative. The other is that the claim that the infinite notion is always determinate with respect to something external, and therefore always only a relative totality, commits us to a bad infinite of progressions from one infinite notion to the next.

To recapitulate: infinite reason is a totality by virtue of being a third term which interrelates its determinate contents. The third term is determinate either because its contents are determinate or because of its own character. But the contents cannot be fully determinate without the new contribution of the third term. How is the third term's contribution determinate? Not by virtue of its contents, and so by virtue of contrasting with what is external to it. But if something is external, the third term is no totality in the required respects. So Hegel's conception is problematic.

Let us then leave the theme of totality in the infinite-finite relation and seek to complement it with an inquiry into the role of totality in negative dialectic. In the infinite-finite relation, totality's role is to sum up or totalize its antecedents, to be the crown of dialectic, as it were. In negative dialectic, however, the role of totality is to present a situation as whole enough to negate, as something firm and complete enough to step on and away from. The totality is necessary in order to move beyond.

This point is worth stressing in connection with the dialectic of history, its paradigmatic instance, I believe, for Hegel. For there to be a spiritual progression from the middle ages to the modern period, for example, the former must be sufficiently whole and integrated, a totality, for negation to be possible. True, the totalization might be accomplished only in the achievement of a successful negation. That is, the superseding stage gives the earlier a coherence it did not have until transcended. The reason or *Geist* which accomplishes the dialectical move achieves its own actuality in the very process of negating the antecedent and fulfilling itself as a successful negation. Whereas some of its own contents might be merely accidental, they are rational because of their roles in the dialectic of negation.

If *Geist* can be modelled on the negative dialectic of history, then we have a new opportunity to address the question of the determinateness of the totality. We may say that the transcending stage is determinate with respect to the stage it transcends precisely in those respects in which it negates the possibility of the transcended stage, annulling the actuality of the earlier stage and carrying its bits along transformed by the determinate actuality of the later stage. The actuality of the moment, then, is determinate not with respect to a possibility that it excluded, but with respect to a past actuality that it negates and subsumes. There may well be many elements in the moment which are not determinate, either with respect to the past or with respect to what is rational in the moment itself. But they might become determinate when the moment itself is totalized and negated by its own executioner. Of course the moment will be negated itself because of the contradictions flowing from the way it achieved negation of its antecedents. But those contradictions do not reconcile themselves automatically. Movement of the spirit is labor and freedom.

Let me point out here that the concept of totality has a different form in connection with negative dialectic than in connection with the infinite-finite relation. For the latter, totality is an inclusive container. For the former, the totality has reason as a selective principle. Reason, which proceeds with necessity, distinguishes within a situation between the truly actual and the adventitious.[7] This is such an important point that it is worth quoting Hegel, from the "Introduction" to the *Lesser Logic:*

> In the preface to my Philosophy of Law . . . are found the propositions:
>   What is reasonable is actual; and
>   What is actual is reasonable.
> . . . For their philosophic sense, we must presuppose intelligence enough to know, not only that God is actual, that He is the supreme actuality, that He alone is truly actual; but also, as regards the logical bearings of the question, that existence is in part mere appearance, and only in part actuality. In common life, any freak or fancy, any error, evil and everything of the nature of evil, as well as every degenerate and transitory existence whatever, gets in a casual way the name of actuality. But even our ordinary feelings are enough to forbid a casual (fortuitous) existence getting the emphatic name of an actual; for by fortuitous we mean an existence which has no greater value than that of something possible, which may as well not be as be. . . . In a detailed Logic I had treated amongst other things of actuality, and accurately distinguished it not only from the fortuitous, which after all has existence, but even from the cognate categories of existence and the other modifications of being.[8]

For Hegel, totalization in reason works by way of distinguishing between the rationally important, that is, the necessary as viewed from the standpoint of the work of dialectical negation, and the rationally unimportant or trivial. This helps us see how totalization might be accomplished as much in the negating of a moment as in the moment's own work of negating its antecedents.

In Hegel's dialectical systematic philosophy, totality in world or in philosophic representation does not suppose that there is some highest category containing all things perfectly related, but only that there is a rational principle which totalizes the things that have bearing necessarily on the principle itself. On the one hand this is a great advance on the popular conception of system as total container. It expresses wisdom's task of distinguishing the important from the trivial. We should learn from Hegel that philosophic system means attaining to a comprehensive view of things ordered as to their importance, with critical reflection on the implied judgments of importance. On the other hand, I fear that Hegel's conception of reason, with its attendant conception of totality, contains a fatal flaw.

Consider the people, events, and institutions that are "fortuitous" on Hegel's view. For him they have existence, but only as appearances. Moreover, they have no necessity as conveyed through their rational successors. That is to say in the latter instance, when the onrush of history totalizes their moment to negate it, they are not included. The selection of what is important doesn't include them. Considering the difference they make to subsequent history, they might as well have not happened. As Hegel says, they have the status of mere possibilities whose existence is so accidental history would be the same if they had not occurred. This means that the victims of history Hegel described so pathetically in his "Introduction" to the *Philosophy of History* are non-entities.[9] So are the institutions that failed without a place in the larger rational order. So are the events that seem so dear and important to their participants but which miss the dialectic. The pathos is that those very accidents might have been heroic elements whose personal passions coincide with the *Geist* if the subsequent movement of history had in fact totalized them into the rational structure of their moment. There is nothing intrinsic to the accidents themselves giving them low value. Rather, it is because of the actual direction taken by history that they are cast into limbo and forgotten. Nor is it the case that dialectic was necessitated to go the way it did. There could well have been other ways of totalizing their moment that would have given them prominence. Spirit is free in this regard, and it is at this point that spirit reduces to force. Its force consists in its power to denude things of actuality by denying them a place in reasonableness.

Even more unfortunate for Hegel's view is that there is more than one way to tell the story of history. That is, each pocket of order, if you will, projects its own perspective over the past and future, a perspective which determines which elements are necessary and actual relative to it, and which can be ignored as accidental. Hegel's reading of Western history seems plausible when reinforced by those institutions he sees as rational. But it surely is Whig history. History from the perspective of the women's movement is very different, with many of Hegel's heroes slipping into fortuitousness. Consider history of science from the standpoint of the alchemical or magical traditions. Consider the importance of European history of philosophy itself from the standpoint of Chinese scholars approaching it with the values of their own tradition.

If reason reduces to force in arbitrarily totalizing the moments of its negation, how much more arbitrary is it if there is not one reason, one *Geist*, but as many as there are pockets of order? As the history of Hegel's thought has shown, his grand historical synthesis could not withstand the creation of alternatives. Kierkegaard and Marx in their own ways preserved something of the form of Hegel's dialectic, but with a radically different story. Emerson, Nietzsche, and Peirce transformed even the dialectical form, and the non-Western thinkers whom we now must take seriously present incommensurable visions.

I believe that with regard to the coherence of system in at least the historical sphere we must abandon the dream of totality and necessity and acknowledge instead that as far as we know there are many pockets of order, sometimes interrelated, sometimes not, often irrelevant and indeterminate with respect to each other, passing with tangential connections, partially overlapping, sometimes in conflict but even then not in coherent agreement concerning what the fight is about. History has many streams, many traditions, rising and falling, entering and leaving prominence, going underground to emerge with new meanings in unexpected places, rarely with the coherence to totalize a period.

Where does this leave us with regard to the question of totality? The world seems to be not one totality but many, and even some of the many are not tightly total. Philosophic system, then, seems wholly relativized, with each pocket of order evoking its own system, its own rationale, and with no particular hope of a super-system. No wonder systematic philosophy is unpopular these days, and even seen as a threat to the integrity of individual pockets of order that might have their own rationale, their own language game.

Before leaving Hegel, however, let us recall his insight that system requires a discrimination of the important from the trivial. System results from a selective ordering of things according to the forms that structure their importance. If things can be systematized, it is because the things themselves have selectively coherent importance. And if this system can be recognized philosophically it is because we have the capacity to appreciate and represent that selection of importance. But how can our pockets of order, each with its own strain of importance, be brought into a system? Is there any sense in which they can be totalized without fiction? To answer this question we turn to Whitehead, whose philosophy is built around the notion of importance.[10]

Whitehead

Like Hegel, Whitehead conceived the processive structure of reality to be continuous with the experiential structure of cognition and philosophy. Knowledge of nature is possible because experience participates in all the elementary structures of nature and, in a sense analogous to Hegel's, human knowing is a complication, enrichment, and fulfillment of processes extending through the world. More than Hegel, however, Whitehead stressed that the selective principles in accumulative process are valuative: his theme was not the necessity of reason but the appreciative valuation of experience.[11]

The data entering experience, for Whitehead, are diverse and disjunct.[12] The activity of experiencing is to order these data so as to make up a coherent individual occasion. At least two kinds of negation are involved in experiencing: the exclusion of data from having any role in the occasion, and the dismemberment of data so as to recombine their elements in new ways. There is also positive creativity in experience insofar as novel forms arise from the recombination. Spontaneous new existence provides a subject entertaining and re-actualizing the given data. Among the creative novelties are intentions toward the future in the case of high level occasions such as found in animal life.[13] In both the negative elements and positive elements, however, the main activity is the creation of orders which grade the data according to importance for the emerging occasion. Masses of data are relegated to triviality while certain other data are featured as so important that their structures set the conditions to which everything else acceptable in experience must conform. The norms governing importance within a single actual occasion are those that have to do with that occasion becoming wholly definite, that is determinate with respect to every possibility and fixed in some position in an existential medium.

It might seem as if the valuing and grading that take place in a moment of process, for Whitehead, are arbitrary functions of the occasion's own need for definiteness. But Whitehead insisted (and here lies perhaps his greatest philosophical contribution) that the data entering experience are themselves achievements of value, and that therefore their own value is grasped appreciatively in the experience of them. They contribute their worth to that which they effect. Now of course the intrinsic worth of a datum might be denied by an occasion that experiences it. This is possible, however, only by dismemberment; the experiencing occasion must transmute the presented value in the datum with some substitute of lesser or different value, as when racists treat others as mere types rather than as full human beings. Distortion of value thus requires positive work, and we may suppose that only sophisticated occasions of experience are capable of it. Unsophisticated occasions in inanimate nature either reject things completely or accept them at pretty much face value. Whitehead's point here is that the value in a thing is given first by the values in the conditions that enter into it, and only derivatively and on the margins by its own creative capacity to loose and join.

The fundamental continuity of value is what undergirds the massive structures of importance in the world: the ancient rituals of human behavior, the more ancient hills, even the highly complicated organic functions of the human body. The grades of importance and triviality embodied in one thing are likely to be reiterated in those things into which it enters as a condition. Put the other way, the readiness of one thing to be conditioned by another depends on its readiness to accept much of the potential condition's expression of importance. The solidity of the world and the intricate workings of natural law express this mutual reinforcement of valuational embodiments from one domain of reality to another. The order of the world, for Whitehead, depends on the mutual resonance of valuations.

Would Whitehead say that there is a single encompassing order of the world, that the world is a totality composed of a univocal, complex super-valuation? Or might he admit that there are only pockets of order? This question must be divided into whether the world is a totality for experiencers, and whether it is a totality in itself.

It is uncontestable for Whitehead that an experiencer, in a single moment, works conditioning data into a single, coherent totality. This is the bearing of all the categorial obligations, especially that of subjective harmony. The structure of experience itself is the total integration of the potential contributors to experience into a world-for-a-perspective: this defines both the locus of the experiencer relative to the perspective and the rest of the more or less distant world; both are contained within the perspectival reality of the experience.[14] The subjective process of totalization is accomplished by integration and synthesis, by dismemberment and reorganization, and most of all by elimination of the unincludable elements. Like Hegel's moment, Whitehead's occasion can render something trivial or even non-functional which in itself is intrinsically important by what can be called, on the human scale, an act of will and, on the subhuman scale, can be called violence.

Significant experiencers, however, are not single moments, but great clusters of moments united by common forms of importance, what Whitehead inadequately called "societies." We identify as human experience nothing that could happen at a moment alone, but rather continuities of occasions that involve thinking thoughts as signs, acting in context, receiving and responding to value-laden information whose own proper locus is at a distance from the experience, and so forth. People organize their experience through such temporally thick valuational structures as bodily sensitivity, responsive sensibilities, needs, desires, orientations to life, sociality, mind, will, personhood, achieved autonomy, responsibility, ego, and self.[15] Do people in this extended substantial sense organize their experience into unified totalities? The question is an empirical one and the answer is, they rarely do. One of the prime motives of philosophy is to achieve greater coherence of experience. From the temporally cumulative standpoint of a human being, the most important things in life exist in pockets of order, linked by crude metrics such as bodily, spatial, and temporal continuities.

The philosophic significance of this point is the question whether this failure of totality (1) is simply because of the feebleness of our capacities of representation (which are so important for being able to integrate distant data) or (2) is the consequence of there being no real totality capable of being represented.

The first alternative can be considered in two steps. To begin with, our mental capacities are indeed feeble relative to what we have every reason to believe can be known with more systematic coherence. Science is far from the end of its task, and Whitehead was sensitive to the ways in which non-scientific cognitive and artistic disciplines have unfinished work in articulating the orders and connections of orders in reality.[16] Whitehead introduces a second step regarding this question, however, namely the consideration of God as an infinite intellect. According to Whitehead's philosophical theology, God at any moment accepts all data which have been actualized up to that time within the divine experience, eliminating none. In contrast to finite occasions of experience which are limited to the integrating forms that are given them in their experienced data, God has access to (or is) an infinite conceptuality, with access to all possible modes of integration. Therefore, argues Whitehead, there is no datum so alien that God can't find some pattern which will intergrate it with the rest, and without dismemberment or diminishment of value. Thus for God at any moment, the past is a totality. Like Hegel, Whitehead believed that totality is created for finite things by the agency of infinite divine reason.

Nevertheless, difficulties analogous to those with Hegel's view arise here for Whitehead's. Is the reference to God's infinity merely a mushy assertion that anything is possible for God, so that there can be divine totalization? No, not for Whitehead any more than for Hegel. But then whence the determinateness of the divine? There are two general possibilities. If it derives exclusively from the actual data God receives, either those data just fit together as they are, or God is limited to the same powers as finite occasions. This makes the question of the coherence of the world an empirical one, and our empirical evidence is that the world is *not* a totality. Perhaps God is like a super-scientist, but still, whether the world is totalizable is contingent upon the world, not on God's necessary infinity (which is what was to be justified). Perhaps as the other possibility, the integrating pattern derives from God's uningressed store of eternal objects rather than from the forms that already had been ingredient in the world. How is this divinely originary pattern determinate? According to Whitehead, eternal objects in themselves are indeterminate, and receive determination from God's primordial act of grading them in a comprehensive vision.[17] As graded, the eternal objects are made determinate as relations between other "things." If those other things are the elements within the actual world, then the determinate eternal objects are precisely those which are ingredient in the actual world, plus their unrealized potentialities. This is no advance upon the suggestion that the divine integrating pattern derives from the actual objects integrated. But if the things integrated by relational eternal objects are other eternal objects, then there must be an infinity of determinate eternal objects. It is no easier to conceive a bottom-most eternal object which is determinate without parts, on Whitehead's view, than it is to conceive a top-most integrating form in Hegel's dialectic of infinite and finite. In addition, if the determinate relations are infinite in a bottomward direction, then all possibilities are structurally present, and the arbitrariness in divine valuation that Whitehead affirmed, rightly, is trivialized; there could be no difference between Whitehead's divinely graded eternal objects and Leibniz's eternal possibilities to whose structural necessities his God must bow.

Not only are there paradoxes in Whitehead's claim that God imposes coherence on the disjunct actual occasions of the world, there are grave difficulties with Whitehead's overall view of God, particularly as the sides of divine envisagement and of worldly appreciation are brought together.[18]

One last and speculative question can be raised regarding Whitehead's views on the totality of the world. With regard to finite occasions, the category of subjective unity delimits the range of data that can condition an emerging occasion prior even to its elimination of what is incompatible with its final synthesis. Are there some occasions which have reached their own actuality but which cannot enter into a later thing's subjective unity? If there are, they could not even be so related to the thing as to be in its past; they would have no relation to it at all. But if there were no such things, then there would be no point to the category of subjective unity; the initial data would consist of all achieved data. Because he did stress the category of subjective unity, I think Whitehead did mean to say that there are some achieved occasions which are not compatible for synthesis even by elimination in a given thing's coming-to-be.

Contrary to some interpreters of Whitehead, in that there may be data which do not enter any later thing's subjective unity, I believe Whitehead meant to say that some things are actual from the perspective of no occasion except themselves (and their anticipatory antecedents).[19] Or to put the point more modestly, achieving actuality within one's own perspective is enough for actuality, regardless of other multiple locations in other later things' perspectives. On this interpretation Whitehead is a radical and irreducible pluralist, or disjunctivist. Wholly disjunct things are wholly indeterminate with respect to one another, and are determinate only within their local pockets of order. Of course there would be no totality in such a world. Those who insist that achieved actuality requires existing in the perspective of some currently subjective occasion either appeal to God to sustain the otherwise facing actuality of past facts, or admit that the past becomes unreal, or say that Whitehead's system is very, very wrong.

If the world is only problematically a totality for a (problematic) God in Whitehead's system, and if it is fragmented rather than total for human beings, in what sense can we speak of a world, and in what sense can there be philosophic system?

World and System

Our world, I shall argue, must be acknowledged to be ontologically vague. Vaugeness is a logical term adapted from Charles Peirce, for whom it meant a sign which tolerates mutually contradictory interpretations. In order to tell what the sign refers to, it is necessary to take an extra step and specify one from among the potentially contradictory interpretations.[20] A term is vague when it requires a further specification to tell in which of several ways it is to be applied. I mean to use vagueness in an ontological way. The world is vague in the sense that its coherence strictly speaking consists in the harmony it allows to be imposed by a finite subject that takes its components in perspective. A finite subject at a moment entertains a totally coherent world, but there is no way within the moment alone to distinguish between the fantasy of subjective creativity and the truth about anything in the world. To assert that a vision of the world is true or that some element of a moment's experience is true, the truth question must be framed outside the single occasion in a complex tissue of moments constituting the whole person as inquirer, and perhaps even in a whole community of inquiry. Only the uncontested commonalities of a few abstract ideas provide grounds for saying there is one world for all elements of an individual's personality, or for a group of inquirers. But those bodies and abstract ideas, the sort carried in language, are vague. In order to specify them so as to refer to something in the world, they must be specified with particular concrete lines of causation that embody massively inherited importance. That is, we engage in perception, refer to the funded experience of common sense, adhere to the exact discipline of some science, or pursue a subject in depth. As soon as we take the line of some specifying discipline we leave the safe vagueness of our unified world and enter some specific world—the world of seeing here now, the world of our tradition, the world of a laboratory science, the world of a specific craft of inquiry. And of course generally there are alternatives to these specifications, any of which is compatible with the vague contours of our common world, and these alternatives might be incompatible with each other and with the ones we have chosen ourselves.

The situation is that we may have one world vaguely, but many worlds concretely. Furthermore, we suspect that people different from ourselves have concrete worlds of their own that we don't share.

Hegel and Whitehead both warned against confusing the concrete with the abstract. One version of this is the confusion of the concrete with the vague. The mistake can be made in two directions. We may begin with vague elements of commonality and believe they are concrete. Philosophers are prone to do this, especially if they contemplate charts of Hegel's system during their formative years. They are rightly criticized by artists, scientists, and working people for not being in *any* concrete world. It is more likely, however, that we begin with our favorite pocket of concrete order and believe it is the universal order, thus denying the other pockets of order. Personal and cultural chauvinism is of this sort, mistaking a specific order for a universal order comprehending all things. Relativism is the recognition that there are fundamentally different and perhaps incommensurable orders; relativism dotes on itself too much, however, when it believes it is the last word. For, in addition to the many pockets of order, the many worlds of specific actuality, there is the vague world we have in common by virtue of our interacting physical natures and our abstract signs.

The function of system in philosophy should now be apparent. It has two parts. The first is to frame a system of categories and articulate the vague world we have in common. The great historical systems, including Hegel's and Whitehead's, are the resources for this, plus our own speculative imagination. Our system should be consistent and coherent, dialectically superior to others, or at least have advantages the other's don't have. There is no reason there should be only one system, one articulation of the vague world; each has different virtues.

As Whitehead said, the system also should be applicable and adequate. But we must stress that the applicability and adequacy are vague. That the applicability of a system is vague means that it requires specification in some particular order if it is to apply to actualities. To apply the vague philosophic notion of person, for instance, it is necessary to speak of the Western person, or the Chinese tradition of personhood, or the Skinnerian, the Freudian, the Kierkegaardian, or whatever. Each of these is a pocket of intelligible order, more specific than the categories of the philosophic system. One should reject those elements in a philosophic system that have no applicability in the specific orders in which we live.

That the adequacy of a system is vague means that it should be specifiable in *any* specific order that we have reason to respect. To put the point in reverse, if any pocket of order seems important, if there is any human culture, or plausible discipline, or poetic world, which cannot specify the system, then the system is inadequate. As pockets of order rise and fall in their claim to actuality, the reference set for a philosophic system changes. There can be no finality with respect to the adequacy of a philosophic system. A philosophic system is vaguely true to the extent that it is adequate and applicable.

The second part of philosophic system is the dialectic of moving back and forth between the system of categories and their potential specification in the pockets of order that seem important in our lives. This is the more extensive part of systematic philosophy, in the face of which the construction of categorial schemes seems brief. Hardly any one person can do it since the pockets of order that are important for our vaguely common world include many that are inaccessible to any one philosopher. Systematic philosophy in this sense is a cultural enterprise, stimulated by the aesthetic attractiveness of the categories on the one hand and the need for common critical vision on the other.

One advantage of this conception of systematic philosophy is that it advertises the importance of life within local pockets of order, legitimating the uses of intelligence that are idiosyncratic to those orders. Cultures are not to be reduced to one another. Poetry is not to be reduced to general formulation. Religions are not be homogenized into a common mush. The various intellectual and scientific traditions are to pursue the specifics of their research enterprises so as to take advantage of advances in instrumentation, serendipidous findings, and the felicities of jargon. More than non-systematic philosophies, which are likely to generalize their special orders as if they were a universal order, this conception of systematic philosophy is best friend to plurality. It stands in stark contrast to conceptions of system such as Hegel's that squeeze the multifariousness of things into the system's terms and exclude from importance the things that don't fit.

An equal advantage of this conception is that it gives shape and discipline to the task of relating our pockets of order to the vague orientations that we take to be our world and that guide our activity. A prime motive for philosophy is curiosity about whether the things that are important and intelligible for us are equally so for others, and whether we are justified in taking them as we do. The form of a total vision is an ineluctable guiding principle, as Kant so well saw. In addition to guiding our inquiry about matters of the whole, this conception of systematic philosophy allows us to see whether and to what extent our various pockets of order are coherent, overlapping, contradictory, irrelevant, or incommensurable. Each can be translated as a specification of the system, and terms there are comparable, even if the assertions when translated into the system's common language are not coherent with one another. So systematic philosophy can provide a map through the vague world from one pocket of important order to another.

As a final consideration, let me point out that this conception of systematic philosophy does not require a conception of totality, where that means a comprehensive coherence of the real items of the world. Neither Hegel's divine infinite reason, I argue, nor Whitehead's divine infinite conceptuality is required for an ontology compatible with systematic philosophy.

Against Hegel we can say that the basic philosophic categories are not infinitely inclusive totalities but rather vague structures requiring external supplementation in order to refer to actual things. With Hegel's victims we can say that their pockets of order have an importance of their own which ought to be registered in an adequate system. Those pockets of order are not reduced to the system; rather the system is supplemented with specifications to reach out to each pocket of order. An implication of this philosophic view is that the field of determining which important pockets of order have claims upon us is thrown open to empirical inquiry. This is a felicitous result in an age characterized by the encounter of world cultures, by the assertion of minority, third world, and female perspectives.

The view of systematic philosophy presented here is closer to Whitehead's than to Hegel's. Nevertheless it differs from Whitehead's by abandoning the conception of totality implicit in his conception of God's conditioned, consequent nature. It differs also by stressing not only the need for generalizing up to abstract categories but also the need systematically to relate to the pockets of order important for our lives. It is clearer than Whitehead about the kind of abstraction involved in systematic philosophy: logical vagueness requiring further specification in order to have real reference. Should Whitehead believe that philosophic abstractions are merely general, referring immediately to actual things, the system of categories might be taken to require a totality in its references which is unjustified by either our experience of our philosophic arguments. The most potent argument against systematic philosophy today is that, since experience shows our orders to be fragmented, any system of categories requiring them to be totalized must be wrong. That argument cannot be made against a system construed as a vague hypothesis. And despite the fragmentation, we vaguely move together in a common world that should be acknowledged and understood relative to those existentially viable pockets of order.

Although totality has seemed to be a concept essential to having a world and a philosophy of that world, in fact it is a liability.[21] The failure of our two great systematizers, Hegel and Whitehead, adequately to defend a conception of totality, marks the liability. By abandoning that conception, we can sustain still their great ideal of philosophic system and yet pay proper tribute to the multifariousness of the world.

Notes

1. See "The Antinomy of Pure Reason," which is Chapter 2 of Book 2 of the "Transcendental Dialectic" of the *Critique of Pure Reason*.

2. One way of understanding the ontological argument is to take it to claim that parts imply a whole. Idealistic descendents of Kant, such as Josiah Royce, often argued that we must presume whatever is necessary to complete something before us so that it is fully intelligible. A refutation of this kind of ontological argument is to point out that some incomplete thing might not belong to anything completing it, incompleteness being the state of things; put another way, the thing may not be fully intelligible, which is the point at issue. Richard Rorty criticizes Paul Weiss along these lines in his remarks in Weiss's *First Considerations* (Carbondale, Ill.: Southern Illinois University Press, 1977), pp. 206f. See also Weiss's reply immediately following. Michel Foucault makes a strong case for the empirically grounded fragmentariness of things in *The Archaeology of Knowledge*, trans. by A. M. Sheridan Smith (New York: Harper, 1976).

3. For a sample discussion by Hegel, see his *Science of Logic*, trans. by Johnston and Struthers (London: Allen & Urwin, 1929), on quantity, pp. 201-332, a passage which contains several discussions of Kant's antinomies as well as a discussion of the calculus.

4. I have learned much on the present topic from Lauer's *Hegel's Concept of God* (Albany: State University of New York Press, 1982), especially Chapter 4, "The Infinite." See also Lauer's *Essays in Hegelian Dialectic* (New York: Fordham University Press, 1977), especially Chapters 1 and 2, and *Hegel's Idea of Philosophy* (New York: Fordham University Press, 1971; revised edition 1974). More than most commentators Lauer stresses

the unfolding of *Geist* as the identity of God; he is extraordinarily acute on the infinity of reason insofar as it attains to a totality of finite determinations. See his *A Reading of Hegel's Phenomenology of Spirit* (New York: Fordham University Press, 1976), Chapters 9 and 10.

5. For a pertinent discussion of the "bad infinite" see paragraph 94 of the *Lesser Logic*, translated by Wallace as *The Logic of Hegel* (2nd ed.; Oxford: Oxford University Press, 1892), pp. 174ff.

6. The dialectical argument which follows here is a short revision of the one I developed extensively in *God the Creator* (Chicago: University of Chicago Press, 1968), Chapter 1. In the discussion of Hegel in that earlier account I limited myself to treating him insofar as he could be construed as saying that being is determinate. The present argument supplements that with a discussion of the process of negative dialectic.

7. This point about the selective character of reason in negative dialectic, its establishment of a distinction between the actual and the irrelevant possible, is central in the work of Thomas J. J. Altizer. Of his many books see particularly *The New Apocalypse* (Michigan State University Press), *The Self-Embodiment of God* (New York: Harper & Row, 1977), and *Total Presence* (New York: The Seabury Press, 1980). For Altizer, negative dialectic is the process by which God achieves actuality and identity.

8. *Lesser Logic*, Wallace translation, pp. 10f.

9. See Hegel's *Reason in History*, translated by Robert S. Hartman (New York: Liberal Arts Press, 1953), pp. 25–49.

10. "Importance" is the initial and dominating concept of Whitehead's *Modes of Thought* (New York: The Free Press, 1968; orig. Macmillan, 1938), especially Chapter 1, "Importance." Chapter 4 "Perspective," is also pertinent to the discussion below. The general problem of an ontological function of value pervades Whitehead's work; see, for instance, *Process and Reality* (Corrected Edition by Griffin and Sherburne, New York: The Free Press, 1978), Part II, Chapters 3 and 4; for value and intelligence, see his *The Function of Reason* (Boston: Beacon, 1958; orig. Princeton University Press, 1929); on the problem of importance in the divine perspective, see his *Science and the Modern World* (New York: Macmillan, 1925) for an early and very interesting view in Chapter 11, "God." My own work has been inspired to develop certain clues about value given by Whitehead, for instance in my *Cosmology of Freedom* (New Haven: Yale University Press, 1974), Chapter 3, "A General Theory of Value," and most especially in *Reconstruction of Thinking* (Albany: State University of New York Press, 1981).

11. The theme mentioned pervades the references in the previous note. But it finds its most striking exemplification in Whitehead's polemic against theologies that represent God as necessitating power. God's proper relation to the world, according to Whitehead, is to appreciate it and reciprocally to represent for the world's appreciation a poetically moving set of worthy possibilities. See, for instance, *Process and Reality*, Part 5, or *Religion in the Making* (New York: Macmillan, 1926).

12. The following discussion of Whitehead's theory of actual occasions, experience, value and determinateness arises from his technical discussion in *Process and Reality*, Part 3, on the categorial obligations. I have given my own technical critical discussion of his view in *Cosmology of Freedom*, Chapters 1 through 7, and in *Reconstruction of Thinking*, Chapters 3 and 4. The discussion in the present text attempts to avoid relatively private technical terms.

13. Whereas it might seem as if Whitehead used the model of human experience to explain the most elementary particles, that is mere appearance. Rather, he constructed a model of elementary particles such that by internal complexification and external combination and nesting, things like people could be modelled, he hoped. Whitehead thus rejected Hegel's sharp distinction between nature and spirit, not because of exaggerations of spirit but because Hegel accepted too much of the mechanistic philosophy of nature for Whitehead's taste. Whitehead's project thus requires showing just what internal complexifications and external combinations and nestings are involved in the "higher" forms of experience such as the human. He did not do much of this himself, and tended to leap to human functions by analogy with the simple processes modelled in single occasions. He does present extraordinary resources for that project, however.

14. The emphasis on perspective is very important in Whitehead's philosophy, as pointed out by Stephen David Ross in *Perspective in Whitehead's Metaphysics* (Albany: State University of New York Press, 1983). Ross finds the emphasis on perspective to be the dominating truth in Whitehead, and thus rejects other elements in Whitehead that are in tension with it. I find this an extreme position, for some of the reasons expressed in the present text concerning actuality in one's own perspective.

15. This list comes from Paul Weiss's fine book, *Privacy* (Carbondale: Southern Illinois University Press, 1983). Weiss has long criticized Whitehead's atomic theory of occasions on the grounds that it cannot account for temporally thick dimensions of human experience. Since Whitehead in fact didn't lay out how those dimensions could be modelled with his theory, Weiss's point is well taken. I have more confidence than Weiss, however, that an approach not too far from Whitehead's can provide an

account of the substantial character of temporally thick realities. Florence Bradford Wallack developed one line of inquiry in her *The Epochal Nature of Process in Whitehead's Metaphysics* (Albany: State University of New York Press, 1980) by suggesting how occasions themselves may be temporally thick, in fact very long. But the dimensions of human reality listed and analyzed by Weiss are not single long occasions but enduring, organically developing structures. More work is required by those interested in testing the Whiteheadian project.

16. The mention of representation in science should call to mind the fact that science is not mere modelling but also interpreting according to the leading principles and biases of its instruments, basic concepts, and habits. This point is best explored by Patrick Heelan in various writings, particularly *Space-Perception and the Philosophy of Science* (Berkeley: University of California Press, 1983). One might think that acknowledgment of the hermeneutical circle obviates the question of totality and eliminates the possibility of system. The former is not so, however, for one of the main insights of hermeneutics is the global orientations of hermeneutic stances; the systematic issue is the merit of the particular stances. The latter is not so because the systematic suppositions of a hermeneutic process need to be interpreted and that interpretation is by means of a system used as a complex sign.

17. Lewis Ford presents a fine analysis of this complex in his "The Non-Temporality of Whitehead's God," in *International Philosophical Quarterly* 13/3 (September 1973), pp. 347–76. For a debate about the bearing of this point on ontology, see my "Whitehead on the One and the Many," *Southern Journal of Philosophy* 7 (1969–70), pp. 387–93; Lewis Ford's "Neville on the One and the Many," *Southern Journal of Philosophy* 10/1 (Spring 1972) pp. 79–84; and my rejoinder, "Response to Ford's 'Neville On the One and the Many'," in *loc. cit.*, pp. 85–86. Revised versions of the debate, which unfortunately downplay the importance of eternal objects, are to be found in *Explorations in Whitehead's Philosophy*, edited by Lewis S. Ford and George L. Kline (New York: Fordham University Press, 1983), Chapters 12 and 13. A more extended version of my side of the debate is in my *Creativity and God* (New York: The Seabury Press, 1980), Chapters 2 and 3 (although Chapter 3 is rather much the same as Chapter 12 in the previous reference).

18. *Creativity and God* is an extended analysis of these difficulties with process philosophy.

19. Charles Hartshorne is chief among those who believe as the truth and as Whitehead's doctrine that the satisfaction of an occasion entails that it must be prehended by a successor occasion, at least by God. My own view

is that in truth and in Whitehead an occasion's satisfaction makes it available for subsequent prehension but whether it is a real potentiality depends upon the successor occasion's subjective unity. For a discussion See Charles Hartshorne, John B. Cobb, Jr., and Lewis S. Ford, "Three Responses to Neville's *Creativity and God,"* Process Studies 10/3–4 (Fall-Winter 1980), pp. 73–88, and my "Concerning *Creativity and God,* A Response," *Process Studies* 11/1 (Spring 1981), 1–10.

20. "Vagueness" is discussed throughout Peirce's writings. See for instance his "Issues of Pragmaticism" and "Consequences of Critical Common-Sensism" in *Collected Papers of Charles Sanders Peirce,* edited by Charles Hartshorne and Paul Weiss (Cambridge: Harvard University Press, 1934), Vol 5, paragraphs 447–50 and 505–06. It is of extremely great historical interest that Hegel gave exactly the same analysis of vagueness as Peirce, but drew the opposite moral from it. See the *Lesser Logic,* paragraph 9, where Hegel says (in Wallace's translation):" . . . the Universal or general principle contained in it, the genus, or kind . . . is, on its own account, indeterminate and vague, and therefore not on its own account connected with the Particulars or with the details." Hegel notes that such vague universals do not allow of necessity in philosophy , and so rejects them as an adequate starting point. Peirce agrees about necessity and affirms "vagueness" as essential to the empirical character of philosophy. My own extensive development of the notion of systematic philosophy requiring vagueness is in Chapter 2 of *Reconstruction of Thinking.*

21. In developing a systematic conception of the world without totality I have learned much from Justus Buchler. See his *Metaphysics of Natural Complexes* (New York: Columbia University press, 1966) and especially his "On the Concept of 'the World'," in *Review of Metaphysics* 31/4 (June 1978), pp. 555–579.

Jan Van der Veken
KATHOLIEKE UNIVERSITIET—LEUVEN

A Plea for an Open, Humble Hegelianism

Whitehead and Hegel seem to have more in common that Whitehead himself could have suspected on the basis of his minimal acquaintance with the texts of Hegel and his indirect knowledge of German idealism. Unbeknown to Whitehead, however, the project of developing a speculative system competent to interpret a broad range of aesthetic, religious, and scientific experiences had constrained both philosophers to fight essentially the same battle.

Hegel is at the origin of everything important which has been going on in philosophy during the last century, e.g., of marxism, Nietzsche, of phenomenology and German existentialism, of psychoanalysis. He instigates the endeavour to explore the irrational and to integrate it in an *enlarged reason*, which remains the task of our century.[1]

The "similarity of methodology, context and results exhibited in the metaphysical systems of Whitehead and Hegel"[2] is striking indeed, and there is no doubt that Whitehead greatly contributed to the exploration of that "enlarged reason" by the broadness of his mature thought which in many respects is "Hegelian" in scope and penetration.

Whitehead lived in an age during which speculative thought of all sort, including especially Hegel's, was distrusted. For that reason, Whitehead himself rejected any claims to finality. In this sense, I will argue, Whitehead's thought qualifies as a kind of "humble and open" form of Hegelianism. Such an "open and humble" approach, moreover, is far more in line with the contemporary awareness of the risks and limitations of all speculative thought. It is also in line with some very mild but authoritative interpretations of Hegel.

On the other hand, a reinterpretation of Whitehead along Hegelian lines promises a broader philosophical perspective on many of the much debated issues in process philosophy itself—e.g., the relationship between God and Creativity, or whether God is *an* actual entity (amongst many actual entities)—contributing to a revision of Whiteheadianism which Whitehead himself might well have found congenial. Some of these crucial problems in the interpretation of Whitehead's metaphysics cannot be solved within the system itself, and may require deeper roots in the mainstream tradition of philosophical thought.

An excellent way to clarify the relationship between Hegel and Whitehead is to call attention to the role played by religion and science in the systematic thought of both philosophers as related to the overall problem of comprehensive philosophical insight or widsom. According to Hegel, philosophy reaches its aim in "Wissen" ("knowledge" is an inadequate translation; "sophia" would be better). Absolute knowledge or absolute "sophia" is the culminating point of the whole system: it really is a "System des Wissens." Because knowledge (I will use this standard translation) is not present to itself from the beginning, it has to pursue for itself the long way, from the first and still abstract figure of sense-awareness to the concluding figure of the *Phenomenology of Spirit:* Absolute knowing. The *Phenomenology of Spirit* is the first part of the *system*, as indicated on the title-page of the first edition.[3] It is in no way a matter of chance that Hegel looks upon *Phenomenology* as the first part of the *System of Science.* When, in a later edition of the *Phenomenology of Spirit* the *Phenomenology* is no longer presented as the first part of the system, the reason very probably is that the *Phenomenology of Spirit* already contains the complete system, from the point of view of experiencing consciousness.

In Hegel's opinion, Absolute knowledge is "Wissen"—knowledge which has come into full possession of itself. Hegel has understood that none of the existing philosophical systems in itself contains the truth and that only the movement of the Spirit coming to full self-awareness through art, religion, and philosophy brings about knowledge. The aim of philosophy is "das wirkliche Erkennen dessen, was in Wahrheit ist."[4] It can hardly be denied that Hegel intended to offer at least an outline of such a philosophy which has become a science—his *Enzyklopädie der philosophischen Wissenschaften.*

Whitehead does not share such high expectations. "There never has been any exact complete system of philosophical thought," he writes.[5] For Whitehead, no philosophical system is ever "science." The term "absolute knowledge" or "science" (in the sense of *sophia*) not only does not occur in Whitehead, but is inconceivable within the parameters of his thought.

The difference in tone between Hegel and Whitehead is nowhere as evident as in the comparison between Hegel's "programmatic" introductions (his *Vorreden*[6]) and Whitehead's concluding remark of the preface to *Process and Reality:* "There remains the final reflection, how shallow, puny and imperfect are efforts to sound the depths in the nature of things. In philosophical discussion, the merest hint of dogmatic certainty as to finality of statement is an exhibition of folly." The author of such a statement does not exude philosophical pretentiousness. What Whitehead actually *does*, however, is not so very different from what Hegel himself intended—to (as Whitehead goes on to say) "frame a scheme of ideas, the best that one can, and unflinchingly . . . explore the interpretation of experience in terms of the scheme."[7] Again, for such reasons, I classify Whitehead's speculative philosophy as a "humble" form of Hegelianism.

Is it possible to interpret Hegel *himself* in this "humble" fashion? The general impression gleaned from reading Hegel's explicit statements on the role of philosophy point in rather a different direction—whence his arrogant reputation for desiring that *his* system be perceived as nothing less than *sophia*, the conclusion and the end of philosophy's quest. Nevertheless, there are presently a number of authorities on Hegel's thought who feel that "Absolute knowing" can likewise be understood as a humble and open search for understanding:

That is absolute knowledge: not the ultimate possession of the keys of the universe, but the very poor ability to take the risk, knowing what one does, of a unifying word which is able to give a meaning to that which arises unexpectedly in the course of the events.[8]

This perspective can be more readily assimilated with the "Whiteheadian" interpretation of Hegel. It is Hegelianism which has become "humble."

Can Hegel's philosophy likewise be interpreted as "open" to new developments? Can "Absolute knowing" be superseded? Hegel, to be sure, perceives himself as in a position to say something definitive about earlier philosophical systems and cultural developments. The phrase "fuer uns aber, oder *an sich*" recurs frequently in his writings. It certainly seems as if Hegel's own standpoint is understood by him as the "an sich." Unfortunately, this appearance has encouraged rigid and finalistic interpretations of his philosophy of history by critics and disciples alike—as though Hegel himself had suggested that philosophy really had come to an end in his day and that in this sense philosophy had really reached a full understanding of the meaning of history.

By contrast, it is quite evident that Hegel was fully aware of the fact that history would go on in its own fashion—indeed, what he says in this regard about the future of the United States as a nation is quite illuminating. One may argue on systematic grounds, however, that Hegel really *had* to be convinced that no new figure or form of *consciousness* could arise in the subsequent historical process. Based upon the inner logic of his system, the rest of history could not be anything other than the propagation (throughout the whole of human societies) of the ideal of the finite "spirit-in-community" which has eventually reached full understanding of itself and of the movement of history.

Here again, however, Pierre-Jean Labarriere advances an unusual interpretation:

The consciousness of the individual who wants to be the equal of the present figure of the Spirit has to reassume at his own cost that long road, as it is present to him in the "recollection of memory" (Erinnerung), so that he may carry further, according to his own poor measure, that burden which is for all of us "the kindgom of the spirits" [Ph. 564/13; "Das Geisterreich"].[9]

This, again, is a very "Whiteheadian"—and a very "open and humble" interpretation of Hegelianism.

Obviously, such sharply contrasting and rival interpretations point to a fundamental unsolved ambiguity within Hegel's system itself. On the one hand, the path of development of Spirit toward full self-understanding appears to be (in some sense, at least) a *necessary*, well-defined path.[10] On the other hand, however, it seems as if the whole philosophical enterprise is to be understood as articulating the manner in which Spirit comes to this full self-understanding *in and through the contingencies of history:*

Is Science the disparition of philosophy in its self-understanding or is it the starting point of a new understanding of the world by the philosopher who seeks and finds its rationality?[11]

The first of these interpretations is certainly the most traditional; the second is truly both "open" and more "Whiteheadian."

This interpretive ambiguity in Hegel had earlier been noticed by Maurice Merleau-Ponty in his inaugural lecture at the College de France. His discussion of the tension between our understanding of philosophy and of history is worth quoting at some length.

Hegel had already identified [history and philosophy] by making philosophy the understanding of historical experience, and history the becoming of philosophy. But the conflict was only masked, since for Hegel philosophy is absolute knowledge, system, totality, whereas the history of which the philosopher speaks is not really history, that is to say, something which one does. It is rather universal history, fully comprehended, finished, dead. But, on the other hand, history as pure fact or event, introduces into the system in which it is incorporated an eternal movement which tears it to pieces. These two points of view both remain true for Hegel, and we know that he carefully maintained this equivocation. At certain times he makes the philosopher appear as the simple reader of a history already accomplished, as the Owl of Minerva who takes flight only at dusk when the work of history is finished. But at other times he seems to make the philosopher the only subject of history, since he alone does not undergo it, but comprehends it by elevating it to the level of the concept. In reality this equivocation works to the profit of the philosopher. Since history has been staged by him, he finds in it only the sense he has already placed there, and in accepting it he merely accepts himself. It is to Hegel, perhaps, that we should apply what Alain has said of the subtler merchants of sleep who "offer us a sleep in which the dreams are precisely the world in which we live." The universal history of Hegel is the dream of a [genuine] history."[12]

Whitehead more successfully surmounts this ambiguity, precisely because his approach is more empirical than is Hegel's.

There is a metaphysical need for a principle of determination, but there can be no metaphysical reason for what is determined. If there were such a reason, there would be no need for any further principle: for metaphysics would already have provided the determination. The general principle of empiricism depends upon the doctrine that there is a principle of concretion which is not discoverable by abstract reason.[13]

In rejecting the notion of prior metaphysical-historical determinateness, Whitehead was likely responding to Spinoza—but his assessment applies equally well to Hegel. This interesting interpretation of "empiricism" makes all the difference: Whitehead's speculative system is (as a result of this commitment) more truly descriptive than is Hegel's. Whitehead accepts the empirical basis, not just for the contingencies of history, but also for the discovery of the specific determinations of the Spirit.

This feature of Whitehead's approach to speculative metaphysics has important consequences with regard to the relationship between religion and philosophy—and it is in this area that the *difference* between Hegel and Whitehead is most clearly evident (even though both subscribe to philosophical variations of the Christian tradition). In Hegel's opinion, Christian religion and true philosophy have an identical *content*. What appears in religion as well as in philosophy is the Absolute Spirit who is the triune God of Christian religion:

> Here . . . God is *revealed as He is;* He is immediately present as He is *in Himself,* i.e. He is immediately *present* as Spirit. God is attainable in pure speculative knowledge alone and *is* only in that knowledge, and is only that knowledge itself for He is Spirit; and this speculative knowledge is the knowledge of the *revealed* religion.[14]

Because of the coincidence in content, the figure of religion in which absolute knowledge appears for the first time (albeit in the guise of representation) is "revealed religion."[15] What Hegel says about "revealed religion" in the *Phenomenology* applies to a *definite* figure of the Spirit, but it is at the same time already a recapitulation of the coming-to-itself of Absolute Spirit.[16]

Why then must revealed religion be superseded, if it already contains the final truth (albeit truth on the level of representation only)? Hegel explains lucidly why in modern times traditional religion was no longer able to reconcile the Absolute and finite, which was the traditional task of religion. Christian religion has understood itself as final, as "absolute." For that reason, it must incorporate in its overall scope a view on the relationship between God and creation (Nature) as well as between God and man (history). In fact, Christianity has presented itself as an overall view on reality, illuminating every aspect of existence. In the ages of faith there was virtually no aspect of human life which did not receive its ultimate significance from the all-encompassing viewpoint of the Christian ("absolute") religion.

In modern times, however, this all-encompassing synthesis no longer determines the self-understanding of western culture, because "absolute religion" has found opposite itself a new kind of knowledge of the finite world, which adopts its own intrinsic standards and methods and imposes them upon all knowledge and experience in direct challenge to religion. This challenger comprises, of course, the disciplines of natural science.

In this conflict, the intellect suddenly finds itself endowed with an overwhelming power: it conceives of all objectivity as something finite. Religion, in order to escape the jurisdiction of a form of the intellect which is opposed to its dearest concerns (namely, the *reconciliation* of the finite with the Infinite) withdraws from all exteriority and objectivity and settles itself in the interiority of eternal longing. The moments of reconciliation in the divine man Jesus and in the Christian community are not understood in their togetherness, because human beings still operate on the level of representation: (in the past) "Jesus died for our sins and was resurrected; we will (in the distant future) partake of the glory of his resurrection." The advantage of this strategic withdrawl to "interiority" is evident: a conflict between religion and the rational intellect is thereby avoided. Religion and the natural sciences each have their own distinct and quite separate domains of definition. The price exacted for this compromise, however, is quite high. Religion loses its reconciling power; it can no longer function to bring together consciousness and the exterior, objective world.

Hegel wants to elaborate a speculative philosophy which will overcome this dichotomy and limit the reductionistic power of the intellect (according to which all objectivity comprises something finite and merely exterior). Hence, in Hegel's systematic deliberations after 1800 (following the move from Frankfurt to Jena) it is no longer religion but *philosophy* which has to perform the all-important task of reconciling the finite and the Absolute.[17] While it is true that so far as its content is concerned, Hegel still considers Christianity to be the highest form of "revealed religion," even Christianity remains a form of representation rather than of "knowledge" *(Wissen)*. Speculative philosophy is necessary in order to raise religious feelings and intuitions to the level of genuine understanding.[18] For Hegel, then, philosophy is religion *understood.*

Whitehead also describes a kind of "rational religion" or philosophical theology in quest of an adequate metaphysics. But, for Whitehead, religion *per se* adds its "own independent evidence which metaphysics must take account of in framing its description" (RM 76). The "religious experience of mankind . . . brings its own contribution of immediate experience" (RM 57, 77). There is, naturally, an attempt to integrate this particular insight, derived from Christianity, into the larger metaphysical scheme of things. Whitehead acknowledges, for example, the important impact of his thought of "the brief Galilean vision." But this section of his major work arguably constitutes a "post-systematic" text. And in any case (it seems to me) it is important to try to decide what can be said about God on metaphysical grounds and what can be said on religious grounds. It is better not to try to "recuperate" in philosophy all that religion says about God, in that the very attempt tends to render the larger philosophical enterprise decidedly less convincing.[19]

I would suggest attending to Whitehead's more edifying statements on this topic in *Science and the Modern World*. There, having introduced the religiously-neutral postulate of a "principle of limitation," he makes the following sharp distinction: "What *further* can be known about God must be sought in the region of *particular* experiences, and therefore rests on an empirical basis" (SMW 257; my emphasis). Whitehead's perspective, in this sense also, constitutes a "humble and open" form of Hegelianism. He leaves more room for religious particularity—including the great non-theistic tradition of Buddhism.

Turning from science and religion to the problem of epistemology in science itself, it is only fair to observe that, to his enduring credit, Hegel was one of the few nineteenth-century philosophers who was not impressed virtually to the point of intimidation by the advances in the store of human knowledge made by the disciplines of natural science. For Hegel, by contrast, the sciences can in no way set the standard for knowledge generally, precisely because their perspective is limited in principle to that which is finite and objective. Only philosophy understands the finite as an exteriorization of the Infinite, and hence as not radically distinct from the Infinite. A genuinely *complete* knowledge of Nature, as a consequence, is only possible within the framework of speculative thought, the only true "Wissenschaft."

One may belabor the important differing understandings of "the Whole" *(das Ganze)* between the two philosophers. But in the main (regarding the relationship of philosophy and the sciences) Whitehead adopts basically the same standpoint as did Hegel. Whitehead likewise believes, for example, that true understanding—valid philosophical knowledge—must be able to conceive a "complete fact." And precisely the inherent limitation of the natural sciences collectively, according to *both* philosophers, is their deliberately partial, and hence abstract, viewpoint:

Philosophy is not one among the sciences with its own little scheme of abstractions which it works away at perfecting and improving. It is the survey of sciences, with the special objects of [bringing about their] harmony and . . . their completion. It brings to this task, not only the evidence of the separate sciences, but also its own appeal to concrete experience. [Philosophy] confronts the sciences with *concrete fact*. (SMW 126ff.; my emphasis)

Many authors have suggested that Hegel's philosophy of nature is the weakest part of his whole enterprise. And, to be sure, Hegel's knowledge of science was limited to a less than perfect comprehension of the sciences of his own historical period. But so far as his philosophy of *nature* is concerned, the limitations and imperfections in his actual acquaintance with the immediate particulars of the sciences may well have proved as much a help as a hindrance, and in any case do not seem to negatively affect his basic philosophical insights.[20]

All this does not entail, however, that Whitehead's is simply a modern and up-to-date version of Hegelianism. Indeed, there are aspects of Whitehead's system which could stand some creative transformation in the direction of Hegel's speculative system. According to Hegel, for example, creativity and God are so related that God cannot be conceived merely as one (finite) reality amongst others. For Whitehead, by contrast, God comes to have the strange metaphysical status of a formative element, which is at the same time *an* actual entity (one amongst a myriad?)—albeit an *everlasting* actual entity.[21] Hegel has perceived (correctly, in my view) that "God," and "what is Absolute or ultimate," cannot be divorced in meaning from one another. God cannot be simply one entity amongst others; God cannot be less than the Absolute.

A re-interpretation of Whitehead's most fundamental insights regarding God and creativity along this more Hegelian line would appear to be all to Whitehead's advantage. Indeed, it seems very nearly the case that a more "open and humble" interpretation of Hegel's view on the relationship between Creativity (as the self-development of the Absolute) and God (as that Absolute which is thus developed) is precisely what Whitehead intended to formulate.

Notes

1. Maurice Merleau-Ponty, *Sens et non-Sens*, 2nd ed. (Paris: Nagel, 1985), p. 109.

2. George R. Lucas, Jr., *Two Views of Freedom in Process Thought: A Study of Hegel and Whitehead*, American Academy of Religion Dissertation Series, n. 28 (Chico, CA: Scholars Press, 1979), pp. 1, 4.

3. *System der Wissenschaft. Erster Theil, die Phänomenologie des Geistes* (Bamberg und Wuerzburg: Joseph Anton Goebhardt, 1807).

4. *Phänomenologie des Geistes*, "Einleitung." Ed. J. Hoffmeister (Hamburg: Felix Meiner Verlag, 1952), p. 63 (6e Auflage).

5. *Religion in the Making* (New York: Macmillan, 1926), p. 139. Following a standard convention, subsequent citations of this work will appear in parentheses within the body of this paper as "RM," followed by the pagination of this edition.

6. Cf. Erwin Metzke, *Hegels Vorreden* (Heidelberg: F. H. Kerk Verlag, 1949), 1970.

7. *Process and Reality* (New York: Macmillan, 1929), p. x. Further references to this work will also appear in the body of my text in parentheses as "PR" followed by the pagination of this edition.

8. Pierre-Jean Labarriere, "La sursomption du temps et le vrai sens de l'histoire conçue," *Revue de Métaphysique et de Morale* (1979), p. 98: "Tel est le savoir absolu: non par la possession dernière des clefs de l'univers, mais le très pauvre pouvoir qui consiste à risquer, en connaissance de cause, une parole unifiante susceptible de donner sens à ce qui survient dans l'inattendu des choses." [my translation.]

9. "La Phénoménologie de l'Esprit comme discours systématique: histoire, religion et science," *Hegel-Studien*, 9 (1972), p. 148: "Et l'individu qui, ici et maintenant, veut s'égaler à la figure actuelle de cet Esprit se doit de reprendre à son propre compte ce long cheminement, tel qu'il se présente à lui dans la "récollection du souvenier," afin de porter plus loin, à sa pauvre mesure, ce fardeau qu'est pour chacun le "royaume des esprits." [My translation.]

10. G. W. F. Hegel, *Reason in History*, trans. Robert S. Hartman (Indianapolis, IN: Bobbs-Merrill, 1953), p. 24: "World history is the progress of the consciousness of freedom—a progress whose *necessity* we have to investigate." [my emphasis]

11. Review of Fulda, *Das Problem einer Einleitung in Hegels Wissenschaft der Logik* by J. Gauvin: *Hegel-Studien*, 4 (1967), p. 249.

12. *In Praise of Philosophy*, trans. by John Wild and James M. Edie (Evanston, IL: Northwestern University Press, 1963), pp. 48–49.

13. *Science and the Modern World* (New York: Macmillan, 1925), p. 257. This work will hereafter be cited in parentheses in the text as "SMW."

14. *Phänomenologie des Geistes*, 530, 1. 11–16. The translation is that of A. V. Miller, *Hegel's Phenomenology of Spirit* (Oxford: The Claredon Press, 1977), p. 461.

15. Cf. Louis Dupre, "Religion as Representation," *The Legacy of Hegel*, Proceedings of the Marquette Hegel Symposium, 1970, Ed. J. J. O'Malley, K. W. Algozin, H. P. Kainz, L. C. Rice (The Hague: Martinus Nijhoff, 1973). Cf. also Kenneth L. Schmitz, "The Conceptualization of Religious Mystery: An Essay in Hegel's Philosophy of Religion," pp. 108–136.

16. Cf. Labarriere, "La Phénoménologie de l'Esprit," *Hegel-Studien*, p. 144.

17. Cf. Peter Jonkers, "Filosofie en Religie bij de jonge Hegel (1800)," *Bijdragen: Tijdschrift voor filosofie en theologie* (1984), pp. 28–42.

18. In an early programmatic text (the first part of the *Differenzschrift*) Hegel assigns to Philosophy the task of suspending the fixed dichotomies between the finite and the Infinite, and of constructing the Absolute for consciousness.

19. Cf. this objection in my essay, "Whitehead's God is not Whiteheadian Enough," *Whitehead und der Prozessbegriff*, ed. Harald Holz and Ernest Wolf-Gazo. "Proceedings of the First International Whitehead Symposium, 1981." (Munich: Verlag Karl Alber, 1984).

20. Milic Capek is quite critical of Hegel's shortcomings regarding the mastery of specific scientific data and theories ["Hegel and the Organic View of Nature," *Hegel and the Sciences*, eds. R. S. Cohen and M. W. Wartofsky (Amsterdam: D. Reidel, 1984), pp. 109–121], in contrast to the sunny assessment of his farsighted competence offered elsewhere in the present volume by J. N. Findlay, as well as that offered earlier by Errol E. Harris ["The *Naturphilosophie* Updated," *Owl of Minerva*, 10 (December, 1978), pp. 2–7]. George R. Lucas, however, demonstrates the basic irrelevance of these perceived insights and oversights to the broader question of the consistency of Hegel's philosophy of nature, which he finds comparable to Whitehead's in important respects: "A Re-interpretation of Hegel's Philosophy of Nature," *Journal of the History of Philosophy*, 22, no. 1 (January, 1984), pp. 103–113.

21. Robert Whittemore appears to agree with this criticism when he complains that "Hegel's conception of deity as self-evolving, universe-encompassing Mind or spirit provides a unity of concept lacking in its Whiteheadian counterpart." Cf. "Hegel's 'Science' and Whitehead's 'Modern World'," *Philosophy*, 31 (1956), pp. 53ff.

Michael Welker
UNIVERSITY OF TÜBINGEN

Hegel and Whitehead: Why Develop a Universal Theory?

Hegelians and Whiteheadians have a common problem, whenever they encounter an interested public. They are both challenged to aid in the decoding of a theory which is (to continue the metaphor) difficult to crack. This challenge entails a particular freedom and a particular risk. The particular freedom comes from the fact that the theories of Hegel and Whitehead—precisely because of their obscurity and need for decoding—leave considerable room to play with possible approaches to reconstruction, to offer one's own proposals for systematic improvements, and to introduce thought experiments of all sorts.

Corresponding to this freedom is a particular risk. The theories of Hegel and Whitehead—precisely because of their obscurity and need for decoding—are notoriously controversial. Their recognition and reputation are chronically endangered. To be sure, some interpreters consider them sources of an endless wealth of disclosure and knowledge. Others, however, see in both philosophies products of both a habit of thought led astray into the realm of the eccentric, and a private language which has lost itself in the clouds. The decision between the two view-points wavers in one direction or the other, depending upon the abilities of the Hegelians and Whiteheadians to unlock the obscure theories and to render their operations plausible.

How are the theories of Hegel and Whitehead to be regarded: as sources of increased knowledge, or as mazes of bad speculation? This question remains as urgent today as ever.

The characteristic risk—that the reputation of the theories is constantly endangered—should not be suppressed by emphasizing their respective "success stories", and repressing the history of their previous failures. Dieter Henrich, a leading Hegel authority, admits: "We know that we still cannot say what is actually going on in Hegel's thought."[1] The Whitehead authority is forced to a similar admission—when, for example, he or she is supposed to give a systematic explanation of the "Theory of Extension" in *Process and*

Reality. At the most, certain regions of the two great theories can be reckoned as available to thought and amenable to mediation and reproduction.

In view of this diagnosis, communicating Hegelians and Whiteheadians might take as their motto the German proverb, "Geteiltes Leid ist halbes Leid" ("Trouble shared is trouble halved").

In fact, however, a comparison of the two philosophies increases simultaneously both the freedom and the risk already mentioned. It augments the freedom, since *two* quite obscure theoretical languages are now at one's disposal. This raises the theoretical possibility of answering the question posed not only by outsiders—namely: "What does expression 'x' or operation 'y' mean in Hegel?"—with the reply, "Well, expression 'x' and operation 'y' in Hegel say the same thing as expression 'η' and operation 'δ' in Whitehead." If we were to succumb to this temptation of merely establishing referential connections between two very obscure theories, we would greatly increase the risk that the interested public would be further alienated from these theories.

How can one prevent the immunization effect which at that point would certainly set in, but which is called forth by the obscurity of the theories themselves? One must squarely apprehend the common problem of Hegelians and Whiteheadians, and not seek to transpose and translate the obscure operations of Hegel and Whitehead directly into each other's terms. Rather, one must insist upon the *delineation of a further theoretical and linguistic level*.

I will attempt to show that precisely this procedure would correspond to Hegel's and Whitehead's style of thought. I would thus like to argue *against* direct contact between the two theoretical languages, which would only increase the hermeneutic complexity. Instead, I will argue *for* a procedure which consciously apprehends a further level of understanding which makes these two great theories accessible and will allow one to work productively with them.

In the first part, I shall discuss some approaches that speak against my proposal: that is, approaches which are oriented towards direct contact and immediate comparison of the theories. Since these approaches are familiar and have been considered and criticized repeatedly in the literature, this part of the discussion can be kept very short. In the second part, I will argue that the procedure which I propose corresponds to the developmental logic of Hegel's and Whitehead's theories. This argument holds, moreover, despite the fact that my procedure recommends reversing, rather than continuing, Hegel's and Whitehead's process of moving away from so-called natural languages and specifically scientific languages into idiosyncratic theoretical languages. In part three, I will evaluate the observations of the two preceding sections and show why Hegel and Whitehead both develop universal theories. It will thereby become clear that analogous motives direct the respective developments of their thinking. Moreover, a difference which often goes unnoticed between the universal theories of Hegel and Whitehead and premodern ontologies will be emphasized.

1. Hegel and Whitehead: The Difficulty of Comparing Their Theories Directly

A direct comparison of the theories of Hegel and Whitehead cannot be justified—so far, at least—by appealing to a historically documented kinship of their thought. Whitehead's assurance that he had not read Hegel's writings has often been quoted. There are, to be sure, traces of Whitehead's contact with English Hegelianism. The Houghton Library at Harvard even possesses a copy of Bradley's *Logic* with a number of critical marginal notes by Whitehead. These traces are not sufficient, however, to suggest the influence of Hegel's *theory* in Whitehead's thought, to say nothing of proving it. We can only vaguely hope that significantly intensified research on English Hegelianism at the beginning of our century[2] will lead to a more favorable situation. If we could render more clearly recognizable the transformations of Hegel's philosophy which occurred in English Hegelianism, perhaps we could distinguish the comparison of Whitehead and Hegel from relations between Whitehead and Hegelians who, be it from strength or from necessity, were often very independent.[3] Unless the state of research undergoes a dramatic alteration, however, the comparison on the historical level will remain basically sterile.

Still more ticklish with regard to a comprehension of specific relationships is the situation on the systematic level. The (so to speak) risk-free observations, kept extremely general, have been uttered often enough: for example, that both thinkers place a process structure in the center of their theory,[4] that they seek to reconcile philosophic and religious thought,[5] that they make similar judgments about many aspects of the philosophic tradition.

To advance to more specific and fruitful theses, on the other hand, is difficult. A consistent examination of the use of basic concepts in Whitehead and Hegel reveals not only commonalities either perceived or conjectured, but also clear differences. This has been demonstrated by Reiner Wiehl and George L. Kline, for example, with regard to the conception of subjectivity.[6] Other studies have, to be sure, done more to obliterate evident differences—as for example Friedrich Kambartel on the heterogeneity of the conceptions of "world" in Hegel and Whitehead.[7] The recognition of clear differences also functions as a deterrent against the unrestrained wish for, or the easy requirement of, reciprocal "supplements" to the theories. How, for example, should Whitehead's theory be "supplemented" with concepts of subjectivity which are centered (or at least capable of being centered) in the theory of consciousness and in individual anthropology—as long as we cannot clearly say whether the mature form of Whitehead's theory is systematically even compatible with such concepts?[8] Yet how could one proceed, if one does not want to lay the foundations of the comparison of Hegel's and Whitehead's theories upon sand?

2. Hegel and Whitehead: Formally Comparable Developments of Universal Theories

Hegel and Whitehead, as is well known, did not develop their universal theories through mere cogitation upon ultimate questions, nor through an immediate striving for general insights applicable to all possible problems. Indeed, at the beginning of their philosophic development, they are far removed from the obscure theoretical language of their "mature" periods, on which we primrily concentrate today. One cannot even say that either philosopher searches for an idiosyncratic theoretical language which could claim universal diagnostic competence. Both believe, rather, in the sufficient power of achievement of the widely recognized theoretical foundations which have been laid before them. For Whitehead, of course, that foundation is the theoretical language of mathematics, and for the young Hegel it is Kant's philosophy. Both Whitehead and Hegel, however, develop a line of inquiry which explodes the theoretical foundations which they themselves had presupposed and accepted at the outset.

Whitehead and Hegel of course pose different questions: Whitehead asks about the knowability and adequate comprehension of the world; Hegel inquires concerning the mutability of the societal world and the bringing about of a world characterized by freedom. Despite these differences, however, the genesis of their theoretical development is formally quite comparable.

At first Whitehead is convinced that an adequate representation of the world is possible only in mathematical language.[9] Moreover, he tries to grasp the world as a *unity* conceived in motion, a unity consisting only of *one* class of entities. Conversely, Whitehead wants to thematize for his investigation the various ways of regarding the "nature of the material world." At this initial stage, in the first decade of the twentieth century, he intends these ways of viewing the world to be mathematical.

Whitehead thus formulates a set of problems which will shape the developmental dynamic of his thought and the fundamental character of his universal theory.[10] The complex of problems is as follows. Suppose that one holds fast to the presupposition of the unity and simple fundamental character of the world. How then can one evaluate different mathematically formulated ways of regarding the world (or even ways not formulated mathematically) without yielding the claim to adequacy and precision? Can one way of viewing the world tolerate the others? Given the presupposition of its own adequacy of the unity of the world, must not each perspective attempt to force the other ways of viewing the world to assimilate? Or rather, should the presupposition of the unity and simple constitution of the world be abandoned, if the presupposition of various adequate ways to regard the "nature of the material world" is to be retained?

We know that Whitehead develops his thought, at the latest from 1905 onward, with a consistency of purpose directed towards responding to this set of problems. This preoccupation also explains why he abandons, from 1911 onward, the monopoly of mathematically formulated theories of the world.[11] Moreover, it provides an internal explanation of his successive integration of philosophic and general cultural questions and problems. Beginning with the very important texts published in *The Organisation of Thought* (1917), Whitehead—true to the logic of his inquiry—holds various conceptions of the world in conjunction which, although internally correct, do not readily admit of agreement among themselves.

Mathematically-educated natural scientists, poets, philosophers, and theologians all comprehend the world in ways which are apparently incompatible and often defined in opposition to one another. How can we correlate these various ways of understanding with one another? By what criteria can we classify one way of comprehending the world in relation to another? How can we establish relations which are not arbitrary and not mutually distorting between the way of comprehending the world in the natural sciences, and the contacts of individual feeling with the world? Such questions determine the course of Whitehead's philosophic development and compel him *to formulate a relativistic and polycontextual theory.* This theory takes into account the differentiation of realms of experience, and the differentiation and apparent incompatibility of scientific and cultural forms of thought and representation. In the third part of our reflections we will have to characterize this theory more closely.

In a way which is thoroughly analogous formally,[12] the young Hegel quickly brings himself into the situation of *having to reconstruct the commonality and the differences of various systems of reference.* These systems of reference, stabilized both internally and over against each other, are at first religious, political, and philosophic. Hegel's development, like Whitehead's, originates with an attachment to a significant theory and to a line of inquiry which explodes this theory on the grounds of heightened claims to concretion and to universality.

The young Hegel expects conditions of world freedom to be procured through the application of Kant's theory, particularly of his mature ethics. Hegel writes to Schelling on April 16, 1795:

I await from the Kantian system and its highest completion a revolution in Germany. This revolution will proceed from principles which are already present, and which only need to be generally worked out and to be applied to all previous knowledge.[13]

Religion and politics, according to Hegel, have conspired in secret to stabilize despotism. In opposition to them, and proceeding from the principles laid down by Kant, the philosophers would prove the dignity of human beings:

The peoples will learn to feel it [human dignity]. They will not demand their rights, which have been trampled in the dust, but rather themselves again assume and appropriate those rights . . .[14]

This rather naive conception of the young Hegel contains an interesting dynamic which is rich in consequences. This dynamic is rooted in a conception of autonomy and its propagation which departs from Kant's theory. Dieter Henrich has called attention to this fact:

For Kant, the categorical imperative was the principle of freedom as well as the ground of a legislation which should bring our life under strict rules. Differently from Kant, . . . Hegel adopted from the morality of reason not so much the ethics of law as the appeal to freedom and spontaneity of action. His overriding intention was to procure the free unfolding of properly human life, and to withdraw the legal basis from all systems of order which place life under compulsion.[15]

But this willfully selective reading of Kant's theory throws open the question of how the feeling of dignity should be communicated, and how the experience of autonomy should be carried over and extended. The young Hegel is of the opinion that a *Volksreligion* could and should accomplish this. He must, however, define the conception of a *Volksreligion* which serves the extension of freedom, over against the established dogmatic religious system.[16] He must show how the extension and social manifestation of freedom through *Volksreligion* is possible without destroying individuality and subjectivity, which are, in his estimation, characteristic of freedom. Hegel therefore attempts to depict the relations and differences between various historical and fictitious forms of religion, which stand in correlation to, or in conflict with, various political systems.[17]

Under this complicated presupposition of various systems of the societal world—systems which penetrate and combat one another—Hegel initiates the development of his mature theory. In a situation formally comparable to Whitehead's, Hegel's theory seeks from the beginning *to take into account the differentiation of individually and socially ordered realms of experience, and the differentiation and apparent incompatibilities of dominant cultural systems of reference.*

On the basis of this analysis of the development of Hegel's and Whitehead's thought, one can draw important conclusions for answering the question, "Why develop a universal theory?" Furthermore, one might also be better equipped to distinguish between meaningful and not so meaningful ways of comparing the theories of Hegel and Whitehead.

3. Hegel and Whitehead: A Common Motive for the Development of a Universal Theory

The expressions and operations of the mature theories of Whitehead and Hegel which have won their way into our hearts—the actual entities, eternal objects and phases of concrescence; or *das Wesen, der Begriff, die Schritte der Dialektik* etc.—can be understood as philosophical reactions and responses to the set of problems and tendencies of thought sketched above. It may occasionally make sense to disregard these problems and tendencies in order to examine the internal coherence of the mature theories of Hegel and Whitehead—to treat them "scholastically" by laying hold of their mature theoretical language directly. But however much this procedure might help in understanding the inner workings of the theories, it would prove fruitless in comparing them.

One should, instead, understand the formulation of the mature theories of Hegel and Whitehead as *constructive reactions* to the problems described above—problems whose diagnosis would of course have to be refined. Such an understanding renders both the analogies and the deep differences between the two theories comprehensible. The related intentions and the specific power of achievement of the respective theories can be comprehended, and our vague impression that we have phenomena before us which are somehow comparable can be clarified.

Hegel and Whitehead develop a particular type of universal theory, which cannot properly be understood according to the model of pre-modern ontologies.[18] Hegel and Whitehead present us, rather, with projects which are in principle left open for their own further development. By their own self-understanding they are "contact theories," designed to mediate between heterogeneous realms of cultural experience.[19] *It is the common intention of both theories to react to the modern process of cultural differentiation both of realms of experience and scientific forms of thought and representation.* This process calls into question the naive presupposition of rationality and reality as a continuum. One is compelled to ask whether the development of a universal theory is not a meaningless undertaking, to which only minds which are both simple and prepared to engage in dogmatic violence could turn their attention.

In opposition to many theorists who have since passed from our memory, and in deviation from the style of thought of many who have appropriated the ideas of Hegel and Whitehead, these two thinkers themselves react *consciously* to the process of the dissolution of the rationality and reality continuum, to the differentiation of cultural and scientific forms of thought and representation. They do not respond to this process by abstractly negating it. Nor do they naively recommend the adoption of a connected system of metaphysical dogmas, in which the separate realms of experience should seek (and with good will could find) their own proper localization. Hegel and Whitehead react to the process of modernity by clearly apprehending the different levels and spheres of experience and the attendant threat of relativism, and by offering intratheoretical reconstructions of the incompatibilities and differences of understanding which they want to overcome. The theories of Hegel and Whitehead deny that the rationality-and-reality continuum is a chimera only by reconstructing a process of differentiation which calls even the theories themselves into question, and threatens their own undertaking.

This type of universality, this polycontextualism, this "performance-claim" of the theories explains why Hegel as well as Whitehead developed a theoretical language whose difficulty continually threatens to discredit the theory itself. The common motive for the development of a universal theory and the emphasized type of universal theory also explain, however, why these theories could test and prove their power of achievement in a variety of areas of application. The genesis of the theories and their type of universality explain why they have won cultural influence precisely as bridges of dialogue between heterogeneous realms of experience, or by the prospect to serve as bridges for dialogue between different sciences and disciplines.

Will the cultural influence of these theories and their power to produce their own schools grow in strength, or will they, living chiefly on credit, go stale? The answer depends, I think, upon our success in decoding the theoretical languages and in bringing their functions into plain view. I would therefore enter a plea against attempting to establish direct referential connections between the theoretical languages of Hegel and Whitehead. The attempt to decode these theories and to illuminate their functions should renounce direct comparison and direct transferral from one theoretical language to the other. One should, rather, recognize in the comparative reconstruction of the genesis of these theories a further, third level, which is capable of contact and communication beyond the circles of Hegelians and Whiteheadians.

The question why Hegel and Whitehead developed a universal theory, and the answer to this question, did not point out a place from which they had come, but which had become foreign and insignificant to them, and to which, in view of the mature systems, we should also be indifferent. The question why Hegel and Whitehead developed universal theories should lead us to a level of interpretation that will permit translation of their artificial languages without sacrificing the intentions or the strengths of the great theories. From this perspective a comparison would not of course necessarily produce universal accessibility to the two universal theories. Yet such a comparison could persistently work towards that accessibility, and with a good chance of success. The undertaking of a universal theory would then be freed from the notoriety of hopeless obscurity and dogmatic lust for power. The particular type of universal theory which Hegel and Whitehead developed would become known as a medium of understanding and enlightenment.

Notes

1. Dieter Henrich, *Hegel im Kontext* (Frankfurt: Suhrkamp Verlag, 1971), p. 7 [my translation].

2. And perhaps also on North American Hegelianism. Cf. George R. Lucas, *Two Views of Freedom in Process Thought. A Study of Hegel and Whitehead*, American Academy of Religion Dissertation Series, no. 28 (Chico, CA: Scholars Press, 1979), p. 8. In any case, the warning of Victor Lowe seems to me to be worthy of consideration: "I suspect that even the analogy to Bradley was somewhat overestimated." *Understanding Whitehead* (Baltimore, MD: The Johns Hopkins Press, 1962), p. 256.

3. It is especially in this regard that I am excited about a recent study by George R. Lucas, which includes an historical re-examination of precisely this transformation: *The Genesis of Modern Process Thought: An Historical Outline with Bibliography* (London and Metuchen, NJ: The Scarecrow Press, 1983), chs. III and V. Robert Ellis has attempted to differentiate the Hegel—Bradley—Alexander—Whitehead line of development: cf. "From Hegel to Whitehead," *Journal of Religion*, 61 (October, 1981), pp. 403–421. He adds six quite general observations (p. 417) to the very cautious and scanty observations which Victor Lowe [*Understanding Whitehead*, pp. 255 ff.] brought forward concerning the specific possibilities and impossibilities for comparison of the theories of Hegel and Whitehead. Ellis most certainly merits assent when he says that Whitehead "may not have read Hegel, but, as we have said, there is much which calls Hegel to mind" (p. 420). Friedrich Kambartel [" 'The Universe is More Various, More Hegelian.' Zum Weltverständnis bei Hegel und Whitehead," in *Collegium Philosophicum: Studien Joachim Ritter zum 60. Geburtstag* (Basel and Stuttgart: Schwabe, 1965), pp. 72–98] has drawn attention to the fact that the report from Bertrand Russell [*My Philosophical Development* (London 1959), ch. 4] is very informative concerning the influence of Hegelianism in Cambridge at the time when Whitehead was teaching there.

4. Cf. Robert C. Whittemore, "Hegel's 'Science' and Whitehead's 'Modern World'," *Philosophy*, 31 (1956), pp. 36–54. F. Kambartel, " 'The Universe is More Various, More Hegelian'," esp. pp. 89 f.

5. Cf. Daniel Day Williams, "Philosophy and Faith: A Study in Hegel and Whitehead," in *Our Common History as Christians: Essays in Honor of Albert C. Outler*, ed. J. Deschner, L. T. Howe, and K. Penzel (New York: Oxford University Press, 1975), pp. 157–175.

6. "Einleitung in die Philosophie A. N. Whiteheads," in A. N. Whitehead, *Abenteuer der Ideen* (Frankfurt: Suhrkamp Verlag, 1971), pp. 57 ff., 66 ff. Cf. George L. Kline, "Life as Ontological Category: A Whiteheadian Note on Hegel," in *Art and Logic in Hegel's Philosophy*, ed. W. E. Steinkraus and K. I. Schmitz (New York: Humanities Press, 1980), esp. p. 159 f.

7. *Op. cit.*, pp. 90 ff., 94 ff.

8. Cf. the uncertain reaction to Whitehead's concept of "subject" in R. B. Edwards, "The Human Self: An Actual Entity or a Society?", *Process Studies*, 5 (1975), pp. 195–203, and in R. L. Fetz, *Whitehead: Prozessdenken und Substanzmetaphysik* (Freiburg and München: Verlag K. Alber, 1981), p. 261. Note also the difficulties of a comparison of theories, which become apparent in George L. Kline's "Introduction" to *Alfred North Whitehead: Essays on His Philosophy* (Engelwood Cliffs, N.J.: Prentice-Hall, 1963/Landam, MD: University Press of America, 1983), pp. 2 ff. See also, however, the excellent contribution from G. Vlastos, "Organic Categories in Whitehead," *ibid.*, esp. pp. 163 ff. Vlastos presents not so much a comparison of theories as a third, integrative conception on the basis of an original concept of "dialectic."

9. Cf. "On Mathematical Concepts of the Material World," *Philosophical Transactions* [Royal Society of London, Series A], 205 (1906), pp. 465–525.

10. I have shown this in detail in *Universalität Gottes und Relativität der Welt: Theologische Kosmologie im Dialog mit dem amerikanischen Prozessdenken nach Whitehead*, Neukirchener Beiträge zur Systematischen Theologie, 1. (Neukirchen: Neukirchener Verlag, 1981), pp. 35 ff. For the following section of the text, cf. "Die relativistische Kosmologie Whiteheads," *Philosophische Rundschau* 32, 1985.

11. Readily apparent in *An Introduction to Mathematics*, 1911. For evaluation of this work, see the essay from Chr. Wassermann, "The Relevance of *An Introduction to Mathematics* to Whitehead's Philosophy: Remarks on Whitehead's Philosophy of Mathematics," which is scheduled to appear in *Process Studies*.

12. Richard Hocking has worked out the persisting difference of content quite clearly; cf. "The Polarity of Dialectical History and Process Cos-

mology," *The Christian Scholar*, 50 (1967), esp. pp. 180 ff. Once again I refer the reader to Victor Lowe, *Understanding Whitehead* (note 3 above).

13. *Briefe von und an Hegel, Bd. I: 1785–1812*, ed. J. Hoffmeister, Philosophische Bibliothek Bd. 235, 3rd ed. (Hamburg: Verlag Felix Meiner, 1969), pp. 23 f.

14. *Ibid.*, p. 24.

15. *Hegel im Kontext*, p. 67.

16. G. W. F. Hegel, "Fragmente über Volksreligion und Christentum," in Hegel, *Werke 1: Frühe Schriften* (Frankfurt: Suhrkamp Verlag, 1971), pp. 9 ff., esp. pp. 33 ff. Cf. the (to be sure, rather uncertain) judgment of Hegel's posing of the problem in Charles Taylor, *Hegel* (Cambridge: Cambridge University Press, 1975), p. 56. See also H. S. Harris, *Hegel's Development: Toward the Sunlight, 1770–1801* (Oxford: Oxford University Press, 1972), pp. 119 ff.

17. In "Die Positivität der christlichen Religion," in Hegel, *Werke 1*, pp. 104 ff.

18. Cf. Hegel's characteristic critique of Aristotle in *Vorlesungen über die Geschichte der Philosophie II*, in *Werke 19* (Frankfurt: Suhrkamp Verlag, 1971), pp. 248 f. Note also, however, the effort to establish a comparison between the theories of Hegel and Whitehead by attributing to them a common Aristotelianism (following Collingwood), in A. J. Mandt, "Aristotle, Whitehead, and Hegel on the Problem of Creativity," *The Modern Schoolman*, 59 (1982), pp. 157 ff.

19. Cf. for example, *Process and Reality. An Essay in Cosmology*, corrected edition D. R. Griffin and D. W. Sherburne (New York and London: The Free Press, 1978), pp. 8, 15 ff., as well as Hegel's thesis of the inherent historical relativity of philosophy, discussed by R. Bubner in "Philosophie ist ihre Zeit, in Gedanken erfasst," in *Hermeneutik und Ideologiekritik, Theorie-Diskussion* (Frankfurt: Suhrkamp Verlag, 1971), pp. 210–243.

George L. Kline
BRYN MAWR COLLEGE

Concept and Concrescence: An Essay in Hegelian-Whiteheadian Ontology

I

G. W. F. Hegel, the major speculative philosopher of the nineteenth century, and A. N. Whitehead, the major speculative philosopher of the twentieth century thus far, have a number of traits in common.

In their creative primes both of them were independent, almost solitary, thinkers, who steadfastly ignored the proscription of speculative philosophy widely current in their time. In Hegel's case the proscription emanated from Kant and his followers, in Whitehead's case from the positivists. (Of course, Kant's philosophy was itself one of the several roots of twentieth-century positivism.) Whitehead, to be sure, wrote his major works before the mid twentieth-century flowering of neo-positivism and linguistic analysis.

Considering how decisively both Hegel and Whitehead swam against the philosophical currents of their respective times, it is perhaps surprising that they should have remained so self-confident, even serene, about their work. In this they were reminiscent of Spinoza, speculative philosopher of an earlier and happier time, before the anti-speculative bias had become dominant.

Both Hegel and Whitehead are encyclopedic as well as systematic thinkers. Both made distinctive contributions to the philosophy of culture, social philosophy, and the history of philosophy. (I shall not consider any of these topics in the present paper.) Both tended to de-emphasize epistemology—at least in the Kantian sense of a close critical scrutiny of the possibilities and limitations of human knowledge. In general, both Hegel and Whitehead are anti-Kantian thinkers, although each accepts and develops in his own way Kant's characteristic stress on the activity and "spontaneity" of the human mind. Hegel, no less than Whitehead, rejects the "Kantian doctrine of the objective world as a theoretical construct from purely subjective experience" (PR viii). Both philosophers decisively reject a materialist ontology with its doctrine of "vacuous actuality"; for both of them actuality (*Wirklichkeit* in Hegel's language) is ontologically non-empty—"filled" with activity, agency, life.

Both thinkers undertake to exhibit, in painstaking detail, the "structure of process" or the "logic of becoming *[Werden]*." This undertaking involves both of them in the enormously difficult attempt (an attempt which Bergson, who is often grouped with the "process philosophers," explicitly renounced) to "eff" the "ineffable," i.e., to articulate the forms, categories, and relations of "arising"[1] (what Hegel called *Entstehen* and Aristotle *genesis*) and "perishing" (what Hegel called *Vergehen* and Aristotle *phthora*).

Despite these important similarities, there are significant differences between their respective philosophical heritages and ontological positions. Whitehead stands in the Pythagorean-Platonic tradition,[2] steeped in mathematics; Hegel stands in the Aristotelian tradition, which is suspicious of mathematics and the "merely quantitative." Although as ontologists both place great stress upon activity, relatedness, and the activity of "self-relating," Whitehead is committed to ontological atomism whereas Hegel is committed to ontological continuity (see Sec. VI below for further details).

Moreover, Whitehead developed a "micro-ontology," a theory of least and last events, of atomic or "epochal" concrescent occasions, whereas Hegel developed a "macro-ontology," a theory of the concept (*Begriff*), idea, spirit (*Geist*), and the Absolute. However, it would be misleading to contrast Whitehead's "pluralism" with Hegel's "monism" without noting the unifying function of creativity, and of the Primordial and Consequent Natures of God, in Whitehead's ontology; and without noting Hegel's voracious appetite for the multitudinous details of natural and historical happening.

One might attempt to restate key points of Hegel's ontology in technical Whiteheadian terms and key points of Whitehead's ontology in technical Hegelian terms. However, I propose, as far as possible, to restate such points in a non-technical, neutral language, avoiding the more forbidding technicalities of both systems.

Certain comments on the specialized terminology of both thinkers will be needed as a propaedeutic to that undertaking.

II

One of the results of the attempt by both Hegel and Whitehead to develop a theoretical account of process in general was their recourse to a technical terminology which was misleading in contrasting ways:

(1) Whitehead used certain traditionally "objectivist" terms—'event', 'process', 'concrescence', 'actual entity'—to designate entities with strikingly "subjectivist" characteristics: experience, subjectivity, immediacy, (ontological) privacy, freedom, purpose.

(2) In contrast, Hegel used certain traditionally "subjectivist" terms—*Begriff, Geist, Idee*—to designate entities with such ontological and, in part, "objectivist" characteristics as historicity, objectivity, and intersubjective validity.

The term 'organism' is a special case, although it might be included in the list of "objectivist" Whiteheadian terms with a partly "subjectivist" meaning. In ontological discussions both Hegel and Whitehead mean by it not 'biological organism', i.e., 'living creature', but something much more general, roughly, 'an organized, self-constituting, inwardly articulated whole'. In this broad sense Hegel can call both the concept and the state an organism, and Whitehead can apply the term to both the concrescent occasion and, in an extreme case, a functioning *factory*.[3] Whitehead, I think, intends the narrower sense, but misleadingly suggests the wider one, when he calls his own position "the philosophy of organism" and uses as the title of a key chapter in *Process and Reality* (Pt. II, ch. 4) the expression 'organisms and environment.' (The context makes clear that he means not honeybees and flowers or trout and trout-streams but "[present] concrescent occasions and [past] concreta": see below.)

The shift of both Hegel and Whitehead away from natural and scientific language toward an "idiosyncratic theoretical language"—as Michael Welker has aptly termed it[4]—involved certain additional ambiguities and *aporiai*.

Although both thinkers place central stress on becoming and development, Hegel uses significantly more categoreal or systematic verbs than does Whitehead as well as a great many more gerunds. (Details in Sec. III below.)

Whitehead uses the quite traditional philosophical term 'actual' in two contrasting senses, which I have inelegantly distinguished by the use of subscript numerals as 'actual$_1$' (='active [but not efficacious]') and 'actual$_2$' (='efficacious [but not active]').[5] Whatever is actual$_1$ involves actuali*zation*, an *act* or *process* of actuali*zing;* whatever is actual$_2$ involves actuali*zedness*, a *state* or *condition* of having-been-actuali*zed*.

That Whitehead makes this distinction, if only implicitly, seems to me to be a result of his having "taken time seriously," i.e., *categoreally*. (Present) concrescences are actual$_1$, whereas (past) concreta ("completed" or "objectified" actual entities) are actual$_2$. The second sense is, in part, a holdover from the objectivist sense of the term (according to which particular *things* are held to be "actual") and is related to the residual objectivist sense of such Whiteheadian terms as 'event' and 'process'.[6]

What justifies Whitehead in using the term 'actual' for both senses is the fact that they have a core of common meaning, which can be expressed by saying that whatever is actual in *either* sense "makes a difference." Partly because Hegel does not take time seriously enough to make ontological distinctions between present and past, he appears to use the term *wirklich* primarily in the sense of 'actual$_1$'. To bring out the fact that *wirklich* means 'active' he sometimes links it to the participial form *wirkend* (cf. PhG 168; Enz. § 142 Zusatz).

III

As John Smith justly notes, for Hegel the *process* of becoming (*[das] Werden*), must issue in a *product ([ein] Gewordenes)*, "something which has become." A *Verwirklichung* must issue in a *Werk*, as, for Aristotle, an *energeia* must issue in an *ergon*. Otherwise, in Smith's words, there would be "sheer [i.e., unstructured and unknowable] becoming."[7]

Hegel's language is generally better suited than is Whitehead's—a consequence, perhaps, of the fusion of the "genius of the German language" with Hegel's own verbal genius—to express the process/product and "-ing/-ed" distinction. As we have just seen, Whitehead uncritically uses the same term 'actual' to characterize both the active process of becoming or concrescence and its passive product or result.

In contrast, Hegel, without calling explicit attention to what he is doing (as, for example, he calls attention to the rich ambiguity of the term *aufheben* [cf. WdL I, 94]), nevertheless makes a consistent distinction between those terms, or forms of terms, which refer to an *act* or *process* and those which refer to the *product* or *result* of an act or process. Key Hegelian terms ending in *-ung*, such as *Bestimmung, Beziehung*, and *Vermittlung*, suffer from the same systematic ambiguity as their English counterparts ending in '-tion/-sion'—in the present case 'determination', 'relation', and 'mediation'.[8] Hegel regularly disambiguates the *-ung* terms by using gerunds and nouns formed from verb infinitives to refer to acts or processes and nouns formed from past participles to refer to states, conditions, or products. The process-words corresponding to (1) *Bestimmung*, (2) *Beziehung*, and (3) *Vermittlung* are: (1) *(das) Bestimmen* (='[the act or process of] determining'), *(das) Bestimmtwerden* (='[the act or process of] becoming determinate'); (2) *(das) Beziehen* (='[the act or process of] relating'); (3) *(das) Vermitteln* (='[the act or process of] mediating').

The state- or product-words are: (1) *(ein) Bestimmtes* (='something which has been rendered determinate') and, more abstractly, *(die) Bestimmtheit* (='the state or condition of having been rendered determinate') and *(das) Bestimmtsein* (='the state or condition of having been determined'); (2) *(ein) Bezogenes* (='something which has been related'); (3) *(ein) Vermitteltes* (='something which has been mediated') and, more abstractly, *(das) Vermitteltsein* (='the state or condition of having been mediated').[9]

The fact that I have been able to provide English counterparts to these German terms, even if some of them are rather cumbersome and all of them are longer and more complex than the German originals, suggests that Whitehead *could* have disambiguated such key terms as 'constitution', 'decision', 'determination', 'objectification', 'prehension', and 'relation'. But in fact he seems to have made very few attempts to do this.[10]

Since Whitehead used the term 'concrete' in two systematic senses, roughly parallel to 'actual$_1$' and 'actual$_2$', I have in discussing Whitehead alone,[11] referred to them as 'concrete$_1$' and 'concrete$_2$'. However, since I wish to compare these senses to Hegel's systematic speculative sense of 'concrete' (=*konkret*), I shall in this paper, despite the unwieldiness of the notation, refer to 'concrete$_{W_1}$' (='experient and actively self-relating') and to 'concrete$_{W_2}$' (='settled and determinate'). Concrescences are concrete$_{W_1}$; concreta are concrete$_{W_2}$. The concrete in the first sense is *quod concrescitur;* that in the second sense is *quod concretum est.*

'Concrete$_H$' means 'many-sided, adequately related, complexly mediated'; this is what Hegel calls "the speculatively concrete," sharply contrasting it to the "empirically or sensuously concrete" (Enz. §§ 164, 505). His characterization of a "concrete entity" (= *ein Konkretes*) includes reference to the "unity of differentiated determinations" (*Einheit verschiedener* [sometimes *unterschiedener*] *Bestimmungen*). Unfortunately, Wallace garbles this badly into "unity of distinct propositions" (Enz. § 82) although in another place he puts "unity of distinct characteristics" (Enz. § 33).[12] Thus Hegel writes that *Dasein*, being "concrete," exhibits "a number of determinations, differentiated relations of its dialectical phases or aspects *[Momente]*" (WdL I, 97). That which is concrete is, in itself, "manifoldly determinate" (WdL I, 59). It is a unity which results from the unifying mediation of differentiated elements or components; it is a universal which contains the particular within itself.

The association of subjectivity with immediacy—cf. Whitehead's much used expression 'subjective immediacy'—is a Whiteheadian theme which is quite foreign to Hegel, for whom immediacy is non-concrete$_H$ (he flatly characterizes it as "abstract"), whereas subjectivity, like the concept, is the paradigm of concreteness$_H$. But perhaps both Hegel and Whitehead might be persuaded to make certain terminological and doctrinal concessions on this point:

(1) Hegel might be willing to admit that the subjectivity of the concrescent occasion is not abstract$_H$ in the sense of one-sided or "thin," since it involves the prehensive unification of differentiated elements—objectified data of categoreally distinct kinds, namely concreta and forms. A coherent combination of the speculative Hegelian sense with the first Whiteheadian sense of 'concrete' becomes plausible—I suggest—if emphasis is shifted away from subjectivity as a simple *state* of immediacy and (ontological) privacy to the subjectivity of the concrescent occasion, seen as a complex *process* of prehensive unification. Then both the concept and the concrescence could be characterized as "concrete$_{HW,}$"—"many-sided, adequately mediated, experient, and actively self-relating."

(2) Whitehead, for his part, might be willing to drop the term 'immediacy', retaining only the terms 'subjectivity' and '(ontological) privacy'. Whiteheadian "immediacy" seems to me to differ in any case from Hegelian *Unmittelbarkeit* in an important respect: the latter, as a deficient mode or manifestation of mediatedness, is something to be dialectically overcome; the former, as the locus of achieved value, is something to be cherished—although Whitehead admits that it can be "preserved" only in the special and limited sense of being made "objectively immortal," which in turn involves objectification and mediation.

One way to put the point at issue is to say that Hegel gives up immediacy willingly, whereas Whitehead gives it up unwillingly. What Whitehead's speculative system *cannot* give up is the non-objectifiability of the concrescent occasion; but this does not have to be identified—as Whitehead himself often identifies it—with "subjective *immediacy*." However, it *does* require ontological *privacy*, which, in contrast to moral or legal "privacy," is not a *need* or *right* to remain unobjectified, hence "unknown" and "unrevealed," but the categoreal *impossibility* of being objectified, hence "known" or "revealed."

The kind of reciprocal terminological and doctrinal concessions which I have suggested would, however, raise a new theoretical problem. The term 'concrete$_H$' names a property which admits of degrees.[13] Hegelian *Konkretheit* is typically a matter of more-or-less—indeed, of the systematic increase, in the course of a dialectical development, of many-sidedness, fulness of relation, and adequacy of mediation.

In contrast, 'concrete$_{W_1}$' names a complex property, one element of which—active self-relation—admits of degrees, although the other element—being experient—does not. A given entity either is experient or it is not; but it may be more or less actively self-relating. The remaining question is whether the all-or-none character of "being experient" overrides or infects the more-or-less character of "being actively self-relating" or rather the reverse. For purposes of comparison with Hegel, in any case, it seems clear that the more-or-less character would come to dominate in concreteness$_{HW_1}$.

Thus, a given concrescence α might be called more concrete$_{HW_1}$ than another concrescence β because it more successfully transformed exclusions into contrasts (to use a Whiteheadian expression) or effected a more complete reconciliation of more sharply opposed dialectical phases or components (to put the point in Hegelian language). Much the same thing could be said of one Hegelian concept as compared to another. This is because the property of active self-relation, a property which admits of degrees, is common to both concreteness$_H$ and concreteness$_{W_1}$.

IV

Both Hegel and Whitehead reconceive the subject-object relation, which for Descartes and Kant had been viewed as essentially cognitive, characterizing it as the "subject-to-object" structure of *experience*. However, as we shall see (Sec. VII below) Whitehead goes further than Hegel in de-emphasizing the *cognitive* dimension of experience. Furthermore, Whitehead's reconception is more radical than Hegel's in another respect: he introduces a categoreal distinction between subjects as *present* and objects as either *past* (concreta) or *timeless* (forms). For Whitehead the future is a realm of pure possibility, whereas the present is the locus of actuality$_1$, as the past is the locus of actuality$_2$. The key point is Whitehead's insistence on the asymmetry of past and future; such asymmetry stands in marked contrast to Hegel's general insistence on reciprocity and mutuality.[14] In particular, as John Burbidge has convincingly argued, for Hegel the past is non-present in the same way that the future is—as a form of "non-being."[15] In contrast, for Whitehead the past, as non-present, is characterized by actuality$_2$, whereas the future as non-present is characterized by nonactuality. In other terms: the past is characterized by "real" potentiality, the future by "pure" possibility, and of course the present by "actuality$_1$." In any case, there is a strong ontological—even categoreal—*asymmetry* between past and future.

Despite this difference, there is a significant similarity in the way that Hegel and Whitehead conceptualize potentiality and actuality. Objects, for both, are potential; subjects are actual (for Whitehead, of course, this means 'actual$_1$'). What is potential for Hegel is merely *an sich*, whereas what is actual (both *wirklich* and *wirkend*), is *an und für sich*. For Whitehead object-forms and object-concreta are potentials ("pure" and "real," respectively) for actualization by subject-concrescences, which, as we know, are actual$_1$. To put Whitehead's position in Hegelian terms: the object, whether (timeless) form or (past) concretum, is only an in-itself *(an sich)*, whereas the (present) concrescent subject is an in-and-for-itself *(an und für sich)*.

For both Hegel and Whitehead the relata of the objectifying relation are, respectively, subjective and objective, actual and potential. The subject is the *active* relatum, the object being *passive*. And the relation, for Whitehead, is constitutive with respect to the subject, although nonconstitutive with respect to the object (whether form or concretum). But this relational asymmetry, this non-reciprocity of constitutiveness ("internality") appears not to be shared by Hegel, with his pervasive stress on mutuality and reciprocity of relations.

Before proceeding to raise (in Sec. VI) the question of Whitehead's ontological atomism (a position which Hegel does not share) and (in Sec. VII) the question of the sense in which both concept and concrescence can be interpreted as "dialectical" processes, I wish to look briefly at an early comparative study of dialectical categories in Hegel and Whitehead.

V

Gregory Vlastos, in a pioneering study of the ontologies of Hegel and Whitehead, characterizes both of them as "dialectical" thinkers, but sees a basic difference between what he calls the "homogeneous" dialectic of Hegel and the "heterogeneous" dialectic of Whitehead. Vlastos means by this that for Hegel all the categories of existence are categories of *Geist*. Every dialectical phase or aspect of the whole is "of the nature of Idea."[16] In contrast, Whitehead's categories of existence are diverse and irreducible: forms and concrescences are ontologically heterogeneous. "Where such heterogeneity occurs," Vlastos maintains, "the second term of the triad cannot be generated from the first term by negation, nor the third from the second. First and second have independent origins."[17]

If Vlastos considers forms to be the "first" terms in the dialectical series and concrescences to be the "second" terms—and he isn't very explicit about this point—we might agree about their "independent origins," if by this he means that forms are timeless and uncreated whereas concrescences are dated, present, and (partially) self-creating. But this strikes me as a difference of ontological *status* between entities which *have*, and those which *lack*, "origins" rather than a difference of *origins*.

Vlastos adds that Whitehead's heterogeneous dialectic

prevents him from pyramiding actual entities to form individuals of higher orders [as Hegel allegedly does]. Two (or more) actual entities could not join to form a higher type of actual entity. The transition from actual entity [i.e., concretum] to actual₁ entity [i.e., concrescence] is a linear transition in time.[18]

Unfortunately, Vlastos makes no clear or systematic distinction between present and past actual entities, in other words, between concrescences and concreta. If he had, he might have seen that concreta are as diverse from, and irreducible to, both forms and concrescences as forms and concrescences are diverse from, and irreducible to, each other—even though concreta, unlike forms, are the *products* of concrescent *processes*. And he might have been willing to add a third kind of entity—the concretum—to the two which he distinguishes in the "heterogeneous" Whiteheadian dialectic, making it no less "triadic" than the "homogeneous" Hegelian dialectic.

But the *rapprochement* between Hegel and Whitehead would be carried a long step further by a recognition—nowhere evident in Vlastos' account—of the importance of certain categoreal distinctions in Hegel's ontology: in particular, the contrasts between subjectivity and objectivity and between internality and externality.[19] These contrasts seem to me to be sharp enough to justify the application of the term 'heterogeneous' to Hegel's dialectic as well.

VI

Walter Jung has referred to Whitehead's speculative system in a suggestive phrase as an *Atomistik der Ereignisse*. Klaus Hartmann, if I understand him correctly, regards Whitehead's ontological atomism as a speculative limitation or weakness.[20] I regard it rather as a strength, for the following reasons:

(1) Whitehead's is a thoroughly *relational* kind of atomism. His concrescent occasions are not windowless Leibnizian monads[21] or self-enclosed neo-Platonic "souls." They are unit-processes which actively prehend ("grasp") both past and timeless objects. Their activities of prehensive unification are constitutive of them as concrescent subjects.

(2) A non-substantialist ontology of process must be atomistic. Alternative, non-atomistic ontologies seem to me to be "process philosophies" only in a broader and looser sense. Such alternatives are of two kinds:

(a) An Aristotelian substantialism, which—in opposition, say, to Parmenides or Zeno—does indeed emphasize change and development, as well as activity and actualization. But the change, development, activity, and actualization are all the doing or undergoing of individual enduring substances *(ousiai)*. I shall call this the "*ousia* version" of process philosophy.

(b) A Hegelian substantialism[22], which adds to the Aristotelian stress on change, development, activity, and actualization a further stress on relatedness or relationality, in particular, the active self-relating of subjects or concepts. The celebrated Hegelian move from "substance" to "subject" is, I suggest, incomplete; it is a move from a *Spinozistic* substantialism—as Hegel quite unfairly understood Spinoza, namely as conceiving substance to be fixed, eternal, lifeless, static, unrelated (or inadequately related) to its modes—to a relational *Aristotelian* substantialism, where the *ousia* is conceived as filled with life, development, and activity. I shall call this the "relational *werdende ousia*" version of process philosophy.

Whitehead rejects every kind of substantialism, and for good reasons. If Hegel insists that the "relational *werdende ousia*" can be conceived as a subject rather than a substance, Whitehead would respond—rightly, in my view—that it is still a *substantial* subject, self, or soul, i.e., a subject, self, or soul which persists through time, however active and changing it may be. This stands in sharp contrast to Whitehead's own atomistic theory of subjectivity and selfhood. What is problematic in Whitehead's position, it seems to me, is not his ontological atomism, but the precise relationship between the evanescent individual units of living process (concrescent occasions) and the relatively stable selves, persons, and things of the macro-world. This is a portion of his speculative system which Whitehead himself left relatively undeveloped.

Partly for this reason, partly—I suspect—because of a lingering commitment to substantialism, certain Whitehead scholars have applied what I am calling the "relational *werdende ousia* interpretation" of process philosophy to Whitehead's own position. I admit that this interpretation facilitates the comparison with Hegel. But I find it unacceptable, for reasons which I have set out in defending my interpretation of concrescence and concretum as distinct *entities* rather than (as the "relational *werdende ousia*" interpretation would have it) distinct *phases* or *aspects* of a single enduring entity: the actual entity as *ousia*.[23]

Despite his occasional characterization of the "free subjective concept" as "impenetrable atomic subjectivity" (WdL II, 484), Hegel rejects ontological atomism. What he refers to as "the Whole" (*das Ganze*) is, in the words of a perceptive commentator, a "continuum-process," a "self-differentiating continuum" of dialectical phases or components.[24] Whitehead, in his assertion of both asymmetrical relatedness (especially that of present subjects to past or timeless objects) and ontological atomism (the "epochal" theory of becoming) departs from Hegel on key points.

Errol Harris has written that for Hegel "each succeeding stage of spirit is subject for which the preceding stage is object."[25] I think that this well captures Hegel's position, but it also shows that Spirit (like the concept) is still an *ousia*, even if both *werdende* and relational.

Consider Hegel's doctrine of active self-relation and his repeated claim that the subject grasps itself, as other, as its object. Slightly formalized, this could be expressed as follows:

Concept C, as subject, takes as "its" other concept C, now as object. C is thus, clearly, an *ousia* which endures through a stretch of time, or else this entire dialectical process is non-temporal.

In contrast, for Whitehead to say that a concrescent occasion is engaged in active self-relation, means something like the following: Concrescence β as (present) subject is actively related to concretum a as (past) object; and a in turn is the product of the (partially) self-creative process of an antecedent (then present) subject α.

Although the object-concretum is an "other" to the concrescence-subject in a general or categoreal sense—concrescences are experient, non-dative, non-repeatable, non-objectifiable, processive, and active in the present, whereas concreta are post-experient, dative, repeatable, objectifiable, product-like, passive, and fixed in the past[26]—one must distinguish between two quite different relationships of "otherness" in the case of particular concrescences and particular concreta. (1) In the example above a is the "other" of β in the sense of being the *object* of β's active prehending relation. (2) But in the same example, a is the "other" of α in the stronger sense of being the *product* of the creative process of α's act of becoming.

This is the kind of asymmetry which Hegel's insistence on mutuality and reciprocity of relations, including active self-relations, precludes. For Hegel the objectification of the concept is ultimately "self-objectification" and a central mode of the concept's activity as subject is its *Sich-Gegenstandsein* (='being an object to itself').[27] In the end Hegel espouses a "subject-object identity" (which is, of course, in Hegel's inimitable phrase, an "identity of identity and non-identity"); for Whitehead the subject-object relation is irreducibly asymmetrical, being *constitutive* for the (present) subject but *non-constitutive* for the (past or timeless) object.

VII

Hegel uses the key term *Begriff* in two senses, roughly parallel to the two senses of 'concrete' noted above (pp. 137f). The ordinary sense of *Begriff*, like the ordinary "empirical-sensuous") sense of *konkret*, is rarely mentioned, and then principally to distinguish it clearly from the central speculative sense, the sense which concerns us here.

Thus Hegel remarks that "what are usually called *Begriffe*," namely, such abstract or general *Bestimmungen* or *Vorstellungen* as 'tree' and 'house', are not concepts at all in the speculative sense (Enz. §§ 162, 164). This "ordinary" non-speculative sense of 'concept' I shall call 'epistemic' or 'methodological' to distinguish it from the speculative sense, which I shall call 'ontological'.

These two contrasting senses of the term *Begriff* are revealed perhaps most clearly in the case of compound terms that *end* with *-begriff* in contrast to those which *begin* with *Begriff-*. Those in the first, "epistemic" group include *Freiheitsbegriff*, *Subjektivitätsbegriff*— to be sharply distinguished from the expression *Begriff als Subjektivität*, in which *Begriff* is being used in the contrasted *ontological* sense—*Systembegriff*, *Vernunftbegriff*, *Wesensbegriff*, and *Wissenschaftsbegriff*. Those in the second, "ontological" group include *Begriffsbestimmung*, *Begriffsbestimmtheit*, *Begriffslehre*, *Begriffslogik*, *Begriffsmoment*, *Begriffsverhältnis*, *Begriffsunterschied*, and *Begriffsurteil*. Note that the expression *Begriff des Begriffes* (WdL II, 219, 220; cf. 432) is quite different from the formally parallel expression *Negation der Negation*. In the first occurrence *Begriff* has the "epistemic" or "methodological" sense; in the second it has the "ontological" sense. But *both* occurrences of *Negation* have the same (ontological/logical) sense.

What, then, is the *Begriff* as an ontological category? If one takes Hegel at his word when he equates concept and subject or self *(das Ich)*, then it is an agent, engaged in active and unifying self-relation. Many texts support this reading, which is the one I here favor. The alternative reading, favored by George Lucas, makes the *Begriff* not an agent but a non-active "principle or pattern of organization for organic [i.e., 'organizing', 'unifying'] activity."[28] He goes on to compare it to the "subjective aim" of the Whiteheadian concrescent occasion. I find this unconvincing on two levels: (1) a subjective aim, like the Hegelian *Zweck*, is an integral aspect or component of the activity of a subject, whereas a principle or pattern is more like a ("conceptually") prehended form or cluster of forms. (2) As already suggested, Hegel regularly characterizes the *Begriff* as a subject, as pure self-consciousness, as a self; as active, creative, self-determining, etc. The speculative concept is an *agent*, which no abstract principle or pattern can be.

I suspect that one of Wallace's many mistranslations may have misled certain readers (perhaps including Lucas) on this point. In a key passage (Enz. § 160), quoted by Lucas at p. 87 in Wallace's version (with 'Notion' changed to 'Concept'), Hegel calls the *Begriff das Freie*, i.e., "that which is free" or "something free." But Wallace twists this into "the *principle* of freedom," although his word 'principle' has absolutely no counterpart in Hegel's text. Hegel goes on to characterize the *Begriff* as *das an und für sich Bestimmte* (="that [or 'something'] which is determinate in and for itself"). Wallace reduces this to "has original and complete determinateness," thus wholly losing the sense of *für sich*, an expression which for Hegel is clear evidence that he is here treating the concept as a self or subject, since it is only selves or subjects which can be *für sich*, although presumably even principles or patterns could enjoy "original and complete determinateness."

Concepts in the ontological sense resemble neither Platonic forms (fixed, eternal, and "in the world") nor Lockean simple ideas (passive, perishing, and "in the mind"). The Hegelian *Begriff* is closer in its intellectual lineage to the Aristotelian *psuchē*—a self-active, self-moving *energeia* or entelechy.[29] Like the Whiteheadian concrescence, it is active, "prehensive" *(begreifend)*, unifying. Its development, like the process of becoming of the concrescent occasion is "dialectical": as the *Begriff* constitutes itself through its (partly negative) relation to its other, so the concrescence constitutes itself through its (partly negative) relation to its other (in one of the two senses distinguished above [p. 144]), namely, its concretum (in the weaker sense of 'its'[30]).

What Hegel calls *Begriffsbestimmungen* (='determinations of the concept') are the functional counterparts of Whiteheadian prehensions; the "negativity" of such *Bestimmungen* is, in part, analogous to that of Whitehead's "negative prehensions." Objectification, for both thinkers, is a unifying process which involves exclusion as well as inclusion.

Hegel asserts that, at a given stage of the dialectical process, the concept is "something subjective—free, self-sufficient *(selbständig*: note the substantialist language), self-determining *(sich in sich bestimmende)*, or rather it is the *subject* itself" (WdL I, 47). Further, the objectivity which is the dialectical "other" of the concept-subject "offers resistance" (Enz. § 195) to the latter's self-activity. In a parallel way, for Whitehead the concreta provide what I have called "unrefusable data",[31] which concrescences in their self-activity cannot fail to take into account. (This is the "causal pressure" of the past.) However, for Hegel stubborn objectivity is ultimately *aufgehoben* and externality is wholly internalized. This would appear to be an irreducible difference from Whitehead.

Three other irreducible differences between Hegel's theory of the concept and Whitehead's theory of the concrescent occasion remain to be mentioned. The first two have been discussed above: (1) that Hegel fails, or refuses, to make the categoreal distinction between subjects as *present* and objects as *past* (or *timeless*) which is integral to Whitehead's position; (2) that unlike Whitehead, Hegel conceives the concept's objectifying activity as a *self*-objectifying activity, asserting that the concept functions as an object for *itself*. Errol Harris formulates this point concisely: the concept's "process of mediation culminates in its own cancellation, and the resolution of the oppositions it contains issues in its own union with its other, which is no other than itself."[32]

(3) The final difference is that for Hegel the unifying, organizing activity of the concept is, in the end, cognitive and self-conscious, whereas for Whitehead the prehensive relation is a more general "taking account of," of which cognition and consciousness are quite special cases. As Düsing puts it: the "absolute identity" of the speculative concept is the "self-relatedness of a subjectivity which thinks itself."[33] And again: through subject-object unity "subjectivity not only knows itself in the object, but in this knowledge is also certain of the producing *(Hervorbringung)* of this object."[34] Other recent commentators add that the concept is not only "a concrete system" but also "a conscious experience . . . , an activity of [cognitive] self-differentiation [or self-specification]"[35]; and that it is a "reflexive or self-conscious grasp by subjectivity of itself as subject-object."[36] I have no quarrel with these interpretations; they make vividly explicit the "intellectualist" or "theoretical" bias of Hegel's theory of the concept as compared to Whitehead's theory of the concrescence.

VIII

In general terms, what for Hegel is the concept's reconciling mediation of contradictory opposites,[37] is for Whitehead the concrescent occasion's reconciling conversion of exclusions into contrasts. John Smith has said that for Hegel philosophy has an "absolute reconciling power."[38] This, I suggest, is precisely the power of the concept.

Although both Hegel and Whitehead place great emphasis on the "power of negativity," the last word in both of their speculative systems is 'harmony' and 'reconciliation'.

Notes

1. The traditional rendering of *Entstehen/genesis* as 'coming-to-be' misleadingly suggests that the present unit-process *becomes* a past unit of being ("concretum": see Sec VI.), thus supporting the *"werdende ousia"* version of process philosophy which I reject in favor of Whitehead's "relational atomistic" version.

2. But note that it was Hegel who first made clear the speculative importance of the late Platonic dialogues, especially the *Parmenides* and the *Sophist*, for the questions of identity, difference, otherness, and non-being. And it was precisely these dialogues which were of central importance for Whitehead.

3. Hegel has the broad sense of 'organism' in mind when he speaks of the state as *ein Organismus* (PhR §§ 267, 269), as he makes clear in his more careful discussion in the *Encyclopedia*, where he calls the state "ein organisiertes, in die besondern Wirksamkeiten unterschiedenes Ganzes" (§ 539), roughly, "an organized whole [which is] differentiated into its particular functioning elements." Whitehead's characterization of a factory as an "organism" is at SMW 287. "Organisms" in the loose sense of 'organized wholes' are *not* characterized by subjectivity, freedom, or (partial) self-creation, although "organisms" in the narrower, ontological sense which applies to "life as ontological category" *(das logische Leben)* and "units of living process," i.e., to concepts and concrescences, clearly *are*.

4. "Hegel and Whitehead: Why Develop a Universal Theory?" this volume, p. 135.

5. See my essay, "Form, Concrescence, and Concretum" in Lewis S. Ford and George L. Kline, eds., *Explorations in Whitehead's Philosophy* (New York: Fordham University Press, 1983), esp. pp. 104–106.

6. Whitehead gives a moderately subjectivist sense to 'actuality$_1$', characterizing it as "self-realizing" (PR 340) and a radically subjectivist sense to 'process', characterizing it as the "rush of feelings" (PR 235).

7. "Religious Experience in Hegel and Whitehead," this volume, p. 304.

8. Even '-ing' words in English may be equivocal as between process and product. Whitehead's punning aphorism: "There is a becoming of continuity, but no continuity of becoming" (PR 53) means: "There is a having-become [=*Gewordensein*] of the (past) extensive continuum of concreta, but there is no continuity of the (present) process of becoming [=*Werden*] of concrescences." In all puns there is a shift of meaning of key terms; here

the shift in the meaning of 'becoming' may be regarded as syntactical rather than semantic.

9. For further examples and detailed references to Hegel's texts, see my essay, "The Systematic Ambiguity of Some Key Whiteheadian Terms," forthcoming in Ernest Wolf-Gazo, ed., *Prozessphilosophie: Eine Einführung.* (Munich: Karl Alber, 1986).

10. An exception: Whitehead says that "a 'prehension' will be analyzed into 'prehending subject' [and] 'object prehended' . . ." (PR 215; cf. also PR 399, 410).

11. E.g., in my "Form, Concrescence, and Concretum," pp. 107–109.

12. 'Proposition' and 'characteristic' are only two of the more than *forty* different renderings of *Bestimmung* offered by Wallace in what is to date the only published translation of the *Encyclopedia* Logic. These range alphabetically from 'attribute' and 'category' through 'formula' and 'function' to 'statement' and 'term'. The consistent and systematic use which *Hegel* makes of the term is thus buried beneath the promiscuous luxuriance of *Wallace's* terminology.

13. Errol Harris nicely brings out the Aristotelian, "developmental" flavor of this term in Hegel when he notes that the relation between the abstract and the concrete$_H$ is "that between the germinal and the mature" (*An Interpretation of the Logic of Hegel* [Lanham, MD: University Press of America, 1983], p. 105).

14. Hegel's stress on mutuality and reciprocity is of great importance and value in the areas of moral, social, and political phenomena (the "macro-level")—and Whitehead shares it—but it becomes problematic from a Whiteheadian perspective, in the area of *ontology* (the "micro-level"). George R. Lucas, Jr., in a spirited discussion of this point, appears both to admit, and to attempt to gloss over, the difference between Hegel and Whitehead. Lucas claims that Whitehead's account of the subject-object relation is a "doctrine of asymmetrical mutual relatedness' " (*Two Views of Freedom in Process Thought: A study of Hegel and Whitehead* [Missoula, Montana: Scholars Press, 1979], p. 33). But I don't see how he can have it both ways: if the relation is "mutual" it is not "asymmetrical"; if it is "asymmetrical" it is not "mutual."

15. For Hegel, Burbidge notes, "The being of the present came from the non-being of the future and goes to the non-being of the past" ("Concept and Time in Hegel," *Dialogue*, vol. 12 [1973], p. 409).

16. "Organic Categories in Hegel and Whitehead" [1937] in George L. Kline, ed., *Alfred North Whitehead: Essays on his Philosophy* (Englewood Cliffs, NJ: Prentice-Hall, 1963), p. 159. Vlastos here ascribes a dialectic of "thesis, antithesis, and synthesis" to Hegel. In fact, as is more widely recognized today than it was in 1937, Hegel *never* uses these terms to characterize his own position. It was Marx who forged this myth (in the opening pages of *La Misère de la philosophie* [1847]), although many non-Marxists have been taken in by it. In any case, this terminological blunder does not undermine Vlastos' main theoretical point.

17. Vlastos, *op. cit.*, p. 159.

18. *Ibid.*, p. 164.

19. Vlastos stresses the fact that for Hegel the "development of individuality is the process by which otherness is internalized and overcome" *(loc. cit.)*. Unfortunately, Vlastos confuses externality with the broader conception of otherness as well as the narrower conception of environment (cf. *ibid.*, p. 163).

20. "Types of Explanation in Hegel and Whitehead," this volume, pp. 61–85.

21. Hence Hartmann's claim that "a diagnosis to fit Whitehead could be adapted from Hegel's treatment of Leibniz" *(ibid.*, p. 71) strikes me as wide of the mark.

22. Klaus Düsing, in an important study, points out that Hegel's theory of subjectivity "beruht auf substanzmetaphysischen Voraussetzungen" (*Das Problem der Subjektivität in Hegels Logik* [Bonn: Bouvier, 1976], p. 243).

23. See my "Form, Concrescence, and Concretum," esp. pp. 135–38.

24. Stanley Rosen, *G. W. F. Hegel: Introduction to the Science of Wisdom* (New Haven: Yale University Press, 1974), pp. 104, 121.

25. Errol E. Harris, "The Contemporary Significance of Hegel and Whitehead," this volume, p. 25.

26. See "Form, Concrescence, and Concretum," esp. pp. 115–122 and 135–36.

27. The terms *Selbstvergegenständlichung* and *Sich-Gegenstandsein* are Düsing's but they accurately convey Hegel's position. Cf. Düsing, *op. cit.*, pp. 271, 326; 250, 271.

28. Lucas, *op. cit.*, p. 135.

29. It is, I think, significant that in the chapter of the *Logic* entitled "Das Leben" (WdL II, 413–29) Hegel uses the term *Begriff* much more frequently than the term *Leben* or *das Lebendige*. The concept, as I have argued elsewhere, is an instance of "life as ontological category," characterized by subjectivity, inwardness, freedom, purpose, and (partial) self-creativity— properties which equally characterize the Whiteheadian concrescence (cf. "Life as Ontological Category: A Whiteheadian Note on Hegel" in Warren E. Steinkraus and Kenneth L. Schmitz, eds., *Art and Logic in Hegel's Philosophy* [Atlantics Highlands, NJ: Humanities Press, 1980], pp. 158–62).

30. See my "Form, Concrescence, and Concretum," p. 143 n.25.

31. *Ibid.*, pp. 105, 127.

32. *An Interpretation of the Logic of Hegel*, p. 248.

33. Düsing, *op. cit.*, p. 235.

34. *Ibid.*, p. 304.

35. Harris, *An Interpretation of the Logic of Hegel*, p. 227.

36. Rosen, *op. cit.*, p. 235.

37. Cf. Errol Harris: "The concrete universal, as particularizing itself, 'has the particulars in itself', and so reconciles the opposites" (*An Interpretation of the Logic of Hegel*, p. 42).

38. "Religious Experience in Hegel and Whitehead," this volume, p. 288.

III

Nature and Mind

J. N. Findlay
BOSTON UNIVERSITY

Hegel and Whitehead on Nature

There are numerous analogies between Hegel and Whitehead, both in their grounding of nature in a metaphysical principle that transcends nature and has many connections with the God of religion, and in their perception in occurrences within the organic and the inorganic world of many analogies with human subjective and intersubjective experience. It is remarkable that Whitehead, who was so well acquainted with Plato's *Timaeus*, as well as with the whole of modern philosophy from Locke to Kant, should have been almost wholly ignorant of Hegel, between whose ideas and his own there are so many resemblances. The philosophical atmosphere of Cambridge, England, and Cambridge, Massachusetts, did not however at that time encourage an *approfondissement* in the writings of Hegel.

The invitation to prepare this paper compelled me to reread Whitehead's *Process and Reality*, a work which, when I first read it fifty years ago, seemed as hard to understand in many places as the Athanasian Creed. Most philosophers in England felt the same, and the immense success of Whitehead in hard-headed Harvard, and his monumental position there as a sage, seemed a wholly incredible state of things. His earlier lectures on the *Concept of Nature* and the *Principles of Natural Knowledge* had been much admired, but *Process and Reality* passed all understanding. At present its panpsychism and panpsychologism strike me as perfectly intelligible and quite arguable: they are the basic insights of Leibniz accommodated to the bizarre novelties of modern physics.

I shall in this paper say more about Hegel than about Whitehead because comparatively few people have any deep understanding of Hegel's *Naturphilosophie*, a work obviously antiquated in its scientific detail, but which I consider deeply right in its interpretative principles. Hegel to an extraordinary degree knew all the physics, chemistry, geology, biology, physiology, and psychiatry of his own time, which is in fact not so far from what we now regard as established as is thought to be the case. I remember in particular a long Zusatz in which Hegel deals with strokes of lightning in North Germany, and another in which he deals with types of fossils in all sorts of strata, and yet another in which he enumerates all the strange components found in human feces—all of which might, I feel, have been written today. Hegel's physics may be speculative in questions of philosophical import, but it is severely factual in questions that are empirical. Few modern philosophers are so well informed as regards the detail of contemporary science. Living before Einstein's relativistic innovations, Hegel's views accord well with their spirit. Living likewise before Darwin's evolutionary teaching, Hegel's views on the ladder of organic forms seem to tremble on the verge of becoming evolutionary.

Hegel's Philosophy of Nature is the middle phase in the dialectical development of his Absolute Idea, a unique kind of philosophical Absolute, which is identified by Hegel with the God of Christianity, but which is quite as far from ordinary notions of that God as the God of Thomas Aquinas is likewise far from the God of Abraham, Jacob and Moses. Hegel has, as the supreme principle of his system, a Concept or Begriff which is simply Universality as such, rather than any specific universal, but which is also held to be such that it has *Besonderheit* or Specificity as one of its essential moments, so that it becomes inseparable from a whole system or hierarchy of specific universals, each of which distinguishes itself from every other, and sometimes even opposes the latter, and which also has the further essential moment of *Einzelnheit* or Singularity, of expressing itself in particular instances, without whose reality or real possibility it would not be a genuine universal at all.

Universality as being the active cause of everything that exists or happens in the world is of course a principle asserted in crucial passages in Plato's *Republic* and his *Phaedo*. Hegel, however, adds to Platonism not only the view that it is of the essence of universals both to have many specific forms and indefinitely many instances, but that it is also of their essence to return to themselves in the form of thinking awareness, states of mind in which universals are envisaged and enjoyed, and envisaged and enjoyed both in their exemplification in instances but also in the very visions and enjoyments that the mind has of them, and in which it also sees and enjoys its own cognitive, spiritual universality.

Hegel's philosophy is accordingly a tripartite Platonism, which starts with a "realm of pure categories" which anticipate the specificities that will afterwards be actualized in the objective world and in the subjective experiences of that world. This realm is the realm of Logic, of pure essentialities as they might be present to a God before the creation of Nature and finite Spirit. From this realm Hegel turns to a consideration of the same categories as embodied in largely unconscious material instances: i.e., the celebrated Philosophy of Nature. From here, Hegel must pass on to the consideration of the same categories, both in their logical and their natural form, as related in the cognitive and volitional activities of minds or spirits in their interactions both with natural objects and with one another, as well as with the societies of interacting spiritual persons that they form. At the end of Hegel's Logic we have therefore the celebrated *Entausserung* or self-externalization of the Asolute Idea.

The Absolute Idea is the Idea of an exhaustively specific Universality which also has indefinitely many actual and contingent instantiations and, being what it is, must accordingly be actively dynamic and not abstract, have all the wealth of concrete instantiation that fulfils it, and represent its notional inwardness completely brought to outwardness and actuality. Logic or the realm of pure forms or categories must accordingly entail a working out in the realm of natural instantiation and of subjective, spiritual instantiation. In other words, Logic, as the philosophy of pure categories, demands supplementation by the philosophies of Nature and Spirit. The transition is not temporal, and it is as much a presupposition as a consequence.

It is here, however, that I must indicate an important feature of Hegelian Platonism: its persistent stress on negation and opposition, its deep persuasion that every universality only can be the universality that it is in standing out as exclusive of, and opposed to other forms of universality. Remove all otherness, exclusion, opposition from experience or thought or being, and it collapses into the completely empty and meaningless, concerning which nothing can be said. This necessity of exclusion and opposition obtains at the humble level of sensuous qualities (a specific color being nothing in the absence of contrasting colors) but it obtains also at the level of the higher categories: each being nothing at all unless associated with other categories which contrast with it, and which serve as its necessary material or its fulfilling complement.

Thus Universality itself is nothing without Specificity and Singularity, and vice versa; the inwardly possible is nothing without the outwardly realized and vice versa; the cogitatively abstracted is nothing without the sensuously illustrated and vice versa; the inwardly felt is nothing without the outwardly executed and vice versa; the precisely bounded is nothing without the open and unbounded and vice versa; and so on in countless other cases. The need of something antithetical to complete the significant content, as well as the value and interest, of everything in thought and being, is built into the Hegelian form of Platonism. It was, however, also built into the unwritten Platonism of the Academy which made all the Eide represent the cooperation of two fundamental Archai or principles, one of Definiteness or Limit and the other of the Indefinite or Unlimited, out of whose interpenetration and interaction arose all the Numbers of Arithmetic, all the Lines, Figures and Solids of geometry, all the patterns imparted of originative Motion, and all the species of self-moving organisms and their souls, and of the societies in which such souls cooperated with one another.

Platonism, like Hegelianism, believes in a mutual interpenetration of opposites which are so essentially interdependent that each may be said, after a fashion, to involve its opposite in itself. What lesson is imparted by Plato's *Parmenides* but that Unity, if considered solely in and by itself, has a perhaps impressive transcendence of all characterization, but that if we once allow ourselves to characterize it, we forthwith have the whole realm of numbers and geometrical patterns and dynamic developments on our hands. Hegel learned his dialectic from the Platonic *Parmenides*, and it is not therefore remarkable to find such a dialectic resuscitated by him. That Motion is in some sense to be found even at the timeless level of the Eide is also the lesson of Plato's *Sophist*, and is likewise the teaching of Hegel. There is nothing absurd and illogical in the manner in which both Plato and Hegel seem to tolerate inner contradiction in what is ideally self-consistent. The fact that such opposites live in peace with one another is a sign that they are not mutually contradictory in a mutually destructive, nugatory sense but that they complement each other in a unity which would be destroyed if either were rent apart from its other.

It is in this logical sense that we must understand the self-externalization of the Absolute Idea in Nature, which occurs at the end of the *Logic*. The Absolute must carry the sense of the eternal vision of its unifying subjectivity into what is utterly opposed to itself, a reality which consists throughout of parts external to other parts, and it stands to reason that a kind of unity that has to see itself in what is thus alien to itself, must indeed be confronted by what is thus alien, if it is to have anything to do or to be. The self-externalization of the Idea is not therefore an inexplicable μετάβασισ ε'ισ 'αλλογένοσ, but a timeless logical requirement that there should be a confronting Other to the Idea in which it can come to see, as in a mirror, the reflection of itself and of its own activity.

The Other which confronts the Absolute Idea must accordingly have the immediacy, the hereness and nowness of the instance, not the everywhereness and everywheness of an ideal category. There must therefore be instances which can be seen *as* instances of universals, if the Absolute Idea, the seeing of its universality in such instances, is to be possible at all. And since the Idea is essentially the Idea of infinitely close, self-conscious unity, it must oppose itself to objective immediacies which have nothing of this close unity, but which are sharply other than and external to one another. And this mutual externality must take the two basic forms of mutual outsideness in space and of before-and-afterness in time.

The two great media of instantial being are therefore dialectically deducible from the Absolute Idea which requires their opposing presence. And Hegel maintains against Kant, and in harmony with what will later be maintained by Whitehead, that there are not merely forms of conscious subjectivity, imposed on a reality which is in itself neither temporal nor spatial, but that they are the essential forms of an objectivity which the Absolute Idea requires as the otherness to which its profoundly unified subjectivity will be antithetically possible. The emergence of Nature is not, therefore, a creative act in time but a timeless positing of what is antithetical to self-conscious subjectivity and that can also be made to mirror the demands of self-consciousness.

Nature being thus essentially antithetical to the unifying universality of consciousness must further reveal infinite regresses in every direction, as the Kantian antinomies make clear, and must likewise reveal itself in contingencies of collocation and mutual interference which we find everywhere in nature, and which neither the philosopher nor the scientist should seek wholly to eliminate. Hegelian Platonism does what antique Platonism never did: it establishes the necessity of the contingencies which will not always aid the instantiation of the Eide. It is only if there are unintelligent necessities that intelligent insight can have something to transform and use. Hegelianism further anticipates Einstein in holding Space and Time to be mutually complementary, and to require as media the presence of material occupants and the mutualities of motion and gravitation.

It is rather touching that Hegel should at this point have further held that the moving material contents of space and time should, despite their mutual externality, have a basic tendency both to repel each other, and also to move towards centers common to one another, and so to generate those systems in which we have a central sun, with planets moving around it and acting as subordinate centers to satellites, while satellites and comets remain the loose individual bodies hanging on the fringes of the whole system. Hegel here permitted himself to prefer Kepler to Newton, and to hold that the heavenly bodies do not experience *two* independent forces of gravitation and inertia, not two independent centripetal and centrifugal tendencies, but that they obeyed a single attractive, repulsive and center-seeking tendency which has organized the whole cosmos in the manner which we, like the Greeks, find so very attractive. Hegel may be quite wrong in the details of his concept of universal gravitation, but his synthesis of gravitation and inertia certainly has a faintly Einsteinian ring. Very modern is also what he says about light, that it is merely a transmissive, communicative function which links everything in the cosmos together, being an assertion of matter's profound identity despite spatial separation, and putting no hard individuality of its own into space, and being quite indivisible into rays, beams, pencils, waves, or corpuscles such as Englishmen like Newton like to believe in.

It will be kind to pass over without detailed comment Hegel's detailed treatment of the peculiarities of many physical substances: his analysis of elasticity, of sound as a periodic shedding by matter of its inherent self-externality, of the geometric regularities of crystals which perform in space antics such as magnets perform in time, or his defense of the color-theory of Goethe as infinitely superior to the theories of Newton. His treatments of chemical processes are likewise interesting, arguing as before that they make apparent the non-independence of spatially sundered bodies. Hegel also defends the Greek view that the true material elements are Earth, Air, Fire, and Water, and that Oxygen, Nitrogen, and so forth are merely artifacts of the laboratory which exist only for short periods. This view is amusingly wrong, but it anticipates the discovery of short-lived varieties of matter.

Hegel further asserts that Nature essentially reveals itself in a ladder of forms from the most self-external to the most organically unified, since the ladder is that of the logical dialectic. But he repudiates the notion that this dialectical ladder must be turned into a historical temporal ladder. We must think neither in terms of emanation nor of evolution. Emanation was the Alexandrian view which saw in Nature a continuous process of degradation. Evolution is the more modern view which, basing itself on a misinterpretation of the geological record, thinks that the higher, more unified forms evolved in time out of the lower, less organized and differentiated ones. Hegel holds that all stages of the ladder of forms coexist in time: their order is logical, not temporal. This position was modified when Hegel, compelled by the facts of the geological record, was forced to admit that life at least, in its higher vegetable and animal forms, emerged out of mere chemistry at a definite point in cosmic history. But even then he preferred to think of all species emerging together much as Pallas emerged fully armed from Zeus's forehead. The Mosaic creation in a week is also preferred to any long drawn out evolutionary story. But plainly an evolutionary theory of natural being would have accorded well with the premises and methods of Hegel.

Hegel declared Life to be the "truth" of the chemical and electrical processes, in both of which matter tries to negate its spatio-temporal self-externality. In Life self-differentiating unity triumps over spatio-temporal diremption, and we have in it the truly infinite process in which the natural individual breaks into many parts and functions, yet always returns to self in and through such divisions, the parts and functions all being means and ends to one another. Individuality thus self-differentiating and self-returning is in a rudimentary sense subjective: the conscious self will be more truly subjective. Life further postulates a universal, imperfectly animated background: the earth is a geological organism with a diffused, spontanteously generated vitality in land, sea, and air, and manifest in such phenomena as honey-dew in the air, and phosphorescence in the sea. The earth is also presupposed by life as having a long pre-vital history, but Hegel does not believe that many of the fossils found in early geological strata ever really lived, they are products of an organic-plastic impulse in inorganic matter which anticipated the lightning stroke of life.

The Hegelian dialectic is here as absurd as are certain modern biblical fundamentalists. Hegel, however, gives a widely ranging dialectical treatment of plant and animal life, based on very accurate information. In plants the category of Being-for-Self is inadequately exemplified; hence plants are imperfectly individuated, so that each of their parts can assume the function of all the others. And this imperfect individuation also shows itself in the inability of plants to separate themselves from their earthy environment, or to move freely about in it and go in search of their food or their mates. They are further not sufficiently self-referring to have one fixed temperature, nor any sensation. Like gravitating bodies they crave for a center, but outside not within themselves; they accordingly turn towards the light. They further transcend themselves genetically in the production of buds and seeds from which new individuals develop. But, since they are imperfectly individual, sexual differentiation and reproduction is a luxury, not a necessity, and they are capably of reproducing themselves without the formation of buds, seeds, and fruits.

The plant therefore passes over dialectically into the animal, where all parts are subordinated to the whole and cannot exist independently, but whose wholly distinct functions none the less gear into each other teleologically. The asunderness of matter is now overcome, and, being free from gross asunderness, the animal organism can move about freely and determine its position in space. It has further a voice in which, Hegel holds, spatio-temporality is overcome; the animal can display itself in a free, inward cohesion, and its nourishment by the environment takes place at times and in ways which it itself determines. The animal further brings the environing world into its self-feeling by way of sense-perception, and by the various forms of organic drive or need and the more elaborate instinctive patterns of response, such as migration, hibernation, nest-building, and so forth. Having overcome the environment, it reinstates it in the form of an environing genus in which the individual is both integrated and negated, but at the same time secures self-perpetuation in other individuals.

The genus is present in the single individual in the form of a straining against its perishable individuality. It has the urge to find itself in another member of the same species and through such union to give the species an extended existence, which can, however, only take the form of a bad infinity of perishable individuals. Animality must further specify itself in a range of species, each fitted to a specific environment, all mainly hostile to one another and liable to die at one another's hands. Disease seizes the animal when a single organic part or function gains dominance over the whole: medicine, as the Greeks held, must restore organic wholeness. Ultimately, however, the organism must succumb to disease or an alternative imbalance. Organisms decay because they are only the Idea in its immediacy. They never reconcile their individuality with their universality which can only be achieved in the inner life of Spirit. The opening phases of spiritual life remain, however, an extension of the natural.

Spirit certainly comes into being as a setting aside of nature's self-externality; in its first emergence it is all potentiality and no actuality. Spirit is at first a natural soul, not as yet deeply individualized, and responsive to all the climates and moods of nature. Differing regions breed differing spiritualities: the Arabian, the African, the English. The soul responds to the organic differences of childhood, youth, manhood, and old age. Sexual and family life are parts of the life of the natural soul. The term "feeling" is used by Hegel in much the manner in which it was later used by Bradley, Whitehead, and others: it is an unanalyzed sense of the world and oneself which lies below referential thought. The feeling soul is held by Hegel to be not sharply separate from other souls, but often has telepathic ties with them. Abnormal arousal of the feeling soul in developed spiritual life is revealed in such phenomena as sleep-walking and mesmeric trances. These do show us Mind or Spirit annihilating the self-externality of matter, but it is wrong to expect important revelations from them. The occult and the paranormal were of course very much studied and cultivated in Hegel's time, but he tends to disparage them. He makes the interesting remark, however, that the lunatic who identifies himself with Julius Caesar at least is aware of the absolute universality and negativity of conscious spirit.

From the anthropological section of Subjective Spirit, Hegel passes on to a phenomenological section which is a resume of his early work on the Phenomenology of Spirit, then on to a detached treatment of Theoretical Spirit, Practical Spirit, and Free Spirit, then on to Objective Spirit which details the development of Spirit through Law, Conscience, and Communal Ethics, which in its turn leads on to the dialectic of Civil Society and the Nation State. The latter develops its own temporalized dialectic in Universal History, which in its turn leads on to the suprasocial dialectic of Absolute Spirit, working itself out in the three cultural forms of Art, Religion, and Philosophy. At the end of the process Spirit is conscious of itself as the goal of all dialectical development, whether on the plane of categorial Logic or of self-external Nature or of conscious Spirit.

For Hegel, as well as for Whitehead at this comparable stage of his interpretation of nature and life, we meet with a highest reality which both thinkers elect to call God and claim to identify with the Object of Religion. His Highest Reality in both cases exists of necessity, since it embraces in itself not only all universal categories, but also all possibilities of their detailed specification or instantiation, and there is nothing whatever, whether actual or possible, which is not in some direct or less direct way present to it, or which could be derived from some source wholly independent of it. It is also, in both cases, a Highest Reality which carries to an unsurpassable maximum every form of positive value towards which any existent entity could aspire or achieve, and so serves as a genuine object of religious reverence or devotion to such existents as are capable of such attitudes. In both cases also the Highest Reality has a primordial nature which could not be other and which covers the general possibilities of any and every world, and also a consequent nature which is illustrated in the world as it is, but which might not have been illustrated in other possible worlds, and so involves much ineliminable contingency, which philosophy must not seek to remove.

Whitehead's Highest Reality is definitely individual, even if it is also categorial, the only possible instance of an all-perfect kind or nature; whereas Hegel's Highest Reality only has its individuation in all actual and all possible singularities in the actual or any possible world, and is, in and for itself, a pure universal or category, the eternal vision of itself in what is other than itself, without restricting this self to any individual self whatever. In Hegel's *Entausserung* we have a purely categorial principle giving itself individual form in the world of nature and finite spirit, whereas in Whitehead's Creativity the principle is already a categorial individual, endowed with consciousness and self-consciousness, and not merely the pure principle of the latter.

In Hegel a Platonic Form of the Good genuinely stands at the apex of everything, whereas in Whitehead it is rather an all-inclusively good individual that stands there. In Hegel, further, the Absolute Idea is creative of all things, not merely of their concepts or universal notions, whereas in Whitehead Creativity is rather a function of *all* the finite actual entities as much as of God. They may be said to create themselves, stage by stage, even if they borrow their individual aims from the all-comprehensive storehouse of God's primordial nature, and they are likewise responsible for helping to create one another, each individual entity being "objectively immortal" in its successors, and growing out of them and in some manner retaining them.

In this process of unending creation of actual individuals by actual individuals, Whitehead's God seems to be largely at the receiving end. If God stimulates the endeavors of finite creatures by providing them with the lure of unrealized possibilities, God does not engineer the fulfillment of this lure, but merely embraces its outcome in what Whitehead calls God's consequent nature. The

God of Whitehead is therefore not merely a conceptual storehouse in which all possibilities are stored: God is also a repository in which the archives of all realized possibilities are likewise stored. Since the world-process is credited with some wholly novel combinations of the original contents of the primeval storehouse, this second storehouse will be constantly enriched by the archives of innovations. God therefore not only enriches but is also enriched by the world. God is further not only the source and ultimate repository of the world's creations, but is also the poet who makes aesthetic sense of them all, or the fellow-traveller who understands and redeems them. In short, Whitehead's concept of God holds more in common with the compassionate Amitabhas, Avalokiteshvaras, and Manujshris of Mahayana Buddhism than with the God of Christianity or even with the Idea of Hegel—both of which are, in direct or indirect fashion, omniresponsible. I am not opposed to these Buddhist divinities; arguably it is best to have Gods who are only in part makers of our sad world.

There is accordingly this profound difference between Hegelianism and Whitehead's Philosophy of Organism that the former makes its Highest Reality a creative Universality which is specified and instantiated in every individual and character in the world, whereas the latter makes its Highest Reality a rather aloof aesthetic and sympathetic presence who inspires it, and who appraises such sense as can be successfully made of it. There is further the profound difference that for Hegel the instantial world comprises many individuals which are in no sense experients or subjects or superjects, even if their role in the world is to lead up to cases of fully self-conscious subjectivity, and even if their reactions evince many anticipations of such subjectivity.

Plants are held by Hegel to be devoid of sensation and feeling, which only begins at the animal level: they turn to the light and find as it were their self in it, but for Hegel they none the less feel not, neither do they think. Whitehead, by contrast, is a complete Leibnizian in that his denial of vacuous actuality means that he locates experients and experience everywhere. Whitehead may verbally deny consciousness to many actual entities in the world and even to God in some of his phases, but his definition of consciousness is highly idiosyncratic, and involves the presence, it would seem, of conception and judgement. He can still suppose that every actual entity duly *feels* the entities which act upon it causally, and dimly feels the trends in itself that will lead on to other entities.

There is in Hegel no trace of this affective monadology, though, as I have said, he acknowledges analogies to it in the relations of inorganic entities and even abstracta to subjects. I myself consider it an unnecessary complication to deny the sheerly *en soi*, and to want to see the *pour soi* everywhere. I value inanimate things precisely because they are honestly what they are without the disturbing self-transcendence of conscious experience. But I am not hostile to the view that there may be vague feeling-experiences in electrons and other charges of energy, or that something like kinaesthetic or organic sensation may be universally present in nature. I only think that such a view is too speculative (in the ordinary, non-Hegelian sense of "speculative") for us to found a world-view on such a supposition.

Ivor Leclerc
EMORY UNIVERSITY

Whitehead and the Problem of the Knowledge of Nature

I

When Whitehead moved to philosophy from his earlier immersion in mathematics, physics, and logic, it was the problem of the knowledge of nature which came to concern him, from his papers on "The Organization of Thought" and "The Anatomy of Some Scientific Ideas" (1916)[1] and his books *An Inquiry Concerning the Principles of Natural Knowledge* (1919) and *The Concept of Nature* (1920); and this remained his preoccupation through *Science and the Modern World* (1925), *Process and Reality* (1929), *Adventures of Ideas* (1933), to *Nature of Life* (1934)—this last being included in *Modes of Thought*, his last book.

This concern with the problem of the knowledge of nature was both fundamental to his philosophical endeavour and determinative of his metaphysics, as had analogously been the case with the two pivotal modern thinkers, Descartes and Kant. Deliberate attention to the role of this problem for Whitehead is as important for the proper understanding of his thought was it is for that of his two great predecessors.

This problem will be receiving special attention in the present paper, but I shall be approaching it from a rather different perspective from that which is usual. I shall approach it from the ontological perspective, and I shall do so historically.

II

Modern science and modern philosophy arose, in rejection of the natural science and the philosophy of Aristotelian scholasticism, upon a new basis, which was the Neoplatonism that had been resuscitated in the fifteenth century, this steadily affecting scientific thought and coming into full effect in the early decades of the seventeenth century.

Fundamentally and especially relevant in this is the Neoplatonic ontology,[2] the basic doctrine of which is that that which 'is', in the primary sense, must be immutable. The Neoplatonic inheritance which had been particularly influential on Descartes, and also other thinkers of the time, was the Augustinian, and according to this the primary 'being', the being which is immutable in the strictest sense, is God. However, since the forms also are changeless in themselves, they too are 'beings'. Further, according to Plotinus, the forms, in enaction, constitute soul,[3] which entails that souls also are beings, the embodied souls being the principles of agency of the physical—the *rationales seminales* of Augustine. Further, in the Neoplatonic doctrine all change, *motus*, including becoming, pertains strictly to the physical, to the realm of nature. Plotinus had made a very clear distinction between, on the one hand, the agency, the acting, of soul and, on the other, the *kinesis*, *motus*, of the physical. That is, the acting of soul, which is thinking, is not a species of change *(motus)* or becoming, but stands in contrast to the *motus*, change, and becoming of the physical. This doctrine, a central tenet of Neoplatonism, was carried over into the modern period.[4]

But a very considerable and crucial modification of the Neoplatonic scheme came to be introduced in the seventeenth century. This was in respect of the status of matter. In classical Neoplatonism, matter pertained to the physical as the recipient of form, and was conceived as having an ontological status the very contrary to that of form, namely that of 'not-being'—for Augustine a *prope nihil*. But in the late middle ages certain developments gradually led to a change in the conception of matter,[5] culminating, in the first two decades of the seventeenth century, in the introduction, through Descartes' elder compatriot Sebastian Basso[6] of the conception of the physical as constituted by matter alone—in contrast and opposition to the antecedent conception of the physical as composite of form and matter.

Descartes was the first to appreciate fully the philosophical implications of this new theory of nature. In this view matter was an ultimate; it was simply matter, being everywhere the same and thereby incapable of changing into anything else. Descartes recognized that since matter is in itself changeless, matter accords fully with the Neoplatonic criterion of 'being', namely immutability, which entailed that, ontologically considered, matter is indeed 'being'—and not 'not-being' or a *prope nihil*. Therefore, in the new theory, matter alone is physical being, i.e. matter per se is substance, a *res*, thus having its own essence whereby it is a *res*.

Now in traditional Neoplatonism 'essence', viz. that whereby a being is what it is, was conceived as necessarily determined and constituted by forms. Further, these forms determining the essence were held to be necessarily qualitative. The reason is that in classical Neoplatonism *anima* (soul) is the paradigmatic being, and when soul is considered in terms of the categories, it is only the category of quality which is relevant—soul is not, for example, quantitative nor in any place; that is, the only categoreal question relevant in determing "what" a soul is, is *qualis*, "of what kind or sort."

But Descartes saw that, since matter does not admit of any differences of kind, the qualitative does not pertain to matter at all. On the other hand, the most completely general feature of matter is that it is extensive, which meant that the category of quantity alone pertained to matter. Accordingly, Descartes concluded, it is extensiveness and that only which constitutes the essence of matter. Thus matter as the physical, ontologically considered, is a *res extensa*. It was further clear to Descartes that the Neoplatonic ontology, applied to the new conception of the physical as matter, ineluctably entailed a metaphysical duality of two separate and mutually exclusive *res:* in addition to the physical or nature as a *res extensa*, there is also a separate realm constituted by souls, the realm of *res cogitantes*.

It is highly pertinent to our concern in this paper to be clear that this metaphysical dualism, which has so profoundly affected subsequent philosophy, involved not only a new conception of nature, of the physical; it also involved a significantly different conception of soul. In the antecedent philosophy—both traditional Neoplatonism and also Scholastic Aristotelianism—which this new metaphysical dualism replaced, *anima*, soul, was included in the physical in the fundamental role of the principle of life, of emotion and feeling, and thus of the agency of the physical. But in the new doctrine, since matter is without any change in itself, and thus devoid of agency, there was no room in the physical per se for any principle of agency. This meant that soul, as thus extruded from the physical, had thereby also lost that part of its nature whereby it had previously functioned as a principle of agency, of life, of the physical. Descartes drew the evident conclusion that soul is left with only the activity of 'thinking', whence it had to be a *res cogitans*. The logic of this carried over into subsequent philosophy; as a consequence of the metaphysical dualism, 'soul' had become *mens*, 'mind', i.e., 'intellect'.

For the proper understanding of modern philosophy it is important to appreciate not only that it involved a rejection of the Aristotelian conception of soul, but also that the conception which replaced it was essentially the Neoplatonic one, which differed from the Aristotelian in a singularly fundamental respect. In the Aristotelian doctrine soul is not an ontologically separate entity but is integral to the physical as the *eidos*, form, of physical beings. A physical or natural being, for Aristotle, was one which has the capacity and power of action *(energeia)*, and it is *psyche*, soul, which is the *arche*, source, of that power in a natural being. Aristotle distinguished natural beings into non-living and living, and in the case of the living its *kinesis*, motion, includes nutrition and sensation as well as locomotion.[7] Man, as a living being, shares these powers of the soul with other living beings, but man's soul, *in addition*, has another power, namely that of *nous*, mind or intellect, i.e. the power or faculty of 'thinking'. The fundamental difference from this of the Neoplatonic doctrine of soul is that what in the Aristotelian theory was an *additional* factor in the soul of man, in the Neoplatonic conception was the very essence of soul. The ontological basis of this is that in Plotinian Neoplatonism 'being' is primarily *nous*, intelligence, and *psyche*, soul, derives from *nous* its essential character, namely 'intelligence'. In Augustinian Neoplatonism, the doctrine historically most influential, it is God which is 'being', and God is 'intelligence', whence the essence of *anima*, soul, too is 'intelligence'. This conception of soul carried through into the modern period. It was this Neoplatonic conception of soul as 'intelligence', i.e. as 'mind', which replaced the Aristotelian conception, not only in Descartes and other thinkers such as Locke, who accepted the new conception of the physical as matter, but also by others such as Leibniz and Berkeley, who rejected the conception of the physical as matter. This Neoplatonic conception of the soul also carried over into the eighteenth century with Hume and with Kant, and consequently into the empiricism and rationalism of the nineteenth century and later.

III

It was this modern form of the Neoplatonic tradition introduced in the seventeenth century which Whitehead came to reject in its entirety. However, because the Neoplatonic ontology and the new metaphysics of nature erected on it as its basis had by the nineteenth century come to be accepted as tacit presuppositions which thus determined the climate of thinking of Whitehead's time, the development of his thought represented a rather gradual process of extrication from that inheritance. This extrication was indeed not a complete one, for some of his thought remained affected by it, as we shall see.

When Whitehead, in his earlier period, in developing a philosophy of nature adequate to the twentieth-century developments in physical science, inveighed against the "bifurcation of nature" and its concomitant theory of "psychic additions"[8] to nature—i.e. the theory of the subjectivity of the secondary qualities—it was basically metaphysical dualism which he was rejecting. He insisted at that time on explicitly placing not only man, but also colours and other sensuous qualities, within nature. But this necessitated, as he soon came to see, a new metaphysical basis in terms of which this was possible. This new metaphysics was first fully revealed in his Gifford Lectures at Edinburgh University in June 1928, published in a somewhat expanded form in his book *Process and Reality* in 1929.[9]

In this book he propounded a theory of an indefinite plurality of ultimate beings, which he termed 'actual entities'.[10] This theory, as he had himself noted, is analogous to that of Leibniz in that Whitehead's actual entities, like Leibniz's monads, are the ultimate metaphysical beings out of which all composite entities are constituted. But the analogy does not go much further than that, for Whitehead's theory differs fundamentally from that of Leibniz in a number of respects, but basically in that whereas Leibniz's monads were conceived as Neoplatonic souls, in Whitehead's doctrine actual entities are *not* souls—the interpretation of Whitehead's position as panpsychist,[11] I shall argue, is consequently a grave error. Whitehead held that actual entities are 'dipolar', physical and mental. To comprehend this doctrine it is essential that both these terms, physical and mental, be properly understood as Whitehead used them.

The meaning of the adjective "physical" underwent a significant change in connotation with the new seventeenth-century conception of nature as matter. In terms of that conception the word "physical," i.e. "natural," came to mean "material"; and since matter is "bodily," "physical" also came to mean "bodily"—but "body" in a sense quite excluding "soul." This meaning of "physical" stands in contrast to the antecedent Scholastic Aristotelianism, in which the "physical" was certainly "bodily," but not to the exclusion of soul.

Whitehead's rejection of the modern doctrine of the physical as matter entailed also his rejection of the modern connotation of "physical" as "material," and also of it as "bodily," as well as of it as essentially "extensive"—Descartes' doctrine.

In opposition to the modern doctrine of the physical as immutable matter, Whitehead maintained that the physical must be conceived as essentially "in a process of becoming." This entailed, Whitehead saw, that fundamental in the physical must be 'acting', this acting, in his theory, being that of 'prehending'. The notion of 'acting', however, requires clarification, for it can be, and has been, differently conceived. Historically first there is the position of Aristotle, he having maintained that 'acting' *(energeia)* is fundamental to the physical. And there is the position which has historically been dominant, that of classical Neoplatonism, according to which 'acting' is essentially and primarily attributable to soul, and to the physical or bodies only derivatively through the acting of indwelling souls. This is the conception which Leibniz had taken over in his doctrine of monads. Modern metaphysical dualism, from Descartes, also maintained the Neoplatonic conception of acting as pertaining only to souls. It is important to appreciate that it was this Neoplatonic conception of 'acting' as fundamentally and primarily pertaining to soul which Whitehead rejected. The position at which he had arrived is close to the Aristotelian one.

Whitehead in his doctrine made a distinction between two kinds of acting, physical acting and mental or conceptual acting—this distinction is there in Aristotle too, although terminologically less distinct. Whitehead explicitly conceived physical acting as being the acting of an actual entity in which that acting is in reference to or involves another actual entity or other actual entities. In contrast to this there is mental or conceptual acting, which is the acting of an actual entity in reference to 'eternal objects' (what in the philosophical tradition had been termed 'forms').

There has, however, been a not inconsiderable amount of confusion respecting Whitehead's conception of 'acting', which is the result of the terminology in respect of this 'acting' which he had developed in *Science and the Modern World* in the context of his consideration of the interrelatedness of physical beings. He began this with a quotation from Francis Bacon,[12] and drew the reader's attention to "the careful way in which Bacon discriminates between *perception*, or *taking account of*, on the one hand, and *sense*, or *cognitive experience*, on the other hand," agreeing with Bacon on the primacy of the former. But because the word "perception" in our contemporary customary usage has the connotation of conscious cognitive experience, Whitehead chose the word "prehension" for unconscious "taking account of."[13] Then, in *Process and Reality*, he used the word "prehension" as the general term for "concrete facts of relatedness."[14] But thereby he became entangled in the presuppositions of Neoplatonism.

To appreciate this it must be borne in mind that, in terms of the Neoplatonic ontology, 'acting' is that of soul: it is soul, as 'being', which 'acts', and it is *only* soul which is, in the primary sense, active. Moreover—and this is a most important feature of the Neoplatonic doctrine—soul is *purely* active, in the sense that it is not able to be 'acted upon'. A clear illustration of this is provided by Leibniz's mondads, which are Neoplatonic souls whose acting is that of 'perception',[15] which, as he stresses, is a completely "internal principle,"[16] this meaning that a monad is wholly active, in no respect being 'acted on' by any other monad. Because of this there can be no causal relatedness between monads, even in respect of perception. Thus perceptions of other monads can arise in the perceiving monad only by its own internal and autonomous activity of perceiving, a consequence of which is that perceptions of other monads are purely subjective to the perceiver, and thus necessarily phenomenal.

We can readily appreciate the extent to which Whitehead, with his use of the term "prehension," became enmeshed in the Neoplatonic position, by noting the similarity of his doctrine in this respect to that of Leibniz. For Whitehead the acting of an actual entity is that of 'prehending', analogously to that of Leibniz's monad being 'perceiving'. Furthermore, Whitehead did explicitly maintain that his notion of 'prehension' is a "generalization from Descartes' mental 'cogitations', and fron Locke's 'ideas' "[17]—both of which are the product of wholly subjective actings, in accordance with the Neoplatonic doctrine which they accepted—Whitehead emphasizing there that his philosophy "starts with a generalization of Locke's mental operations." Moreover, in *Process and Reality* Whitehead also used the word "feeling" as a synonym for 'prehension', the word "feeling" having, in recent times, come to acquire a very largely subjective connotation.[18] The implication is readily drawn that the 'prehending' of a Whiteheadian actual entity is to be conceived as a wholly subjective acting, with the actual entity, like the Leibnizian monad, not being capable of being 'acted on'—this being so since an actual entity can prehend only other actual entities which are in its past, i.e. ones whose acting is over, and which are thereby unable to act on the present prehending actual entity. The outcome thus is the conception of 'prehension' as an essentially "mental" act. This is indeed the basis of the interpretation of Whitehead's position as "panpsychist."

But as against that, Whitehead did insist, contrary to Leibniz and others in the Neoplatonic tradition, that 'prehensions' cannot be wholly subjective, originating entirely in the experiencing or prehending subject. The subjectivism of the modern tradition had necessitated, for the veridicality of experience and knowledge, having to have recourse either to God (explicitly in Descartes and Leibniz, implicitly in very many others), or to transcendental categories (Kant), or to mere pragmatism or "animal faith" (Santayana). Whitehead, on the contrary, maintained a necessary objectivism as to the "data" of prehension. Of special concern to Whitehead in his insistence on the necessity for the objectivity of the data was that unless that objectivity were able to be validly maintained, there would be no foundation for any claim to scientific knowledge.

The question is whether this insistence by Whitehead on objectivity constitutes a fatal incoherence in his system, as would be the case if his conception of 'prehensive acting' were indeed essentially that of the Neoplatonic tradition. The issue is how, in terms of his conception of the acting of an actual entity, that objectivity of the data is to be secured. Whitehead was well aware of this issue, and of the problem it constituted for him, and he clarified his position in his chapters on "Objects and Subjects" and "Past, Present, Future" in *Adventures of Ideas*. He pointed out there that for an actual entity to be an 'object' for a prehending actual entity necessitates the former being 'given', which means that it is antecedent to the latter, and experienced as such,[19] affirming that "thus an object must be a thing received, and must not be either a *mode* of reception or a thing *generated* in that occasion."[20] The emphasis is on the object as 'received,' and this is crucial.

Two pages later he observed that the "objects are the factors in experience which function as to express that that occasion originates by including a transcendent universe of other things."[21] This is essentially the Aristotelian position—to be seen as standing in contrast to the Neoplatonic one. The issue, for Whitehead, is how precisely this "receiving" is to be understood. Whitehead argued here against the supposition "that an occasion of experiencing arises out of a passive situation which is a mere welter of many data,"[22] which entails that for him the things as data must themselves be active. This again is the Aristotelian position. The issue then is what exactly is the relation between those active things, which constitute what Whitehead terms the 'actual world' of the perceiver, and the 'receiving' by that perceiving subject. Whitehead's analysis is as follows:[23]

> The initial situation includes a factor of activity which is the reason for the origin of that occasion of experience. This factor of activity is what I have called 'Creativity'. The initial situation with its creativity can be termed the initial phase of the new occasion. It can equally well be termed the actual world relative to that occasion. It has a certain unity of its own, expressive of its capacity for providing the objects requisite for a new occasion, and also expressive of its conjoint activity whereby it is essentially the primary phase of a new occasion.

It is clear from this that Whitehead did not conceive of that 'receiving' as being a quasi-mental "grasping" of the antecedent data—as he would have done had he proceeded on the Neoplatonic conception of 'acting.' It is to be emphasized that Whitehead was explicitly concerned here with *physical* acting. He maintained that the initial situation in the prehending actual entity includes a factor of *physical* activity, which is 'conjoint,' i.e. it is the activity not only of the prehender but also that of the prehended; and it is a 'physical' acting, i.e. one of each actual entity in reference to the other. In other words, at that juncture the physical activity of the antecedent and of the consequent actual entity is 'common.' This means that what we have here is a *continuity* of physical activity constituted by a 'contiguity' of the two entities at a crucial juncture, at which, as Aristotle argued,[24] it is necessary that they have their 'point of contact' in common. This common activity, for Aristotle, is to be analysed as constituted by the antecedent thing 'acting on' the perceiver, and the latter 'being acted on.' This 'being acted on,' however, is not to be construed as mere and sheer 'inertness,' but as indeed as 'activity,' the activity of 'receiving'—the contrary presupposition derives from the Neoplatonic conception of 'acting.' My point is that Whitehead's position in this argument is essentially that of Aristotle, which means that the 'initial situation' of the prehending actual entity is a 'being acted on'—which entails an 'acting on' by the object actual entity—and this means that the 'initial situation' is an 'interaction;' a 'giving' and a 'receiving,' and in that 'receiving' the given actual entity is 'objectified.'

Thus, despite his confusing term 'prehension', Whitehead has in fact avoided being trapped in a Neoplatonic position. Nevertheless it seems to me that that term (and its synonym 'feeling') is further unfortunate in that it is a hindrance to the conception of *physical acting* as an 'interacting' of actual entities—for this 'interacting' is essentially what for Whitehead 'physical prehension' is. I would suggest that this is much more effectively conceived in terms of the generic term 'act': 'interacting' is both an 'acting on' *and* a 'being acted on.' This is the Aristotelian conception of physical acting,[25] and Whitehead's position is in fundamental agreement with this.

This conception and analysis of physical acting, in Whitehead's theory, becomes further intelligible in contrast to his conception of 'mental prehension'. Whitehead defined 'mental' or 'conceptual' prehension as that in which the data are 'eternal objects', i.e. 'forms'.[26] For Whitehead, as for Aristotle, eternal objects or forms are the determinants of the definiteness of physical beings. As such these forms are 'particular'; i.e., each is "this" definiteness to the exclusion of "that" or any other definiteness. These are the forms *(eide)* which for Aristotle are the forms of sensible things *(ta aistheta)*. In contrast to these are the eternal objects or forms which, for Aristotle, are 'universal' *(katholou)*[27]—Whitehead's prefereed term is 'pure potentiality'.[28] Aristotle held that the latter forms are, "in a manner, in the soul itself,"[29] in that intellect *(nous)* is not dependent for these upon sensible perception. It is by virtue of this that Aristotle held that *nous* is a distinct activity of *psyche* which alone is capable of 'separation' *(chorizesthai)*;[30] in contrast, that activity of *psyche* which is sensible perception *(aisthesis)* is not independent of body. This means that forms as universals are not derived by *nous* through its being 'acted on' by body.[31] On the contrary, these forms are 'conceived'—in the etymological sense of "grasped," "held"—by its own autonomous acting; this is the point of Aristotle's doctrine that "it is this *nous* which is separable, and impassive, and unmixed, being in its essential nature *(ousia)* an activity *(energeia)*."[32]

Whitehead's position is similar to Aristotle's in that for him *pure* mental or conceptual prehension is the prehension, i.e. the "conceiving," "grasping," of forms in their sheer generality and pure potentiality. This pure mental or conceptual prehension is an *autonomous* 'act'; it is not a 'being acted on.' Whitehead did indeed hold that in pure conceptual prehension the forms or eternal objects are 'derived' from the eternal object or form determinant of the definiteness of an actual entity or nexus of actual entities physically prehended,[33] but this "derivation' does not consist in a 'receiving' of those forms in the sense of mental activity being initially a 'being acted on' as in physical prehension; mental prehension per se is an autonomous "grasping," "conceiving," of the forms in abstraction from their physical determination of actual entities. This is the essence of *mental*, i.e. *conceptual*, acting in Whitehead's doctrine, which is clearly very close in this respect to that of Aristotle. But Whitehead proceeded to a distinction which is only implicit in Aristotle. Whitehead termed this mental "deriving" of a form or eternal object, in the way just indicated, a 'conceptual valuation',[34] distinguishing it from the further autonomous mental act of 'conceptual reversion', i.e. conceiving a form which is 'reverse', viz. opposite or contrary to that in conceptual valuation.[35] It is by virtue of this latter mental power that possibilities divergent from those deriving from the data become conceptually accessible. This mental power is, in Whitehead's theory, the basis of 'imagination'.

In Whitehead's philosophy, therefore, although mental acting is analysed as being distinct and different in kind from physical acting, Whitehead does not ascribe to mental acting an independent ontological status, as does Neoplatonism. He maintains that that which is ontologically independent, an actual entity, requires *both* kinds of acting, since both are necessary for the philosophical understanding of "what is," and neither of them is derivable from, or reducible to, the other. Thus in Whitehead's doctrine an actual entity is "dipolar," physical and mental, which means that it is *one* actual entity which is the subject of both physical and conceptual acting. To characterize this position as "panpsychist" is entirely incorrect: the mental "pole" is not a *psyche*, and it is not a "being"; nor is physical "prehending" accurately to be understood as a quasi-mental "grasping." For Whitehead the actings of these "poles" of an actual entity are both intrinsically different, but they are also interconnected and complexly interdependent. A fully systematic analysis of this interrelationship will not be possible within the scope of this paper; I shall concentrate on only one pertinent aspect of it.

IV

On the basis of this metaphysical position of two poles of acting involved in every actual being, Whitehead developed an epistemology in terms of which he was able to evade the kinds of difficulties involved in the epistemologies of empiricism and rationalism. For Whitehead a major consideration in this—and on which I shall particularly concentrate—was the problem of the knowledge of nature.

This had indeed been a primary consideration for historical empiricism; it had been this which had led Locke to carry over the Scholastic Aristotelian position that *nihil est in intellectu quod non prius in sensu*. Locke, however, did not appreciate the fundamental incompatibility of this Aristotelian position with the Neoplatonic subjectivism involved in his acceptance of metaphysical dualism, and this inevitably landed empiricism in a fatal epistemological difficulty.

In Whitehead's view, what is crucially necessary to examine in this empiricist position is its conception and analysis of sensuous perception. As we have seen, on the basis of the Neoplatonic ontology sensuous perception is a purely *mental* act, i.e. an autonomous act of the mind (mind not "being acted on" by matter, as Locke was very clear), giving rise to "ideas" of sensation, these being "qualities" inhering in the mind alone, and not in material things. Further, these sensuous "ideas," Whitehead emphasized,[36] are essentially universals. This entails that on that position, contrary to Aristotle, sensuous perception *(aisthesis)* cannot be of particulars which are, in Whitehead's words, "other things which are in the world in the same sense as we are."[37] In this empiricist theory, therefore, there is no basis for any knowledge of physical things other than by inference. Locke recognized this, and indeed maintained that a valid inference can be made from the occurence of sensuous ideas in the mind to *"the particular existence of finite beings without us."*[38] Whitehead has insisted that there can be no such valid inference—as had indeed been clear to Hume. For Hume, consequently, there could be no genuine knowledge of nature, but only a probability.

This empiricist doctrine, Kant saw, in effect left natural science without a foundation, and it was a primary concern of his critical philosophy to provide such a foundation to secure genuine scientific knowledge, which he did by grounding it in the mind. For Whitehead, however, this version of the rationalist position was subject to the same fundamental objections as had to be directed against that of Descartes. Descartes, with much greater perspicacity than the empiricists respecting the implications of the Neoplatonic ontological foundations which they shared, saw that on that basis knowledge of nature had to be grounded, not on *sensuous* ideas, but on *intellectual* ideas. But these are necessarily universal, and the difficulty is that from universality there can be no inference to any particular entity—this is why Descartes' pure mathematics cannot be knowledge of particular physical things. Kant, being clear that the universal categories of the understanding cannot give knowledge of particular things, held that for knowledge there is also is required sensibility, by means of which there is 'intuition' *(Anschauung)* of objects. But he accepted the modern Neoplatonic conception of sensibility as strictly subjective,[39] which entails that 'things-in-themselves' cannot directly be objects; they can be objects only by inference. We shall return below to the issue whether this does indeed enable Kant validly to have "knowledge" of particular things.

Adequately to appreciate Whitehead's criticism of both the rationalist and empiricist positions, it is necessary at this point to pay particular attention to two features of the conception of knowledge as carried over by Descartes from medieval thought, and which were crucial not only to Descartes' philosophy but also to that of subsequent thinkers, rationalist and empiricist, including Kant. Whitehead found it necessary to question and reject both these features as traditionally maintained. One of these is that of genuine knowledge as necessarily intuitive. The other feature of this conception of knowledge is that it be certain.

The former conception, that knowledge is necessarily intuitive, derives from Plato's *noesis* of the forms.[40] This accorded fully with the Neoplatonic doctrine of the soul as mind or intellect, and thus was accepted by Descartes. Consistent with this, Descartes held that knowledge is essentially mathematical—for it is mathematics which is the exemplification *par excellence* of knowledge as intuitive—and he accordingly developed the conception of knowledge as a general mathematics, this encompassing metaphysics. On this basis he was then able consistently to hold that physics, i.e. the knowledge of nature, is no other than "geometry or abstract mathematics."[41]

The second feature of this conception of knowledge, viz. that it is certain, also derived from Plato, but it underwent a significant change effected by the Neoplatonic subjectivist position. Plato had spoken of knowledge *(episteme)* as per se true and thus as infallible or "not false."[42] This 'infallibility,' however, is significantly different from 'certainty,' for the concept of 'infallibility' is a logical entailment of 'truth', whereas 'certainty' has an essential reference to the thinking subject: it is the thinker which has the subjective feeling or conviction of 'certainty'. Descartes, with his Neoplatonic subjectivism, required this feeling of 'certainty' as the warrant of authentic knowledge (as had Augustine). He maintained further that it was this 'certainty' that attested mathematics as being genuine knowledge, and this was accepted by subsequent thinkers in the Neoplatonic tradition, including the empiricists. Kant carried this to its logical conclusion: taking the term *scientia* strictly as the Latin rendering of *episteme*, he held that "only that can be called true science whose certainty is apodictic,"[43] and consequently maintained, like Descartes, that science in this strict sense had necessarily to be mathematical.[44]

We can now return to the issue raised above, whether Kant, with his doctrine of sensibility, is indeed able to have genuine knowledge of particular things. He believed himself able validly to maintain this because of his conception of knowledge as 'apodictic certainty', such knowledge being mathematical. Against this Whitehead argued that, on the basis of Kant's Neoplatonic subjectivism the objects are universals, both in mathematical thought and in sensibility. But, as Whitehead retorted in a characteristic epigram: "You cannot know what [thing] is red by merely thinking of redness";[45] and, we can add, you cannot know what thing is of a certain particular mathematical quantity by merely thinking of mathematical pattern or equations. On the contrary, Whitehead insists, "You can only find red things by adventuring amid physical experiences in *this* actual world. This doctrine is the ultimate ground of empiricism."

V

Whitehead concluded that, in order validly to have knowledge of the physical or nature, it is necessary to have a conception and an analysis of knowledge different from that of the traditional modern one. We will concentrate here on the problem of the knowledge of nature.

Having rejected Neoplatonic subjectivism, Whitehead was not in need of 'certainty' as the criterion of knowledge. As to the conception of knowledge as 'intuitive' (i.e. a direct, non-discursive "seeing"), Whitehead held that 'intuition' pertains primarily to *pure* mental or conceptual prehension.[46] Thus this 'intuitive' grasping of the forms or eternal objects would hold only in respect of pure possibility—which for him is the concern of, for example, pure mathematics.[47]

This, however, as a kind of knowledge, is to be distinguished from the knowledge of nature—and not confused with it, as had occurred, for example, in the systems of Descartes and Kant—and also from that knowledge which is metaphysical—metaphysics, for Whitehead, being the science which seeks to understand all "that which is" in terms of its most general features.[48]

Whitehead's basic insistence is that if there is to be valid and genuine knowledge of nature, then the first requirement is to admit—what the Neoplatonic ontology and its concomitment subjectivism precludes—a physical acting of the perceived actualities on the perceiver. It is this requirement which has been rendered impossible by the post-Kantian subjectivism which has been dominant in this century. In that doctrine scientific theory is wholly mental, entirely subjective, the actual physical entities which are the objects of scientific inquiry being only putatively referred to.[49] With that position a state of crisis has arisen in respect of the knowledge of nature, especially the outcome of the realization and acceptance of scientific method being hypothetico-deductive. For if a scientific theory is essentially an hypothesis, there are competing hypotheses, none of which can strictly be verified, but are only capable of falsification, with relativism as the consequence, for it renders truth in respect of scientific theory merely chimerical.

This epistemological impasse, Whitehead maintains, can be escaped only by an explicit turn to metaphysics. What is indispensably requisite is a metaphysical theory in terms of which perceived physical entities act on the perceiver. This is what Whitehead's metaphysical doctrine secures by its conception of physical entities as all 'active', 'acting on' and reciprocally 'being acted on'. By this physical interaction the perceived entities are objectified for the perceiver. And by the integration of the physical interacting with the conceptual acting, the objectified entities become the subjects of the propositions constituting scientific theory.

What we have here is a new conception of 'propositions', differing radically from the dominant subjectivistic conception of propositions, a new conception grounded in a metaphysics not only of the physical interaction of actual entities, but also, in each actual entity, an 'integration' or 'synthesizing' of the physical acting with conceptual acting. This is Whitehead's metaphysical doctrine of every actual entity being dipolar, physical and conceptual, and this integration of the physical and conceptual acting being an indispensable requisite for the becoming of the actualities. In high-grade actualities, those capable of knowledge, there occurs an integration of the propositional kind, i.e. of actual entities as 'objects', received in physical interaction, with 'concepts' *proposed* as hypothetical predicates, of those entities as 'subjects'. Scientific theories are, in this theory, general propositions—as opposed to singular propositions. With this philosophy we have the greatest attempt after Kant to provide a solid and secure foundation for scientific theory and the knowledge of nature.

Notes

1. Both reprinted in *The Organization of Thought* (1917) and in *The Aims of Education* (1932).

2. I have shown this in some detail in my paper, "The Ontology of Descartes," *The Review of Metaphysics*, Vol. XXXIV, 1980–81, pp. 297–323.

3. Cf. Plotinus, *Enneads* VI, 6. 6.

4. Cf. e.g., Descartes, *Principles of Philosophy* II, 25.

5. See my *The Nature of Physical Existence* (London: Allen & Unwin; New York: Humanities Press, 1972), Part II, pp. 101–148, for this development.

6. Sebastian Basso, *Philosophia naturalis adversus Aristotelem Libri XII. In quibus abstrusa veterum physiologia restauratur, et Aristotelis errores solidis rationibus refelluntur* (Geneva, 1621).

7. Cf. e.g. Aristotle, *De Anima*, 413b11–13. Hereafter cited as DA.

8. A. N. Whitehead, *The Concept of Nature* (Cambridge: The University Press, 1920), Ch. II.

9. A. N. Whitehead, *Process and Reality* (Cambridge: The University Press; New York: The Macmillan Company, 1929). Hereafter referred to as PR, and the pagination respectively to these two editions.

10. This theory had been first somewhat sketchily introduced in *Science and the Modern World*, as a development of his earlier theory of "events", and in this work also referred to as "primates"; and then adumbrated in *Religion in the Making*, where they were referred to as "a multiplicity of occasions of actualization" and as "epochal occasions" (p. 78).

11. The issue of "panpsychism", as we shall see, is complex. A distinction can be made between an actual entity as "being" a soul, and its "having"

a soul. But the crucial issue is whether the "acting", i.e. "prehension", of an actual entity is to be understood as essentially a "mental" act.

12. A. N. Whitehead, *Science and the Modern World* (Cambridge: The University Press; New York: The Macmillan Company, 1926), Ch. 3, p. 52. Hereafter cited as SMW.

13. SMW, Ch. IV, p. 86.

14. PR I, II, II, "The Categories of Existence", C 29, M 32.

15. G. W. Leibniz, *Monadology*, para. 16.

16. *Ibid.*, para. 11.

17. Pr I, II, I, C 26, M 29.

18. This is not the case in the earlier use of the word (cf. *O. E. D.* "Feel", verb, Art. I). Whitehead's use is in fact in this original sense.

19. A. N. Whitehead, *Adventures of Ideas* (Cambridge: The University Press; New York: The Macmillan Company, 1933), p. 229. Hereafter cited as AI.

20. This is an obvious reference to the Kantian doctrine.

21. AI, p. 231.

22. AI, p. 230.

23. AI, p. 230.

24. Aristotle, *Physics*, Book V, Ch. 3.

25. Cf. DA 417a13–18.

26. PR I, II, I, "Categories of Explanation" xi, C 31, M 35.

27. DA 417b16–26.

28. PR I, II, I, "Categories of Existence v", and "Categories of Explanation vii", C 29, 31, M 32, 34.

29. DA 417b23-24: "ταυτα δ'έν αύτῇ πωσ έστι τῇ ψυχῇ." Tr. R. D. Bicks, *Aristotle De Anima* (Amsterdam: Adolf M. Hakkert, 1965).

30. DA 413b22-27.

31. Cf. DA 429a10-429b9.

32. DA 430a17-18: "καὶ οὗτοσ ο νοῦσ χωριστὸσ καὶ ἀπαζὴσ καὶ ἀμιγήσ, τῇ οὐσία ὢν 'ενέργεια". Tr. Hicks, *op. cit.* Whitehead seems to have been unaware of the similarity of his position to that of Aristotle in this, as in so many other respects. He does not appear to have made a study in depth of Aristotle—as he did of Plato, especially the *Timaeus*—but to have relied considerably on the exposition and interpretation of Sir David Ross.

33. PR I, II, III, Categoreal Obligation iv, C 36, M 39-40.

34. *Ibid.*

35. PR I, II, III, Categoreal Obligation v, C 36, M 40.

36. Cf. PR II, I, VI, C 72, M 82; II, VI, II & IV, C 203, all, M 221, 230; II, VII, I, C 219, M 239; II, IX, II, C 269, M 289.

37. PR II, VII, I, C 221, M 240.

38. Locke, *Essay* IV, II, 14.

39. Cf. Kant, *Critique of Pure Reason*, B 45: "For these [colours, taste, etc.] cannot rightly be regarded as properties of things, but only as changes in the subject, changes which may indeed, be different in different men" (tr. Kemp Smith).

40. E.g. as brought out in the simile of the divided line at the end of Book VI of the *Republic*, in which *noesis* is the direct apprehension of the forms per se.

41. Descartes, *Principles of Philosophy* II, LXIV.

42. 'αψεῦδοσ. Plato, *Republic* 485c, *Theaetus* 160d. This means "infallible" in the sense of "not liable to be deceived or mistaken" (*O. E. D.*).

43. Kant, *Metaphysische Anfangsgründe der Naturwissenschaft*, Vorrede: "Eigentliche Wissenschaft kann nur diejenige genannt werden, deren Gewissheit

apodiktisch ist". Engl. tr. by James Ellington in *The Metaphysical Foundations of Natural Science,* The Library of Liberal Arts (Bobbs-Merrill, 1970).

44. Unlike Descartes, for whom pure mathematics was identified with physics as a general conception of nature, for Kant there is a "science" (in the strict sense) of nature only if the phenomena of nature be understood in terms of mathematics—cf. *Metaphysische Anfangsgründe,* Preface, and *Prolegomena zu einer jeden künftigen Metaphysik,* Part II, esp. Section 24. Engl. tr. by Lewis White Beck, *Prolegomena to Any Future Metaphysics,* The Library of Liberal Arts, No 17 (Bobbs-Merrill, 1950).

45. PR III, IV, I, C 362, M 391.

46. Whitehead also admits "intuition" in respect of one kind of "impure" prehension, that constituting an "intuitive judgment"—see below p. 25.

47. Cf. SMW, Ch. II, p. 44.

48. PR I, I, I, C 3, M 4.

49. A good exemplification of this is Albert Einstein's statement in his Herbert Spencer Lecture (1933): "The natural scientists of those days were . . . most of them possessed with the idea that the fundamental concepts and postulates of physics were not in the logical sense free inventions of the human mind but could be deduced from experience by 'abstraction'—that is to say by logical means. A clear recognition of the erroneousness of this notion really only came with the general theory of relativity. . . . the fictitious character of the fundamental principles is perfectly evident from the fact that we can point to two essentially different principles, both of which refer to experience to a large extent. . . ."

Quentin Lauer, S. J.
FORDHAM UNIVERSITY

"The Life of Consciousness and the World Come Alive": Nature and Self-Consciousness in Hegel's *Phenomenology*

There is in Hegel's *Phenomenology of Spirit* a relatively brief passage (eight pages) at the beginning of Chapter IV, "Self-Consciousness," which may well be one of the most difficult passages in the whole Hegelian corpus, but which is also of supreme importance for coming to grips with the movement of Hegel's thought, not only in the *Phenomenology* but in the entire "system." It is precisely the difficulty of the passage, it would seem, that explains why it has not been given by commentators an attention proportionate to its significance. So much attention has been focused on the "independence of self-consciousness," expressed in the sections on "Lordship and Bondage," "Stoicism and Skepticism," and "The Unhappy Consciousness"—which are, it is true, important and which lend themselves most readily to extended interpretation—that not enough attention has been given to the introductory section, entitled "The Truth of the Certainty of Self," in which are enunciated the principles which regulate the whole movement of Hegel's thought. The section might be described as the indispensable transition from those forms of consciousness which are merely "objective" yet try to give themselves off as authentic knowing, to what Hegel considers to be the only possible way of authenticating the objectivity of human consciousness, i.e., the self, which claims to know, progressively coming to know itself, a self-knowing which will be knowing at all only if it culminates in "absolute knowing." Only in the light of this section will the preface (as prologue-epilogue) be intelligible; only in its light will the whole of the *Phenomenology* hang together.

Most of the commentators, it is true, refuse to throw up their hands, as does Norman, who says, "The section on 'Self-Certainty' is extremely unrewarding, and since I find large parts of it unintelligible I shall say little about it."[1] Nevertheless, I find that many of them are simply guessing. They do not quite know (small wonder) what Hegel is saying, and so they surmise what his words *would* mean, if they themselves were to say something like this. Without discounting the significance of intelligent reflections *on* Hegel's text, there seems to me to be no substitute for extremely careful analysis *of* the text itself. In attempting to provide such a careful analysis, I shall look for elucidation principally in the paragraphs which make up the corresponding section in the *Encyclopedia* (##424-30), the introduction to the whole "Philosophy of Spirit" in the same *Encyclopedia* (##377-86), and the preface to the greater *Phenomenology of Spirit*. There are two basic assumptions operative in an endeavor such as this: (1) If one works long enough and hard enough in trying to come to grips with a passage such as this, it will turn out to be intelligible (whether or not one agrees with what it says); and (2) to understand what is most difficult (in any thinker) is to find the key for really understanding what *seems* to be less difficult.

Hegel begins his transition to *the* rational mode of thinking by reminding us that up to this point we have been dealing with modes of "certainty" regarding the objectivity of the content of consciousness, whether it be the certainty that the content of consciousness is most authentic when it is presented immediately through the senses, or that when consciousness reflects on the sensory content thus given it can justifiably connect it with "things" out there (reflective certainty), or that consciousness is justified in inferring a supra-sensible something (e.g., a "force") which is explanatory both of the consciousness had of reality and of the truth of that consciousness (inferential certainty). In short, consciousness has been quite sure that what it is conscious of is true independently of the consciousness *of* it. But, the very experiencing of this kind of truth has revealed that it is not true, that "certainty" is simply not enough; it must yield to a truth that is not what it thought it was. As Hegel expresses it in EpW, #424, consciousness is coming to the realization that it must look into itself, not outside itself, to find the truth of whatever content it has.[2] Kant had already recognized that it was vain to look for a validation of knowing outside the knowing process itself, but he contented himself with establishing the necessary subjective conditions for knowing to be knowing, without trying to establish that what is known really is the way it is known to be. Fichte had correctly seen that the only possible foundation for objective knowledge is self-knowledge, but he had then sought to validate the former by "deducing" it from the latter. Schelling had correctly seen that only if reality as known is the same as reality as it is, can the validity of objective knowing be established, but he had simply posited the identity of the two, without articulating the process of identification. Hegel will undertake the laborious effort of showing *how* this identification comes about.

But, in seeking to establish this, Hegel has a number of hurdles to get over—precisely the ones that, he felt, Kant, Fichte, and Schelling did not get over. It is not sufficient simply to be *certain* that this is the way it must be; he must *show* how this is the way it is.

My task in the rest of this paper, then, will be to detail the manner in which Hegel clears (or is convinced he clears) the hurdles in his path. (1) He must show that consciousness, naively presumed to be objective, not only does not cease to be objective in becoming self-consciousness, but rather realizes the truth of objective consciousness in becoming aware of what the objectivity of consciousness truly is. (2) On the other hand, he must show, contra Kant, that the essential subjectivity of conscious activity (e.g., conceptualization) does not cease to be subjective in being objectified—nor is it any the less objective in being subjective.[3] (3) This, in turn, means reconciling the subjectivity of conscious activity with the objective truth of its content. (4) More than that, he must show that the kind of conceptualizing which is reason's activity can be objectified in such a way that the objectivity of its referent is guaranteed—as it is not guaranteed when it is simply naively assumed to be objective—and that it does more than merely posit objects—which is but another way of saying that its certainty is true. (5) Further, since to be object is to be *for another*, it must be shown that its being *in itself* is both distinct and not distinct from its being for self (my object must be both distinct from me, or it is not an *object*, and it must not be distinct from me, or it is not *mine*).[4] (6) This means giving careful attention to the functions of the *Aufhebung* of "moments" in a process: (a) The naive certainty of objectivity must be *canceled* in such a way that the objectivity of the content is *retained* by being *lifted up* to a higher level; (b) it must be shown that reason (ultimately spirit) is objective in a way that understanding is not and that it is only as rational *self-consciousness* (for self-conscious *reason*) that it is thus objective.[5]

To get back to Hegel's text: What we now observe is the emergence of *a* certainty which is the same as its truth, because the certainty is itself the object of investigation, and the truth of this certainty is consciousness itself.[6] In this, of course, consciousness must make itself its own object; it cannot be object merely for us (philosophical) observers. Thus, Hegel tells us, consciousness in making itself its own object makes itself both distinct and not distinct from itself. Initially, we can simply call *concept* the activity of knowing, and we can call *object* the *knowing* which we objectify (Hegel calls it *das Ich*). This is, so to speak, the paradigm case of the object—the "I" conceptualizing—which is at once *in itself* and *for another* (itself as other), a distinction which is not a distinction because its otherness is a self-othering; what consciousness is in itself and for another is the same. We might call it the originary identification of *in itself* and *for self*. What consciousness finds in looking into itself, then, is itself as both the content of the looking and the looking itself. Thus is revealed to consciousness where it must look for objectivity, i.e., in self-consciousness, where truth is at home (the truth of all that went before), which Fichte had seen so clearly but, according to Hegel, had been unable to develop adequately.

The question now becomes that of finding how self-consciousness (*diese neue Gestalt des Wissens*) presents itself to itself and, in so doing, validates its own objectivity, at once canceling the otherness of consciousness' object and retaining its moments as moments in continuity with the concrete process of self-consciousness. Granted that this raises the spectre of solipsism, what Hegel calls the "motionless tautology,"[7] which says no more than "I is I" (see *EpW*, #424, Zus.), but Hegel is not fazed. Only by consciousness making itself its own object can it validate its own objectivity, but initially it does this only in the mode of certainty (that this is the way it ought to be), which must be raised to the level of truth (that this is the way it is). The otherness of objectivity has disappeared, but is "moments" have remained—present as they are *in themselves*—the *being* of sense certainty, the singularity and universality of perception, and the empty interior (out there) of understanding; they remain however as "moments" of one and the same process, that of self-consciousness, and are abstract distinctions which in the continuity of concrete process are not distinctions. Self-consciousness, then, is the return to self from the putative otherness of a world of which consciousness is conscious. But, Hegel is not out of the woods yet. Even granting that the "moments" make the inward turn inevitable, how can this be other than hopelessly subjective, as Hegel claims it is for Fichte? Hegel, in fact, states quite explicitly that the subject immediately making itself object accomplishes little; it comes up with the previously mentioned "motionless tautology" (we can call it an unmediated identity), which says no more than "I is I," and this sort of content is *not* self-consciousness; it provides no more than distinguished "moments," which by themselves say nothing.

But, all is not lost; it may well be that *by themselves* the moments say nothing, but they do point a direction, and, if it be permitted to anticipate, the direction they point is the validation of the objectivity of consciousness by progressively sloughing off the abstractness of successive forms of consciousness in a movement of concretization (concrescence?), in which objectivity and subjectivity (being and knowing) are mutually mediating (see *EpW*, 425, Griesheim). Hegel is unquestionably trying to show that knowing can be self-authenticating, provided it keeps moving—refusing to stop short of "absolute knowing," where the identification of the knowing and the known is complete ("absolute").[8] Here it is that Hegel steals a march on Kant—and to a great extent on Fichte and Schelling—in seeing two moments essential to the whole process, as operative throughout: (a) the self, and (b) all that the self is conscious of, which moments constantly need each other in the process of mediation whereby they grow into what they are to be. A self which withdraws itself from the reality (being) of which it is conscious is not a self-conscious self, and a reality which does not manifest itself through the medium of a self conscious of itself is no more than abstract *being*. This is but another way of saying—and it is important to say it if solipsism (mere subjectivism) is to be avoided—that the *Aufhebung* of moments in a process can never be merely their cancellation; it must be their retention, precisely as "moments" and their being raised up to the level of truth, ultimately in the Truth which is the absolute subject-object.

Given what has been said thus far, it begins to become evident that no solution to the dilemma of the objectivity in question is to be found, if the inquiry is confined to the level of cognitive consciousness only. The task at hand is that of examining consciousness in such a way that its objectivity is assured, without appeal to what is not consciousness. Along the lines of cognitive analysis thus far pursued the whole world of sensible objectivity has become a world of mere *appearance* (in the sense of that which *appears* but effectively *is* not). Cognitively considered, the sensible object—à la Hume (or even Kant)—yields only sense data, the concrete individual thing underlying these data, and understanding's abstract universal inferred from what the senses present. It is all very well to see cognitively *that* essential to the concreteness of this is the unity of self-consciousness with itself (see *EpW*, 425, 427 *Zus.*) and *that* this provides the only way to authenticate the true objectivity of consciousness; it does not get the authenticating done. Here we come upon a Hegelian insight, which at this point is *only* an insight, i.e., that the object of cognitive consciousness ceases to be *merely* an object only when it becomes an object of appetite, which, as Hegel sees it, is the mediation whereby self becomes object to itself (see *EpW*, 426 *Zus*); it is appetite (subjective) which makes the object capable of mediating objective consciousness with consciousness of self.[9] Appetite is revelatory of selfness in a way that mere cognition is not, provided, of course, that we are aware that appetite and cognition are inseparable—*ignoti nulla cupido*. The nut which now has to be cracked, and which in Hegel's opinion Kant, Fichte, and Schelling had not succeeded in cracking, is that the object merely as object over-against a subject takes on the negative character of being simply the non-subject, and the self becomes the *essential* object, where objectivity is to be looked for. The question, then, is how to look. The object merely as dead abstraction will reveal nothing either of itself or of the self of self-consciousness.[10]

Thus, not only has objective consciousness turned in on itself (inchoately), but the object, negatively over-against self-consciousness, in the consciousness had of it, i.e., *for us*, and as that of which we are conscious, i.e., *in itself*, is seen as in a sense reflecting back on itself and has, thus, "come alive" *(Leben geworden)*; it has, so to speak, been infused with life in the consciousness had of it—as part of a concrete organic whole it can mediate self-recognition in a way that dead abstraction cannot, as Hume, Kant, and Fichte had seen so well. This is to say that the object of consciousness is more than the object of sense or perception—even of understanding—and thus begins to contribute to overcoming the naiveté of merely objective consciousness *(natürliches Bewusstsein)*. As an object of immediate appetite it is reflected back into itself and is alive *(ein Lebendiges)*—consciousness has infused it with life and is thus over-against a *living* reality.[11] This is important: Consciousness beginning to make the transition to self-consciousness begins to comprehend that the distinctions understanding had made and had taken to be distinctions in the cognitively apprehended object have turned out to be merely *posited* distinctions, which understanding can see *only* as distinctions not as organically interrelated moments of a dynamic whole. What we have to recognize is the role of the appetitive relationship in overcoming this *mere* positedness, which is what Hegel means by saying that the object of appetite is "independent"—precisely as having "come alive," being active, not *on* but *in* consciousness.[12] This means that the opposition now is not between consciousness and its object, but between self-consciousness and *life*, which is not simply *conferred* on the object by consciousness—objectivity and subjectivity are not yet identified, but they are at least partners in a dynamic (concrete) relationship. Understanding had merely imposed distinctions on an undifferentiated whole; because real differences are united in a dynamic process, and the mutual mediation of reality and self-consciousness—the organic unity of living reality making possible consciousness of self, and consciousness of self making possible the self-revelation of the real.

It is in this way that Hegel can account for the independence of objectivity over against subjectivity and the independence of subjectivity over against objectivity—which does not mean that they do not work together in a common project. Here is where appetite comes in: It is appetite which bears witness to the independence of the object of cognitive consciousness, even though as object it is *for* the subject (Thus naive objectivity is overcome). Appetition, then, is the experiencing of the independence of the object. It is not enough, however, that the objectivity come alive in self-consciousness be seen immediately as a dynamic unity; merely as dynamic unity the activity of objectivity is no more than indeterminate movement which needs determination, and the latter bespeaks consciousness. It is a mistake, however, to conceive of the indeterminate movement as "receiving," so to speak, determination *from* consciousness; rather it is *in* consciousness—as self-consciousness—that reality determines itself, again a kind of partnership relation.

It is here that Hegel's thought becomes particularly difficult to unravel. Almost surreptitiously he introduces a concept which necessarily sends us back to the preface to the *Phenomenology*, if we are to make sense of it, the concept of the indispensable "fluidity" (*Flüssigkeit, Flüssigwerden*) of the indeterminate movement, if determination is to be concrete differentiation and not merely the abstract fragmentation operative in the distinctions posited by understanding.[13] What follows can, perhaps, best be understood as a kind of dialecticization of the opposition of a Parmenidean infinity of sameness which is pure being without intrinsic differentiation and a Heraclitean infinity of difference which is pure change without the all-embracing unity of the matrix wherein change occurs and makes sense. The resolution of this conflict, it would seem, demands a *logos* which at once differentiates the undifferentiated and reintegrates the differentiated, reminiscent of the threefold movement of the *Science of Logic* expressed in a "Doctrine of Being," a "Doctrine of Essence," and a "Doctrine of Concept." In the passage before us Hegel seeks to articulate the "moments" of an indeterminate movement progressively determining itself in the dynamic relationship of consciousness and objectivity. This movement is "essentially" pure motion as such, the infinity which transcends all differentiation, the "simply circular motion" which is "rest of itself as absolutely restless infinity" (one is reminded of Whitehead's "rest as motion of zero velocity"). This is independence as such in which the differences inherent in the movement are resolved. None of this, however, can make sense except in the framework of space-time which is the necessary condition of objectivity.[14] This brings us back again to "universal fluidity" *(diese allgemeine Flüssigkeit),* wherein are *aufgehoben* what were differentiated, i.e., raised to a new level of concreteness without cancelling differentiation. The "fluidity" in question, then, is at once the enduring of the self-identical independence of the original unity of objectivity, and it is the "substantial" whole whose parts are independent *(fürsichseiende),* i.e., independent yet organically interrelated members. As a result objectivity is no longer mere abstract being ("Doctrine of Being") nor abstract essentiality ("Doctrine of Essence"), but rather the fluid substance of pure movement within itself, which makes for dynamic concretion. The distinct parts in this whole, then, are simply moments in the pure movement of dynamic concretion (might one say once more "concrescence"?).[15]

Is all this utterly unintelligible? Well nigh. Perhaps, however, it will be possible to go back to the preface and there find the key (or keys) which will help to make what has been said not hopelessly obscure. There it is abundantly clear that, for Hegel, both unity without diversity and diversity without unity are equally unintelligible (Since paraphrasing Kant has become the mode, might we not say, "Unity without diversity is empty; diversity without unity is blind"?). It is also clear that the greatest obstacle to coming to terms in consciousness with reality is *fixedness,* whether it be the fixity of sensible reality or the fixity of the thoughts in which reality is conceptualized, hence "fluidity"; to let being be is to not let it be pinned down, to let the living whole which reality is reveal itself, and it is the function of human consciousness to enable reality to do precisely that.[16] Reality, then, reveals itself as an organic whole, each of whose parts is necessary to the whole. This means that reality shapes *(Gestaltung)* itself in the consciousness had of it; a consciousness which is not consciousness of the real is not consciousness, nor is a real which is unrelated to consciousness real; the relation is a two-way street. For this, however, an original unity of the totality of reality is not sufficient; it must break itself up in order to reintegrate itself in the unity of consciousness. Its forms *(Gestalten)* must reveal that they need each other in the formings *(Gestaltungen)* in the world of consciousness—which is the meaning of the oft-quoted remark that the true must be seen not only as substance but also as subject.[17] The key to this is to be found in the recognition that to know self, which is essential if there is to be knowing at all, it is equally essential to know self in knowing what is other than self. Thus, once again, the "fluidity," primarily of thoughts, which comes about when thought recognizes the immediately given as only a moment in the process of the self revelation of reality, which process cannot be, if truth is looked upon as "a minted coin" which can be kept in one's pocket without changing its value; the true simply does not stand still, it is a "bacchanalian revel" where all is constantly moving.

In both the preface and the passage we are examining it is clear that what Hegel is attempting to describe is the movement of consciousness toward knowing in the fullest sense of the term, *Wissenschaft*. In both, too, it is clear that *Wissenschaft* is possible only if reality is conceived of as "alive." What is more explicit, however, in the preface than in our passage is that the very life of the real is its concept, not the concept (or concepts) in any individual mind, or in the sum-total of individual minds, but the conceptual structure which constitutes the very lifeblood of reality. "Science can organize itself only through the concept's own life. In science there is the determinateness, which from the point of view of the schema is externally plastered on determinate being *(Dasein)* but which is [actually] the self-moving soul of the fulfilled content" *(PdG,* 44, 53). And, it is precisely because the real, its substance, is itself subject that the entire content of science is this subject's own reflection on itself—the self-revelation is reality's own reflection on itself, *in* thought. To know in the strict sense, then, is to comprehend the rationality of the real, what Hegel calls "the rhythm of the organic whole," which is but another way of saying the "concept" which is the "essence" of the content of thought (47, 56). It is in this sense, too, that we must understand the remark about the knower (philosopher) taking upon himself *"die Austren-*

gung des Begriffs" (48, 58). All of this bespeaks the dynamic character of that which knowing knows, not a conceptual form imposed by thinking, but the living concept vitalizing objective reality: "Insofar as the concept is the very self of the object *(Gegenstandes)*, the self which presents itself as the coming to be of the object, this self is not a passive subject which carries accidents without moving, but rather the concept moving itself and taking back into itself its determinations" (49, 60).[18] The language is hard to unravel, but says Hegel, that is as it should be, when the language in question is philosophical (52, 63).

To get back to the text we are examining, Hegel tells us that, although reality is not one single unified object but many objects, each independent *(für sich)*, nevertheless the independence *(Fürsichsein)* proper to a plurality of objects is just as much a reintegration *(Reflexion)* into an overall unity as it is a breaking up into independent forms *(Gestalten)*. The kind of unity in question, i.e., the unity proper to totality, is "absolutely negative or infinite unity," i.e., embracing all opposites as complementary moments.[19] Now, because this unity is the constant, differences of the plurality of objects make sense only within the overarching unity. Once more the emphasis is on the organicity of the whole, since the "fluidity" of the substantial whole is the continuity of the forms into which it has been broken up. As a result the unity in question is an "infinite" whole embracing the "independence" of both subjectivity and objectivity over against each other, and we are back again with the self-consciousness which is both subjective and objective.[20]

This, then, brings us to a new—perhaps the most important— question: how does the self come to grips with itself in its authentic selfhood and not simply as a particular instantiation *(Gestalt)* of selfhood? This question can be read in two ways: (1) How does the individual who is immediately conscious of itself come to authentic consciousness of self, which is not individual but universal (concretely)—the question Kant did not even ask: and (2) since all consciousness is *in truth* self-consciousness, how does human consciousness transcend its particularized manifestations *(Gestalten)* in order to culminate in a consciousness which is completely identified with self-consciousness in that the content of the one *is* the content of the other? The first of these questions will be answered in the movement subsequent to Chapter IV from individual reason to abstractly universal reason, from abstract reason to concretely universal reason in collective spirit, from merely collective spirit to absolute Spirit, the object of religious consciousness (i.e., religious self-consciousness), and from the realization, expressed representationally in religious consciousness, that only when finite spirit is embraced in absolute Spirit will it be authentically spirit and thus authentically self-consciousness and authentically rational, to the ultimate authentification of self-conscious spirit in a knowing which is absolute precisely because it has as its source the Absolute and because what it knows is absolute, which is, after all, what absolute knowing is. The answer to the second question will in a sense be the same as the answer to the first, though its focus will be different. Here the emphasis will be not on individual consciousness but on the particular manifestations *(Gestalten)* of consciousness, each of which in succession is to be recognized as only a moment in the process, to be superseded yet retained and lifted up to the ultimate synthesis of all the forms. Here, as will be clear to those familiar with the text we are examining, I have departed slightly from a detailed exegesis of the text in order to see it more emphatically as a transition to what is to follow. We can return to the text once more by pinpointing the theme of "life" as the organic process of wholeness realizing itself and as the quasi-organic process of consciousness becoming aware that to be conscious of this organic whole is to be wholly conscious of itself. This, of course, is anticipating, but since the interpretation of any step in the phenomenological process makes sense only from the vantage point of its culmination, it is legitimate to see in this transitional movement the adumbration of the whole route to be traveled, which will be true also of the introductory paragraphs of the "Philosophy of Spirit," which we shall see later—what is explicit at the end is already implicit in the beginning.

It is in this way that we can see the overall process at any stage along the way as, in Hegel's words, "the simple universal fluidity" which, so to speak, sorts itself out in the distinct forms it takes, each implying its other in the process. The distinct stages in the process are "other" than the process itself, but by the same token the overall process is "other" than the sum total of stages as distinct. None of this, however, is going to make sense, if it says nothing about the individuals in whom consciousness (self-consciousness) resides; hence the return of the emphasis on "appetite," which pertains to the individual as individual and constitutes a relationship to the object of consciousness completely different from the relationship of cognition. When Hegel speaks of the "limitless movement" which "devours" the fluid continuity of the process, he himself is seeing "life" as concretized in the "living being," which as such is individual and in whom the determinateness of the object is realized,[21] even though in the remainder of the chapter on "Self-Consciousness"—and indeed in the remainder of the *Phenomenology*—individuals turn out to be *types* (of consciousness) which may either be combined in one individual (e.g., master and slave) or characterize classes of individuals (e.g., unhappy consciousness).

In Chapter III, "Force and Understanding," Hegel had spoken of the abstract world which understanding constructs for itself as a "reversed" *(verkehrte)* world, whose characteristics could be the exact opposite of those of the real world, thus making it impossible for mere understanding to come to terms with reality as it is in itself. Here he speaks of a "reversal" *(Verkehrung)* which turns into "reversedness"—or, perhaps, "contrariness"—*(Verkehrtheit)* which clings to abstract universality which is not concretized through mediation of individuals, but by the same token he sees individuality as itself abstract if not sustained by the concrete universal of total interrelatedness and mutual complementarity. At this level we can say that the individual that recognizes itself as an operative factor in concrescence is on the way to realizing itself as a true self, whereas the individual that merely universalizes itself abstractly trails off into the indefinite "I," which is powerless to effect any determinateness. The individual cannot escape the universal (the life which embraces all that is living) which is essential to individuality, but it can lose itself in the direction of abstract universality instead of finding itself in the direction of concrete universality.[22] Individuals must be differentiated from each other, which they are in the concrete universal of complementarity, and which they are not in the abstract universal of indeterminacy (undifferentiated "fluidity"). There is, then, a distinguishing which unites, i.e., a distinguishing which is "articulation" *(Gliedern)*, and a distinguishing which merely separates. The former preserves, cancels, and elevates differences, the latter merely makes them indifferent. It is only with the former that the different moments of the total movement come together in a "forming" *(Gestaltung)* which is at the same time a transcending of any fixed "form" *(Gestalt)*—a transcending which is also an articulation. Back and forth it goes, and the whole is intelligible only as the putting together of all the distinct moments, a self-developing and a dissolution of development, a totality preserving itself in this movement which cannot be pinned down.

It may come as something of a surprise that not until this point (para. 7) is the activity of consciousness itself recognized explicitly as a form of life; is it not precisely in conjunction with consciousness that reality comes alive? The point, however, is that life and consciousness are not the same; to be alive is not necessarily to be conscious, even though to be conscious is to be alive. More than that the life of consciousness is other than the all-embracing life of which consciousness is conscious; to be conscious of its own life is something special, and it is proper to self-consciousness at a more advanced stage than the initial immediate "certainty" of self which yields no more than a vague "I." What emerges, then, is that in the consciousness of which self-consciousness is conscious there is a union of the manifestation *(Gestaltung)* of life *for* consciousness and the life *of* consciousness, a union which contributes to the ultimate identification of reality and thought. The process of concretizing the initial immediate consciousness of a mere "I" is well on its way. It will be a process of explicating the implications of self-consciousness as life. This will mean that, for consciousness to be fully aware of what it itself truly is, the otherness of life as simply the object of consciousness is to be *aufgehoben* in a process which is self-determination, the coming together of objectivity and subjectivity not simply by fiat. The danger is that the "I" be conceived of as merely abstractly universal—a kind of transcendental ego. The key to overcoming this danger is once again that the relation of consciousness to life as other (objective) passes from the merely cognitive to the appetitive (self-referential). Thus, certain of the nothingness of the other as simply *op-posite,* consciousness *posits* the other (the *of* of consciousness-of) as its own truth; it is related to its own truth in being related to its other as not simply independently other. This is but another way of saying that the self in recognizing its subjectivity as essentially related to objectivity (a sort of "intentionality"?) is objectified without its subjectivity being annihilated. The objectivity of the self is no longer merely immediate, a certainty; it is the truth of that certainty, having overcome the arbitrariness of mere positing.

It could well seem that at this point Hegel is becoming needlessly repetitious in once more ringing the changes on appetition, but it must be recognized that he is not simply saying the same things over again; what he now says takes on richer meaning by virtue of the development up to this point—appetition is revelatory of selfhood in a far more significant sense than initially. A subtle change occurs when Hegel tells us that what appetite desires is not so much the object in question as it is the desire for the satisfaction of appetite. This satisfaction can be attained, of course, in the consumption of the object, a negative relation to the object, but we must be ready to think too of an appetitive negative relation to the object which can be satisfied other than by consumption of the object. In any event, what is important is to recognize that satisfying appetite means both to experience the independence of the object desired and to experience the self as desiring. But, where the desired object is consumed, the satisfaction is temporary, and, thus, generates further appetite to be satisfied (see *EpW*, 428). Thus, both appetite and the certainty of self achieved in its satisfaction are conditioned by both the object of appetite and by the *Aufhebung* of the object—whether this be simply consuming it or in a more significant sense canceling its otherness, retaining it as object, and raising it to a higher level of significance—but the object can be *aufgehoben* only if it is more than an abstract object. More than that, the connection of appetition and self-consciousness is heightened by the realization that just as consuming the object means producing again the same appetite, so too the self-consciousness of subject-object cannot be achieved without relation to another object-subject—a self-conscious object.[23] By the same token, while it is the essence of appetite that it be in relation to what is other than the self, at the same time it must be oriented to the *Aufhebung* of otherness, if it is to be the affirmation of self. We are now faced with negation which is not the consumption of the other but self-negation which can be achieved only by another self. This brings with it the realization that a single self-consciousness makes no sense whatever—either more than one self-consciousness or none. Thus, self-consciousness becomes a sort of class designation, which, however, is not simply the expression of an abstract universal; a multiplicity of self-consciousness is significant only if they interact; the other self-consciousness is essential to the satisfaction of the appetite which triggers authentic self-consciousness—the trinitarian overtones are obvious.

All of this now permits Hegel to summarize the three "moments" proper to the "concept" of self-consciousness—not, be it noted, self-consciousness as simply the object of conceptual thinking, but the very rationale which makes self-conscious being to be what it is. Initially what consciousness is conscious of in being self-conscious is a pure undifferentiated "I"—no more than a vague awareness of being a subject which thinks and acts, a self immediately present to itself, with little, if any, awareness of what that implies. But, this immediacy, since it is a return from mere objectivity, is out-and-out ("absolute") mediation, since it is achieved through the *Aufhebung* of the independence of the object of appetite in the satisfaction of appetite, the awareness of self that satisfaction brings, the reflection into self which is inseparable from the satisfaction. This, Hegel tells us, is self-certainty realizing (inchoately?) its truth. Its truth (the process of becoming what it truly is) cannot stop there; only if there is a multiplication of the kind of reflection in question can the reflection make sense. Self-conscious being can be neither a mere object nor a mere subject; rather what is required is an object of consciousness which is another self-consciousness, which itself negates its mere objectivity. Each self-consciousness implies its other, and thus emerges the community of self-consciousnesses which is the very truth of self-consciousness. The world we previously saw "come alive" in consciousness cannot just be alive, just a living object, just an organic whole. It cannot be any of these, cannot be world, unless there be in it consciousness; consciousness and world are inseparable. By the same token, it is essential to consciousness that it be self-consciousness, and thus the very truth of world and consciousness, the all unifying "concept" is self-consciousness. The life of the world, then, is self-consciousness, and the life of self-consciousness is the concrete interrelationship of self-consciousnesses.[24]

It will be the task of the remaining chapters of the *Phenomenology of Spirit* to spell out the implications merely adumbrated in this transition from the abstractness of merely objective consciousness to the ultimate concreteness of the truth of all reality—spirit—"an *I* which is *we* and a *we* which is *I*," fully realized only in "absolute Spirit." Here, I think, we are inevitably sent to the ten opening paragraphs of the "Philosophy of Spirit" in the *Encyclopedia*, where in a most forceful way Hegel outlines what spirit is going to have to mean, if human knowing *(Wissenschaft)* is to come to terms with integral reality. As befits an introduction, what Hegel says here is only asserted, not proved; the proof is in the entire working out of the philosophy of Spirit.[25]

#377, *Zus.*: Knowing in the full sense *(Wissenschaft)* is the essential activity of spirit, but this knowing is truly knowing only as spirit's knowledge of itself. Thus, for spirit there is no "totally other" to be known. This is the teaching of religion and it applies paradigmatically to the infinite divine Spirit. The Christian doctrines of the Incarnation and of the indwelling of the Holy Spirit in the community, however, make it clear that the relation of the human spirit to infinite Spirit "has made possible comprehensive knowledge of spirit in its absolute infinity." This, then, becomes the goal of human endeavor.

#378, *Zus.:* The self-knowing in question, therefore, can make sense only as the self-manifestation of infinite Spirit, not, however, as though spirit were an entity which manifests itself; self-manifestation is the very being of spirit. Thus, even human knowing is not to be separated from the self-knowing of infinite Spirit in its fullness.

#379, *Zus.:* It will be seen as the end result of the philosophy of spirit (absolute Spirit) that the self-knowing of absolute Spirit, the absolute logical Idea, contains all truth. "Philosophy, then, must comprehend spirit as a necessary development of the eternal Idea and must allow what constitutes the particular parts of the science of spirit to unfold out of the very concept of spirit." Just as in the realm of the organic the seed is oriented to bringing forth the full-blown plant, so in the realm of spiritual activity spirit is oriented to bringing forth its own adequate concept, the concept of all concepts; "its goal has been attained when its concept has been completely actualized, which is to say when spirit has achieved complete consciousness of its own concept."

#381: So true is this that the truth of nature itself is to be found in spirit and in spirit alone, which is to say that only if, in knowing nature, spirit knows itself does it truly know nature.

#381, *Zus.:* This addition contains a further elaboration of what we saw in the addition to #379. The concept of spirit reveals spirit to be the self-knowing actual idea. It is philosophy's task to demonstrate that all conceptual knowledge is implicit in this. Thus, although philosophy of spirit has both logic and philosophy of nature as its presuppositions, neither of these can be validated short of the coping stone of the philosophy of spirit. Ultimately, then, philosophy is knowledge of spirit, or it is not knowledge at all. This is so, because only in spirit in the fullest sense does the concept succeed in overcoming both finitude and externality—obstacles to full-fledged knowing. It is the function of spirit in its own self-determining activity to internalize—idealize—what initially seems to it to be external, merely objective. This internalization—idealization—however, has to be more than the representational activity of finite spirit, as though the latter could *derive* its knowledge of all that spirit implies from a consideration of things; only the self-revelation of the absolute Spirit dwelling in external reality, who is also religion's object, can actualize this knowing. Finite spirit can *begin* its quest for knowledge by looking into itself, but it will find what it is looking for only in the knowing of absolute Spirit (both objective and subjective genitive), without whom this reality is not fully real.

#382, *Zus.:* It has often been objected that Hegel plays fast and loose with the principle of non-contradiction, but the objection is based on a misunderstanding of what Hegel means by contradiction. The spirit which is truly spirit is the fully self-determining spirit, not at all determined by what is other than itself. If, then, it finds its own thought determinations contradictory, it can tolerate the contradiction, precisely because, having posited the contradictories, it can resolve the contradiction; in fact, resolving the contradiction is the movement toward getting at the truth which the opposition in question signifies. This is what it means to say that spirit is free, self-determining; in what is given to it immediately it is not free, only in its appropriation of what is given, in producing it as its own *(proprium)* in thought is it free. Thus it is in thinking, producing its own thought determinations, that it liberates itself, and the process of spirit's development is the process of making itself free from whatever does not correspond to its concept, which is to say actualizing what it thinks in such a way as to transform seeming contradictions into forms thoroughly consistent with its concept. It, so to speak, makes use of contradiction to resolve contradictoriness.

#383, *Zus.:* To the extent that spirit corresponds adequately with its concept, then, it contains in itself the "possibility" of self-revelation, i.e., the manifestation of the truth of reality, and its activity is the actualization of that possibility. Only absolute Spirit, however, is the absolute unity of its actuality and its possibility, i.e., the resolution of contradiction.

#384: Nothing of what has been said will make sense unless it is possible to identify what is seen as other than spirit with the self-revelation of absolute Spirit, and that is what "creation" means. But, "creation" is not only the bringing into being of a world of nature; it is the bringing into being of that same world in thought.

#386: To bring this down to the level of finite spirit, it must be said that its being determined to knowledge of a world is not the work of its finitude but the work of Spirit in its infinity of which finite spirit is the active manifestation.

#386, *Zus.:* This, of course, means that finitude is not a fixed determination of spirit, beyond which it cannot go (as Kant would have it), but only a moment in the process of spirit's coming to the realization of what it truly is to be spirit. Spirit precisely *as* spirit is not finite, because the ideality which is spirit's defining characteristic cannot be confined within fixed boundaries; finitude, on the other hand, is only a reality not adequate to its concept, and spirit, even finite spirit, is adequate to its concept only in relation to infinite Spirit.

So much for Hegel's introduction to the philosophy of spirit. What does it tell us about the text we have been examining? It tells us that the self-consciousness whose "certainty" has been under scrutiny will know itself as what it truly is when it recognizes itself as spirit. There it will be able to emerge both from the illusions of sense which confine it to what is immediately given to it and from the emptiness of a suprasensible which is inferred as being out there, thus emerging into the spiritual light of the *Gegenwart*, which is both the "present" (of developed spirit) and "presence" (of infinite Spirit).

Notes

1. Richard Norman, *Hegel's Phenomenology: A Philosophical Introduction*, New York: St. Martin's Press, 1976, p. 46.

2. The presupposition here is that, from the very beginning, what is being traced is the emergence of human consciousness which is simply not a function of nature. The transition under investigation, then, is not merely to self-consciousness but to reason, which is objective in a way that mere understanding is not.

3. What will gradually become clear in the grasp of the truth which replaces mere certainty is that the true for consciousness is not something other than the consciousness had of it. Thus, the truth is to be found *in* consciousness, not *over-against* it; the *Gegen-stand* is not *outside* consciousness.

4. See M. J. Petry, *G. W. F. Hegel: The Berlin Phenomenology*, London: Reidel, pp. 62–63. The text in question is from the notes of Major Giesheim who, Petry tells us, took down Hegel's lectures practically verbatim, here as an addition to *EpW*, 424. Future references to this text will be placed in parentheses in the text.

5. To be objective is to be *for* a subject which is other than the object. Where, however, the object is the concept itself, its "otherness" constitutes a distinction which is not a distinction. It will gradually become clear that,

for Hegel, this will ultimately make sense only when the subject in question is "absolute."

6. We see here the first emergence of spirit as more than an empty "I." Spirit here is standing, as it were, on the threshold of a series of experiences which will gradually reveal both a world and the self which is spirit as the actuality of that world. Granted, the term "Spirit" does not yet appear.

7. In the words of Merold Westphal, "It is tautology because it expresses identity without difference. It is motionless because the mediating process between self and other has been excluded" (*History and Truth in Hegel's Phenomenology*, New Jersey: Humanities Press, 1979, pp. 125–26).

8. The point is that, as Hegel sees it, consciousness is activity (subjective), and being is activity (objective), and the activity is one and the same. This is but another way of identifying the vital process of the real becoming actual and the conceptual process of comprehending the real, where both share in the dynamic life of the Concept.

9. Although, it is true, the majority of commentators translate *Begierde* as "desire," the somewhat weaker term "appetite" seems preferable, precisely because Hegel is referring only to an initial move outward toward the object, which involves an inchoate recognition of selfness on the part of the subject appetitively related to the object of cognitive consciousness. The "I" implicit in wanting is more concrete than the "I" of cognizing.

10. Concrete reality, then, analyzes itself. In abstract thought the real becomes unreal, dies only to be vitalized in self-conscious spirit. The dead object whose analysis is posited in abstract thinking becomes the living subject which differentiates itself.

11. This is an extremely important point in Hegel's position: the thinking subject does not impose determination on its object; its relationship to the objectively real is one of continuity, allowing the real to determine itself by turning back (reflecting) on itself.

12. It is practically a truism that the only world consciousness can deal with is the world it finds when it looks into itself. It is anything but a truism, however, that consciousness will not be able to look into itself without the mediation of appetite. Still less is it a truism—in fact it can seem a contradiction—that consciousness as merely cognitive can find no way to negate the otherness of its object and thus come to terms with it. The world of objectivity, then, is a world vitalized in the consciousness had of it, which can then sort itself out in our activity which is at once different from and identical with the activity of consciousness. It is this

activity of the world in consciousness which is the actuality of the world as world and of consciousness as self.

13. Understanding can fragment its world by positing fixed distinctions which are its own work only. Reason, on the other hand, can dissolve the fixity of posited distinctions, thus permitting "flowing" reality to determine itself, which is to say, manifest its determinacy in the actuality (activity) which is consciousness.

14. This is, it would seem, needlessly obscure, nor does Hegel enlarge on it. It is obvious enough that space and time are inseparable—we can, with Kant, call them the necessary conditions of experience—and in this sense we can, presumably, say that they condition the objectivity of experience. If, then, the consciousness of a world and the consciousness of self are continuous, then the space-time matrix is inseparable from both. For Hegel, of course, space and time are not merely necessary forms of subjective experiencing.

15. To be concrete is to be alive, to be self-determining, mutually co-determining. "Aber ihre [der Formen] flüssige Natur macht sie Zugleich zu Momenten der organischen Einheit, worin sie sich nicht nur nicht widerstreiten, sondern eins so notwendig als das andere ist, und diese gleiche Notwendigkeit macht erst das Leben des Ganzen aus" (PdG, 10, 2). In all references to the text of the *Phenomenology (PdG)* the first number designates the page in the Hoffmeister edition, the second designates the paragraph in Miller's English translation.

16. "Es ist aber weit schwerer, die festen Gedanken in Flüssigkeit zu bringen, als das sinnliche Dasein" (PdG, 30, 33). *Gedanken* becomes *flüssig* when thought as merely unmediated recognizes itself as a "moment" in the overall process (PdG, 31, 33).

17. "Dadurch überhaupt, dass, wie oben ausgedrückt warde, die Substanz an ihr selbst Subjekt ist, ist aller Inhalt seine eigene Reflexion in sich" (PdG, 45, 53).

18. In a certain sense the thinking subject could be said to discover the objective determinations of reality. In a more important sense, for Hegel, the determinations are contained in the concept which reveals itself and its determinations in rational thought.

19. A totality of selfness (ultimately "absolute") to which corresponds a world as totality (the real).

20. Hegel definitively rejects the Kantian contention that a finite subject can have only a finite object. In a sense Hegel bases this rejection on Kant's own principle that practical reason can, so to speak, have the infinite as its object. More importantly, however, Hegel contends that the infinite object infinitizes the subject, since finite and infinite are continuous.

21. Remembering, of course, that individuality is concrete only as sustained in the concrete universal, which is subject rather than only substance.

22. Concrete universality ultimately betokens the concrete totality of interrelatedness. There is a sense in which any concept in its truth is such a totality, and there is a sense in which there is a world of absolute totality, which, it would seem, is possible only for a consciousness which is absolute, i.e., absolute Spirit, and absolute knowing, which is philosophy's goal, is a sharing in absolute knowing.

23. Hence it is nonsense to speak (or think) of a self-consciousness in isolation. There can be self-consciousness, it is true, only if consciousness is both subject and object, but it must be at once object for itself and for another consciousness which is also self-consciousness. Once again, the trinitarian foundations for Hegel's thought are obvious. There can be spirit at all, only if there is absolute Spirit, and absolute Spirit bespeaks a plurality of relatedness.

24. Hegel's *Phenomenology of Spirit*, then, is more than just a preamble to his "system," more than a *Wissenschaft der Erfahrung des Bewusstseins;* it is the masterplan for the study of spirit, for the whole of philosophy, and it is the constant underpinning, without which the entire system would be unintelligible—philosophy, for Hegel, *is* the study of spirit, and the study of spirit is the study of the totality of reality, which lives the life of spirit.

25. We should remind ourselves at this point that "proof" does not mean for Hegel what it means for the natural scientist, the mathematician, or the formal logician. One would, in fact, look in vain in the whole of Hegel's system for formal-logical entailment in the sense in which we understand it. For Hegel proof is the gradual explication of what is implicit in what we cannot but think, cannot but know. It is the progressive self-revelation of the real in the consciousness had of it. It may well be that we can refuse this kind of proof; we may refuse to call knowing what is not proved in a more exact way; but it may also be that the price we risk paying for this kind of knowing is the trivializing of knowledge itself.

Ernest Wolf-Gazo
UNIVERSITY OF MÜNSTER

Negation and Contrast: The Origins of Self-Consciousness in Hegel and Whitehead

Both Whitehead and Hegel seem to agree that consciousness is a form of human experience. The essential difference between the two philosophers at the outset is that Hegel considers consciousness as a *necessary* expression of Mind, while for Whitehead consciousness is merely a *possible* form of human experience. For Whitehead, it is of utmost importance in attempting to construct an "organic" philosophy that the idea of possibility take on an *ontological categoriality*, in order to account for the phenomenon of novelty (or better, creativity). Consciousness, in the Whiteheadian context, is but one possible form of novelty in the world and thus contributes to creativity in the form of judgement, evaluation, intuition, or simple reflective awareness.

It is possible to show, to a certain extent, that Hegel's notion of consciousness comes close to some aspects of what Whitehead describes in Part III, Chapter V of *Process and Reality* as "The Higher Phases of Experience." I would like to examine the question of how such Whiteheadian "higher phases of experience" might be accounted for in Hegel's system.

I

Hegel proposes that real knowledge is only possible in the form of a *System of Wissenschaft* (*Phänomenologie des Geistes*, Vorrede). Yet, in order to arrive at the standpoint of Wissenschaft, we must, according to Hegel "work at it" (herausarbeiten). We must work ourselves out of the chaos of immediacy (Unmittelbarkeit) and up to a higher level of conceptuality (Begrifflichkeit; cf. *Wissenschaft der Logik* II, 242ff.). Immediate sense perception for Hegel does not qualify as real knowledge, in contrast to Whitehead, who considers the immediacy of "presentationalism" (as we might call it) an abstract perceptive act. For according to Whitehead, in "presentational immediacy" the perceiver is already engaged in the network of geometrical formation.

The Hegelian understanding of immediate experience can be equated with Whitehead's notion of *causal efficacy*. However, the epistemological value and the ontological status of immediate experience (or causal efficacy) differ in Hegel and Whitehead. Reaching the heights of immediate experience in the form of real knowledge in Hegel's System means *work* (Arbeit): it means education (Bildung) as a *program* of work (Bildung als Arbeit); it means, that the human organism has to develop its perspective from an apparent "useless" immediate experience to the heights of consciousness, self-consciousness, and Mind (absoluter Geist). The fact that the ontological as well as the epistemological values of immediate experience are evaluated differently by Hegel and Whitehead affects their respective perspectives regarding the phenomenon of consciousness. Hegel considers consciousness a necessary precondition for genuine and fully determinate actuality, while Whitehead regards consciousness (and especially self-consciousness) only as a *possibility* in the world—a possibility among many alternatives amidst the wide spectrum of human experience.

II

An essential notion for the interpretation of Hegel's System is the function of Negation (*Logik* I, 35–38; 100–102; II, 494–499). The act of negation is a self-conscious mental act exclusively in Hegel; whereas for Whitehead such self-conscious acts are included within the scope of the theory of prehension, but negative prehension is not limited exclusively to this class of acts. For Hegel, negation is a systematic treatment of the overcoming of contradictions in the world. For Whitehead, in contrast, negation is a manifestation of mental cogitation within the wide spectrum of man's mental activities. For Whitehead, conscious negation is one form of the possible "higher phases of experience," but not the exclusive case, since bare perceptive acts may themselves exhibit features of negative prehension.

The background of the Hegelian notion of negation can help us more fully to appreciate its function not only in Hegel's system, but also in Whitehead's categorial scheme in terms of *Contrast*. In order to come to terms with Hegel's notion of negation we must briefly examine Hegel's critique of Spinoza (cf. *Vorlesungen über die Geschichte der Philosophie*, III, 157–197). According to Hegel, thinking as self-consciousness cannot be accounted for in Spinoza's monistic substance-attribute theory. Thought must be an attribute of Substance, according to Spinoza; yet, attributes do not exhibit the essential characteristic of self-reflectivity. Thinking entails negation for Hegel, and such activity cannot take place in Spinoza's system since (according to Hegel) there is no possibility of accounting for the necessary transference between substance and its attribute of thought. Spinoza might conceive of this transference as a kind of *passive* negation—a conscious negation of something other (ein Anderes), but *not* of consciousness itself. But, according to Hegel, it is the activity of *self* negation which is the essential and defining characteristic of self consciousness. Hence, Spinoza's substance-theory is unable to account for the most characteristic feature of subjectivity.

The logic of the negation of something other is merely a sequence of negations: A, being the negation of B, while the negation B is A; the negation of A and B together is C, the negation of C is D, the negation of D is C; the negation of C and D together is E; and so on. In every item of the universe there is a contradiction to be unravelled—in Spinoza's famous dictum, "Omnis determinatio est negatio" (All determination implies negation). Yet, Spinoza's system itself merely exhibits a structure of geometrical relatedness, which is neither dialectical nor negative. Spinoza lacks, as it were, the one essential element of the Hegelian system: the notion of a dynamic, creativity activity of negation.

One of Hegel's central presuppositions is that every basic principle has its own contradiction. Thus, the negative behavior of a reflecting subject initiates the negative *activity* of negation. However, this subject needs a mediation (Vermittlung) in order to arrive at the moment where the subject develops its own momentum in terms of reflection (Reflexion an sich selbst) as *pure* negativity. For instance, Whitehead's human organism, seen against this Hegelian background, is itself already a mediation of contrasts between consciousness and non-consciousness, between the simple and the complex structures constituting the organism. The experience of the Whiteheadian organism is manifold and multifarious—as also is the case with organic human experience according to Hegel. But the Hegelian organism always requires *mediation* in order to channel the chaotic impressions of immediate experience into the mold of reason.

Hegel's conception of a human being is basically expressed in terms of the Aristotelian definition as "animal rationale." In that sense Hegel was a traditionalist. The embryo is a *Mensch an sich*, but not yet *für sich*, for the *Mensch für sich* can be defined *only* in terms of "die gebildete Vernunft"—which is in turn the product of *Arbeit an sich*. This work-in-itself qualifies as Reality (Wirklichkeit). This disciplined, formative process of work *an sich* is purposive and teleologically structured. There is the "Arbeit" which is pure purposive action (zweckmässiges Tun) which, however, can be carried out even at the relatively undeveloped stage of immediate subjectivity (bare, unreflective consciousness). The stage of *Vernunft*, however, turns out to be identified with pure negativity—what Hegel terms *Being-for-itself* (Fürsichsein). The development of pure negativity makes possible the dialectical process of Becoming at the level of "Geist," and it is this dynamic and dialectical process of pure negativity which characterizes human subjective experience (the Self). Selfhood is that "higher phase of experience" which inaugurates the realm of genuine self-consciousness as pure *Fürsichsein*.

Again, Hegel pointed out that in Spinoza's system, Substance and its attributes do not account for the specific nature concatenating Negation and Contradiction. Spinoza's principle "Determinatio est negatio" is translated by Hegel as "Bestimmtheit ist Negation" (*Logik* I, 100; II, 164). In Spinoza, according to Hegel, we find only the aspect of *simple* negation of one substance as an exemplification of the manifold of the accidence of that very substance. Hegel suggests that this exhibits a static view of the nature of things—when what is wanted is a *transformation* of static Spinozistic Substance into a dynamics of Subjectivity involving Negation. Hegel here proposes his famous formula "Negation of Negation" (*Logik* II, 166). It is in this so-called "double negation" that we find Hegel's fulcrum for his theory of the dynamic development of Geist through self-negation.

Spinoza, by contrast, cannot explain how the determinate modes of Substance are themselves constituted out of undifferentiated Substance itself. Indeed, as a pantheist Spinoza is unable to avail himself of an external standpoint from which (as it were) to gain the necessary leverage to activate his objective reality. Lacking both an external "first cause" beyond itself, and an internal dynamic power of self-differentiation (such as Hegel's power of double negation), Spinoza's substance must remain forever lifeless, inactive, and indeterminate—substance which can never be "subject" as well. Thus, Hegel's theory of "double negation" was intended to overcome this perceived deficiency in Spinoza by accounting for the dynamic self-generation of the Determinate Modes (Bestimmungen). World history as the self development of Spirit thus has its beginning in double negation: conceptualization is basically a diachronic affair. The process of thought itself is enmeshed in contrary phases of thinking. Positing and negating—whereby the substance is transformed into the subject in terms of "Ansich" and "Fürsich"—is the activity of consciousness which is itself rendered the object of conscious reflection, through which self-consciousness or cognition can be understood to evolve. This cognition is heightened into absolute knowing (*absolutes* Wissen), or conceptualized knowing (*begreifendes* Wissen), which is the highest exemplification of the Concept in-itself as well as for-itself (Begriff an und für sich).

Through this exemplification of the natural movement of the concept (Begriff) in terms of "An-sich-sein," Hegel achieves a conceptualization of the world. The Concept turns out to be the structure of thought itself and the process thereof portrays Hegel's version of "nature in the making." Thus, Hegel's concepts are "snapshots" of a world in the making. Mind in itself is only a transitory phase in this process of conceptualization, which never rests but always moves on, achieving its final goal of "absolutes Wissen" in the form of "begreifendes Wissen"—expressed in terms of Art, Religion, and ultimately Philosophy. In modern terms we might classify Hegel's as a theory of "meta-knowledge" attained through the process of "double conceptualization," namely, the knowledge of knowledge, or (in Hegel's terms) "die Negation der Negation."

III

In view of this interpretation of Hegel's theory of the development of self-consciousness, we can see that Whitehead was attempting also to solve the problem of the emergence and development of consciousness through his theory of prehension. For one of the most essential problems in Whiteheadian metaphysics is the evolution and ontological status of consciousness within the prehension theory. But, how *does* consciousness arise in the acts of prehension? We have noted that in Hegel's thought we find the quintessential function of negation which accounts for the emergence of novelty solely in terms of conceptual thought, which Whitehead does not accept. Do we find nonetheless a notion equivalent to Hegel's negation within Whitehead's scheme?

I would like to propose that Hegel's notion of "negation" seems to have an equivalent in Whitehead's last category of existence, namely *Contrast*. Whitehead describes Contrast as "Modes of Synthesis of Entities in one Prehension, or patterned Entities" (PR 33). He adds, "The eighth category includes an indefinite progression of categories, as we proceed from 'contrasts' to 'contrasts of contrasts,' and on indefinitely to higher grades of contrasts."

This description of Contrast seems to have its analogy in Hegel's Negation. We might also speak, for example, of an "indefinite progression" of negations of negations encompassing everything from immediate experience to absolute knowledge. For Whitehead, contrasts of contrasts actually involve all sorts of experiences— anything from simple sensation to the most sophisticated of those "higher phases of experience" characteristic of human experience.

We find an even more Hegelian tone in Whitehead's thinking if we follow the account of feelings, prehensions, subjective forms, and the categories of the scheme themselves. The categories of existence, for example, also share this characteristic of indefiniteness in terms of the types of possible feelings, which are indefinite in number "according to the complexity of the initial data which the feeling integrates, and according to the complexity of the objective datum which it finally feels" (PR 354). Prehensions are also indefinite in number, "overlapping, subdividing, and supplementary to each other" (PR 359), as are the evolution of subjective forms which exhibit the emergence of prehensions in terms of emotions, valuations, and judgement (PR 108). Finally, the categories themselves are endless in number—although Whitehead restricts himself somewhat arbitrarily to eight categories of existence and twenty-seven categories of explanation.

Yet, in the seventeenth category of explanation, Whitehead gives us a hint as to the nature of the relationship between the categories and the notion of Contrast:

That whatever is a datum for a feeling has a unity as felt. Thus *the many components of a complex datum have a unity: this unity is a 'contrast' of entities.* In a sense this means that there are an *endless number of categories of existence,* since *the synthesis of entities into a contrast in general produces a new existential type.* For example, a proposition is, in a sense, a 'contrast.' . . . The most important of such 'contrasts' is *the 'affirmation-negation' contrast* in which a proposition and a nexus obtain synthesis in one datum, the members of the nexus being the 'logical subjects' of the proposition. (PR 36; my emphasis)

Clearly, if we read these Whiteheadian passages carefully we do find some striking analogies: specifically, structures woven into the whole fabric of the categorial scheme of *Process and Reality* which resemble the function and nature of Hegel's "Negation." Particularly, the "affirmation-negation" contrast exhibits a form of Whiteheadian higher phases of experience resembling Hegel's process of "double negation." Both operations are logical in function but ontological in import. An Hegelian negation may appear in the form of a "feeling of negation" (PR 244) eliciting consciousness in terms of a "negative perception" such as suggested by Whitehead's example of "perceiving this stone as *not* grey" (PR 245). For perceiving this stone as grey means (in Whitehead's terms) that there is an "ingression" of one particular eternal object or form of definiteness taking place (to the deliberate exclusion of other possibilities) so as to formulate a determinate experience (or judgement of experience) in one of many possible worlds.

IV

The nature of negation for Hegel involves dynamism in the forms of thought exclusively, while for Whitehead "negation" may involve feelings in terms of awareness of contrasts. In Hegel's worldview, thought becomes conceptual and thereby perpetuates the process of thinking. Negation is reality as actuality. Hegel impresses upon us that there is no such thing as "pure positivity," as we might call it. For "pure positivity" is a myth created by those who claim that the observer of the world is just a passive bystander in the world of ontological affairs. The observer, in fact, is an integral component of the natural world; negation takes on the role of the devil's advocate. The observer will never be permitted to rest and will be pressed to attain absolute truth, while every provisional candidate for "absolute truth" is revealed as mere fiction. Negation attains a universal categorization turned into a necessary operation giving birth to a new concept and thereby a new object. It is a logical operation with ontological import. The simple mode of negativity reflects the structure of self-consciousness, while "real" negativity exhibits the dialectical process of consciousness in the world. It is negativity *as a unity* of the negative as well as the positive which addresses what Whitehead considered the essential problem of a natural philosophy—"the bifurcation of nature" (or, as Hegel called it "Entzweiung und Zerissenheit").

Negativity posits, preserves, negates, and sublates the entities that constitute the world.

Such a description also holds true of Whitehead's notion of Contrast, applicable particularly to the area of aesthetics and the philosophy of art. Yet, there is an essential difference between Hegel and Whitehead on this point. For Hegel, self-conscious thinking has inherited exclusively the function of negation, while for Whitehead, negation is already present in simple perception, which takes place in the form of differentiation, configuration, contrasting, and mainly in the process of Gestalt. Whitehead's reality is contrastive; while Hegel's reality lies in the cradle of dialectic as a process of negativity. Basically speaking, we may say that Spinoza's Substance, dynamized, turns out to be Hegelian "Mind" inaugurating adventures of ideas.

In Whitehead there is no simple contrast possible, but always a contrast of contrasts. Likewise, in Hegel's worldview, there seems to be no simple or isolated act of negation possible, for there always follows another negation, a "negation of negation." It seems that the essence of contradiction lies in the very interdependence of the relevant entities in question. It is, perhaps, the secret of Hegel and Whitehead that they discovered the nature of contradiction in the world, each in his own way: the one in terms of negation, the other in terms of contrast. In the last analysis Hegel holds on to the maxim that the World as Reality is Rational, while Whitehead responds that what is Real *can* and *may* be rational, but need not be. Yet, the whole is a circle of process constituted through separation and contradiction on the one hand, and, on the other hand, reconciliation and reunification—basic "ontic motions" steeped in negations and contrasts aiming teleologically towards Geist, conceived in terms of the Absolute, or, in terms of the philosophy of organism, Mind prehending itself.

References

Alfred North Whitehead, *Process and Reality.* New York: Macmillan, 1929.

G. W. F. Hegel, *Phänomenologie des Geistes.* Eds. W. Bonsiepen and R. Heede. Band 9, der Rheinisch-Westfälischen Akademie der Wissenschaften, Gesammelte Werke. Hamburg: Meiner Verlag, 1980.

———. *Wissenschaft der Logik.* Eds. F. Hogemann and W. Jaeschke. Band 11/12, Gesammelte Werke. Hamburg: Meiner Verlag, 1978/1981.

———. *Vorlesungen über die Geschichte der Philosophie (III).* Frankfurt: Suhrkamp Verlag (Band 20), 1971.

IV

Moral, Aesthetic,
and Religious Experience

Thomas Auxter
UNIVERSITY OF FLORIDA

The Process of Morality

> Reality is not what it is.
> It consists of the many realities
> which it can be made into.
> *Wallace Stevens*

I

The process of morality begins with the first experience of discord and ends with a specific resolution to bring into existence a new way of acting. Between the beginning and the end, and to the extent that a real change is sought, one must appeal to principles which allow a separation of what is desirable from what is not. Here lies both opportunity and danger. The opportunity is to conceive of, and publicly agree upon, a new structure for social relations that precludes the frustrations in past ways of acting at the same time as it expands the range and depth of experiences. The danger is that 'good' and 'bad', or 'right' and 'wrong', may harden into tablets of stone restricting behavior so severely that even development is thwarted. When guidelines for fulfillment within a specific context of struggle and change degenerate into codifications of behavior expected of all people at all times, the process of moral experience changes from a quest for the good life to an endurance test to see who can best live within extreme limitations. In this case morality becomes a self-frustrating process and terminates without reaching its end.

When we look back into the Western philosophical tradition from the vantage point of the twentieth century, we typically find three radically different approaches or schools of thought that purport to make sense of moral experience. Textbooks conveniently sort these out for us and deliver suitably idealized versions of teleological, deontological, and utilitarian ethics. Commentators usually leave the impression that these three schools of thought are incommensurable and that these schools offer competing approaches no one of which is free of anomalies or capable of covering all of the hard cases. In this reconstruction of the Western moral tradition there has been a decided tendency to treat each of the three basic approaches to morality as if it were unequivocally delineated *sub specie eternitatis*. The premise has been that there is one correct ethical position that is timelessly true. Corollaries are that the correct position is incompatible with other ethical positions which are understood as essentially different, that any position permitting historical and cultural variations in moral values invites relativism, and that the correct position is directly applicable to all societies and cultures at all times. Ironically, the pedagogical effect of this standard academic survey of the Western moral tradition is to confirm a skepticism about values among students who, as the immediate recipients of a culture shaped by positivism, are prepared to be skeptical about "value judgments" anyway. Indeed, if we assume that the correct ethical position is timelessly binding on everyone (the exclusive basis for eliciting commitments, conscripting resources, and mobilizing energies), an emphasis on differences in the moral tradition should foster skepticism. Such differences are insurmountable in the eternal present, i.e. without reference to history and change, because there can be no process of mediation to reconcile them. Furthermore, those with anthropological sensitivities will be irritated to find a culturally-conditioned formulation of morality presented as a universal requirement and will likely perceive this ethnocentric posturing as evidence against the claim that there is any universal sense of morality whatsoever.

When ethical positions are presented as cross-culturally invariant and incompatible with alternative positions, the result is a dilemma concerning the acceptability of moral values. While it is possible to construe this dilemma as an inescapable result once individuals in an "age of analysis" come to terms with their failure to locate and agree upon a source of value, it is also possible to construe the dilemma as resulting from an age peculiarly prone to adopting ahistorical perspectives—even when it examines materials from other periods. Such an age will be more likely to consider the alternative formulations of morality produced by different societies at different times as competitors in an on-going debate over what is eternally true rather than as historically-conditioned articulations of a fundamental sense of what the moral life is about. Speculation about why our age has developed in this way would have to include consideration of the early false promises of the natural sciences (giving rise to positivism), the impact of industrialization (reinforcing the notion that specialization is the path to knowledge), and the continuing influence of the inverted moral world passed on to us by the Victorians (so that morality becomes the will to limitation rather than the desire for fulfillment, and we must repeatedly explain why anyone would want to be moral). Although there is not room here to go further into the causes of this twentieth-century phenomenon, it is interesting to note that the more we inquire into causes the more we discover that the prevailing conception of morality is linked to what the historical process has been. This should provide an additional incentive for turning to philosophers who explore the connection between morality and history.

II

It is one of the manifold ironies of the age that information proliferates as never before and that anti-intellectualism is rampant. No doubt contemporary attitudes toward the intellect have something to do with the uses to which the intellect has been put in recent times. A world using information to make nuclear weapons—with nations threatening universal annihilation if others do not conform to requirements—creates an example hard to ignore when evaluating the tendencies to which the intellect contributes. In general, the specter of reason inventing and producing every conceivable implement of control and destruction makes it difficult to appreciate the claim that there is an essential connection between reason and the good life, or between reason and morality. It seems more obvious that reason is a threat to the decent treatment of others when reason is so often the instrument for sharpening plowshares into swords.

But beginning with Plato, the major moral philosophers in the West have held that reason is central to the pursuit of the highest good for human life and that it is a serious mistake to transform reason into a supposedly neutral instrument capable of promoting any end. In this sense, Western moral philosophy is "a series of footnotes to Plato." When Plato discusses the highest good in the *Philebus* he introduces a method of amplification which becomes the prototype for the process of moral evaluation.[1] The method, which is sometimes called "the method of isolation," demands that one ask of any given candidate for the highest good whether human life could take place on this basis alone, with no other features or dimensions added to it, and be wholly satisfying, with nothing missing and no nagging frustrations. If not, then the candidate should be amplified by whatever else it would take to make human life the most complete it could be. The process of amplification continues until we arrive at a conception of the highest good that is in no way constricting and provides for unimpeded activity and fulfillment. Of course, if this were some eclectic assortment of heterogeneous goods, we would have no way of assuring that the pursuit of one would not interfere with the pursuit of others. Reason is essential for a process of adjusting desires to one another. Through this process of mediation, whereby we determine what we want and how much we want it, reason guides us to the satisfaction of "the deepest wish of the soul." Reason is central to the process of evaluating norms for experience because it adjusts human values to each other and steers us away from overly general conceptions of the good that unnecessarily rule out other important values.

In this process of evaluation implicit in the ampliative method the values of autonomy and community become pivotal. As Plato suggests in the *Sophist*, that which is a function of a more basic, independent mode of being—an epiphenomenon—is less substantial than a self-determining being.[2] In the *Metaphysics*, Aristotle puts forward this same doctrine in terms of the concept of self-sufficiency.[3] Although these observations are offered in the context of metaphysical discussions, they have direct relevance to the status of the value of autonomy in the moral life. Indeed, much of the discussion of the ethical life in Greek philosophy revolves around this concept. Mere compliance with a moral code advanced by others, i.e., becoming a moral epiphenomenon, cannot be an authentic moral achievement. What makes human beings special, and what needs addressing, is the power of coming to decisions autonomously. It is not enough that people come to the *right* conclusion; they must come to it in their own ways and for reasons they can appreciate. Consequently we find in Greek ethics a heavy emphasis on deliberation as a process of forming judgments.

Yet within the context of the rational pursuit of the highest good, autonomy cannot be an exclusive value. Because Plato frequently resorts to myth when he wants to find a way to express the most general and profound truths, it is instructive to consider Platonic myths that bear on the interconnection between autonomy and community. In the *Phaedrus*, for example, we find the spectacle of souls that are crude and clumsy in their pursuit of the highest good trampling on and mutilating one another in the effort to get there while those with knowledge settle into patterns and rhythms emphasizing the natural affinities among beings.[4] The implication is that egoism and isolated individualism are not only *not* paths to the highest good; these patterns of selfishness and exclusivity are self-defeating as well. Likewise, in the *Republic*, the myth of the cave and the myth of Er emphasize community as a central value.[5] Those who climb out of the cave must return to assist others. Those who, in the cosmic lottery, draw the lots of tyrants and other self-indulgent and abusive characters are destined to discover that omnivorous appetites bring with them a life of violence and misery. In Aristotle's writings similar points are made in discussions of friendship and of the nature of the *polis*.[6] The conclusion is that reason cannot coherently be used to enforce autonomy *qua* separation; reason adjusts autonomy and community to each other through a process of deliberation.

The centrality of the values of autonomy and community in the rational pursuit of the highest good through an ampliative method constitutes the core of a moral tradition that continues through the modern period in philosophy. I will illustrate this point by referring to two modern philosophers, Kant and Mill, who have illuminated fundamental aspects of the moral life to an extent sufficient for whole schools of moral thought to grow out of their work.

Because it has been common, until very recently, to ignore or dismiss the teleological elements in Kant's thought, and indeed to present Kant as the paradigm case of a deontological (anti-teleological) moral philosopher, it may seem odd to place him in the same tradition with Greek ethical thinkers. We are all familiar with the image of Kant as the stern moralist who cares only about "duty for duty's sake." In this view Kant is a "rigorist" who believes we should do the right thing exclusively from the motive of love of duty and regardless of the consequences. This means that happiness cannot be a primary goal in life and that we must await an afterlife for virtue to be rewarded with happiness. If this interpretation were correct, it would be impossible to locate Kant in a tradition accepting as legitimate a variety of human desires and satisfactions and holding that right actions must be adjusted to one another for a fully moral world to emerge. However, as I have argued elsewhere,[7] Kant is not a "dispositional rigorist" who claims there is only one legitimate motive—nor is he a "procedural rigorist" who claims that certain general types of action are simply right and ought to be performed regardless of the consequences. On the contrary, he puts forward a teleological conception of the organization of emotional dispositions (based on the integrity of the good will) instead of a mechanical conception in which the love of duty suppresses other motives. Furthermore, the universalization procedure presupposes reference to an historical context in which actions occur, allows for right actions to reflect differences in context, and requires a continuity in choices of action (as opposed to viewing each action as a discrete, isolated choice between right and wrong). Happiness need not be deferred to another life; it is organized in this life on the basis of the human moral identity. Unfortunately, commentators have focussed on Kant's otherworldly summum bonum, which does not even meet Kant's own specifications for an ideal that can guide practical judgment.[8] They have thereby deflected attention from Kant's alternative conception of the highest good as both ectypal world and realms of ends and have reinforced the stereotype of Kant as a rigorist who cares only about purity of will (to be rewarded in an afterlife) and will not adjust values to one another in this life. I have argued, on the other hand, that in emphasizing the importance of the good will Kant is making sure that questions of the attractiveness of a proposal for the highest good do not obscure questions of autonomy and respect for others.[9] In a way, he is warning us about a precaution we should take when applying the method of amplification: while completeness is desirable, it cannot be simply an assortment of wishes projected by superficial beings inspired by narrowly-defined possibilities of gratification. In the world of experience, breadth and depth are correlative notions; only those choices deeply consistent with human autonomy can do justice to the breadth of experience in the good life. Kant's ectypal world and realm of ends give us a better sense of the relationship between autonomy and community than do his arguments about a transcendent highest good. This interpretation of what is most fundamental in Kant also has the advantage of allowing us to appreciate his continuity with the moral tradition.

If it stretches the credulity of the twentieth-century reader to view Kant in this light, it will surely seem farfetched to place Mill in a line of succession with Plato, Aristotle, and Kant. After all, doesn't Mill open the door to hedonism, in spite of all his talk about qualitative differences between pleasures? How can this square with either the classical emphasis on character development or the idea that morality should constrain people from violating the rights of others? Yet, there has been a tendency recently, among utilitarian commentators, to discount the interpretation of happiness as pleasure and to read Mill in terms of the concept of the greatest balance of good consequences over bad consequences. The advantage of this reading is that it allows us to appreciate Mill's approach to moral reasoning while at the same time leaving open the possibility of a pluralistic conception of the diverse values that might count as good. Thus we can attend to procedures for making comparisons and to a number of important moral insights without getting bogged down in a debate about the nature and status of pleasure in moral theory. What we find is that Mill has indeed both affirmed and developed the cluster of values at the center of the moral tradition. An elaborate and open-ended process of comparing and adjusting values to one another is the essence of deliberation. The goal of maximizing these values is an extension of the ampliative method. Moreover, while Mill strongly affirms the value of autonomy in his formulation of the harm principle, he notes that selfishness is self-defeating. The selfish rob themselves of enjoyment by "caring for nobody but themselves," while those who develop a sense of community and cultivate themselves with a strong interest in nature, art, poetry, and the ways of humankind will find "sources of inexhaustible interest."[10] The essentials of the moral tradition are all there, and Mill carries it a step further by sharpening our awareness of the implications of this tradition for formulating social policy.

III

If we notice development in the moral tradition, instead of fixing on differences in approaches as if they were bones of contention that harden into irreducibly distinct ethical positions, we will not find ourselves left with ossified moralities that compete for ultimate honors by discrediting each other, while in the process discrediting themselves by calling into question the very acceptibility of moral values. The method of amplification encompasses the values at the center of this tradition, which receive development and refinement throughout some rather dramatic changes in historical conditions. The ampliative method is a general strategy for living well and for eliciting agreement among human beings about how to go about this. It posits as important values the desire for completeness, the need for autonomy and community, the role of reason in adjusting potential satisfactions to each other, and the importance of learning from experience in the entire process of moral evaluation. Moreover, because the ampliative method involves learning from experience, it is a proto-historical method. At the same time as it posits completeness as the ideal, it depends on historical experience to furnish examples that will prompt us to augment the definition of the ideal. This in turn raises questions about the relationship between morality and history. How do changing historical conditions affect our ability to give a sense of the moral life? In what ways, and for what reasons, are thinkers able to expand the moral consciousness of the species? How do these factors bear on our ability to make critical decisions in the contemporary context?

So far this paper has been an attempt to recover the essentials of the Western moral tradition. We will now turn to two thinkers from the late modern and early contemporary periods in philosophy, viz. Hegel and Whitehead, who help us to answer the questions raised by this recovery. These two philosophers stand out from most others of the same period who talk about the relationship between morality and history. Unlike others, e.g. Marx and Nietzsche, who survey the same terrain and readily identify moral pretense but cannot locate authentic moral awareness, Hegel and Whitehead find a developing moral consciousness, and by taking it seriously, make a number of suggestive comments about the relationship between morality and history that help us to explain why development has occurred in the way it has and why we ought to be concerned about certain historical trends that place further development in great jeopardy.

Hegel and Whitehead share an approach toward history that makes the moral tradition accessible. While many of their contemporaries, impressed with the successes possible through the rigorous application of methods in the natural sciences, are inclined to view history as little more than a chronicle of prejudice and error, occasionally interrupted by inexplicable flashes of insight, both Hegel and Whitehead believe there is a logic of historical development, in which discrete events reflect larger patterns and stages of development, although this in no way implies that outcomes are predictable or that progress is inevitable. This movement in history, to the extent to which it occurs, is motivated by an urge toward completeness of experience that necessarily involves projecting or appealing to a norm for what will count as genuine satisfaction. This norm is not explicitly present to human consciousness from the beginning but develops through a dialectical process in experience. By making explicit how this process occurs in historical terms Hegel and Whitehead have extended and refined the use of the ampliative method.

Hegel's goal is "to know spirit as spirit" by traversing the historical path of consciousness through the forms of alienation resulting from various one-sided interpretations of life.[11] This, he believes, will enable him to determine how an expansion of consciousness is possible and what it would mean for a human consciousness to overcome alienation and be at home with itself in the other. By dwelling in each finite form of consciousness we come to appreciate both the germ of truth present in it and the consequences of insisting that this form of consciousness is all there is to life. Later forms of consciousness grow out of and are predicated upon overcoming the inadequacies of earlier forms—even when there is no explicit memory of them. A retrospective account of the entire process expands our awareness of the many truths incorporated into a complete account, sharpens awareness of transitions and successions necessary for consciousness to reach fulfillment, and helps us to elaborate what is involved in the highest good for human life as a comprehensive unification of formerly opposed interpretations of life. Thus Hegel's approach to experience can be viewed as the logical culmination of the ampliative method inasmuch as he suggests how we can fill out our conception of human identity—and what it would take to achieve full human satisfaction—by coming to appreciate and affirm human differences, the many sides of personality, as they are reconciled through historical experience. Because history is "a conscious, self-mediating process" the goal of which is "revelation of the depth of spirit,"[12] it is a process that amplifies our knowledge of who we are and how satisfaction is possible for us. Throughout this process reason functions as "purposive activity"[13] directed toward the highest good. Reason mediates among differences so that the truth of each is taken up into the effort of the Concept to be true to life and thereby true to the whole. It is only when we have a "comprehended History"[14]—filled out and organized in this manner—that we have amplified the highest good to a point at which human values and interpretations will, in their new historical alignments, throw off the appearance of exclusivity and opposition and form a mediated, well-rounded whole. In this situation no one interpretation will constrain us, ruling out a range of experiences, and we will fully enjoy the freedom to recognize and respond to all of life in the right measure at the right time. In this way the comprehension of historical experience is necessary for completing the task proposed by the method of amplification.

Hegel also contributes to our understanding of the role of the values of autonomy and community in the context of the highest good. It is impossible to be autonomous—i.e., truly self-directing—when a one-sided interpretation of what life is and what promise it holds, limits what one can experience and choose. Thus the self-knowledge that comes from Hegel's phenomenological excursion into the breadth and depth of the human spirit is directly relevant to the aim of leading an autonomous life and choosing a personal identity that genuinely fits what one knows about self and others. Reason's purposive activity, introducing mediations into the search for the highest good, is an essential component of self-knowledge and the choice of a personal identity. The existentialist charge that reason threatens the individual with anonymity is so far from being true that if reason's role in fashioning an individual identity were denied, the individual would be little more than the sum of attractions and repulsions in the immediate environment.

Hegel values autonomy because individual expression is necessary for "the strength of the spirit" to emerge. The demand of social conformity at the expense of autonomy can only result in inquisition and destruction, not in the encouragement of life through a social ideal, as Hegel makes plain in "Absolute Freedom and Terror."[15] Culture, too, is more than a catechism; it must be recreated and advanced under contemporary conditions by each person who selects and combines aspects of the common legacy through the background and unique set of strengths of each interpreter. On the other hand, autonomy is meaningful only in relation to community. This should be apparent from the various stages of the *Phenomenology* in which the narrowly self-seeking individual frustrates its own aims. Whether the goal is power, pleasure, recognition of achievement, or moral rectitude, the atomic individual cannot lay hold of a world that yields to its demands. As Hegel concludes in "Lordship and Bondage", demanding recognition from one who is not allowed an independent consciousness results only in coerced and servile words and deeds—the reverse of the genuine recognition the lord desires.[16] Or, as we discover in "Pleasure and Necessity," "the absolute unyieldingness of individual existence is pulverized on the equally unrelenting but continuous world of actuality."[17] The world does not yield to isolated demands. Satisfaction requires adjustment, integration, and mutuality. Desire and the restlessness of the soul can only be satisfied through the mutual creation of a social world in which each has room for authentic expression.

Neither autonomy nor community is achieved at the expense of the other.

Whitehead shares Hegel's basic attitude toward the ideal implicit in the classical method of amplification and, like Hegel, adds to it historical and metaphysical refinements. He states the connection between the individual good and the general good at the beginning of *Process and Reality:*

Morality of outlook is inseparably conjoined with generality of outlook. The antithesis between the general good and the individual interest can be abolished only when the individual is such that its interest is the general good, thus exemplifying the loss of the minor intensities in order to find them again with finer composition in a wider sweep of interest.[18]

Moral experience is not separable from larger considerations of the kind of milieu into which decisions are assimilated. This entails responsibility for the kind of society, the kind of civilization, and ultimately the kind of reality we are creating. Understandably, then, Whitehead is more concerned with elaborating the kind of reality in which we are implicated, and through which we define choices, than with writing a dissertation on morality as such. But it would be wrong to conclude that moral questions are tangential to basic concerns. Whitehead's occasional remarks show he is squarely within the tradition we have been discussing. "The whole point of moral responsibility," he tells us, is to act in a process in which the indefinite is made definite.[19] Principles of morality guide us in this venture by expressing "the requisites for depth of experience."[20] Evil occurs when "the characters of things are mutually obstructive."[21] If we are to struggle with evil, we must enter into "a process of building up a mode of utilization by the provision of intermediate elements introducing a complex structure of harmony."[22] In this struggle it is the task of reason "to fathom the deeper depths of the many-sidedness of things."[23]

From these passages we can gather that the greatest achievement of value occurs when individual interest is aligned with the general good inasmuch as the intensities of life gain a "finer composition" as they are coordinated with the good of others. (From one point of view, *Process and Reality* is a series of metaphysical arguments for this claim.) This highest good, which is amplified so that the good of each both allows for and benefits from the good of all, is "that union of harmony, intensity, and vividness which involves the perfection of importance for that occasion."[24] But this good is not simply defined in terms of the immediate occasion. It is always the orchestration of factors and forces in the local environment that are the product of long historical preparation. Whitehead explicitly states that Plato first formulated the ideal and that "the cultural history of Western Civilization" has developed in the context of this "lure to perfection."[25]

> Plato conceived the notion of ideal relations . . . based upon a conception of the intrinsic possibilities of human character. . . . The story of Plato's idea is the story of its energizing within a local plastic environment.[26]

The long process of civilizing the species draws its energy and sustenance from this ideal. It is only by becoming aware of the continual struggle throughout this history to organize a local environment through reference to the ideal that we can know what it means to incorporate the ideal—and how far we still have to go. Without knowledge of the historical forms this struggle has taken, we fall prey to the illusion that the presuppositions of our own period are timeless and that current proposals for behavior systems, which are based on contemporary presuppositions, can be evaluated without reference to "the greatness" that has been "nerving the race in its slow ascent."[27] Whitehead says emphatically,

> There is no one behavior system belonging to the essential character of the universe, as the universal moral ideal. What is universal is the spirit which should permeate any behavior system in the circumstances of its adoption.[28]

A knowledge of cultural history is important for exercising moral responsibility. We will remain unaware of the extent to which we are victims of the assumptions of our own age unless we gain some perspective through cultural history. The consequence of ignorance is that we restrict choices and possibly even lose sight of the most fundamental moral principles. When we understand the difference between the universal human spirit and particular behavior systems, we can judge these systems by asking about the extent to which they admit of a quickening of the spirit that will advance the ideal of harmony, intensity, and vividness. At the same time we can struggle against the evil of mutual obstruction resulting in "the loss of the higher experience in favor of the lower."[29] Reason is the key to this process of amplifying the good that can be achieved. Through reason's mediation we can draw out and adjust to each other the various aspects of "the many-sidedness of things." Through this process of mediation and adjustment we can introduce into our local environment that "finer composition" of the general good possible when we weave together the diverse and colorful threads of the past into the tapestry of human self-consciousness and achievement called "civilization."

Whitehead, like Hegel, fills out the historical dimension of moral choice and thereby amplifies the highest good. Whitehead also argues, in a manner reminiscent of Hegel, that reason is not a threat to individuality. On the contrary, reason is a precondition for the realization of individuality. This should already be apparent from the discussion of the function of reason in selecting and combining elements of the past to carry with us into the future. Reason is an irreplaceable ally in the exercise of freedom that constitutes moral responsibility. Through historical experience reason enables us to reconcile positions that would be inconsistent in a timeless realm. Because "process is the way by which the universe escapes from the exclusions of inconsistency,"[30] reason is not an agent of exclusion and narrowness of possibility; it selects and re-selects, combines and re-combines, to foster ever anew the novelty and freshness of experience that goes into genuine individuality. Whereas a static metaphysics assigns to reason the function of exclusion, a process metaphysics assigns to reason the function of integration that must occur with each evolving individual. "Process and individuality require each other."[31] The expression and spontaneity associated with autonomy and individuality presuppose a world of process informed by the inquiries and reconstructions of reason. Without "the unity of the Universe," we would lose "the individuality of the details."[32]

So far we have attended only to those aspects of the thought of Hegel and Whitehead that contribute to the development of the method of amplification. Before closing we should take note of a conviction they share about the degeneration of moral experience. Both Hegel and Whitehead are concerned about the phenomenon of intellectual pathologies. Cultures sometimes fall into diseased conditions. Just as these maladies destroy the liveliness of the species, they also destroy the development of culture. Intellectual pathologies are ways of becoming dead to the world. Although neither Hegel nor Whitehead always diagnoses such problems as moral problems, it follows from what has already been said that the choice of whether or not to accept the pathological condition is indeed a choice between good and evil.

Intellectual pathologies are one-sided interpretations of the world that present themselves as total explanations containing a set of requirements concerning action. In Hegel's *Phenomenology* each of the dialectics begins with an interpretation that inspires development (organizing a life-world in terms of the interpretation) and ends with the emergence of a contradiction that, if suppressed, would inhibit further development; in other words, it has become an intellectual pathology. Whether or not to allow a pathology to maintain a hold on us, after we have recognized that it cannot encompass the full range of human experiences and inhibits further development, is a moral choice. It is a choice between expansion and development, on the one hand, and "withdrawal into itself," on the other.

> Since this withdrawal into itself or self-centeredness of the existent consciousness immediately makes it self-discordant, Evil appears as the primary existence of this inwardly-turned consciousness; and because the thoughts of Good and Evil are utterly opposed and this antithesis is not yet resolved, this consciousness is essentially only evil.[33]

Although this description of evil occurs in the passage on "Revealed Religion" and might be thought to be peculiar to that dialectic, the description fits what Hegel says elsewhere about evil. Evil means shrinking from the growth and development of life and inhibiting growth in others as well. It is no coincidence that Hegel's dialectics frequently end with explicit choices of life against death—with adherence to the old framework signifying relinquishment to the grip of death. Even so-called moral frameworks can have this effect, as Hegel repeatedly makes clear in his contrasts between *Moralität* and *Sittlichkeit.*

While Hegel explains, with reference to internal contradictions, the ways in which partisans of one-sided interpretations act against themselves and others when they advocate a "total explanation" that actually inhibits further inquiry, Whitehead makes the point about intellectual pathologies, which he sometimes calls "dogmas," with reference to their overall impact on the advancement of civilization. We have already seen why no single behavior system is morally required for all time. Yet opponents of authentic moral choice often pose in the garb of morality (pretending to be "the moral majority"). Whitehead has an answer for those who insist on conformity to moral codes that are supposedly timeless.[34] All such codes are abstractions relevant to specific environments and are necessarily restrictive of growth when the environment changes. There is no simple formula for the right answer. There are great differences in backgrounds and circumstances. In making choices a person is responsible for interpreting a situation, for considering how the action will affect others, and for planning a future that brings about development and fulfillment. Facing up to these choices, and taking personal responsibility for them, is what it means to be a mature moral being. Those who find it too terrifying or too burdensome to take personal responsibility for deliberating, planning, and creating the future in which they will live may look to moral codes to relieve them. But the rest of us need not approve their choice by agreeing that they are moral.

What moral codes do to morality, dogmas do to the comprehension of life.

The history of thought is a tragic mixture of vibrant disclosure and of deadening closure. The sense of penetration is lost in the certainty of completed knowledge. This dogmatism is the anti-christ of learning.[35]

Dogmatism halts probing into "patterns of connection" in the characters of things. While dogmas may initially present some insight, dogmatism eventually leaves us to minister over "a dull accumulation of minor feats of coordination."[36] It is deadening to inquiry that might uncover novelty of pattern because this has the potential for challenging established truths. Consequently, dogmatism limits itself to codification—merely extending existing doctrine to new cases and closing off the possibility that experience could suggest the need for a new theory.

It may be that each moral code or dogmatic position represents a hard-won truth learned through agonizing experiences. Human beings tend to record painful experiences in moral rules written in bold letters. But it often happens that circumstances change, and rules remain. Hegel and Whitehead alert us to conditions under which an initially acceptable intellectual framework degenerates into an intellectual pathology. They show ways of criticizing the historical presuppositions of the fixed truths that bind us and make us insensitive to life. They also show how we can identify an amplified alternative. In effect, they present us with the ultimate moral choice: either advance the process or bring it to a halt, thereby turning it into its opposite.

What, then, are we to make of the process of morality in our own age after studying Hegel and Whitehead?

(1) By analyzing historical and cultural differences as preconditions for the development of moral consciousness, Hegel and Whitehead free us from the grip of the relativist contention that a succession of alternative moral positions shows morality itself to be a phantom and a hopeless enterprise. The ability to give a sense of the moral life should not be undercut by historical experience. On the contrary, a discovery of the shapes and forms of authentic moral awareness under changing historical conditions should awaken us to the nature of the moral life and deepen our commitment to it.

(2) By emphasizing that historical and cultural analysis adds to the ability to make moral decisions, Hegel and Whitehead help us to expose and discredit ethnocentric definitions of morality, which would have all societies and cultures evaluated by a formulation of morality created by a single one of them. In this way they not only challenge ethnocentric positions; they call into question the relativist rejection of morality motivated by a dislike of ethnocentrism.

(3) The historical and cultural amplification of the method of amplification provides a source for the dialectical expansion of the moral ideal. This ideal is not simply discovered and fixed for all time. It evolves as we discover modes of fulfillment not obstructing or invalidating other types of fulfillment, while expanding what we can experience. Consequently, we are able to accept completeness as an ideal—desiring experience to be ever more complete—without supposing that we already know about everything that will make experience more complete.

(4) Because reason is essential as the agent of mediation in the creation of the highest good, we can appreciate reason's value as a means of integration without falling into the supposition that reason is strictly a neutral, instrumental value. An integrative reason closes the distance between means and ends. In the process it takes the edge off of a contemporary anti-intellectualism that observes reason entering with the pretense of neutrality and leaving after inventing instruments of destruction at the service of appetites for power.

(5) Reflecting on Hegel and Whitehead in the context of a developing moral tradition enables us to ask questions about the continuity of this tradition that might not otherwise occur to us. It might, for example, suggest ways in which changing social conditions both pose threats to the integrity of moral experience and awaken us to the full dimensions of what we value in such expe-

rience. Thus we might very well read Kant as, *inter alia*, a moral response to new pressures of commercialism—defending the moral status of human beings at a time in which there are new incentives to treat them as instruments—rather than as a petty bourgeois intent on rationalizing trade relations. Or, we might read Mill as repulsed by prevailing attitudes of revenge toward wrong-doers and indifference toward human misery during a period of industrialization in which increased social coordination was morally required. Instead of reading Mill as a disingenuous hedonist, we might read him as a moral reformer advocating the rationality of an all-things-considered, deliberative approach to decision-making.

(6) By identifying symptoms of self-frustration by which we can identify intellectual pathologies Hegel and Whitehead provide evidence for the classical thesis that evil is self-destructive. Of course, we must be careful not to overgeneralize from this conclusion. It does not mean, for example, that good will win out over evil. In an era of nuclear weapons we must realize that in destroying itself evil can destroy good as well.

(7) Hegel and Whitehead provide phenomenological and metaphysical arguments for the interdependence of autonomy and community. Through these arguments they demonstrate that these values are meaningless in isolation from one another and that both are essential ingredients in the highest good. They carry the method of amplification a step further by showing that these values are rooted in the nature of human becoming.

(8) By developing this classical thesis in modern terms they give us a basis for criticizing the two ideologies, capitalist competitive individualism and coercive collectivism, that currently have a stranglehold on the world. Ironically, capitalist individualism frustrates the exercise of the individual's autonomy just as coercive communism frustrates the sense of community. Autonomy without community is empty; community without autonomy is blind. A more bitter irony is that we are on the threshold of annihilation singing the anthems of these two ideologies.

(9) If we draw a "moral" from reading Hegel and Whitehead, I hope it would be that no one value is so important that all others should be sacrificed for it. They teach us that mediation as a process of adjusting values to each other is crucial to the moral enterprise and is the pathway to the highest good. This should give us new energy for establishing (a) conflict resolution centers for neighborhood disputes, (b) legislative agendas to insure that all social groups have their needs adjusted to the needs of others, and (c)

constant international efforts to get the major powers to be more reasonable in adjusting their weapons policies to the goals of the rest of the world. Anything less than this is to miss the point about mediation.

(10) The process of morality begins with discord and ends with a new way of acting that precludes past frustrations and expands what we can experience. Hegel and Whitehead give us new reasons for believing this, if we doubted it before, and as a consequence help us to see that there is truth to the experiences of other societies and cultures. We should respect and pay attention to other societies not only because mutual destruction is possible but also because human identity manifests itself in different ways depending on time and place. They are us under different conditions. Morality is not a bludgeon for beating on people who are different. If the process of morality is allowed to run its course, the experience of each amplifies the experience of all the others. In Whitehead's words, we take "the journey of the soul to the source of all harmony."[37]

Notes

1. Plato, *Philebus* 60.

2. Plato, *Sophist* 247E.

3. Aristotle, *Metaphysics*, XIII, 1077b.

4. Plato, *Phaedrus* 248.

5. Plato, *Republic*, Books VII and X.

6. Aristotle, *Nicomachean Ethics*, Book IX, and *Politics*.

7. Thomas Auxter, *Kant's Moral Teleology* (Macon: Mercer University Press, 1982), Chapter IX.

8. Cf. Thomas Auxter, "The Unimportance of Kant's Highest Good," *Journal of the History of Philosophy* (1979), 121–134.

9. Cf. Thomas Auxter, "Kant's Conception of the Private Sphere," *The Philosophical Forum* (1981), 295–310.

10. John Stuart Mill, *Utilitarianism* (Indianapolis: Bobbs-Merrill, 1957), p. 18.

11. G. W. F. Hegel, *Phänomenologie des Geistes* (Hamburg: Felix Meiner Verlag, 1952), p. 564. Hereafter the abbreviation '*PhG*' will be used to refer to this edition and will be followed by the relevant page number. A second number refers to the translation by A. V. Miller, *Hegel's Phenomenology of Spirit* (Oxford: Oxford University Press, 1977).

12. *PhG* 564; 492.

13. *PhG* 22; 12.

14. *PhG* 564; 493.

15. *PhG* 413; 355.

16. *PhG* 141; 111.

17. *PhG* 265; 220.

18. Alfred North Whitehead, *Process and Reality* (New York: Harper and Row, 1960), 23. Hereafter the abbreviation '*PR*' will be used to refer to this text. Other abbreviations referring to the works of Whitehead are as follows: *AI Adventures of Ideas* (New York: The Free Press, 1967) *MT Modes of Thought* (New York: The Free Press, 1968) *RM Religion in the Making* (New York: The Macmillan Company, 1926).

19. *PR* 390.

20. *PR* 483.

21. *PR* 517.

22. *Ibid.*

23. *PR* 519.

24. *MT* 14.

25. *AI* 43.

26. *AI* 42.

27. *AI* 18.

28. *MT* 14.

29. *RM* 95.

30. *MT* 54.

31. *MT* 97.

32. *MT* 8.

33. *PhG* 537; 468.

34. *MT* 1–19.

35. *MT* 58.

36. *MT* 57.

37. *AI* 18.

Curtis L. Carter
MARQUETTE UNIVERSITY

Hegel and Whitehead on Aesthetic Symbols

The focus of this paper is aesthetic symbols, the types of symbols which originate in the various media of the fine arts. I will use the terms 'aesthetic symbols', 'works of art', and 'art' interchangeably.

The views advanced by Hegel and Whitehead on this topic converge on many issues. For instance both recognize that the arts arise out of a certain advanced stage in the development of consciousness, and both give a very high place in their conceptual schemes to art. Moreover, the two philosophers see art as a link between nature and the primitive states of preconscious being, and a higher realm of mind or spirit. They also recognize that aesthetic symbols have important historical and societal functions that help to define the qualities of the various civilizations, in so far as such symbols refer in some sense to ultimate purposes.

Historically it is interesting to remember that both philosophers were influenced by romanticism. The German Romantic philosophers, Hegel's contemporaries, had developed a philosophy of nature that is essential for Hegel's discussion of the fine arts as a bridge between nature and spirit. His close friendships and intellectual exchanges, particularly during his student days and early career, with the poet-philosophers Hölderlin and Schelling provided an integral link to romanticism. Hegel drew upon his friend's image of "a universal spiritual force which manifests itself in all things and uses them for its own purposes" and incorporated their proposal for a synthesis of nature and spirit into his program for aesthetic symbols.[1] The connection of Whitehead to romanticism would be less obvious were it not for Mary Wyman's suggestive account of his intense study of Wordsworth, which draws our attention to certain parallels between, for example, *The Prelude* and Whitehead's approach to aesthetic symbols. Of particular interest is a common treatment by Whitehead and Wordsworth of the human body as the central ground underlying symbolic reference and their use in art of recollected feelings of the past.[2] Their respective encounters with romanticism help to explain the importance of feeling in their two philosophies, a subject that I will take up in a later section.

My main interest in this paper is to argue that both Hegel and Whitehead offer essentially cognitive approaches to aesthetic symbols as distinct from an expressionist or a formalist approach. In this respect they differ from romantics like Hölderlin and Schelling who advanced feeling over reason and ranked art over philosophy, as well as from later expressionists like Leo Tolstoy who believed that art exists solely to express and arouse feeling.[3] Hegel and Whitehead also differ from Immanuel Kant, who accentuated the formal, internal properties of design and developed a theory of aesthetic judgments leading to a notion of art for art's sake.[4] Neither Hegel nor Whitehead followed Kant in these matters, since both recognized that aesthetic symbols have a role to play in human history. They exist for the purpose of providing us with knowledge: knowledge, for example, of our past feelings and experiences (Whitehead)[5] and of absolute spirit itself (Hegel).[6]

A cognitive approach to art may take many forms—for example, Plato's and Aristotle's views that art imitates nature, or the modern semiotic theories of aesthetics advanced by philosophers from Charles Peirce to Nelson Goodman. Adherence to one or more of the following general claims is normally characteristic of a cognitive approach to art: that art is in part a process or product of human reason; that art is judged in respect to its ability to provide knowledge in some form or degree; that art works are considered as symbols or signs; and that aesthetic symbols formulated in various media are analogous in some respects to language. While it would be possible to show that Hegel's and Whitehead's approaches to symbols in the fine arts qualify as cognitive on most of these counts, I will support this thesis primarily by examining the distinctive ways in which the two develop their respective approaches to art. Hence it is not only because Hegel and Whitehead happen to include the arts among the functions of human reason, recognize art as a form of knowledge, discuss art as symbolic form, or discuss art's relation to other types of symbols (such as language) that their views can be considered cognitive. Rather, their entire presentations of the nature and functions of aesthetic symbols support classifying their views as cognitive. Accordingly, an interpretation of their views that concentrated exclusively upon the expressive features of art, or upon formal properties, without assessing the role of these elements in reference to cognition would be unable to do justice to the views of Hegel and Whitehead. In the course of clarifying the cognitive nature of aesthetic symbols, I will, therefore, secondarily draw a comparision between the aesthetic theories of Hegel and Whitehead.

I. Hegel and Aesthetic Symbols

According to Hegel, aesthetic symbols originate in the "productive power of imagination" and may invoke "recollected intuitions" from past experience as well as the creative powers of imagination.[7] They arise out of the activity of the "free intelligence of thought" acting upon "determined" states of natural materials. The human body, which incorporates certain spiritual properties in a material form, is a useful model for understanding the mixture of corporeality and spirit in art. As interior ideas and feelings exteriorize themselves in facial expression, gesture, or movement, the body literally expresses certain properties of spirit.[8] This expressive power of the body is analogous to the expressive power which attaches to aesthetic symbols when they have resulted from an artistic fusion of sensuous materials and the properties of spirit.

Aesthetic symbols display spirit in the material sensuous forms provided by artistic media such as architecture, sculpture, painting, music, and poetry. In so doing they vividly bring to our minds the deepest spiritual interests of mankind—the aesthetic symbols created in these artistic media enable absolute spirit to penetrate the world of nature.[9] Art does not, qua art, imitate nature, according to Hegel. Rather, it fuses natural materials with feeling and thought, appropriating shapes, colors, and movements to it own ends. Art may *appear* to speak the language of nature just because it appropriates existing natural materials and forms, but art is art only in so far as colors, shapes, and movements are used to express a spiritual content that is merely foreshadowed in natural materials.[10] Art may serve ancillary purposes such as play, recreation, entertainment, or decoration, but the highest role played by aesthetic symbols in Hegel's view is the expression of spiritual content.

Hegel examines aesthetic symbols in the context of his various analyses of the subjective, objective, and absolute manifestations of spirit in human experience. His discussions of aesthetic symbols in relation to each of these aspects of spirit reveal the cognitive aspects as well as the functions of art. From the shorter *Logic* we learn that understanding, that is, subjective reason, is instrumental in the formation of individual works of art.[11] Subjective reason facilitates the beauty and perfection of a work, for instance, by assuring that the aesthetic elements are joined together with consistency and clarity. Hegel explains in his *Philosophy of Subjective Spirit* that producing a poem or a painting requires thought not only prior to but during the execution of the work.[12] In his *Philosophy of History*, which outlines in part the workings of objective spirit, Hegel recognizes that works of art are essential vehicles for expressing community and national values.[13] His *Lectures on Aesthetics* provide the most complete account of how absolute spirit expresses itself in the form of aesthetic symbols.[14] Indeed, in the *Lectures on Aesthetics* Hegel explicitly compares the role of aesthetic symbols in bringing forth absolute spirit in sensuous form to what philosophy does at a higher level of thought.[15]

In addition, the *Lectures on Aesthetics* provide the technical distinctions necessary to a full understanding of Hegels cognitive view of aesthetic symbols. Hegel introduces a dual role for the term symbol: first, as a term applicable to all of art, and secondly, as a term restricted to a particular stage or mode in the development of art.[16] The first, more general sense is the primary sense for him of the term symbol, the sense that concerns us here. He also distinguishes symbols from signs. Symbols precede signs in the evolution of intelligent functions, and, unlike signs, are at least not initially conventional.[17] The manner of symbolizing in aesthetic symbols is immediate (or motivated, as we would say today).[18] Signs, however, are images which take on an independent presentation of intelligence. Their ability to refer, or otherwise function as signs, requires no connection between form and meaning other than convention or rule.[19] This purported distinction between symbol and sign is not as clear in Hegel's writings as it might be, or in anyone else's for that matter, because symbols are also *prima facie* signs in the sense that they may come to function according to convention when the original base in immediacy is forgotten or no longer important. The distinctions mentioned here between symbol and sign are not so significant for our purposes, but I introduce them in order to point out that a broader inquiry into such questions would lead to a consideration of Hegel's relation to our modern semiotic movements.[20]

It is necessary, however, to note certain limits placed upon aesthetic symbols with respect to their adequacy for fulfilling their cognitive purposes. First, Hegel warns us that their very closeness to nature prevents artistic symbols, whether in architecture, sculpture, painting, music, or poetry and related theatrical forms, from presenting a true picture of spiritual reality. The sensuous immediacy of the symbols in these forms does not allow for the symbol to correspond completely to spirit in its truest form. Their "truthfullness" depends upon the sensuous natural properties being taken as a negative, and merely a passing, state, a state which is only a moment in the dialectic of absolute spirit.[21] In these words Hegel is reminding his romantic colleagues—and us—that art cannot offer the final understanding of spirit. Nevertheless, aesthetic symbols are not without their cognitive merit. They give a truer picture of reality than do the immediate appearances of our ordinary "nonaesthetic" experiences, which falsely present themselves in a raw and natural state as the real and true, and they are also superior to historiographic interpretations, because art points beyond itself and gives us an idea of spirit.

Secondly, aesthetic symbolization does not depend entirely upon the will of the individual artist, any more than the symbolization of internal spiritual content by a human body depends upon the individual person's will.[22] Symbolization in a human body is a function of common properties of spirit shared by the external body and its internal spiritual content. The symbolization of a work of art is involuntary because it represents the working of absolute spirit manifesting itself through the spirit of an individual artist. Art thus retains a certain mystery and unpredictability in its individual forms and styles, according to the variety of ways in which spirit chooses to present itself.

A third limitation placed upon the cognitive efficacy of aesthetic symbols concerns the problem of interpretation. Works of art in any mode pose problems of interpretation, and they are capable of concealing as well as revealing absolute spirit in its fuller developments. Hegel's insights into the problem of interpreting aesthetic symbols display a considerable awareness. He recognized, for instance, that because the sensuous form of a work and its meaning (spirit) are not related by convention, interpretation depends in part on the actual properties of spirit that are immediately present in a work.[23] The problem of interpreting aesthetic symbols is further complicated by ambiguities that must be resolved or at least acknowledged. Since a work may include properties that can be organized conceptually according to more than one frame of reference, a judgment is required as to how the properties must be read. For instance, a work consisting of a triangular shape can be read as a set of converging lines, as an abstract geometric form symbolizing a mystical truth about numbers, as a Platonic form, or as a symbol of the Holy Trinity. Hegel is aware of such problems and also of others that emerge when we compare works of art from many different cultures. The works of China, Persia, India, and Egypt were especially troublesome for Hegel. How, for instance, does one go about discerning the nature of absolute spirit as expressed in the art of cultures other than one's own? One problem that Hegel faced was whether to attribute his difficulties of discovering spiritual meaning in the arts of these various cultures to deficiencies inherent to the art forms themselves or to inadequacies in the understanding of spirit available in these cultures. Hegel implies a little of both, and his answers on such questions were probably no more satisfactory to himself than they are to us. The complexities of interpreting aesthetic symbols increase when Hegel reminds us that a picture or a poem can be understood literally, metaphorically, or both.[24] Such problems are not unique to a particular stage in art. Rather, they appear again and again in every stage of art including the historical manifestations of Hegel's symbolic, classical, and romantic art. Such limits and difficulties with interpretation are not unique to aesthetic symbols, however, and our awareness of them should not in itself dissuade us from a cognitive interpretation of aesthetic symbols in so far as Hegel is concerned.

II. Whitehead and Aesthetic Symbols

Whitehead's principal ideas concerning symbols are outlined in his book, *Symbolism: Its Meaning and Effect;* there he explains that symbolism is based on the mind's activity of selecting some components of experience (symbols) to elicit other mental components (meanings).[25] The most obvious examples of symbols would include language units and works of art, and their corresponding meanings would include the beliefs, feelings, and other associated responses or usages. According to Whitehead, human symbolism originates from the interplay of two more basic modes of perception, "causal efficacy" and "presentational immediacy." Causal efficacy supplies to the symbol a consolidation of relevant past experience representing "the hand of the settled past in the formation of the present,"[26] and presentational immediacy, which is a higher grade of experience, represents the perceiver's contribution to a particular moment of experience.[27] These two modes of perception are already differentiated forms of consciousness, that is, removed from that direct preconscious encounter with "the world" which Whitehead considers infallible and not subject to verification.[28] Symbols, according to this view, are thus the product of a high level function of the human organism, and they are in part abstracted from prior stages of experience that are at once richer in content though more vaguely formed.

For the purpose of comparing Whitehead's and Hegel's approaches to aesthetic symbols, I will concentrate on works of art. It is important to note, however, that Whitehead provides an important role for aesthetic properties throughout his system. Aesthetic properties such as feeling, harmony, and unity are an integral part of all conscious experiences from the barest instances of presentational immediacy to the most expansive metaphysical insights. Before turning to a discussion of works of art, we should also be aware that Whitehead uses the term 'art' in several different senses.[29] On one level, 'art' refers to the works of painting, sculpture, music, poetry, and dance that artists produce. At a metaphysical level, he also uses the term 'art' to express the harmonization of appearance and reality, which are different levels of reality in his system.[30]

According to Whitehead, the origin of works of art is to be sought among the cravings generated by the physiological functions of the human body.[31] The desire to produce art represents a craving for symbolic reenaction of the past, "so as to relive the emotional life of ourselves and our ancestors" freed from the constraint of practical life that accompanied their prior occasions. Art makes "a vivid experience flashed out from the necessities of daily life." It is articulate as opposed to a dim, unconscious reality of the body from which it emerges.[32]

A comparison of their views at this particular point might suggest that, while both consider art as a cognitive activity, Whitehead's idea of art aims in a backward direction towards a more primitive natural state of experience, seemingly just the opposite of Hegel's intent to direct art toward a higher rational consciousness. The comparison of Hegel and Whitehead's views on aesthetic symbols does not end here, of course. It is nevertheless of interest to note that Whitehead follows the inclinations of romanticism on this issue, while Hegel moves in the direction of the rational.

The societal functions of aesthetic symbols are especially important for Whitehead, as for Hegel. Whitehead maintains that works of art heighten our sense of humanity by exemplifying a conscious realization of "a self-contained end, timeless within time."[33] He also believes that works of art stimulate human beings to realize their potential for developing civilization. In their expressions of cravings for freshness and change, works of art continuously remind societies of the need to renew their symbols at all levels in pursuit of new ideals for the future. Because of its novelty, therefore, the immediate effect of art upon a particular society may be disruptive, facilitating changes necessary to future advances, in a manner not unlike the workings of Hegel's dialectic.

Whitehead's optimism about the societal efficacies of aesthetic symbols is constrained by a larger context—art is only one among several important factors that he considers necessary for any civilized society. Truth, beauty, adventure, and peace are the others. Art is not necessarily the most important of these, and it must be set aside at certain times in favor of other interests.[34] He cautions, moreover, that aesthetic symbols, like all other symbols, can be manipulated for truthful or misleading purposes and are subject to periodic corrections or revisions in a healthy society.[35]

Were it not for this metaphysical analysis of art, which he sketches only briefly in two chapters on beauty, Whitehead's understanding of aesthetic symbols would fall short just where Hegel's is most strong; namely, in linking art to the highest forms of reality. Unfortunately, Whitehead says little on this subject except to note that works of art at their highest exemplify in some way the metaphysical harmonies that exist elsewhere in the process of "the interweaving of absoluteness upon relativity" which takes place in various stages of appearance and reality.[36] Such interweavings, in conjunction with human intelligence and imagination, supply the purposes which are essential to the enjoyment of art, as they do for all other activities on a human level.[37]

A relative scarcity of remarks from Whitehead has not discouraged philosophers such as Donald Sherburne from attempting to fill the gaps required to form a "Whiteheadian" account on the ontology of works of art. This sparsity has no doubt encouraged the followers of Whitehead, who wish he had said more on aesthetics, to fill in Whitehead's work with their own inventions, developed in the Spirit of Whitehead's expressed views. In his very useful book on Whitehead's aesthetics, Sherburne, for instance, argues that works of art have the status of a Whiteheadian proposition.[38] Others are less successful; Eva Schaper, for instance, fails in her attempt to show that aesthetic symbols elicit only the formal features of experiences as initially felt.[39] Her interpretation does not take full cognizance of the societal or the metaphysical roles that are suggested by Whitehead. No critical discussion of Sherburne's or of Schaper's views will be attempted here, except that

I wish to note that Sherburne's thesis apparently is compatible with a cognitive interpretation of Whitehead's views on aesthetic symbols, whereas Schaper is suggesting a noncognitive role for works of art. For our purposes these views are set aside in favor of Whitehead's own remarks, however far from a complete view of aesthetic symbols this might leave us.

III. Issues of Contemporary Interest for Aesthetics

A. Expression of Feeling in Hegel's and Whitehead's Aesthetic Symbols.

Expression of feeling as it relates to works of art remains a topic of importance for every major theory of art. On numerous occasions in the history of modern aesthetics, an association of feelings with works of art has resulted in the conclusion that they are noncognitive in character. My approach to Hegel and Whitehead's aesthetics already indicates a belief that such a conclusion is false and misleading. My aim, therefore, is to show here that Hegel and Whitehead both approach aesthetic symbols as a matter of cognition. Were it not for the fact that, in the end, Hegel found it necessary to abandon some of the exalted claims of the romantics in favor of an approach to art that recognizes the priority of reason over feeling, my interest in the cognitive aspects of his aesthetics over the "expressive" might appear misplaced. The influence of "romantic" notions in Whitehead's aesthetics might also give pause to any effort to assign to him a priority of the cognitivist moment in his theory of aesthetic symbols over the expressive moment. He very explicitly makes feeling an important element of contemplating and appreciating art. He points out that in literature, for instance, the words of a text gather their emotional symbolism from past history and from their significance in a present literary context.[40] Accordingly, the words intensify our feelings as we contemplate the meaning of a literary text. The symbolic transference of feeling, which also applies to music and the other arts, thus makes feeling a central aspect in Whitehead's account of aesthetic symbols. The central place of feeling in Hegel's aesthetics is widely recognized by such prominent interpreters as Charles Taylor,[41] and Sherburne offers a parallel interpretation affirming the prominence of feeling in Whitehead's aesthetics.[42] Taylor and Sherburne both recognize that in the aesthetic theories of these two philosophers feeling is very important, but that it has its effect through its relation to cognition.

My own position will be that neither Hegel nor Whitehead treats the question of feeling-cognition in art as involving two independent activities. There are good reasons for taking this position. First, their views of body-mind as a continuum of emergent states of conscious behavior, rather than as a relation between two separate substances, allows for the incorporation of feeling into cognition. Their anti-dualistic approaches to body-mind issues, which also carries over into their approaches to aesthetic symbolism, does not allow for any radical separation of feeling and thought. Taylor has pointed out this fact especially clearly with respect to Hegel.[43] The same is true for Whitehead, who believes that feeling is inseparable from the conceptual aspects of works of art, as Sherburne has noted.[44] Secondly, there is no such thing as a simple, direct expression of feeling of the type implied in certain modern expressionist theories, because a transmission of feeling does not exist apart from complex body-mind processes and a shared network of meanings, as John Gilmour has pointed out.[45] Not all expressionist theories of art assume a simple and direct transmission of feeling, but such an assumption is found in several leading versions including Tolstoy's. Thirdly, works of art, as they are represented by Hegel and Whitehead, carry out purposes other than the expression of feeling. As we have already noted, Hegel, for instance, believes that the central purpose of art is to present absolute spirit for human understanding, and Whitehead provides for art societal and metaphysical roles that extend beyond the mere expression of feeling.

Finally, their particular treatments of feeling in relation to aesthetic symbols support a cognitive interpretation. Hegel's extensive discussions of music and poetry, for example, remind us again and again that feelings and emotions are shaped by human imagination in these art media. In speaking of lyric poetry, he states that expression in art is not a matter of bare expression of an individual's inner life, but of a poetic mind's *artistic* expression.[46] Hegel means that the feeling in a lyric poem must appear as having been subjectively felt *and* thought prior to its presentation. Whitehead also recognizes that works of art present feeling in a clarified and harmonious form, selected and abstracted by reason from a more complex and vague primitive state.[47] Feeling and emotion do not, therefore, provide for their own selection and ordering at a conscious level; they serve as a part of the content which art brings to attention for such purposes as contemplation, clarification of the self, and enjoyment.

Judging from the comparison offered here I conclude that Hegel's and Whitehead's views on the role of expressive components of works of art are quite similar in all important respects. They do not recognize the many distinctions that contemporary philosophers have introduced for discussing feeling and expression—for example, whether a feeling experienced in conjunction with a work of art is simply a property of a spectator's inner experience or is a property of an art work which is being perceived, and whether expressive properties are literal or metaphorical, or both. Hegel and Whitehead nevertheless do offer important insights that complement discussions of such topics. Their insights into the cognitive role of feeling are especially useful.

B. The reflexive character of Aesthetic Signs.

As we have seen, Whitehead and Hegel agree that art is conceptual and that it functions as a symbol on the individual, societal, and metaphysical levels. In the remaining two sections I will examine certain areas of difference in the views of Hegel and Whitehead. These differences concern the semantic features of aesthetic symbols: the reflexive character of aesthetic symbols (Hegel), as well as their radical arbitrariness, and "double reference" (Whitehead). Our discussion of these matters will highlight notable differences in the two approaches, and also will draw attention to issues that are of significant interest as topics for present day aesthetics.

The term 'reflexive' refers in general to the mental operations wherein mind attempts to gain knowledge of itself and its own operations. In grammar, 'reflexive' implies that the subject and the object terms in an expression have identical referents. Hegel's discussion of aesthetic symbols incorporates both senses of 'reflexive'. Art, he says, is a development of absolute spirit, out of itself, into the forms of sense and feeling. Thus, in creating art, absolute spirit confronts itself "in its opposite" of sensuous form. When we apply the term reflexive to art, at the level of metaphysics, the purpose of art is seen as reflecting absolute spirit, as it exists in the phenomenal world, "back into itself." A form of imageless, purely spiritual, absolute spirit thus contemplates itself in a sensuous form provided by art. A reflexive relationship between absolute spirit and art does not imply strict identity between the two, because art incorporates sensuous elements borrowed from nature. These elements are changed by their fusion with absolute spirit, but they do not entirely lose their character as sensuous objects. Similarly, absolute spirit encompasses significantly more than can be presented in any single work of art, or in the entire collective output of the art of all times. Otherwise there would be no need for Hegel to introduce religion and philosophy in order to provide additional insights into the nature of absolute spirit.

The primary manifestation of reflexiveness in art is in reference to the activity of absolute spirit as we have outlined above. Works of art also can function reflexively at other levels, according to Hegel. They are reflexive with reference to individual subjective spirit and also to the spirit of a nation. That is, the work of art reflects the activity of a human spirit (an artist's) symbolizing itself. Through the collective activity of its artists, the spirit of a nation on a civilization can be reflected in the highest artistic products produced by that nation or civilization.

In certain of its stages, art may also be reflexive in yet another sense for Hegel: that is, when art assumes the task of saying "philosophically" what art itself is about. In such instances, the self-reflexiveness of art is analogous to the self-reflexiveness of absolute spirit when spirit is looking to art as a means of gaining knowledge of itself.[49] This self-reflective feature of art has become a major topic of consideration for artists, critics, and philosophers in the twentieth century. Today it is common for serious paintings, films, and even broadway musicals to comment on the arts of painting, film, and the musical respectively. Hegel was not the first to be aware of the possibilities inherent in the ability of the arts to become self-reflexive. (This notion was also implicit, for instance, in the approach of the romantic philosophers, particularly Schelling.) Nevertheless, his treatment of the reflexive nature of art, especially when he ponders art's role in giving a philosophy of art, anticipates a major preoccupation of late among major artists in all media with theoretical issues concerning the nature and significance of art itself. A failure to appreciate that art in our time is heavily theoretical, and thus reflexive in its comments about art, would result in our missing the point of a significant amount of art from Marcel Duchamp to the present. Hegel's belief in the reflexive, self-interpreting capabilities of art coincides, moreover, with a common belief shared by many artists, critics, and spectators that many works of art supply their own conceptual frameworks.

C. The Arbitrariness of Symbols and Symbolic Reference.

Insofar as I can determine, Whitehead does not consider the reflexiveness of aesthetic symbols, which is a key element in Hegel's aesthetics. Their different conceptions of the purposes of aesthetic symbols lead them in different directions. Hegel's view that aesthetic symbols are intended primarily to present absolute spirit requires a reflexive account of works of art. Whitehead is more broadly concerned with aesthetic symbols expressing emotion, referring to physical or mental entities, or influencing human actions.[50]

The particular features of aesthetic symbols that I wish to draw attention to now are concerned with Whitehead's notion of symbolic reference. My aim is to show that whereas reflexiveness is the principal semantic feature of Hegel's view of aesthetic symbols, arbitrariness and "double reference" are the principal semantic features of Whitehead's aesthetic symbols.[51] As a result, Whitehead has a view that encompasses a potentially greater range of aesthetic symbols. His view also allows for a more flexible subject matter for works of art, allows him to recognize as art entities that Hegel can recognize as art only in a particular stage of civilization where art no longer fulfills its highest calling as a symbol of absolute spirit.

Whitehead distinguishes symbolic reference from "direct recognition," which yields immediate acquaintance with fact. He advances the notion that symbolic reference derives from a merging of causal efficacy and presentational immediacy, as we noted earlier, and that its validation depends upon verification supplied by these prior mental functions which connect percepts in the modes of direct recognition.[52] Symbolic reference thus consists of a mental transition wherein some components of mind (symbols) elicit in consciousness certain other components constituting the meaning of the symbols.[53] Such transitions require a common element, perhaps simply a feeling. The existence of a common ground, such as a shared feeling or a similar structure between two aspects of experience, however, does not in itself establish a symbolic reference apart from the conscious intervention of a percipient who determines what is symbol and what is meaning.[54]

The arbitrariness of the symbols consists in the fact that no element of experience, in itself, is a symbol, and none is necessarily a "meaning." As a corollary, it follows that all symbolic references are in essence "double references." Whitehead supplies various examples drawn from language; the most pertinent example for us is of a poet who writes about trees. He maintains that the trees that a poet perceives directly, are the symbols, and the words in a poem about trees are the meanings. On the other hand, a poet's words are the symbols for the readers, and the trees that motivated him to write the poem are the meanings.[55]

By his emphasis upon the arbitrary character of aesthetic signs, and upon the fact that references between symbols and their meanings may incur double reference with respect to each other, Whitehead introduces a new approach to aesthetic symbols, which offers a significant departure from Hegel. Aesthetic symbols are not arbitrary on Hegel's view in the sense that a work of art and its "meaning," which is normally understood as absolute spirit, are not interchangeable. A work of art refers to absolute spirit, which supplies its meaning, but Hegel's absolute spirit does not function in the same sense as a symbol referring to a work of art.

There are reasons for this non-reversibility of symbolic roles on Hegel's view. Absolute spirit, in a pure sense, does not have the requisite properties to become an aesthetic symbol, because it lacks the necessary sensuous form. More importantly, Hegel does not include any form of reference corresponding to Whitehead's "double reference." Hegel believes that the reference of an aesthetic symbol runs *from* the work of art *toward* absolute spirit, but not the reverse. When we experience a work of art, therefore, we are expected to read the symbol with the thought in mind that the work of art is absolute spirit's way of drawing our attention to itself as the "meaning" of the work of art. On the other hand, an experience of absolute spirit can take other forms, including forms appropriate to religion and philosophy, forms which do not necessarily refer back to any work of art.

The effects of Whitehead's insights into those aspects of symbols that introduce arbitrariness and double reference anticipate an interest in the particular features of aesthetic symbols that has been widely discussed among contemporary philosophers. Just as Hegel's concern with the reflexive nature of aesthetic symbols is reflected in certain contemporary discussions, it is also true that Whitehead's ideas on aesthetic symbols underlie the reflections of certain contemporary philosophers on the cognitive character of aesthetic symbols.[56]

Notes

1. F. W. J. Schelling, *Werke*, Stuttgart, 1856–1861. Also: Christopher Middleton, tr., *Hölderlin and Mörike* (Chicago: Univ. of Chicago Press, 1972.)

2. Mary A. Wyman, *The Lure for Feeling* (New York: Philosophical Library, 1960), pp. XI, 129, 137. Wyman argues that, although no written acknowledgement by Whitehead exists, Whitehead studied Wordsworth's *The Prelude* intensively and was substantially influenced by Wordsworth's ideas on art, nature, and human consciousness. Wyman bases her claim on testimony from family members and upon a comparison of Wordsworth's ideas in *The Prelude* with such Whitehead categories as creativity, eternal objects, actual occasions, and prehensions. Her comparison of Wordsworth's and Whitehead's views on the place of recollected feelings in art and on the body as a source of preserving and presenting such feelings for symbolic purposes is of special interest for our discussion of aesthetic symbols.

3. Leo Tolstoy, *What is Art? Essays in Art*, trans. Aylmer Maude (London: Oxford Press, 1932).

4. Immanuel Kant, *The Critique of Judgment*, trans. James Creed Meredith (Oxford: The Clarendon Press, 1952).

5. Alfred North Whitehead, *Adventures of Ideas* (New York: Macmillan, 1933), p. 349.

6. G. W. F. Hegel, *Aesthetics*, I, translated by T. M. Knox (Oxford: Clarendon Press, 1975).

7. G. W. F. Hegel, *The Philosophy of Spirit*, trans. M. J. Petry, *Hegel's Philosophy of Subjective Spirit*, 3 vols. (Dordrecht: Reidel, 1979), II:143.

8. *Ibid.*, II:413–414.

9. G. W. F. Hegel, *Encyclopedia of Philosophy*, pars. 458, 558, translated by Gustave Emil Mueller (New York: Philosophical Library, 1959).

10. *Ibid.*

11. G. W. F. Hegel, *The Logic of Hegel*, translated by William Wallace, (Oxford: Oxford University Press, 1873, 1959), Ch. VI, par. 80.

12. Hegel, *Encyclopedia*, par. 460.

13. G. W. F. Hegel, *Lectures on the Philosophy of World History*, translated by H. B. Nisbet (Cambridge: Cambridge University Press, 1975), pp. 56–58. Also: Hegel, *Encyclopedia*, par. 458.

14. Hegel, *Aesthetics:* 1:7f.

15. *Ibid.*, I: 7, 13.

16. *Ibid.*, I:303f.

17. *Ibid.*, also, Hegel, *The Philosophy of Spirit*, III:175.

18. Hegel, *The Philosophy of Spirit*, II:185.

19. *Ibid.*, III:175.

20. See, for instance, Martin Donougho, "The Semiotics of Hegel," *Clio*, XI no. 4, 1982, 415–430. Also: J. Derrida, "Le Puits et la Pyramide. Introduction à la semiologie de Hegel," in Jacques d'Hondt, ed., *Hegel et la Pensée Moderne* 1 Paris: P. U. F., 1970), pp. 27–83, and Max Bense, *Aesthetica: Einführung in die neuen aesthetik* (Baden Baden: Agis, 1965). Derrida, Bense, and others have recently made suggestive explorations into possible connections between Hegel and the modern semiotic movements in Europe and America.

21. Hegel, *The Philosophy of Spirit*, 11:423.

22. *Ibid.*, II:187.

23. Hegel, *Aesthetics*, 1:307.

24. *Ibid.*, I:306.

25. Alfred North Whitehead, *Symbolism: Its Meaning and Effect* (New York: Macmillan, 1927), p. 8.

26. *Ibid.*, p. 50.

27. *Ibid.*, p. 22.

28. *Ibid.*, p. 5.

29. *Ibid.*, pp. 83–88; Whitehead, *Adventures of Ideas*, pp. 341–345.

30. Whitehead, *Adventures of Ideas*, p. 339.

31. *Ibid.*, pp. 347–349.

32. *Ibid.*, p. 350.

33. *Ibid.*, p. 348.

34. *Ibid.*, pp. 345, 353.

35. Whitehed, *Symbolism*, p. 88.

36. Whitehead, *Adventures of Ideas*, p. 339.

37. *Ibid.*, p. 340.

38. Donald W. Sherburne, *A Whiteheadian Aesthetic* (New Haven: Yale University Press, 1961), pp. 45, 46–127. Sherburne argues that art objects have the ontological status of Whiteheadian propositions. A proposition for Whitehead is a coupling of concrete and abstract experience, incorporating subjective aims, past experience, and relevant future possibilities revealed in part by a primordial vision of God (Sherburne, p. 46). A proposition is also described by Whitehead as the objective datum of a propositional feeling, which is a complex feeling derived from the integration of a physical feeling with a conceptual feeling, Whitehead, *Process and Reality*, p. 391. Sherburne further argues that a performance is an objectified proposition: p. 107.

39. Eva Shaper, "Aesthetic Perception," in Ivor Leclerc, ed. *The Relevance of Whitehead* (New York: Macmillan, 1961), pp. 278–280.

40. Whitehead, *Symbolism*, pp. 83–85.

41. Charles Taylor, *Hegel* (Cambridge: Cambridge University Press, 1975), pp. 21, 22.

42. Sherburne, *A Whiteheadian Aesthetic*, pp. 55–71. Shaper, "Aesthetic Perception," pp. 268, 278–281, also affirms the priority of feeling in Whitehead's aesthetics, but she distinguishes cognitive symbols, which she describes as serving the purely theoretical ends of recognition and understanding of things in their general form, from aesthetic symbols, which are directed toward the formal features of things as initially felt.

43. Taylor, *Hegel*, pp. 21, 22. Also: Shaper, "Aesthetic Perception," p. 268.

44. Donald W. Sherburne, "Editor's Preface," *The Arts, Aesthetics, and Process Philosophy*, Special Issue of *Process Studies*, XIII, no. 1 (Spring, 1983), pp. 6, 7. Also: Sherburne, *A Whiteheadian Aesthetic*, pp. 55–71.

45. John C. Gilmour, "Art and the Expression of Meaning," *Process Studies*, XIII, no. 1 (Spring, 1983), p. 82.

46. Hegel, *Aesthetics* II:809, 1123.

47. Whitehead, *Adventures of Ideas*, pp. 347-349.

48. Hegel, *Aesthetics* I:11.

49. *Ibid.*, I:371, 519.

50. Whitehead, *Symbolism*, p. 73.

51. *Ibid.*, p. 7.

52. *Ibid.*

53. *Ibid.*, p. 8.

54. *Ibid.*, p. 10.

55. *Ibid.*, p. 12.

56. The efforts of Hegel and Whitehead to characterize aesthetic symbols are reflected in the principal discussions of mid-to-late twentieth-century aesthetics. Michael Fried (*Three American Painters*, exhibition catalogue, The Fogg Art Museum, 1965, pp. 5, 7, 8); Clement Greenberg (*Art and Culture*, Boston: Beacon Press, 1961, p. 6; and *Post Painterly Abstraction*, exhibition catalogue, Los Angeles County Museum, 1964) have argued, with an acknowledged debt to Hegel, that the meaning and significance of modern "abstract" painting (Jackson Pollock, Kenneth Noland, Frank Stella, and others) is found in its preoccupation with the processes and problems intrinsic to art itself. Hegel's and Whitehead's interest in the cognitive character of art has been a topic central to the interests of Nelson Goodman (*Languages of Art*, Indianapolis, Bobbs Merrill, 1968) and others. Goodman introduces into the discussion of aesthetic symbols two distinct modes of reference: denotation and exemplification. Denotation runs only from the symbol to its referent or denotatum, and is grounded in a language or language-like system. Exemplification, which also is used in conjunction with metaphor to account for expression in art, accommodates reference "in both directions" and especially references running from what is denoted back to the symbol. See especially p. 59ff. Whitehead's discussion of the arbitrariness and the double reference aspects of symbols anticipate Goodman's interests in related properties of symbols.

Brian Leftow
FAIRFIELD UNIVERSITY

God and the World in Hegel and Whitehead

The claim that God is wholly independent of the world is a consequence of a claim basic to "classical" theism, that God is really simple, or without real parts. In this paper, I will outline this classical argument, sketch the ways Hegel and Whitehead deny divine simplicity, compare their positions on God's relation to the world, and offer some suggestions to further the debate between process and classical theism.

I

Classical writers who exempt God from having parts do not as a rule merely mean by this that God is not made up of chunks of matter. Discussions of God's simplicity deny as well that God is "composed" of essence and accident, essence and existence, etc.[1] The relation "is composed of" links wholes to parts. Evidently "classical" writers take not just material but metaphysical constituents as in some sense parts of their subjects. Their denials that God has (or can have) parts, then, include denials that God can have distinct properties or other metaphysical "parts."[2]

If God cannot have distinct properties, then God cannot have contingent properties. For suppose that God has F necessarily and G contingently. If so, in some possible world God has F but not G. Since necessary coextensiveness is at least necessary for attribute-identity, it follows from this that F and G are distinct. If God's properties are all really identical, then, if God has any properties necessarily, God can have none contingently. But God is necessarily self-identical.

A being without contingent properties can in no way really depend on any contingent existence or property-exemplification. Just what it is for one thing to depend really on another is a large, complex topic. But clearly if A depends on B for existence, necessary property or non-necessary property, one either can or must invoke B to explain these aspects of A.[3] Let us say that A strongly depends on B if one must do so and weakly depends on B if it is possible that one do so. Strong dependence entails weak. So if a simple God cannot weakly depend on any contingent existence or property-exemplification, God can in no way depend on one.

To explain the existence of some property of A by invoking B, one must deduce a statement which would be made true by the state of affairs to be explained alone from a set of premises whose truth-conditions are appropriately related to the explanandum and include the obtaining of B. What "appropriately related" means is another large, complex topic. But we recognize that to deduce "Johnny can't read" from "Either some bachelor is married or Johnny can't read" is not to explain why Johnny can't read. Now in any normal modal logic, necessary truths follow from anything whatsoever. But we recognize that not anything whatsoever explains the truth of necessary truths by referring to this fact as a paradox of strict implication. In particular, no contingent truth explains the truth of any necessary truth. But any statement made true only by a simple God's having a property or existing must be a necessary statement.[4] And any set of premises whose truth-conditions include a contingent existence or property exemplification can explain only a contingent statement. The upshot is that no contingent state of affairs can explain a necessary one, and so no necessary one can depend on any contingent one, including necessary states of affairs involving a simple God.

The main stream of classical theism contends that whatever other than God exists has been freely created by God. This entails that the actuality of every existence or property-exemplification other than God's is contingent.[5] If by "the world" we mean whatever other than God is actual, then, divine simplicity conjoined with divine free creation or at least what it entails about the world's status entails God's complete independence of the world. God's complete independence of the world in turn entails divine simplicity given the assumptions that whatever has parts must in some way really depend on them and that whatever is not wholly identical with God is identical with a part of the world.[6] The first is clearly true: whatever has a part strongly depends on that part for the property of having that part. The second was widely assumed in medieval debate over universals, divine Ideas, and theistic predication.[7]

The thesis that God is simple has some claim to be the most basic note of classical theism. It entails God's timelessness, for what is in time must be temporally divisible. It entails God's immutability, both because no timeless thing can change and because to speak of a thing as surviving change one must distinguish a "part" of the changing thing which persists from that "part" which passes away.[8] God's timelessness and changelessness in turn shape most of the features which seem distinctive of classical theism. But timelessness and immutability seem not to entail simplicity in turn. We seem able to conceive of timeless, changeless, yet complex things: e.g. classes, numbers, and propositions. Thus it seems that the doctrine of divine simplicity is logically more basic than the doctrines of divine timelessness and changelessness in classical theologies which contain all three. Further, if Whitehead's view of God is coherent, "God is timeless and immutable" entails neither "God is simple" nor God's being as classical theism depicts Him. For if Whitehead's God is a single actual entity and ordinary time is a function not of the becoming of actualities but of the transition between them, Whitehead's God is timeless, immutable relative to the change which takes place in and through ordinary time, yet complex, composite, and dependent.

All this suggests that the doctrine of divine simplicity is conceptually the most basic element in theologies in which it figures and also forms the dividing-line between classical and Whiteheadian claims about God's nature as apart from the world. If it is fair to say that classical theism determines what must hold of God's relation to the world on the basis of what is true of God apart from the world, it seems also that the doctrine of divine simplicity is where classicists and Whiteheadians part company on the God-world relation. We have in fact already seen that this is so. For we have seen that conjoining the claim that God is simple with the claim that the actuality of every existence or property-exemplification apart from God's is contingent yields the classical claim that God is wholly independent of the world. And the premise about the contingency of nondivine actuality is one any Whiteheadian (or Hegelian) would grant. Thus the doctrine of divine simplicity must be the battleground on which classical and Whiteheadian philosophers contest the nature of the God-world relation.

II

If we assume (what may well not be correct) that Hegel has something which it is not incorrect to call a concept of God, we can say that both Hegel and Whitehead deny God's simplicity. For Hegel, Absolute Spirit—that to which Christians pictorially refer as God—develops through time toward full realization. This suffices to render it composite and complex.

Whatever acquires an attribute is "composed" with that attribute, and by extension whatever depends on another thing for an attribute is composite, for to say that "it" depends is to distinguish the thing which depends from that for which it depends and consider them as in effect brought together. Whatever is composite (made up of distinct parts) is of course complex (multiparted).

Now for Whitehead, God stands in relations for which God depends on nondivine relata. Whitehead holds that God is a single actual entity which is timeless, in that God's relations to "pure potentials" are constant. Whitehead insists that these could exist if God did not (though not if there were no actualities).[9] If so they are really distinct from God, and God strongly depends on them for attributes involving them. Thus, as primordial, God is composite and complex. God obviously strongly depends on actualities for attributes consequent on prehending them, so as consequent God is again composite and complex. Any direct relation to a potentiality is obviously distinct from a relation to an actuality; the latter are "added to" God as things become, and so are "composed with" God's primordial nature. God's primordial and consequent natures are again distinct from and "added to" what Hartshorne would call God's abstract pole—necessary, nonrelational attributes (such as being) such that for all x, if x occurs, God experiences x.[10]

While both Hegel and Whitehead deny divine simplicity, it is not a prime concern for them. Both seem to speak to the subject only in consequence of their views of the God-world relation. Classical theism's commitment to divine simplicity made it problematic that God could know things other than Himself. Divine simplicity, for instance, forces Aquinas to argue in effect that God can know other things while in no way experiencing anything other than Himself.[11] For Hegel and Whitehead, by contrast, God includes the world precisely as an experience includes its objects, and is "ontologically structured" accordingly. Whitehead and Hegel may also score a dialectical point by treating God's complexity only as an implication of His relation to the world. Talk of God as simple or complex is talk which abstracts from His relations to the world. Thinkers who wish to depict God as thoroughly interwoven with the world may downgrade such talk to emphasize its distance from God's concrete reality.

Regardless, we have found reason to say that disciples of Whitehead or Hegel must address God's simplicity. As they are committed to divine complexity, they must ask three questions: (1) what intuitions motivate the doctrine that God is simple? (2) how do these intuitions lead to the doctrine? (3) how can one undercut the doctrine—i.e. how can one construct a genuinely "process" philosophical theology which will give these intuitions maximal play and so render the claim that God is simple otiose? We need not address (2) here. As to (1), medieval arguments for divine simplicity take (among other things) "pure actuality," aseity, necessity, being the first cause, maximal goodness and immutability as premises.[12] Thus the intuitive bases of the doctrine of divine simplicity seem to be God's transcendence, independence and superiority. To approach (3), let us see whether Hegel or Whitehead gives these intuitions fuller play in treating the God-world relation.

III

For Hegel, the real referent of "God" is a living process of bringing together the surd contingency and external relatedness of nature with the Idea, Logos or "rational structure"—"God before the creation of the world."[13] This process is the goal of history and is progressively realized throughout history. It is completely actual if and only if finite minds realize that (a) human rational intercourse with nature presupposes that the "rational structure" of nature is identical with that of the human mind (b) that this reveals the meaning of nature and man—that they exist to bring reason to full flower (c) that reason with (b)'s self-awareness is God fully actual.[14]

The identity of the rational structure of mind and nature thus is a necessary condition of God's full actuality. This identity is "concrete:" it involves and is constituted by the existence in different ways and degrees of rationally apprehensible structure in nature, minds and God. Grasping the Idea's sameness in nature and Spirit, then, is not so much seeing properties both share (though it involves this) as seeing that one goal, the Idea's full actuality in Absolute Spirit, is worked out through both.

The Idea, then, is a universal partly actual in nature and finite mind and fully actual only in Absolute Spirit.[15] Thus, the Idea is in a way common to God, and to the world as distinct from God, though only God can perceive this commonality.[16] Divine, "absolute" or "infinite" experience and its contents differ from any possible non-divine experiences and contents. Only divine or absolute experience perceives the fully actual Idea—for only in the attaining of such experience is the Idea fully real. Only divine or absolute experience perceives the world as fully one—for the world is fully one only in the existence of Absolute Spirit, and this existence is constituted by the having of experiences of the world as thus unified.[17]

Now Hegel reiterates that things are "untrue" as apart from God. To be apart from God is to be other than as in the self-experience which is God's full existence. Thus Hegel tells us that things appear differently in divine experience than elsewhere—that God's experience and its contents are not literally identical with others. Rather, the "untruth" of things is a just necessary condition of the existence of their "truth." This is Hegel's "theodicy," and it reinforces the message of God's discreteness from and dependence on the world.

Let us explore this dependence. As Absolute Spirit exists fully when human minds have a certain attitude toward nature and themselves, its full existence presupposes that they exist. The needed attitude is that the contingency of nature is necessary to reason's full flowering.[18] Thus God presupposes nature precisely as contingent, or able to be other than it is. If so, God presupposes not precisely *this* contingent nature but just some contingent nature. If God presupposed precisely this nature, God would then necessitate it, and—presuming that it is in some sense necessary that God come fully to be—God's existence would abolish contingency rather than overcoming it by presupposing it. If God's full existence is the overcoming of contingency, it is the overcoming of *any* contingency, not just the contingency which actually exists.

Finite mind is natural and contingent. If we say that mind and nature constitute the world, then for Hegel the existence of God strongly depends on the existence of *some* world but weakly depends on the existence and precise character of *this* world. God's non-necessary properties weakly depend on the world which gives rise to God. It seems, however, that to add that God's contingent properties strongly depend on the world's precise character would restrict the freedom of mind to make the world what it will. Hegel considers God's full actuality the goal at which the world-process aims. If so, the world is *for the sake of God*. Now if necessary properties are properties, affirmations of which of their subjects are de dicto necessary, all statements of necessary properties strictly imply one another. But if the world is for the sake of God, there is a strong though nonformal sense in which God's necessary properties are prior to, determine and render strongly dependent the world's necessary properties, and so its very existence.

Whitehead's treatment of the God-world relation parallels Hegel's in some ways. For Whitehead, God at t + 1 brings together in a single actuality the nondivine world at t and God's experience at t, which includes God's vision of the realm of "pure potentiality." As primordial and as a single continuing actuality, God is "before" each new phase of the world. Thus in each new phase of divine experience, God does (according to Whitehead) what (according to Hegel) God does over the course of world history: unify the concrete world with "the nature of God before the World." For both Hegel and Whitehead, the world becomes one in God's experiencing it. For Hegel, though, this means that a world which already is one in having a single goal has that goal fully actualized. For Whitehead it merely means that a world whose final truth is atomism is experienced as a whole.

For Whitehead as for Hegel, God "overlaps" the world by exemplifying universal(s) which the world exemplifies. For Whitehead, "pure potentials" haunt time in changeless self-identity. If I and Ferdinand the Bull see daisy-yellow, on Whitehead's account some single entity is literally identical in both of our experiences, and so in us. Of course, Ferdinand and I have distinct relations to daisy-yellow, and it has a different significance for each of us. But either Whitehead means to say that the same entity ingresses my experience and Ferdinand's nonetheless, or he must give up his claim that pure potentials act as (abstract) universals. Now God's complete experience of the realm of pure potentials assures that every such entity ever figuring in any experience also figures in God's. So as primordial, God's experience (which is His being) contains entities also contained by worldly experiences (or beings).

The realm of "pure potentiality" gives the "rational structure" of things in this sense: whatever reason can in any way apprehend in reality is an exemplification of or is some combination of "pure potential." For Hegel, the Idea gives things "rational structure" in that whatever reason can apprehend is somehow an exemplification of the Idea. We can say, then, that for both Hegel and Whitehead God alone perceives the full rational structure or Logos of things. For Hegel, God is in addition the Logos fully actual. Whitehead's Logos is a disjunctive totality involving mutually incompatible possibilities—so full envisionment is perhaps the closest to full realization (at once) that Whitehead can allow the Logos to come.

For Hegel and Whitehead both, God and world overlap only in the Logos. Whitehead's God experiences but is literally discrete from other concrete actualities. God's experience of concreta is for Whitehead necessarily all-inclusive: God has no "negative prehensions."[19] If so, the world's being different entails that God becomes different. For Hegel it is possible that the world be different and yet have the selfsame God emerge from it. But for Whitehead, God's non-necessary properties strongly depend on the world's.

To Whitehead, God's existence strongly depends on the existence of some world. If God is by nature an all-inclusive experience, God could not exist unless objects of experience did. God's existence weakly depends on the existence of precisely this world. God's necessary properties do not seem to determine and be prior to those of the world, as in Hegel. While in Hegel the world is for God and God is for nothing beyond Himself, in Whitehead God and the world are for the sake of each other, and both are "instruments" of Creativity.[20]

To see this, consider that for Whitehead, God is greater than the world because of the way God depends on it.[21] For Hegel, God is greater than the world because He is living reason, that the actuality of which is an end in itself. Though reason requires the world to be actual, its value simply is self-grounded and the standard and justification of all other value.[22] For Hegel, God is the Good. For Whitehead, God is just good, and is so by serving the Good and its servants. That God is Goodness itself is a central affirmation of Anselm, Aquinas, and other partisans of divine simplicity. However much alike they are in other respects, then, Hegel seems here to have captured a classical intuition of divine transcendence which escapes Whitehead.

On the other hand, it is unclear whether one should say that Hegel's deity is like an Aristotelian substance the matter of which is the world, or is like a quality which some substances in the world acquire. If Hegel sees God the latter way, we must say that his world-picture allows for the existence of things that are more ontologically basic than God. Classical theism would object to this. For Whitehead, by contrast, God is at least as basic ontologically as anything else in reality.

To fully judge the relative merits of Hegel and Whitehead on God and the world, then, one must judge whether Hegel's God is more like a substance or a quality. This would amount to trying to decide between left- and right-wing readings of Hegel. There is no need to try so vast a task. Our question was how a process philosopher may undercut the core doctrine of classical theism, the claim that God is really simple. One answer has presented itself: modify a Whiteheadian concept of God in light of those Hegelian insights which one can apply without deciding the interpretive question of left and right. This paper suggests that one can do so by allowing negative prehensions in God, reconceiving divine perfection and seeking a stronger sense in which God is the realization of or even identical with the Logos. Another suggestion might be to allow God literally to share creatures' immediate feelings and so to occupy what Hegel would call an infinite or absolute standpoint. One could perhaps work this out by analogy with Aquinas' theory of "simultaneous" divine and creaturely agency of single creaturely actions. But that is another task.

Notes

1. Cf. e.g. Aquinas, *Summa Theologiae* Ia, Q. 3, passim.

2. Cf. e.g. Anselm, *Proslogion*, ch. 18, passim.

3. Here I am merely appealing to our intuitions about "dependence." I am also of course simplifying matters by not considering the possibility that A really depends on B but some limitation in our own conceptuality or experience prevents our explaining A by B.

4. For God conceived as simple, "essence" is identical with "existence." Such a being thus exists necessarily, whether or not we can produce an ontological argument to prove this and whether or not we can formulate a proposition made true by God's existing alone (in contrast to God standing in some relation to creatures).

5. That is, "mainstream" theism conforms to its roots in the "mainstream" tenets of Western religions. Even if one were to affirm emanationism, so long as one held that creatures are only "conditionally necessary" but in themselves contingent, one could still accede to the text's claim. (This was Avicenna's position).

6. I.e., that whatever is either a part of God or a part of the world is a part of the world.

7. For discussion of some of this debate see my doctoral thesis, *Simplicity and Eternity* (Yale University, 1984), chs. 2, 4, and 7.

8. That this is so on an Aristotelian analysis of change is clear from *Physics* I, 7, 190a14–18. On a Russellian or Whiteheadian analysis of change, the "parts" that continue are the properties or eternal objects a momentary subject exemplifies, and the "part" that passes away is the subject itself.

9. Cf. A. N. Whitehead, *Religion in the Making* (New York: The Macmillan Co., 1926), p. 150; *Science and the Modern World* (New York: Macmillan Co., 1925), p. 252; Donald W. Sherburne, "Whitehead without God," in Brown, James, and Reeves, eds., *Process Philosophy and Christian Thought* (New York: Bobbs-Merrill, 1971), p. 326.

10. This is a nonrelational property because God could have it even if nothing occurred.

11. *Summa Theologica*, Ia: 14, 5.

12. Cf. Aquinas, *Summa Contra Gentiles* I, 18; Bonaventure, *Disputed Questions on the Mystery of the Trinity*, Q. 3, a. 1, args. pro.

13. Cf. *Encyclopedia*, secs. 214 and *zusatz;* 247 and *zusatz.*

14. *Enc.* sec. 212, *zusatz.*

15. Compare the realization of an Aristotelian species: universal in varied members of a species at varied stages of their development.

16. Other beings can see what are in fact "traces" of the Idea. But to see them as such would require grasping the Idea as such. To do so is to be having divine experience.

17. Cf. *Enc.* secs. 576, 577.

18. Cf. E. Fackenheim, *The Religious Dimension in Hegel's Thought* (Boston: Beacon Press, 1967), pp. 114–115.

19. Cf. discussion in William Christian, *An Interpretation of Whitehead's Metaphysics* (New Haven: Yale University Press, 1959), pp. 344–349. I call God's experience *necessarily* all-inclusive on the assumption that Whitehead would accept some formal gloss on statements like "God . . . loses nothing of what can be saved." (*PR* 525).

20. Creativity, not God, is Whitehead's "ultimate category." For God-world mutuality cf. *PR* 527–528.

21. Consider Hartshorne's development of this as God's "surrelativity."

22. *Enc.* sec. 212, *zusatz*.

David A. Pailin
UNIVERSITY OF MANCHESTER

Narrative, Story, and the Interpretation of Metaphysics

During his *Lectures on Modern Idealism* Royce remarks that "under the influence of the literary habits of the time" Hegel attempts to portray "the *Geist*" by means of "a connected series of stories." The result is that the *Phenomenology* might be viewed as "a sort of biography of the world-spirit."[1] Since something similar might plausibly be said of Whitehead's treatment of the primordial and consequent natures of God in the process of reality, the question arises if any insight into the metaphysical positions of Hegel and Whitehead can be gained by considering them as "stories"—stories which offer ultimate understanding of the whole of reality. In this paper, then, I want briefly to indicate how the notion of telling a story may contribute to our appreciation of the works of Hegel and Whitehead. First, though, it is probably necessary to indicate some of the characteristics of a story and what is involved in seeing metaphysical understanding as a story.

I

Discerning the story is not merely an attractive way of coming to know someone or something: it is the basic form of understanding for whatever is actual (and hence has a history). In its narrative a story discloses its subject in its wholeness as, in the light of its context, it relates its origin, development and end—or, instead of its end, its present state and prospects. When these are sufficiently grasped, there is nothing more to inquire into.

Stories have narrative form. As such they are diachronic, ideally comprehensive, social, directional, and synchronic. A story is diachronic in that it reports a sequence of events. It is comprehensive in that it seeks to include all that is relevant for a satisfying understanding of its subject. It starts and ends at points which it is not useful to go beyond; between these points it aims to cover all the factors which were significantly involved in the process. These factors are not merely listed as discrete items. A story presents a social view of reality, connecting its parts to show how its outcome is an intelligible product of their interactions. Furthermore, it presents the social character of the process as being directional. It is not a mere recital of a chain of random consequences. At a minimal level the directionality may be the description of how various factors unwittingly led to a certain result. Where this result is shown to be the consequence of how things are, given the starting-point of the story and the interplay of necessity and chance among its factors, such an indication of directionality may be intellectually satisfying in its exposure of brute reality. On the other hand the directionality of a story may be presented as more or less intentional and thus partly but importantly intelligible as a matter of internal relations. Notions of meaning, value, choice and purpose may then enter into the description. The preference for such understanding of directionality is a consequence of the judgement that intentions provide the ground for a final intelligibility whereas the identification of stark chance and necessity does not. Finally a story as having narrative form is synchronic: it presents the sequence of its story as a whole. Thereby it expresses an overview which may only be perceptible from the standpoint of the end of the story and hence which may combine its items in a coherent pattern which was undetectable to the actors *in mediis rebus.*

Narrative form, however, is not the only characteristic of stories which needs to be considered. Another quality which a story may have is indirectness of reference. In some cases a story provides a way of grasping what cannot be directly apprehended. As a result different stories, using incompatible thought-forms, may nevertheless express the same basic understanding.[2] Whereas Hegel suggests that in philosophy we can pass beyond pictorial representation to grasp the thought which is the real, it may be rather that we are limited to moving in our apprehension of the ultimate nature of things from a less adequate to a more adequate but nevertheless indirect story. If so we are in danger of confusing the form with the content—a content which may not be expressible except indirectly—whenever we are tempted to treat such stories literally.

As well as being indirect, a story may also be its own meaning in the sense that the only way to express its point is to tell it—or another story. This is not the case with all stories. Some stories are used to express intellectual or moral insights which can, if less interestingly, be expressed directly. In other cases, though, it is not possible to divorce the point made by the story from the story itself. The foundation stories by which people understand reality and orient themselves within it may well be of this type. Faiths such as Buddhism, Christianity, and Islam find their point in clusters of stories and cannot be grasped apart from them—just as the point of a biography cannot be independently expressed. The story of the life of John Smith is the meaning of John Smith.

A stimulating story not only provides understanding. It has an occult quality which provokes the imagination of its readers to interpretative development. In this way stories may foster as well as express understanding. Especially where they are appreciated to be indirect means of apprehension, they are open to adjustment, correction, elaboration, and adaptation in order to produce hopefully more satisfying insights into their subjects. A literalist approach to their foundation stories, whether by biblical or by metaphysical fundamentalists, may thus do injustice to the richness of their materials.

Important stories, finally, are self-involving. Not only do they compel as they provide a synchronic and comprehensive understanding of their subject. They also disturb. They demand a response to what they relate—whether a resignation which accepts what they tell as being how things are or a contentment which finds satisfaction in discerning that matters necessarily must be so or a Promethean refusal to be cowed into endorsing the inevitable or a reforming determination to bring about changes. Telling the story may not be the end but, in a way, the start of a story!

In comparing metaphysical understanding with story-telling, I am not claiming that the two are to be identified nor that all cases of the former are to be judged by their success in satisfying the demands of the latter. What I am advancing is the less ambitious suggestion that in cases where the actual is perceived to be in process of becoming, and being is always an abstraction from a process, there the consideration of story-telling may throw some light on the character and appropriate treatment of metaphysical understanding.

Stories about the real are unavoidably selective. Narrators have to choose from a host of items those which they consider to be important. This judgement is made in the light of the ends of the story, items being given significance according to their supposed influence on what occurred. The narrator's pre-understanding of the start and finish of the story thus largely determines how its directivity is perceived and what is worth mentioning in it. One result of this is that the adopted termini may so control how the constituents of a story are presented that its outcome appears inevitable. Intellectual satisfaction may then be achieved through a methodological selectivity which illusorily confines the story to what tidily makes sense of its development[3] Furthermore, what are treated as the termini of stories are not absolute end-points but interim stages within other stories. A choice of different termini can provide a radically different perception of the directivity of the process and hence of the significant factors in its development. The satisfaction that arises from "understanding" the story of the real is therefore to be qualified by the recognition that it is a product of a selectivity guided by its chosen termini.

When metaphysical understanding is regarded as the story of the whole which discloses its meaning by telling its tale, narrative-form is seen to be appropriate for disclosing its processive, interconnected and directive nature. In principle, furthermore, this story should not be subject to the distortions which arise elsewhere when interim points are the termini. The metaphysical story aims at completeness, using—and disclosing—as its termini that beginning and end of which nothing further can be asked since by definition the former has no intelligible antecedent and the latter no consequent. The story is also unqualified in its comprehensiveness since nothing can be outside its perimeters, undistorting since it perceives what is important from the perspective of absolute ends, and ultimately satisfying since it relates the whole story of the whole.

What is the aim in principle is not obviously attainable in practice. The dimensions involved in metaphysical understanding and the desire to render the intelligibility of the whole intellectually satisfying produce problems. While, for instance, the metaphysical story may seek to be diachronic and social in its appreciation of the processive structure of reality, it faces the difficulty that if the process is to include genuine novelty, it cannot be rendered totally intelligible. If, on the other hand, it is seen as being totally intelligible, it is in danger of appearing to be meaningless as a process since its end is perceived as inevitable. A satisfying metaphysical story thus has the difficult task of finding a way to combine the intelligibility of the process with contingency in its events. The comprehensiveness required by the story is another source of difficulty. It demands that the narrator envisage ends which can only be imagined by projections from what is observable within a very limited horizon. These ends, though, determine how the directivity of the process is perceived and hence what is important within it. The metaphysical story-teller needs to establish a convincing way of talking about the whole, a way whose synchronic character does not merely absolutize a current standpoint nor prevent the possibility of recognizing further developments. The 'story' that is sought, in other words, is a story about a reality which is far from finished, whose extensiveness challenges the capacity of coherent imagination and to whose directivity human awareness can provide only uncertain hints.

It might seem that the sensible response to such difficulties is to give up the attempt, even though it would mean that we could not warrantably claim to find ourselves in an intelligible universe which is supportive to human values rather than in a multiverse of pointlessly interacting items. Difficulties, though, do not entail impossibility. Other characteristics of the story-form, furthermore, suggest that such a response may not be the only appropriate one. The quality of indirectness of reference indicates that such stories are perhaps not to be treated as literal descriptions. Although references to non-literalness may be used to cover all kinds of speculative nonsense, there is an opposite danger that literalist restrictions may hide genuine insights into what is obscure. Tentativeness and occult qualities in a story may also be positive virtues, not only because they prevent the story's being treated as an infallible disclosure but also because they stimulate an imaginative apprehension which develops its insights. Difficulties in discerning the metaphysical story need not, therefore, be regarded as posing insuperable obstacles to considering the reasonableness of holding that we find ourselves in an intelligible universe.

In the end, though, the success or failure of the imaginative enterprise of metaphysics depends upon finding grounds for holding that it is reasonable to regard a particular satisfying story as the way to understand the whole. The probable indirectness and openness of such a story will make its testing elusive. On the other hand a plausible story is not to be accepted just because it appears convincing. Among the criteria to be applied to it are those of internal coherence, external fit, universalizability, and intellectual fruitfulness and ability to adapt without degeneration to new insights into reality. Such tests cannot avoid the charge of circularity since any story upon which they are used as a test will provide a fundamental understanding of the reality by comparison with which the story is to be vindicated. They may, though, rule out certain options and indicate how some other possibility does make satisfying sense of various aspects of reality which cannot be ignored.

II

So far, then, as metaphysical systems can be regarded as stories, is it possible to discern a common theme underlying the stories of reality presented by Hegel and Whitehead? The answer to this question cannot be straightforwardly answered by comparing their doctrines individually to see if they agree. Since they offer all-embracing ways of understanding, their individual metaphysical doctrines can only be appreciated in terms of the whole to which they belong. Among the exponents of each system, furthermore, there are considerably divergent interpretations of the doctrines. What can be done, though, is to consider their "stories" to see whether the overall pictures tally in significant ways even though the details may at times appear remarkably different.

Hegel and Whitehead seek to identify the ultimate structure of reality in terms of which all its constituent events become intelligible. In both cases the structure is diachronic: reality is a process involving interactions, change, development, and emergence. Some of the differences of presentation of this structure are attributable to the different aspects of reality which provide their models. Hegel is considerably influenced by history in his identification of the story of the whole of reality. While he speaks of nature as "the development of the Idea in Space," his primary insights are more the product of his view of world history as where the absolute *Geist* develops in time.[4] Whitehead's story in comparison is rather moulded by his perception of the processes of nature. The story of reality is the story of the actualization of contents of the primordial nature of God to enrich his consequent nature. The differences, though, are largely differences of presentation of a common theme.

In both cases reality as a whole is presented as constituting a universe. Hegel, for example, affirms that the study of world history shows that it is not the product of "mere chance." It has "proceeded rationally" since it "represents the rationally necessary course of the World Spirit, the Spirit whose nature is indeed always one and the same but whose nature unfolds in the course of the world."[5] In this process nothing is lost for the "present stage of the Spirit contains all previous stages within itself." What it seems to have abandoned as past in fact "it still possesses in the depth of its present."[6] For Whitehead reality is not only totally interconnected so that each event "modifies to some extent the character of every event."[7] The many find their unity and preservation in the relationship of God and the World in which "each temporal occasion embodies God, and is embodied in God."[8]

This understanding of the underlying unity of things means that the ultimate structure of the process lies beyond what is described by secularist studies of natural science and human history. For all the insights that such studies provide, the processes which they seek to identify are ultimately pointless. The natural order, for example, may be seen as working out the successive interactions of chance and necessity or expressing some implicate order in the universal flux, but what is sought are relations that obtain *semper, ubique, et in omnibus*. These are brute facts which give intelligibility to the events occurring within the natural order but they do not render that order itself a satisfyingly intelligible structure. It just is. History, in contrast, can be satisfyingly intelligible as its study indicates that the human actions which are being examined are the expressions of value-guided purposes. It is a purposing, however, which is finally pointless when humanity ceases to exist as this planet, whether through human actions or through natural processes, ceases to be capable of producing and sustaining human life. The fate of Ozymandias is the fate not only of all individuals but of the reality that the natural sciences and historical studies describe:

> Round the decay
> Of that colossal wreck, boundless and bare
> The lone and level sands stretch far away.[9]

What both Hegel and Whitehead seek to identify is the story that comprehends the patterns of events investigated by the natural sciences and by historical studies and which is partially and distortedly perceived through their perspectives. This story discerns underlying those patterns and their events a source of movement which gives to the whole, and hence to its constituents, overall directivity, purpose and value.

The process of reality is thus presented as a story with directivity. Its outcomes are not the unintended product of the interplay of chance and necessity but the outworkings of activities influenced by a goal. Whatever accidental features may characterize any individual event, there is a basic rationality about whatever happens. Hegel puts his thesis thus:

It was for a while the fashion to admire God's wisdom in animals, plants, and individual lives. If it is conceded that Providence manifests itself in

NARRATIVE, STORY, AND INTERPRETATION   275

such objects and materials, why not also in world history? Because its scope seems to be too large. But the divine wisdom, or Reason, is the same in the large as in the small. We must not deem God too weak to exercize his wisdom on a grand scale. Our intellectual striving aims at recognizing that what eternal wisdom *intended* it has actually *accomplished*, dynamically active in the world, both in the realm of nature and that of the spirit.[10]

Whitehead himself compares his understanding of the concrescence of a *res vera* to "the Hegelian development of an idea" and sees "the whole story" as being "comprised within the account of the subjective concrescence of *rēs verae*."[11] In this story "God and the World are the contrasted opposites in terms of which Creativity achieves its supreme task of transforming disjoined multiplicity, with its diversities in opposition, into concrescent unity, with its diversities in contrast."[12] God is "the lure for feeling, the eternal urge of desire" which has "particular relevance to each creative act,"[13] drawing the World unceasingly according to that "creative advance into novelty" which is "the ultimate metaphysical ground."[14]

Whether the goal of the directivity is seen as the self-conscious actualization of the absolute Idea or the unresting expression of creativity where the idea is "beyond realization" while "yet it moulds the form of what is realized,"[15] the directivity gives to the story an ultimate meaningfulness. Not only does it describe what ultimately is so; it sees in it a character which is intrinsically satisfying as well as intelligible. Here is found that ultimacy in being, value and rationality which, as "that than which a greater cannot be conceived," marks the completion of the quest for understanding.

In order to establish the coherence of this theme, both Hegel and Whitehead find the final clue to the character of reality in the notion of mind. As a process in which the Absolute achieves self-consciousness[16] or as a process in which the "really actual" completes "the deficiency of his mere conceptual actuality,"[17] the value-seeking directivity of reality only makes sense in terms of the activity of mind. As all-embracing this mind, furthermore, is to be understood theistically—or, perhaps more accurately, panentheistically. According to Hegel, for instance, "mind is essentially active," not "a processless *ens*"[18] and God is to be understood accordingly as "the eternal Process."[19] Although in Hegel's day as well as in ours, there is "so little consciousness of God, and his objective essence is so little dwelt upon,"[20] the notion of God is "the quasi-pictorial representation" of that which is "the essential and actual spirit of nature and spirit"[21] which philosophy recognizes must also be unified in "the simple spiritual vision."[22] In Whitehead it is the activity of God which ensures that the creative process is unending by being "the organ of novelty" for each concresing actuality[23] as well as its fulfilment through its reception as actual into his consequent nature.[24] In both stories the notion of God may have characteristics which are not in accordance with traditional theistic thinking but the notion is crucial for the story and it is a notion of what is defensible as a notion of the divine.

III

Hegel and Whitehead offer, then, stories whose themes challenge the secularism which dominates much recent Western thought about nature and history. Their stories are complete in that they seek to make sense of the whole in terms of that which is intrinsically satisfying. The problem of the alienating effects of the transcendent or the necessary is effectively overcome when the ultimate not only is held to be immanent in all but also is recognized to be in principle unsurpassable in value, in actuality the all-inclusive repository of achieved values and in intention the promoter of the maximum expressions of value. There are, however, points at which the stories call for development either to clarify some matters or to overcome infelicities in their classical presentations. As has been noted, the possibility of such developments is a consequence of the imaginative openness belonging to stimulating stories. The diversity of interpretations which attend the works of Hegel and Whitehead indicates, further, that willy nilly this is what they produce in readers as the latter struggle with the texts to discern what the former were seeking to perceive and express!

Leaving aside points of detail, there are some general issues in the stories presented by Hegel and Whitehead which warrant further attention. In one way or another they concern the directivity and completeness of those stories. Stories that are satisfying do not just stop; they reach an end which marks the intelligible completion of a process. Earlier it was suggested that metaphysical stories have the advantage—and the problem—that their termini are not interim stages in other stories. The danger is that the desire to find completeness may lead to its being considered that the metaphysical story must lead to and specify a material end-point of the process which it describes if it is to be satisfying. This, though, is not a necessary entailment of the desire for what Kermode has called "a sense of an ending." The "end" of a process which allows a complete story to be told about it may be a formal goal which is never finally attained: among such possible goals are "unceasing creative activity" and "the proliferation of aesthetic experience." If such were the goal of reality, its story could be considered to have completion, in that its final aim would be known, while it would not therefore be completed, in that its activities in response to that aim were not exhausted (and, if the aim had unlimited potentialities, might never be). It seems, furthermore, that a process of reality which could be understood to be materially completeable would not be finally satisfying. The writing of a final "finis" to the story—though presumably it would only be done by imaginative anticipation—would not mark a climax but an emptiness of the "death" of God where all is gone.

Accordingly, in developing the Hegelian story, those points where it is suggested that the process has reached an end in the attainment of self-consciousness by the Absolute perhaps ought to be interpreted not in terms of the story of reality being completed but rather in terms of the recognition of the formal goal which is to be everlastingly pursued. On this understanding Hegel's remarks about the end of the process seem to be compatible with his other comments about the unending character of the process—as when he writes that "the eternal Idea, in full fruition of its essence, eternally sets itself to work, engenders and enjoys itself as absolute Mind."[25] Similarly what Whitehead says about the primordial nature of God is to be interpreted not as restricting possibilities to a fixed, if unimaginably huge, number but as holding that God is the inexhaustible source of novelty which stirs the processes of reality. It is a point that Whitehead makes: "The immensity of the world negatives the belief that any state of order can be so established that beyond it there can be no progress."[26] In any case the satisfaction of love does not lie in the achievement of some final state of affairs but in what is there to be cherished "in the immediate present."[27]

The synchronic character of stories is always subject to the danger that it unwarrantably makes the standpoint of the narrator final. This is particularly the case when a narrative continues up to the present or extends into the future. Previous events are then most likely to be evaluated according to their contribution to the present (or the presently envisaged future) and are seen as finding their fulfilment in the present understanding of such matters. Histories written in earlier times are revealing in the ways that they show how different perspectives, determined by earlier points in the ongoing series of events as well, perhaps, as by different cultural evaluations, lead to very different views as to what is significant and hence to what past events are important. The danger for the metaphysical story is that it may be influenced unwarrantably, though perhaps not always avoidably, by the point of view of those who discern it. Whitehead in this respect makes an important point when he remarks that "the chief danger to philosophy is narrowness in the selection of evidence"—a limitation that arises from personal and social provinciality.[28]

A credible metaphysical story needs not simply a move from the culturally blinkered (as when the goals of reality are seen in terms of aesthetic enrichments that are appropriate only to that minority of humanity which is relatively wealthy materially and intellectually) to human values as such. It needs a move from the human to the cosmic—to a recognition of ultimate values which do not, consciously or unconsciously, presuppose that the point of the story of creation is what is good for humankind. Whether or not we are imaginative enough to reach such insights, to be sought is a story about the whole which makes sense of it when humankind is recognized to be a temporary presence on a planet of one of billions of stars. The result may be less comforting than we might hope for but claims which assume that the divine and human have the same interests are liable to be seen as too anthropocentric to be metaphysically—or theistically—credible. When Hegel remarks that "the divine nature is the same as the human,"[29] he may be making a valid point about the (limited) way in which we can apprehend the divine nature but so far as the story of reality as a whole is concerned, "the Good" that is "the general final-end of the world"[30] and "the poet of the world" who "with tender patience" leads it "by his vision of truth, beauty, and goodness"[31] must be perceived cosmically. Humankind will make a contribution to the actualization of parts of that vision but it is only a contribution. It will not satisfy the vision and it is only significant as part of that vision—as means to its attainment, not as an end in itself. Hegel may disturb us, but he properly sets a question-mark against our self-centered concern that the ultimate foster human values, when he writes that

The particular in most cases is too trifling as compared with the universal; the individuals are sacrificed and abandoned. The Idea pays the tribute of existence and transience, not out of its own funds but with the passions of the individuals.[32]

A further point concerns the intrinsic meaningfulness of the story of reality. The requirement of intelligibility is always liable to render apparently inevitable any pattern of development of which we seek to make sense. Chance or contingency appear as surds. They leave us dissatisfied; we consider that we have not fully understood a story in which there are events so describable. Accordingly Hegel may seem to indicate what a satisfying story demands when he states that "it soon becomes evident that thought will be satisfied with nothing short of showing the *necessity* of its facts, of demonstrating the existence of its objects, as well as their nature and qualities."[33] If, though, the necessity were intrinsic in what was reported as the story and not just a matter of the narrator's perception of what was happening, the story of reality as a whole would be a valueless charade since all that is apparently achieved within it would be determined from the beginning. Indeed, if it were accepted that the move from the future to the past is the movement from possibilities to determinate actuality, then its diachronic character would seem to be illusory. On the other hand, should the necessity be held to be a matter of the narrator's way of making sense of what occurred but not an intrinsic character of the events reported, then the events are possibly made intelligible by the imposition of a mode of understanding which misrepresents them.

On reflection, furthermore, it appears that the requirement of intelligibility is not that all relationships and so all events in a process must be necessary but that what is necessary in the process be intelligible as such and what is contingent likewise be intelligible as such. Another, more radical way of putting it is that the necessary structures must be seen to be necessarily necessary and the contingent necessarily contingent. From this it follows that a story's conclusion does not have to be shown to be inevitable in order for it to be intelligible: what is required for intelligibility is that elements of chance and decisions involved in the story be appreciated to be such. Whether, on the other hand, in every event "there is always a contingency left open for immediate decision,"[34] as Whitehead argues, depends among other things on the possibility of establishing a coherent sense for the notion of "decision" in relation to every kind of event. So far as stories are concerned, though, it is the totality of the story and not the necessity (or the partial contingency) of each of its constituent events that is required for it to be intelligible.

There is also the question of the directivity of the story. As it moves towards some cosmically appropriate formal goal or goals, how is its directivity to be understood? Hegel, for example, speaks of "the *cunning of Reason*" as it "sets the passions to work for itself, while that through which it develops itself pays the penalty and suffers the loss."[35] Whitehead writes of "the subject's prehension of the primordial nature of God" in terms of "a lure for feeling":[36] the source of creative novelty acts quietly and tenderly, not enforcing its will but influencing the course of events "in the patient operation of the overpowering rationality of his conceptual harmonization."[37] Such comments raise questions about the self-consciousness and mode of activity of the directing agent. So far as the agency is held to be either "cunning" or non-coercive, the stories may maintain that its non-recognizability as an identifiable factor in the course of events is no overwhelming objection to its reality. At the same time it does suggest that the ultimate acts as a kind of cosmic Svengali, manipulating others—by cunning or by lure—to do more or less what is desired by that ultimate. Admittedly Hegel's cunning reason is apparently much more determinative than Whitehead's lures; nevertheless in both stories the ultimate seems to act in ways that are not directly detectable.

It is possible, though, that the desire to speak of directivity in this way is a product of the view that has earlier been criticized—namely, the view that the goal of the process of reality is a materially determinate one. If such were the case, then it would have to be envisaged, presumably consciously envisaged, by that which sought to direct all things towards its actualization. If, however, the goal is understood formally in terms of the continual appearance of novelty and the proliferation of value, such a self-conscious source of direction may no longer be required. All that may be needed is a force, tendency, or desire for change which ensures that every concrescing event has the possibility of instantiating new values. In that case the theistic or panentheistic notion of a self-conscious ultimate agent—God—would not be demanded by the directivity of the story of reality as we are aware of it (although it would be compatible with such a story). The directing agency would not be seeking at any point a specific material goal, long-term or short-term. What it would be seeking are expressions of value. "God" would then be seen not as a self-conscious agent attempting to fulfill specific material goals but as the persistent urge for novelty as value-enriching which is found within the creative process. The point—and the finally satisfying point—of the story of reality is that it is persistently disturbed by a challenge to produce what is novel and valuable. The figure of "God" which emerges is less personally-related and comforting than the God of many religious believers. It is a "God" who is forever disturbing the process.

The question which may remain is whether the metaphysical stories presented by Hegel and Whitehead have a genuinely (panen) theistic theme. Both authors give a central role to the notion of God. Hegel writes of a correct perception of the "idea of God" and of "the relationship of God and the world" as the basic need of "all philosophies and all religions."[38] Whitehead envisages God, with primordial and consequent natures, as the origin and fulfilment of the processes of reality. On the other hand in both stories the concept of God is treated in ways which involve revisions of the classical way of understanding what is meant by "God". In the end, though, the question of labels is not important. Both authors provide stories about reality that suggest that it is to be understood as processive, creative, and directional. Underlying its nature as such is that which continually stirs it towards novel expressions of value. In this reality humankind makes its contribution and may find comfort in the recognition that what it achieves is forever preserved—the "zest of existence" is "refreshed by the ever-present, unfading importance of our immediate actions, which perish and yet live for ever more."[39]

Notes

1. J. Royce, *Lectures on Modern Idealism* (New Haven: Yale University Press, 1919), p. 149.

2. Cf. how Bultmann sees the same basic understanding presented in what he calls "mythological" terms in the New Testament and in existentialist terms in modern theology.

3. This is an illusion which may arise from the application of Occam's razor as a principle in the selection and use of evidence about events.

4. G. W. F. Hegel, *Reason in History*, translated by R. S. Hartman (New York: Liberal Arts Press, 1953), p. 87.

5. *Ibid.*, p. 12.

6. *Ibid.*, p. 95.

7. A. N. Whitehead, *The Concept of Nature* (Ann Arbor: University of Michigan Press, 1957), p. 159.

8. Whitehead, *Process and Reality*, edited by D. R. Griffin and D. W. Sherburne (New York: The Free Press, 1978), p. 348.

9. From 'Ozymandias' by Percy Bysshe Shelley.

10. Hegel, *Reason in History*, p. 18.

11. Whitehead, *Process and Reality*, p. 167.

12. *Ibid.*, p. 348.

13. *Ibid.*, p. 344.

14. *Ibid.*, p. 349; cf. p. 88. Although Whitehead writes on p. 349 of God's being "in the grip of the ultimate metaphysical ground" and on p. 88 of God as "the outcome of creativity" (cf. p. 7 also when God is said to be the "primordial, non-temporal accident" of the "ultimate" that is termed "creativity"), such statements need not be interpreted as implying that "God" is not "ultimate" but derivative from something prior. It can be argued that what Whitehead here describes, in a possibly misleading manner, is the essential nature of God. God, that is, is neither prior nor posterior to "the ultimate metaphysical ground" but inescapably *is* that ground. Statements which describe that ground are necessary, a priori truths *for* us which express what is embodied *in* God. The relationship of what they express to God is therefore not to be understood in voluntarist terms (for they are not dependent on God's choice of them) nor in intellectualist terms (for they are not imposed on God by some principle(s) which is beyond and over-against God). To identify these truths is to identify what in part God is in himself. Some such interpretation of Whitehead's remarks about God is necessary if they are to be theistically appropriate and, I suggest, can be warranted by his overall position.

15. A. N. Whitehead, *Modes of Thought* (Cambridge: Cambridge University Press, 1938), pp. 164ff.

16. Cf. G. W. F. Hegel, *The Phenomenology of Mind*, translated by J. B. Baillie (London: Swan Sonnenschein, 1910), p. 822.

17. Whitehead, *Process and Reality*, p. 349.

18. G. W. F. Hegel, *The Logic of Hegel*, translated from *The Encyclopaedia of the Philosophical Sciences* by W. Wallace (Oxford: Clarendon Press, 1892), p. 69.

19. G. W. F. Hegel, *Lectures on the Philosophy of Religion*, translated by E. B. Speirs and J. B. Sanderson (London: Kegan Paul, Trench and Trübner, 1895), Vol. III, p. 13.

20. G. W. F. Hegel, *Philosophy of Mind*, translated from *The Encyclopaedia of the Philosophical Sciences*, by W. Wallace (Oxford: Clarendon Press, 1894), para. 554, p. 168.

21. *Ibid.*, para. 565, p. 176.

22. *Ibid.*, para. 572, p. 181.

23. Whitehead, *Process and Reality*, p. 67.

24. Cf. *ibid.*, p. 350.

25. Hegel, *Philosophy of Mind*, para. 577, p. 197.

26. Whitehead, *Process and Reality*, p. 111.

27. *Ibid.*, p. 343.

28. *Ibid.*, p. 337.

29. Hegel, *The Phenomenology of Mind*, p. 770.

30. Hegel, *The Philosophy of Religion*, Vol. III, p. 345.

31. Whitehead, *Process and Reality*, p. 346.

32. Hegel, *Reason in History*, p. 44.

33. Hegel, *The Logic of Hegel*, pp. 3f.

34. Whitehead, *Process and Reality*, p. 284.

35. Hegel, *Reason in History*, p. 44.

36. Whitehead, *Process and Reality*, p. 189.

37. *Ibid.*, p. 346.

38. Hegel, *Philosophy of Mind*, para. 573, p. 192.

39. Whitehead, *Process and Reality*, p. 351.

John E. Smith
YALE UNIVERSITY

The Meaning of Religious Experience in Hegel and Whitehead

In order to avoid misunderstanding, I wish to make clear at the outset that the expression "religious experience" in my title is not meant to denote only personal episodes in individual life but rather the entire range of phenomena in and through which religion manifests itself and becomes available for reflective interpretation. Whitehead did, of course, use this expression in *Religion in the Making* and, in fact, it had become by that time a household word among philosophers largely because of its central place in the most widely-read book on the philosophy of religion in this century, James' *Varieties of Religious Experience*. That some such counterpart expression as "religiöse Erfahrung" was not current in Hegel's time need occasion no difficulty since his approach was thoroughly experiential in the sense that it requires the philosopher to immerse himself in the subject matter, as it were, so as to comprehend what religion actually shows itself to be.

It would, I believe, be generally admitted that the religious dimension of experience figures prominently in the systematic philosophy of both Hegel and Whitehead. The interesting question concerns what may be learned about their thought, about religion, philosophy, and the relations between the two, by a comparison of the ways in which these thinkers treated the subjects. Hegel repeatedly maintained that the supreme object of philosophical thought is Truth in that sense, as he said, in which God and God alone is Truth, and throughout his system he reiterated the claim that the content of religion and philosophy is the same, the difference residing in their respective modes of expression. Whitehead, in addition to developing a doctrine of God within the framework of a metaphysics of organism, insisted that the phenomena of religion must be taken seriously into account by any philosopher hoping to arrive at a conceptual scheme adequate for the interpretation of everything that happens.

In order to reduce a near-infinitude of detail to proportions adequate for our purposes, I shall start with a brief anticipation of where I shall end. Given Hegel's conception of the task of philosophy and the method he pursued, it was inevitable that he should attempt to construe religion, and especially Christianity, within the scope of his philosophy of Absolute Spirit. As I shall point out, however, this does not mean what is so often said by those who have not read Hegel but know nevertheless what he "must" have said, that he simply defined religion to suit the needs of his metaphysics. Something more profound than that is involved. Hegel could not, however, leave religion standing with its own autonomy, since it was his ultimate aim to make it intelligible in a way that transcends any intelligibility religion can attain from its own resources. Whitehead, on the other hand, imposes no such demand on his enterprise. He can, so to speak, let religion *be*, free to contribute its own distinctive voice to the chorus that alone is adequate for expressing the full spectrum of experience which must be the philosopher's primary concern.

The difference between the two thinkers in this regard stands out even more clearly when we consider that, for Hegel, religion is a determinate phase of consciousness and a mode of apprehension in the process whereby Absolute Spirit reaches that self-consciousness in which form and content have become fully in accord with each other. Whitehead, by contrast, although he marked out particular stages in the historical development of religion, did not regard religion itself as a stage in a linear progression issuing in any form of consummation beyond it. This difference in philosophical aims is by no means inconsiderable and serves to explain the divergence in their treatment of religious faith and practice. Hegel's later interpretation of religion as the self-elevation of subjective Spirit to God is a conception necessary for understanding how religion can be the penultimate form of self-consciousness in the final transition to philosophy. In this sense Hegel was constrained and could not avoid making religion subject to the demands of his philosophical vision; and while, like Kierkegaard, one may object to the subordination, there is much to be learned from suspending disbelief for the purpose of seeing how religion actually fills the role assigned to it. Although Whitehead was no less concerned than Hegel to develop a comprehensive categoreal scheme for interpreting the full scope of becoming in its creativity, the fundamental realism of his position does *not* impose systematic demands on the constituents of experience so that they come to have an independence and exercise an autonomy in the way of contributing distinctive evidence for the construction of the metaphysical scheme. It is for this reason that Whitehead was able to pursue a philosophical inquiry into the ultimate and pervasive quality of the cosmic scheme and then consult the deliverances of religious insight for the purpose of comparing the results.

In presenting Hegel's interpretation of religion, I wish to call attention to what I take to be a neglected but most important factor in his treatment of the subject, namely, his tendency to pass too quickly over the nature of theology and the role it performs in the life and development of the religious community. If one supposes, as Hegel does throughout his system, that religion possesses a content which it apprehends only in the form of images and pictorial thought, and that it is the task of philosophy to bring this content to its full conceptual expression and to show its truth, then it seems that theology must be subsumed under religion (taken in Hegel's broadest sense) and no attention will be paid to the distinctive function of theology *within* the religious community in conceptualizing and systematizing religious insight. Even if, as was undoubtedly the case with the three Western religious traditions, theology for the most part was made possible as a discipline through the use of philosophical categories and principles derivative from the schools of ancient philosophy, the fact remains that the task Hegel assigned to philosophy *vis à vis* the religious content was already being discharged in its own way by theology. In short, the religious community did not have to wait for philosophy, and certainly not for Hegel's philosophy, to express its own affirmations in conceptual form. Hegel can scarcely have been unaware of this fact, but he seems to have blunted its edge by incorporating within religion the body of theological construction which was an integral, although distinctive, part of the Christian heritage. Thus in considering such doctrines as the Trinity and the Incarnation, Hegel was availing himself of the work already done by theologians, but he makes no special acknowledgment of this prior intellectual activity. The reason for this oversight is probably to be found in his belief in the universality of reason and the supposition that there is no need to distinguish the self-understanding of religion in theology from an interpretation provided by an autonomous philosophy. I cannot pursue this theme further under the circumstances, but it is far from unimportant since the chief source of tension between philosophy and theology has always been the question as to which is to have the priority. If each claims to be ultimate and each in turn demands the subordination of the other, how is a direct conflict to be avoided? This question will serve as an introduction to the discussion of Hegel since in the course of working the matter out he developed both alternatives, holding in his earlier writings prior to the Jena period that religion surpasses philosophy and then reversing the relationship in his mature system where philosophy is clearly established as the ultimate reconciling power.

As a prelude to a summary account of Hegel's odyssey in interpreting religion and determining its proper relation to philosophy, it will be helpful to distinguish three closely related senses in which religion is understood in his writings. There is, first, what he called the "subjective" dimension of religion manifest in the relation of the individual to God in faith, love, and devotion. In describing religion in this sense, Hegel usually had Pietism in mind and, while he criticized the adequacy of this form when taken all by itself, it is an error to suppose that he did not take it seriously as a "moment" in the total pattern of religion. Second, there is religion on its "objective" side, which is its manifestation in the spiritual community structured by doctrine, worship, and community service. There is, in addition, a third sense of religion encompassing the other two in which it is seen as a total phenomenon or phase in the process whereby Absolute Spirit attains to self-consciousness. This is religion in that exalted sense in which it figures along with art and philosophy in the ultimate triad that expresses the truth and reality of the Absolute Idea. All three senses are important, but it is obviously the third conception of religion that is paramount in Hegel's final determination of its relation to philosophy.

Hegel's struggle, sometimes intensely personal, to plumb the depths of religion in order to determine its nature and proper place in the scheme of things has been recounted by a number of thinkers, including especially Richard Kroner and James Collins,[1] who have succeeded in showing how Hegel worked his way through Pietist, Enlightenment, and Romantic approaches to religion, declared the inadequacy of Kant's pure, moral religion, and finally came to the conclusion that divine love must be the ultimate principle, a conclusion set forth in *The Spirit of Christianity and its Fate*. Although Hegel claimed that the love at the core of the religious teaching of Jesus cannot finally be expressed in the community—the "fate" of Christianity is that it fell into an objectivity of creed and dogma which made this impossible—he nevertheless steadfastly maintained that the love proclaimed by Jesus and exemplified in his relation to the Father is the apex of religion. "Is there an idea," he wrote, "more beautiful than that of a nation of men related to one another by love? Is there one more uplifting than that of belonging to a whole which as a whole, as one, is the spirit of God whose sons the individual members are?" (*Spirit*, Knox, p. 271) Having said this much, however, Hegel was not entirely satisfied with this view of the matter; love, he declared, is a divine spirit, "but it still falls short of religion" (*Spirit*, Knox, p. 289) which requires both an objective form and fusion with the universal, an idea, uniting the subject with an objective reality or God. The "fate" and thus the tragedy of Christianity is that it was forced to form a separate and particular community, something that militates against the uniting of *all* beings.

Further insight into Hegel's interpretation of religion at this point is to be found in the *Fragment* of 1800, where the concept of life plays a central role and the relation between religion and philosophical thought is further defined. He speaks of the impulse of all individuals to raise themselves from "transience" to the level of an all-living and all-powerful infinite life, one that is not "a [bare] unity, a conceptual abstraction" (*Fragment*, Knox, p. 311), in a process where we are no longer merely "thinking or contemplating" (*Ibid.*) because the infinite life does not contain anything reflected or, what is the same, anything dead. "This self-elevation of man," Hegel writes,

not from the finite to the infinite (for those terms are only products of mere reflection, and as such their separation is absolute), but from finite life to infinite life, is religion. . . . When man takes this animated manifold as a multiplicity of many individuals, yet as connected with the animating spirit, then these single lives become organs, and the infinite whole becomes an infinite totality of life. When he takes the infinite life as the spirit of the whole and at the same time as a living [being] outside himself (since he himself is restricted), and when he puts himself at the same time outside his restricted self in rising toward the living being and intimately uniting himself with him, then he worships God. (*Fragment*, Knox, pp. 311-12)

In attempting to interpret further the meaning of life, Hegel engaged the problem that was to occupy him for so much of his life, namely, the dialectic of the opposites and the possibility of their unification. Life, he says, is the union of union and nonunion and neither element can be denied; the problem, however, is how this can be rationally and consistently apprehended. In attempting to answer this question, Hegel was led to a most important observation about the nature of reflection itself. "Every expression, whatsoever," he wrote, "is a product of reflection, and therefore it is possible to demonstrate in the case of every expression that, when reflection propounds it, another expression, not propounded, is excluded." He concludes:

> Reflection is thus driven on and on without rest; but this process must be checked once and for all by keeping in mind that, for example, what has been called a union of synthesis and antithesis is not something propounded by the understanding or by reflection but has a character of its own, namely, that of being a reality beyond all reflection. (*Fragment*, Knox, p. 312)

Finite life, Hegel continues, is always partial in the literal sense that in the individual there is something not living but dead and this something is also dead for all the other individuals. This partial character of finite life, Hegel says, is "transcended in religion" through the rising of finite life to infinite life. The priority of religion over philosophy at this point is quite clearly stated in the sequel. "Philosophy therefore," he wrote,

> has to stop short of religion because it is a process of thinking and, as such a process, implies an opposition with nonthinking [processes] as well as the opposition between the thinking mind and the object of thought. Philosophy has to disclose the finiteness in all finite things and require their integration by means of reason. In particular, it has to recognize the illusions generated by its own infinite and thus to place the true infinite outside its confines. (*Fragment*, Knox, p. 313)

The enormous difference between the Hegel of the early theological writings and the *Fragment* just cited and the Hegel of the *Encyclopedia* and the *Science of Logic* (the transformation had, of course, already taken place in the *Phenomenology*) is striking in the extreme. It is difficult to imagine the Hegel of the mature system proposing that philosophy should stop short of anything or of allowing that the true infinite is beyond the reach of reason.

As Kroner has pointed out, this solution could not permanently satisfy a thinker with such lofty speculative ambitions. Hegel set out, therefore, to find a new solution, but not without having learned much from his early studies. To begin with, despite his assigning to religion the ultimate place, his historical analysis of Christianity convinced him that religion does not provide a final reconciliation precisely because "church and state, worship and life, piety and virtue, spiritual and worldly action can never dissolve

MEANING OF RELIGIOUS EXPERIENCE 291

into one." (*Spirit,* Knox, p. 301) And in this conclusion he was comparing the fate that befell Christianity with his vision of Greek religion as the synthesis of the life and *ethos* of a people. Hegel's task was to find a way of preserving and reconciling the truth of the national religion, the truth of the Gospel, and the demands of speculative thought. His early analysis of the structure of religious experience did, however, leave him with a fundamental insight that was to direct his further thought, and it may indeed have been the first apprehension Hegel had of the idea that was to receive its elaboration in his distinctive doctrine of the *Begriff.* In reflecting on the doctrine of the Trinity and on the celebration of the Lord's Supper, Hegel detected a development or cycle in the latter that has its counterpart in the former. Spiritual life, he claimed, goes out of itself, objectifies itself in the symbolic, and then returns to itself in a movement that is grasped by the mind as the passage from a subjectivity made objective in the outer act of the Sacrament and back to subjectivity again in the form of the individual experience or the outer world become subjective. The Trinity manifests the same process whereby an original unity of life is dirempted only to be restored again in the loving community of the three Persons. The principle that was in time to make its way into the foreground of Hegel's *Logic* and philosophy of Spirit is that neither life nor love can exist and be understood without a disunion following on an original harmony and the recovery of that harmony in a circle that is the union of union and disunion. It is not insignificant that this germinal idea came to Hegel in the course of his examination of the religious consciousness as expressed both in thought and devotion.

The path leading from Hegel's early thought to the position attained in the *Encyclopedia* and the *Lectures on the Philosophy of Religion* where philosophy is definitely established as the final and only fully adequate form for the expression of Absolute Spirit is long and has been well charted. It is sufficient to call attention to three central insights or factors that determined the development. The first is expressed in a passage from Anselm's *Cur Deus Homo?* cited twice by Hegel in the *Encyclopedia;* it runs as follows:

It seems careless for us, once we are established in the faith, not to aim at understanding what we believe.[2]

In arguing against various forms of the opposition between knowing and believing, Hegel suggests on the basis of this passage that philosophy is the making explicit of what is implicit in religion; philosophy is religion understood. The same person who says the Creed as a young person also recites it as an old man and between the two there is a world of difference in comprehension and personal significance. Although this view points in the direction of what is to come in the relations between the two, it suggests not so much a subordination of religion to philosophy as a mutual development in which the religious impulse in man to become related to infinite life takes the lead, as it were, and is followed by a reflective effort to grasp the truth of this relationship. As Collins (*Emergence*, p. 216) rightly points out, this conception of the relation between religion and philosophy is not an instrumental one since the two are seen as phases in one process of awareness. Here, as throughout Hegel's thought, religious reality serves both as a source of experience and a goad for philosophical reflection.[3] One has the distinct impression that in the total dimension of religion Hegel saw a monumental challenge to the speculative thinker to permeate it with a form of knowledge superior to any religion might provide for itself.

The second idea that contributed to the development of Hegel's later position *vis à vis* religion is to be found in his brilliant dialectical treatment of the opposition between Pietism and Enlightenment in their conceptions of religion.[4] In this account Hegel is motivated by a concern to show the inadequacy of any position that would locate religion in a sphere inaccessible to rational comprehension. We may foreshorten Hegel's argument and concentrate on the essential point, namely, that Pietism and Enlightenment, although outwardly antithetical, must be understood as a meeting of extremes resulting in the same erroneous conclusion. According to Hegel, the rationalism of Enlightenment and the elevation of feeling and immediacy in Pietism both lead to agnosticism and the denial that the content of religion can be articulated intelligibly. In retreating within feeling, Pietism thwarts any advance to conceptualization; in rejecting feeling in favor of the understanding, Enlightenment is unable to think what Hegel calls the "proper infinities" expressed in Kant's Ideas. Both fail to advance to the truth of the Concept and neither appreciates the presence of Spirit in the community which itself is founded on the religious content. Pietism *refuses* to develop its rationality and Enlightenment *cannot* do so; both standpoints, says Hegel, fail to rise above abstract subjectivity and individual arbitrariness. Hegel's belief in the power of the philosophy of Spirit and the concept to reconcile these opposites becomes clear in his reconstruction of the situation. True to his principle of finding and preserving the element of truth in every inadequate spiritual form, Hegel claims that Pietism was right in demanding a place for feeling and in refusing to accept the identification of religion with abstract dogma alone. Enlightenment, on the other hand, was also right in insisting on the importance of freedom and the need to express the religious content in some form of rationality. But, again, the abstract understanding is not adequate to the task. It is at this point that Hegel begins to speak in earnest about the role of a philosophy of Spirit. The ultimate opposition to be reconciled turns on freedom; Pietism, in rejecting the demand of rationality, negates freedom, whereas Enlightenment retains a freedom that is merely abstract. Only a philosophy of Spirit, he claims, can preserve the truth and cancel the falsehood on each side. "That is the standpoint of philosophy," he writes, "that the content of faith takes refuge in the concept and through thought *(Denken)* is restored and justified."[5]

The third and certainly most important factor entering into the formation of Hegel's conception of philosophy as the ultimate form for the articulation of Absolute Spirit and hence as the standpoint encompassing the religious consciousness was his reconstruction of philosophy and the recovery of the metaphysical tradition in accordance with the requirements of speculative reason. The underlying belief of Hegel was that the truth of religion can be given adequate expression only if it is possible to recapture the ancient principle that "the order and connection of ideas is the same as the order and connection of things"—a principle demonstrated in his ontological logic—and yet at the same time to reconceive reason in such a way that full justice is done to the reality of Spirit as life, subjectivity, freedom, individuality and self-consciousness on many levels. Again, this ground has already been well charted; it is sufficient to note the central points as a prelude to a brief summary statement about where religion stands in the system purporting to express its intrinsic truth and at the same time the truth concerning Absolute Spirit in its self-related totality.

Hegel's recovery of metaphysics and his development of a positive reason capable of resolving the problems posed by the antinomies precisely because it has become dialectical in form, were accomplishments he achieved by uncovering the limitations of the metaphysics of both modern rationalism and of classical empiricism, together with his criticism of the more subtle empiricism represented by the Kantian transcendental philosophy. The metaphysics of modern rationalism, though correct in its concern to understand God, the human self, and the structure of the cosmos as an integral system, fell short because it trusted in abstract thought with its static and fixed predicates, its tendency to view the infinite and the finite as standing outside each other, and its capacity to distinguish what it had no power to unite in a living whole. This metaphysics was justified, in comparison with empiricism, because it acknowledged the reality of the proper infinities but it failed as the result of accepting an abstract conception of reason. Empiricism, although Hegel commended its demand for the concrete and its refusal to remain content with abstractions, nevertheless falls short because of its limitation of experience to the bounds of sense and its belief in the ultimacy of a form of thought whose chief merit is the capacity to analyze and to separate unaccompanied with a corresponding power to synthesize and unite.

Most important of the factors that led to Hegel's rehabilitation of speculative philosophy was his critique and transformation of the Kantian philosophy. The crucial point of this critique is to be found in Hegel's refusal to accept the validity of the transcendental approach and the idea of a preliminary knowing not put forward as such, or the position described by Hegel as "knowing before you know." It is an error to express this point by saying that Kant insisted on criticism while Hegel rejected it; not only did Hegel not reject criticism, he even commended Kant for proposing to inquire into the validity of the categories. The real issue between them concerns the manner in which the inquiry is to be carried out. For Hegel, the categories criticize themselves in the dynamic process of thought where they are engaged in the actual thinking of Being and thus reveal their meaning, scope, and adequacy in the actual articulation of the content. Kant, according to Hegel, was concerned instead to consider only the question of the subjectivity and objectivity of the categories and was forced to treat them, not in their concrete cognitive activity but rather as functions merely idling in the understanding. Hegel, moreover, was the first to point out the incipient dogmatism in the critical philosophy represented by Kant's having *opted* for the priority of understanding over reason so that, instead of assigning the limitation revealed in the antinomies and the total phenomenon of dialectic to understanding, Kant charged reason with the defect, retreated to the standpoint of understanding, and left reason with no more than a practical reach.

Hegel attained the all-important conception of a form of thought capable not only of distinguishing but also of uniting when he envisaged positive reason as a power that, far from eschewing dialectic, has the resources to overcome the dialectical oppositions. In short, for Hegel, reason becomes dialectical precisely because that is the very nature of becoming, life, spirit, and indeed of all reality. With this conception of reason in hand and the conviction that nothing can thwart its speculative advance, Hegel turned again to the interpretation of religion. His early position is now reversed; religion is no longer the ultimate source of reconciliation. On the contrary, it is the task of philosophy to exhibit the intelligibility of religion and express its truth in the conceptual mode. Although the forms of Art, Religion, and Philosophy are at one in relating man to the Absolute Spirit, it must not be supposed that this identity is more than something abstract because it does not express the essential differences involved. There is clearly an asymmetry in the order of the moments constituting the ultimate triad and, even if it is true that the Absolute Idea is present as a *whole* in each moment—something that cannot be said of any other triad— there is a crucial difference in the mode of expression which determines the asymmetry. Philosophy, and philosophy alone, attains knowledge of the universal, organic totality and, in the form of the Concept, articulates this knowledge in a fully adequate way. This is, however, no reciprocity because neither Art nor Religion is capable of apprehending the unique form in which Absolute Spirit expresses itself in Philosophy. Religion must stop short of Philosophy and that is Hegel's ultimate conclusion; it is not in any way qualified by the consideration that the content of both is the same. The implication is that religion, while it may indeed provide the content, does not *know* this content in its truth from its own standpoint. What this means concretely for the interpretation of religion is a matter far too enormous to be treated here, but perhaps one representative illustration will serve to show the consequences.

As was noted earlier on, I am determined to avoid the superficial and ill-informed view according to which Hegel simply construed religion out of rational, whole cloth to meet the demands of his system. Such a view is contradicted by the mass of phenomenological description presented by Hegel in his careful account of religious forms, and in this regard he fulfilled his own requirement that we allow the subject matter to reveal itself in its actuality without restrictions imposed by the special interests and biases of individual interpreters. There is absolutely nothing in Hegel's writings corresponding to any sort of personal or private opinion which might sarcastically be called "my view of religion!" Having said this, however, it will not do to ignore the underlying and more difficult problem posed in Hegel's ultimate solution, namely, that while Religion does indeed manifest itself in its Being and Essence, it remains for Philosophy to articulate it in its Truth. That is where the strain on religion becomes most evident; Hegel cannot let religion merely *be* in the end, precisely because it is a phase, no matter how important, in a more encompassing development that finds its culmination in philosophy. Consequently, he was forced to interpret the transitions in the dialectical development of religion in such a way as to bring out their truth, a truth, however, not uniquely determined by the reflective religious consciousness but only by the demands of Absolute Knowledge. The following illustration, chosen for the clarity with which it brings home the point, is taken from the *Lectures on the Philosophy of Religion* where Hegel is tracing the dialectic of the truth that the individual is free through his religious destiny and how this is related to the reconciliation of the religious community with the world beyond.

Freedom, understood by Hegel in this context as the relation of the individual to actuality such that subjectivity is "at home with itself," must be related to all cultural and historical forms if religion is to find its proper connections with the secular order. The first moment is the immediacy of asceticism where the spiritual stands apart from the world and remains within itself as if social life, art and science were without value. This moment is unsatisfactory because it is of the nature of Spirit "to develop and differentiate itself until it reaches the worldly sphere."[6] The second moment, far more complex, is manifested in the existence of sacred and secular side by side; this relation, unlike asceticism that rejects the world, implies that each side has value and that they must be related in some positive way. Religion, in the form of the ecclesiastical institution, proclaimed its sovereignty over the secular, which, however, remains in unreconciled form. Consequently, the worldly or unreconciled secularity, is taken into the church and the result is corruption and a form of life in which man is no longer free. In seeking to dominate, the church becomes secularized and Spirit is in contradiction with itself; man becomes involved in purely worldly interests and the sacred is set aside. The resolution of this tangled state of affairs is achieved in ethical life; the argument depends totally on Hegel's claim that the principle of freedom is the *sole* truth of reconciliation so that, having identified the substantial truth of the revealed religion as the freedom of reason, the problem of reconciliation is solved by the passage from the abstract form of this freedom to its concrete realization in ethical life. The divine, by breaking into actuality in the State, justifies the secular in and for itself because of its foundation in the divine will. In ethical life in the state religion and secular life are brought together.

The point of direct relevance to the foregoing is the extent to which Hegel simplified his problem by determining the principle of revealed religion in accordance with his speculative philosophy. He omits the negative side of the religious insight and fails to see that freedom also means the capacity of the being who is free to *misuse* that freedom in defiance of divine law, which is precisely why the forgiveness of Grace is necessary in the first place. If freedom in its wholly positive sense is made the basis of the secular, there inevitably develops that pride and self-sufficiency of both freedom and reason in the secular city which lead to a denial of the need for the reconciliation offered by the spiritual community. This is an exceptionally clear case of the strain placed upon the religious content when it receives its final articulation at the hands of Hegel's philosophy. He could, of course, reply that that content does not contain a clear and definitive *doctrine* of the relation between sacred and secular of the sort represented, for example, by a doctrine like the Trinity, and hence that the defining of the relations between the two is a legitimate philosophical task. That is a justifiable response, but it does not follow that the principle of freedom, said to be the *sole* truth of the reconciliation of the individual and God and also to serve as the basis for the reconciliation of secular and sacred, is adequately expressed from the religious standpoint when the positive side of the principle is emphasized and the negative factor omitted. The omission, moreover, is all the more significant in view of the fact that tensions between sacred and secular have most often been the result of a refusal on the part of the secular mind to acknowledge the truth of the religious insight into the ambiguity of freedom and its misdirection.

The interpretation just considered is thoroughly representative of Hegel's approach to the religious consciousness and reveals clearly what is bound to result from the total incorporation of religion within the bounds of an all-encompassing metaphysical system. There can be no question that Hegel's insight into the nature of religion generally and into the special claims of revealed religion provide a valuable source of illumination for religious intelligence committed to the enterprise of faith seeking understanding. In the end, however, the theoretical and speculative demand of reason triumphs over the distinctive stance of religion so that it becomes a subordinated phase in a more comprehensive process, a phase in which its being coincides entirely with its being understood. Knowledge supersedes love.

In turning now to Whitehead's treatment of religion in relation to metaphysics, it will be necessary to limit the discussion to the fundamental ideas articulated in *Religion in the Making*, a book which, as we are told in the Preface, was meant to represent the application to religion of the same train of thought used to elucidate science in *Science and the Modern World*. There is to be sure material in Whitehead's other writings which bears on our main theme and there has been, moreover, an extensive development of "process theology" inspired by Whitehead's philosophy which a more complete account would have to reckon with. Since, however, the primary emphasis must be on the interpretation of religion as an enduring historical form and on religious experience both in itself and in its contribution to metaphysics, most of what is essential for these purposes is found in *Religion in the Making*.[7]

Let me begin by modifying slightly a statement made at the beginning of this discussion concerning the autonomy accorded to religion by Whitehead's approach. In saying that, in comparison with Hegel, Whitehead could let religion *be*, I did not mean to imply that his own philosophy of organism and creativity plays no part in the interpretation of religion because it obviously does, especially in connection with the conception of God but also in connection with the ideas of value and creativity. It is rather that Whitehead acknowledged the autonomy of religion in its primary experiences, in what he calls its "intemediary representations" and finally in dogma, which he regarded as a form of self-understanding arising within the religious community. But most important, there is no hint in Whitehead's treatment that religion is a limited or inferior form of some other kind of truth that in the end surpasses it, nor is it seen as a phase among others in a more encompassing process of development.

The first question is, what did Whitehead take religion to be and to mean and how did he understand its historical development as manifest both in the progression of its own forms and in its mutual relations to philosophy and science within the total fabric of civilization? In answering the first part of this question, two considerations are paramount. There is, first, the close connection Whitehead envisaged between religion and individual *character* and, second, the all-too-well-known identification of religion with what the individual does with solitariness. As regards the first, the central point is the *transformatory* character of religious belief; the general truths of religion are not merely entertained or contemplated but are a force for "cleansing the inward parts."[8] Secondly, the connection of religion with solitariness is meant to express Whitehead's concern to focus on the ultimate fact of the individual alone for its own sake and at the same time to deny that religion is primarily a social fact.[9] The important fact about the solitariness—the famous passage is not without its cryptic side—is what the individual "does" with it as is suggested in the prior statement that "religion is the art and the theory of the internal life of man."[10] The "does" means how the individual becomes related to what is permanent in the nature of things or God. This relationship is said to pass through three stages—from God the void to God the enemy and finally to God the companion—and Whitehead describes the last stage as a "final satisfaction." The suggestion here of a progressive development invites us to interpret the four factors of religion—ritual, emotion, belief, rationalization—in a similar way since, we are told, only when the last two stages were reached did it become apparent that *solitariness* is "the heart of religious importance."[11] In view, however, of the central role played by religious communities throughout the history of religion, the question has been raised whether Whitehead's insistence on solitariness and the individual is not less the product of an historical analysis than it is a contribution of his own metaphysics. I believe that this is correct and that the claim about solitariness cannot be regarded simply as the result of a critical history.

On the other hand, however, Whitehead's idea of the importance of the individual alone and for itself is not entirely derivative from his metaphysics because what he had in mind was manifest in certain features of the development of Western religion. As anthropologists and historians of religion have pointed out, in many traditions the "we" language of the community takes precedence over the "I" language of the individual in the order both of time and importance. The point is well illustrated in the history of Hebraic religion where the radical emergence of individual consciousness took place only after the destruction of the Temple and, as recorded in the writings of Jeremiah, the question was asked whether God could visit his people *individually* in the *Diaspora*.

Jeremiah's answer was yes and helps to illuminate Whitehead's basic point. Since it is the character of the individual that is of the ultimate importance there must come a time in the development of communal religion when this fact is recognized and a new level of spiritual awareness is attained. As Whitehead's subsequent acknowledgment of the social dimension of religion shows, the issue is not a simple contrast or opposition between individual and communal but rather the achievement of a higher form of community embracing individuals whose ultimate value has come to be fully appreciated. Thus Whitehead can say, in accordance not only with his social metaphysics but with his conception of expression as well, that

> expression, and in particular expression by dogma, is the return from solitariness to society. There is no such thing as absolute solitariness. Each entity requires its environment. Thus man cannot seclude himself from society.[12]

I have dwelt on the preceding point at some length for at least two reasons. First, Whitehead's repeated emphasis on religion as solitariness and his basically negative view of communal religion have led to the belief that his position is sheer individualism. This, of course, is not so. In the second place, the recognition that Whitehead's evolutionary account of the development of religious forms is too sketchy and without sufficient documentation to be taken seriously as an historical explanation has prompted the view that his conception of what is essential in religion stems exclusively from his metaphysical position and has no historical roots. As against this view I am suggesting that Whitehead's basic conception of religion reflects both the value assigned to individual existence in his philosophical scheme and the historical facts about the emergence of individual consciousness over against a monolithic communal reality.

Since it was what he called *rational* religion that Whitehead was chiefly concerned to interpret and to relate to metaphysics, some attention must be devoted to the meaning of this particular form. To begin with, religion, having attained rational form in Whitehead's sense, has nothing to do with the natural religion or the religion within the limits of reason alone associated with the Enlightenment philosophers. For him rational religion is one whose beliefs and rituals have been so ordered as to fulfill the aim of providing a "coherent ordering of life"[13] including both thought and conduct. The prerequisites for the attainment of rational religion were the ability to handle general ideas accompanied by the development of a language with a sufficient fund of general terms to express these ideas and a literature to preserve and help to define them. It is clear that Whitehead was here thinking of what has been called, especially in connection with the Western religions, "religions of the Book" or traditions deriving their identity, inspiration, and endurance from sacred scriptures. More important, however, is the unique status assigned to rational religion; it is said to stand between abstract metaphysics on the one hand and particular principles that apply to some limited region of experience, on the other. As a result, religion becomes, in James' expressive phrase, a "double-barrelled affair," since, in selecting for its foundation a small portion of human experience, it becomes a specialized interest among others, but in insisting that the experience it selects should have universal validity, religion transcends particularity. Stating the point more formally, Whitehead claims that rational religion looks to the insight of special occasions for the concepts with which to elucidate all occasions; what was special in origin becomes universal in import. The outcome is a kind of "supernormal" metaphysics based on those insights of founders and prophets from which rational religion continues to draw its life.

Of great importance to rational religion is the development of a world-consciousness that goes beyond both a tribal and a social consciousness. Interestingly enough, the solitariness theme resurfaces at this point. Rational religion is responding, not to a tribe, ethnic group, or nation, but to the universe in an effort to attain the conception of an essential rightness in all things. To rise to the level of world-consciousness requires a detachment, "a disconnection from immediate surroundings"[14] which Whitehead associates with solitariness in search of something permanent and capable of interpreting the confusion of immediate detail. A model of this detachment Whitehead finds in the book of Job, where in his view the concern is neither with transforming society nor with expressing religious feelings but with the apprehension of general principles, and, in this particular case, with interpreting the contrast between a long standing dogma about the nature of God and the plight of Job.

Whitehead's general description of religious experience harks back once again to the fundamental character of solitariness and, while we are told that the three concepts ingredient in religion—the value of an individual itself; the value of the individuals for each other; the value of the objective world—occur together "in one moment of self-consciousness," we are also told that "the moment of religious consciousness *starts* from self-valuation."[15] It is difficult to avoid the conclusion that an ontological priority is assigned to the individual, especially if one adopts the view that Whitehead did not regard the communal religion that falls short of rational religion as religion in any genuine sense at all[16] but merely as a stage in its development. On this view, religion in the proper sense comes on the scene only when the value, freedom, and creativity of the individual have, as it were, been released and freed from the strictures of tribal religion. There is no question that this interpretation has a foundation in what Whitehead wrote, but, as was noted previously, criticism of communal religion must not be construed to mean rejection of the social principle. For, as Whitehead continues, the self-valuation at the start "broadens into the concept of the world as a realm of adjusted values"[17] which, of course, includes both the value of the individuals for each other and the value of the objective world itself. The religious quest of the individual, moreover, initiated by the question, "What, in the way of value, is the attainment of life?" issues in what Whitehead calls "world loyalty" or the merging of the individual claim by the solitary self with that of the objective universe. "The spirit," he writes, "at once surrenders itself to this universal claim and appropriates it for itself."[18] Life under the aegis of religious experience is conditioned by this formative principle, which is said to be not a dogma but an intuition of immediate occasions with respect to their success or failure in realizing the relevant ideal. Essential to any such appraisal is the permanent rightness of character in the nature of things which Whitehead takes to be the central deliverance of religious experience. And, in the name of universality and consensus, he maintains that such experience does *not* include the direct intuition of an individual or definite person. What is disclosed is the character of rightness such that the harmony in the actual world is derivative from conformity with this character.

In support of the contention that the intuition of an individual in religious experience is not universal, Whitehead cites the predominance of the impersonal mode in the religious traditions of Buddhism, Confucianism, and Hinduism and further claims that, as regards Christianity, belief in a personal God is a matter of inference and not intuition. I believe it would be generally admitted that Whitehead was justified in drawing this conclusion, even if the case of Christianity is more complex than he makes out. In the end it was the need to preserve the consensus with respect to religious experience that prompted Whitehead to insist on the concept of a rightness in the nature of things; the attempt to incorporate the intuition of a personal being would destroy the consensus and leave us without a discernment that can be universalized. His final comment on the deliverance of religious experience is that it discloses a type of character in things, not a form of words.

With the description of religious experience as a background the next consideration is Whitehead's understanding of the interplay between religion and metaphysics. Stated in the most general terms, his view is that rational religion must turn to metaphysics for the determination and clarification of its basic terms, while religion contributes "its own independent evidence"[19] to be used in the articulation of the categorial scheme. In setting forth these relations, Whitehead reflects both the historical facts about the interaction between religion and philosophy in Western civilization and his own conception of the connections between metaphysics and the particular dimensions of experience. Any attempt to express a doctrine of God will involve the use of such terms as "personal," "impersonal," "individual," "existence," etc. and, according to Whitehead, their meanings will depend on a metaphysical description of the universe. Religion, in its turn, affords the insight that human existence is more than a succession of bare facts, that it embraces a common world of valuations, purposes, successes and failures, joy and grief; religion, in short, tells us that there is a quality of life "beyond the mere fact of life" and contributes this quality "as an immortal fact to the order which informs the world."[20]

The foregoing general account of the interplay between religion and metaphysics has now to be supplemented by what is the most illuminating part of the entire discussion, namely, Whitehead's idea of offering a metaphysical description of the universe which is then to be compared with the content of religious experience. It is important to bear in mind that this description, although clearly in the same vein as the fully developed position set forth in *Process and Reality*, is, by comparison, no more than an outline. Under the circumstances, however, no attempt can be made to coordinate the two versions especially in view of the fact that even the outline must be trimmed of some details in order to elucidate the intended comparison between the metaphysical scheme and religious insight.

A metaphysical description, according to Whitehead, is subject to tests of accuracy—here he mentions only logical coherence, adequacy and exemplification—but, since it arises from a special field of interest, its confirmation requires exemplification in other fields of interest. The point is important because, insofar as religious insight is in accord with the metaphysical description, religion acquires the rational safeguard needed to contend with the intense emotions it elicits, while, on the other hand, metaphysics, in showing its exemplification in another domain of experience, receives its measure of confirmation.

While the entire analysis offered in the chapter, "Body and Spirit," is relevant for the outcome which is the confluence of the religious insight and the metaphysical vision, I must assume that the conceptual scheme is familiar and that it is sufficient to concentrate on what I take to be the most relevant for religion—God, the moral order, the purpose of God in the realization of value. To begin with, there is for Whitehead the actual world passing in time, or the all-inclusive universe, and the formative elements which are themselves not actual and passing. The latter are creativity or temporal passage to novelty, the ideal forms exemplified always according to a scale of relevance and God as the actual but non-temporal entity whereby the primal indeterminacy that attaches to creativity is, as Whitehead says, "transmuted into a determinate freedom."[21] I take this to mean that the actuality of God ensures that, with respect to every process and its outcome, it is not the case either that anything you please can eventuate or that only one thing can happen—in short, a rejection of both chaos and determinism.

Whitehead's further elucidation of the formative elements leads to the introduction of the occasions of actualization, creatures or epochal occasions in community, and the temporal, creative advance wherein the ingredience of God determines that there will be a definite *result* in the form of a limitation that is coincident with value. It is interesting to note in passing that Whitehead, in insisting on the necessity for a limitation and result, is pointing to what also concerned Hegel when he claimed that in becoming there must always be a result—something that has become—if we are not to be left with sheer becoming. For Whitehead it is the ingredience of God imposing "unchanged consistency of character" which directs the "boundless wealth of possibility in the realm of abstract form" to a determinate result.[22] At this point Whitehead poses a basic problem: if a complete determinism prevailed, the temporal world would indeed be self-consistent, but the demand that it be in conformity with the nature of God leads to the consequence that the evil in the world conforms to the nature of God, a conclusion no less to be avoided than the occurrence of evil itself. Although recognizing evil as positive but destructive, Whitehead laid great store by his view that evil is unstable and promotes its own destruction in contrast to good which is characterized by an inherent self-preservation. God, however, in being exempt from internal inconsistency is also exempt from evil as can be seen from Whitehead's claim that the order in the temporal world shows that its creativity is conditioned by the immanence of God, while the evil in the world indicates the presence of other formative elements not to be defined in terms applicable to God.

There, nevertheless, remains God's purpose which is the attainment of value; apart from God there would be no creatures because there would be no harmonious order. For, as Whitehead says, there is not an actual world which just happens to manifest order; on the contrary, an actual world requires an order to be at all, and, since there is such a world, the order follows. In maintaining that the ordering element is a necessity, Whitehead claims that he is extending the argument of Kant except that, unlike Kant, the order is in the cosmos and is essentially esthetic and embraces the moral order, both derivative from the immanence of God. The upshot of this part of the discussion is the return to the content of religious experience. "The order of the world," Whitehead writes, "is no accident"[23] and, he continues, "The religious insight is the grasp of this truth"—the order, value, beauty, the zest and peace of life, the containing of evil are all connected essentially because the universe exhibits a creativity with infinite freedom, forms with infinite possibilities, actualized through the ideal harmony which is God. Thus the route of religious experience and the way of metaphysical description meet in the mutual apprehension of a permanent rightness in the nature of things.

The final section of *Religion in the Making*, "Truth and Criticism," is concerned not so much with religious experience as such as with the implications of Whitehead's metaphysics for the doctrine of God. The account, though a highly condensed version of the philosophy of organism set forth in *Process and Reality*, is still too long to be summarized here and, in any case, the ground covered is well known. I shall, therefore, single out what I take to be the signal turns in the description as a prelude to making a concluding comment about the extent to which the process conception might be said to intrude upon the traditional Christian conception of God.

Since in Whitehead's theory of creativity, actuality, limitation, and value are closely intertwined, the crucial role of God is to provide "a measure of harmony in the ground" that ensures "rightness of limitation."[24] As Whitehead says, "Unlimited possibility and abstract creativity can procure nothing" without the limitation stemming from God "who is the ground antecedent to transition" and who includes all possibilities of physical value and thus can hold the ideal forms apart so as to produce "equal, conceptual realization of knowledge." Since, in Whitehead's happy phrase, God is *something decided*, God is limited by his goodness or harmony of valuation. Stated in other terms, God is "the one systematic, complete fact, which is the antecedent ground conditioning every creative act."[25] Thus apart from God there would be no actual world and apart from that world and its creativity there would be "no rational explanation of the ideal vision which constitutes God." God is not the world, "but the valuation of the world." Central to this entire conception is the emphasis Whitehead places on the reality of time, creative advance, and novelty. "The passage of time," he writes, "is the journey of the world towards the gathering of new ideas into actual fact."[26] The decay and physical wasting of the world is offset by the spiritual ascending order grounded in God who constantly passes into his next relation to the world with the increment of value preserved from what has gone before.

Earlier on I maintained that Whitehead, unlike Hegel in this respect, could allow full autonomy to religion, to let it be as it were, since rational religion and its doctrines do not represent a phase in a more encompassing development. It must be said, however, that the early response to Whitehead on the part of many theologians was one of uneasiness if not dismay at the thought that so much emphasis on time and becoming must result in what Tillich then called "changing God." A symposium at the annual meeting of the Metaphysical Society of America held some decades ago was devoted to the merits of "Being vs. Becoming" in relation to the doctrine of God; this proved to be a confrontation between Tillich and Maritain, who had joined forces in defense of Being, and Hartshorne, who was upholding the process view. In short, the standpoint of Whitehead and his followers was seen initially as revisionist and for two reasons. First, before the standpoint of process philosophy with its novel ideas and intricate language became better understood, the critics were convinced that it meant injecting time into God, a thought bound to be disturbing to those wedded to the conception of God as "pure actuality" or as the

One in whom "there is no shadow of turning." In the face of their uneasiness, they failed to see the deeper meaning of the attempt to discover the implications concerning the relations between God and the world which must follow from taking seriously the reality of time and its novel increment. The second, and closely related, reason prompting the initial response to Whitehead was, ironically enough, a failure on the part of some theologians to take into account a fundamental emphasis in the biblical tradition itself, namely, the idea of a *living* God and the large commitment running throughout the Bible to the reality of time, history, providential development, and individual creativity. Whatever the proper interpretation of this oversight may be, the fact remains that many theologians did not grapple with the important problem of considering what *difference* the reality of the historical increment both in individuals and in the cosmos at large would make to God. What I am suggesting is that, far from being a revisionist, Whitehead was laying the ground for the recovery of one of the distinctive beliefs of the Western religious tradition. In this sense he was helping the tradition to recover itself in its full dimensions, that is, helping it to be what it essentially is.

Notes

1. See Richard Kroner's Introduction to *Hegel's Early Theological Writings*, Tr. T. M. Knox (Chicago, 1948), pp. 1–66 and James Collins, *The Emergence of Philosophy of Religion* (New Haven, 1967), pp. 212–253.

2. This passage, in slightly different wording, is to be found in *Cur Deus Homo?* Book I, Ch. ii Translated by S. N. Deane, *Saint Anselm* (Chicago: Open Court, 1939), p. 179. Hegel, *Encyclopedia* (*Logic*) Trans. Wallace, Second Edition (Oxford, 1892), Sec. 77 (1) N. 1.

3. Throughout the *Encyclopedia* Hegel claims that philosophical thought must always find its substance in our ordinary experience of ourselves and the world and in the faith and thought of religion. Consequently, he invariably emphasized the implications of a principle, a category, a moment, a phase of development, for the conception of God and religious experience.

4. *Hegel's Lectures on the Philosophy of Religion*, Ed. and Tr. Rev. E. B. Spiers and J. B. Sanderson, 3 Vols. (London, 1895), III, pp. 138ff.

5. *Lectures on the Philosophy of Religion*, III, p. 145.

6. *Lectures on the Philosophy of Religion,* III, p. 137.

7. A. N. Whitehead, *Religion in the Making,* New York, 1926.

8. *Religion in the Making,* p. 15.

9. Whitehead, it appears, was uneasy about those theories of religion which exaggerated the social dimension and even suggested that, contrary to the belief that the Founder of a tradition also founds the community, the community as the primary fact functions as the "creator" of the Founder. It is also likely that Whitehead was echoing James and his claim that the social expression of religion is always something "second-hand."

10. *Religion in the Making,* p. 16.

11. *Religion in the Making,* p. 19.

12. *Religion in the Making,* p. 137; cf. "The topic of religion is individuality in community" p. 88.

13. *Religion in the Making,* p. 31.

14. *Religion in the Making,* p. 47.

15. *Religion in the Making,* p. 59, Italics not in the original.

16. This interpretation has been advanced by Donald A. Crosby in "Religion and Solitariness," *Explorations in Whitehead's Philosophy,* ed. Lewis Ford and George Kline (New York, 1983), p. 150.

17. *Religion in the Making,* p. 59.

18. *Religion in the Making,* p. 60.

19. *Religion in the Making,* p. 79.

20. *Religion in the Making,* p. 80.

21. *Religion in the Making,* p. 90.

22. *Religion in the Making,* p. 94.

23. *Religion in the Making*, p. 119.

24. *Religion in the Making*, p. 152.

25. *Religion in the Making*, p. 154.

26. *Religion in the Making*, p. 159.

Conclusion

George Allan
DICKINSON COLLEGE

The "Conning" of History

I shall argue two points. First, Hegel's profile of historical change, sketched in the introductory remarks to *The Philosophy of History*, is remarkably like the profile Whitehead developed a century later.[1] For both history is a process of clashing differences that constantly give rise to a reconciling new achievement and then the emergence of new differences. But, second: both Hegel and Whitehead wish to rescue from perishing the values inherent in this process. God is called upon to play this saving role. As a result, their philosophies are both rendered profoundly anti-historical.

I

Let me start by summarizing Hegel's views as they appear in *The Philosophy of History*. Those familiar with Whitehead's description of concrescent process will hear it reverberating as a harmonic overtone to the Hegelian claims.

The past, says Hegel, presents us with an unrelieved panorama of sin and suffering. Selfish passions and narrow purposes are everywhere ascendant; even the "finest exemplars of private virtue" act from essentially selfish motives. The result is inevitable: disagreement, violence, and immorality, leading to failed purposes, the death of accomplishment, the collapse of hope. What is true of individuals is all the more true of nations and civilizations. The ruins of Carthage, Palmyra, Persepolis, and Rome offer mute testimony to the narrow-visioned ways by which even values of the greatest importance are too soon sacrificed "to an infinite complication of trifling circumstances."

What is the past for us? A cacophony, a confusion of conflicting values that simultaneously demand our allegiance and threaten our survival. In Hegel's account of it, our reaction is deeply emotional and deeply negative. Our reaction might well be one of "moral embitterment," a jeremiad of condemnation at so much unnecessary loss. Or, in a more reflective mood, our reaction might be "disinterested sorrow" at the wasting of past glory. But in either case the basic feeling is of "the profoundest and most hopeless sadness, counterbalanced by no consolatory result."

Such powerfully negative emotions require relief. Our response is obvious. We withdraw into our own subjectivity, seeking the "quiet shore" of our private aims and interests, finding in them a refuge from the dolorous vistas provided by our inheritance. This self-indulgence is a balm that eases the pain of such endless public tragedy. But this is a counsel of despair, a form of fatalism. We have allowed our aspirations to be imprisoned by the past. Its givenness has circumscribed us. We have made a separate peace with human history, on terms that give us some momentary personal happiness but that do nothing to arrest the widespread and ongoing social decline.

This inward-turning response is what Hegel calls "natural death," for when an individual or a people succumb to the constraints imposed on them by their past they merely contribute to the enlargement of those negativities. If this reaction is reiterated from individual to individual, generation to generation, the result cannot but be a downward spiral ending in our own individual despair and our nation's dismemberment.

Hegel's antidote to historical entropy is to propose that we become aware of the positive reality lying behind all this apparent negativity. We are, says Hegel, to recognize the presence of a "universal principle," the ideal of human fulfillment in community, a concrete achievement that is self-sufficient, all encompassing, fully comprehending. This ideal, termed Spirit, is an active principle, realizing its abstract perfection in time, functioning as the final cause of historical change by the steady transformation of its ideality into the concretely actual.

From the perspective of any particular agent within history, there is thus an ideal for it which is not reducible to those already actualized by the world it is inheriting. Always a "higher, more comprehensive" aspiration presents itself, a new order of principle by means of which the limitations of the past can be transcended. In the absence of any awareness of Spirit, says Hegel, our achievements like the work of Chronos rise in splendor for a moment and then perish without a trace. But for those who grasp the world-historical significance implicit in the ideal of Spirit, their efforts will be like that of Zeus whose creations are centers of human community set firmly amid the abiding harmonies of universal order.

The empires and nations of the world perish, to be sure, but phoenix-like there rises from the dust of that destruction new forms, forms often better than the old: "exalted, glorified, a purer spirit." Historical loss is not an occasion for despair. The perishing of old achievement is the opportunity for the emergence of new efforts, ones that use the old as building blocks for something better. Thus runs Hegel's phenomenological account in *The Philosophy of History* regarding how human beings experience the past and respond to its significance. The account is startlingly similar to Whitehead's analysis of concrescence, as the following glosses on the Hegelian account make clear.

One. In this Hegelian profile, the past presents itself to the emerging subjectivities of the present as a plurality of unharmonized and perishing achievements. The occasions of the immediate past are available for the living present in the form of a swarm of specific, parochial realities, each in conflict with the others. The past is initially prehended by its successors as a problem.

Two. The very existence of this problem evokes subjective purpose. The past must be taken account of in a manner that requires the present subject to act, to make decisions, to solve the problem with which it is confronted. Thus present activity is a response to past achievement. The concrescence of a new world begins in the realization that something must be done about the old one.

Three. The past is always experienced emotionally, in terms of its felt relevance to the needs and desires of the experiencing subject. The form of its subjectivity, the specific passion it has for its own well-being, defines how each existing subject will deal with its heritage.

Four. Were this all, then history would be entropic. A new subject would seek as directly as possible to eliminate threats to its satisfaction by ignoring whatever is inconvenient, by narrowing its aspirations to some subset of the available opportunities. This would mean settling for less in the present than had been available in the past, a strategy that would carry succeeding generations to ever lesser levels of accomplishment.

Five. Fortunately this is in fact not the full truth about the world. At minimum, the entropic wasting away of things implies prior achievements of a higher order that must be accounted for. And in our planetary biosphere, especially in the regions of human activity, it is clear that natural transformations have been in the direction of increasingly self-conscious and significant forms of individuation and social order.

Six. God's abstract reality, the principle of perfection He timelessly is and exhibits, functions as the central element in this metaphysical counterforce to entropy. God's primordial presence, tailored to the peculiarities of a given context and perceived by its inhabitants from the perspective that context has defined, provides refreshment to the world. It provides an ideal which if taken as the subject's initial aim frees it from bondage to the limited options available through past imagination and accomplishment. Experience of the divine ideal permits the emergence of higher aspirations.

Seven. The existing subject works out its purposes as best it can, passionately pursuing ends which in minor ways involve creative departures for the past. Some modicum of satisfaction is obtained, although always far short of what the initial possibilities seemed to promise. When the individual at last perishes, it makes room for successors who are now in their turn perplexed by the seemingly insoluble difficulties which have come about as a result of such novel reconciliations to old conflicts. The past is once more a problem for the present.

II

So far so good. Here in both a Hegelian and a Whiteheadian mode we have an analysis of the structure of historical change. A dialectical interplay of perishing past and passionate present gives rise to human agents in time and to the cultures articulated by their mutual interactions. For Whitehead, an analysis of the process of concrescence, in conjunction with God's primordial nature functioning as a principle of concretion, seems sufficient to provide an adequate account of both natural and historical transformations. Similarly, Hegelian Spirit, functioning as a regulative principle only, provides a fully adequate account of time's arrow and the dynamics of Being.

But both of these philosophers have a longer agenda in mind. As Hegel says,

Our mode of treating the subject is in this aspect, a Theodicaea—a justification of the ways of God— . . . so that the ill that is found in the World may be comprehended, and the thinking Spirit reconciled with the fact of the existence of evil. [*Phil. of Hist.*, p. 15]

Hegel's "hypothesis" that Reason governs the world entails for him the further belief that its goodness will ultimately be triumphant, that the evil involved in human sorrow, loss and death can be explained. The ways of God are to be defended against the moral criticism implied in the spectacle of suffering humanity.

For Whitehead similarly, the perishing of all accomplishment in the moment of its prehension by the emerging future cannot be the final disposition of its value. Some larger appreciation is required, a cherishing that transforms even suffering into its relevance for enduring harmony. God is evoked for a purpose not strictly metaphysical:

The ultimate evil in the temporal world is deeper than any specific evil. It lies in the fact that the past fades, that time is a 'perpetual perishing'. . . . But there is no reason, of any ultimate metaphysical generality, why this should be the whole story. [PR 340]

Hegel has no hesitation in taking the first crucial step required by any journey into theodicy. He shifts the locus of intrinsic value away from the individual and locates it in the whole. Spirit becoming concrete is the good to be discerned amid the wreckages of time, and so the value of individual passion lies primarily in its contribution to such enlarged achievement. Hegel envisions the "vast altar of the earth" as a "slaughter bench" upon which individual passions are sacrificially offered for the propitiation of Spirit. God, being at first too abstract to provide the passional intensity needed for material transformation in time, requires the burnt offering of human selfishness in order—across the incense of its stinking flesh—to realize a transcendent perfection. We are not to attend to the particular tragedies. They are, after all, the consequence of selfish passions and so have their own reward. Our eye is to be upon the work of God as it comes to self-realization, the "glory of the Idea mirroring itself in the History of the World."

Whitehead is more hesitant, more sensitive to the particular tragedies. But in his cosmology as in Hegel's the intrinsic value of the individual subject perishes inexorbly as subject, its passionate effort to achieve completion a sacrifice for the sake of the future that succeeds it. Whatever the benefits may be of one occasion's brief life as objectified in the life of its equally brief successor occasions, the religious demands to which Whitehead succumbs is that human value have some sort of "ever-present, unfading importance," that though it perish yet shall it "live for evermore." This, argues Whitehead, means that God must be the direct and especial beneficiary of all accomplishments. As the "divine companion" that prehends all occasions in the moment of their completion, God develops in concreteness while the spindle of time plays out its skein of possibilities, His consequent nature translating the abstractions of the primordial nature into appropriate realization.

What the parochial occasions do parochially, the divine occasion does superbly. What perishes subjectively but is of value nonetheless lives on forever objectively, transfigured as an element in the complex everlasting harmony of the divine life. We struggle to fulfill our narrow aims, we feel sorrow or despair, joy or ecstasy, and then we die. What is ultimately important about this brief moment lies in its contribution to the deeper, wider enjoyment which is God's trans-historical reconciliation of the world's incompatibilities.

Thus for both Whitehead and Hegel an individual's value ultimately lies in the ends it serves. Each actual occasion, each historical individual, each world-historical people work out in some way the problems set them by the past. In doing so, if their efforts are informed by some sense however dim of the divine ideal, if their efforts are Zeusian and not merely Chronistic, the result will be that they have contributed to lifting up the world to a new level of integrative accomplishment. Whitehead's God may be more compassionate than the Hegelian Spirit, agonizing empathetically with our agony, but the fact remains that in the end we perish and God endures. Whitehead's God like Hegel's Spirit is the persisting beneficiary of the perpetual perishings of all persons and all peoples. We are, all of us, in the last analysis means for transforming abstract ideality into concrete actuality.

For Hegel the historical process is such that, at a given stage or epoch in the world's development, the reigning character of past accomplishment will have defined a checklist of problems and a palette of relevant possibilities, a contrast between is and ought that requires action and challenges individual passion to its realization. Eventually these problems find their proper resolution, the immediate carriers of the achievement pass over into the natural death of their complacency and a new grouping of the peoples arises, a new national spirit emerges, in whose eyes the values and aspirations of the past seem too confining.

This ascent of Spirit to full self-consciousness thus has, unavoidably, a geographic dimension. The "great Day's work" of Spirit begins, according to Hegel, in Asia and progresses ever westward as the centuries pass. The absolute East of Chinese culture is where the bright light of Spirit first bursts forth. Here historical individuation is still submerged in rigidly circumscribed institutional structures, the principle of Spirit but barely imprinted into the recalcitrance of Nature. But as each people spin out their perspective on this principle as fully as they can manage, their accomplishment becomes the basis for a new and less abstract grasp of Spirit. And so a new culture is bathed in light, one located in an ever more westerly terrain than its predecessor, until in the high noon of the Germanic world what was first glimpsed in the Eastern sunrise shines forth in maximal brilliance, Spirit now fully articulated in history as the sublime unity of individual freedom and social order.

The backwaters of history surround this island of grandeur in embarrassing profusion, however. The tropics and the polar regions are deemed by Hegel unfit places for self-consciousness to thrive, and the need for large landmasses excludes the whole of the southern hemisphere from consideration. America and perhaps Russia lie in the future and so are not the concern of a philosophy of history. Moreover, China first and each world-historical people thereafter have their brief moment on the stage decked out in the persona of Spirit. But for centuries before and forever after that hour of glory, they have no intrinsic meaning either. All these individual lives, these many passions pursuing selfish ends, thus lack even the relevance accorded sacrificial victims. Like the flowers of the field, they merely spring up and fade as a part of Nature, of Nature not come to self-consciousness or Nature truncated at some intermediate stage in its journey to full realization as Spirit.

And so for Hegel humanity is for the most part excluded from Spirit's saving Work. On the altar of history a few are sacrificed that God might be born, but most perish having served no higher purpose. Perhaps a very few, an elect, are transfigured, those Germanic folk who have managed to incorporate divinity fully in the webwork of their cultural existence as a people. But clearly the justification of God's ways has in Hegel's philosophy led to the repudiation of individual human beings in their individual, idiosyncratic particularity. We are left with the edifying vision of eternal Spirit, now concrete rather than merely abstract, its implicit perfection now made explicit. History and human suffering, having been catalyst and conductor for this transformation, disappear. What always was now is, the circle of Spirit fully revealed in its timeless perfection.

Whitehead was never able to embrace explicitly this Hegelian notion of historical progress. The divine ideal for each occasion, says Whitehead, is that it maximize the intensity of satisfaction available for it under the given conditions it has inherited. This as such carries with it no progressivist implication. But if the world does not progress, at least God does. The consequent nature of God is like a snowball, rolling up past experience into itself, becoming ever more complex and profound in its concrete unification of that inheritance. In Hartshorne's phrase, God has relative perfection. He is a self-surpassing perfection that in each new moment of the world's history becomes more than He was before, qualitatively more: more intensely a harmony of the enormous diversity of all inherited experience.

If the consequent nature of God thus progresses, and if that nature is itself a lure for the aspirations and efforts of the creatures, then perhaps a Whiteheadian ideal would be the eschatological apotheosis of the world into a cosmos without conflict, the parallel in the philosophy of organism to the Hegelian ideal of the concrete universal. But even if this be impossible, if the ideal is regulative but not constitutive of history, the divine self-surpassing apotheosis in the form of the consequent nature is real enough. No wonder some contemporary Whiteheadians would like God's prehension of an actual occasion to involve subjective as well as objective dimensions. For them God would be the Kingdom of God in which all creatures are subjectively immortal, all tears wiped dry, all conflict harmonized. Time and history are the arena making possible this incremental growth in God's concreteness; but the only true value, the value that endures, is God. Time and history endure only so far as they are comprehended within the divine concrescence.

III

Both Hegel and Whitehead thus turn out to be religious mystics. This is an ironic turn of events, to be sure. Each philosopher trumpets the centrality of time, the primacy of Becoming, and the importance of history. Each sketches surprisingly similar epochal theories of temporal change, theories able to account for the antientropic character of organic life on Earth and for progress in human history. By giving these theories a fully metaphysical interpretation, they have given us the two most distinctive philosophic expressions of post-Enlightenment sensibility. Western thought from the Greeks to Kant is plagued by viciously incoherent dualisms: time and eternity, the perishing material body and the transcendent rational mind. Hegel and Whitehead each offer a way to overcome this bifurcation by making temporality the fundamental category for metaphysics and relegating timelessness to one of its abstract elements.

But their dread of time and of history, their failure to shake off the deepest emotions of the tradition they sought to overcome, disclose themselves in the need each has to secure human accomplishment in some reality immune to the ravagings of time. God is assigned this salvific role. Traditional religious convictions insist that despite the world's perishings God endures. Hegel and Whitehead go one step further. Because of the world's perishings, they argue, God flourishes. But this means that time is an instrument for divine development, a necessary but not ultimate reality. Human reality has ultimacy only insofar as it is taken up into divine reality. What is essential is therefore whatever is God, whatever becomes one with God. What is not so transfigured perishes and is thus unessential, of apparent but not real significance. Yet this is precisely transcendental mysticism. What seems *sub specie temporalis* to be vital and fundamental, the desires of finite individuals, the yearnings of the creatures throughout the cosmos, becomes *sub specie divinitatis* transitional and unessential.

Hegel and Whitehead need to be rescued from this betrayal of their deepest metaphysical vision. Time, process, becoming, and the structures it grounds, must be reinstated as fundamental reality. We need Hegel and Whitehead, purged of their transcendental mysticism, to help us understand that all value is the work of liberty, of choices made amid the flux of time, choices unavoidably involving loss and resulting in accomplishments which can endure only across further choices that necessitate further losses. We need to realize that created value is always and irredeemably incomplete, but that it is always unique. Its value is that it is unique, the result of a freedom that cannot be fully anticipated nor replicated. Created value is valuable because it is partial, inessential, brief. Finitude is the price we pay in order to find for a fleeting moment the precious joy of real accomplishment, definiteness wrested from the indefinite.

To take history seriously this sense of value must be affirmed against the illusions of transcendent value. Hegel and Whitehead have given us the metaphysical tools for constructing just such an understanding of temporal reality and real value. But history can only be grasped for what it truly is if the notion of God as hidden savior is repudiated as a false concept. The dignity and creative power of human suffering, of the suffering of the whole creation, must be understood as being the sole agency for the fleeting achievements that comprise our world.

Notes

1. G. W. F. Hegel, *The Philosophy of History*, tr. J. Sibree (New York: Dover Publications, 1956), Section III of the Introduction, especially pp. 17–27, 72–79; Alfred North Whitehead, *Process and Reality*, ed. D. Griffin and D. Sherburne (New York: The Free Press, 1978), Parts I and V.

Index

Absolute, 41–43
Absolute Idea, 156–159, 288, 295
Absolute Knowledge, 110–111
Absolute Spirit, 23–27, 195–196, 200–203, 240, 249–252, 259–262, 286, 288, 291–293, 295. *See also* Geist, Spirit
Adventures of Ideas (Whitehead), 8, 31, 167, 174
Alber, Verlag Karl, 6
Appetite, 191–200
Aquinas, St. Thomas, 260, 265
Aristotle, 42, 45–47, 65, 70, 170–172, 174–177, 222–223, 240
  Metaphysics, 45, 49, 222
Art, 239–252
Augustine, St., 168
Autonomy, 222–223, 228–229, 235

Bacon, Francis, 172
Basso, Sebastian, 168
Bohm, David, 10
Bradley, Francis Herbert, 5, 26, 29, 31–32
  Logic, 123
Burbidge, John, 140

Cassirer, Ernest, 40
Christianity, 114–116, 286–291
Collingwood, R. G., 3, 17
Collins, James, 288
The Concept of Nature (Whitehead), 18, 155, 167
Consciousness, 186–203, 207, 211, 227
Contrast, 212–214

Descartes, René, 30, 32, 46–47, 167–173, 178–180

Dialectic, 18–19, 23, 72, 79, 80, 140–142
Diethey, Whilhelm, 7
Dubos, René, 10

Einstein, Albert, 159
Encyclopedia (Hegel), 62, 73, 187, 290, 291
Epistemology, 32, 34–35
Eternal objects, 21–22

Fichte, Johann Gottlieb, 31, 187–191
Findlay, J. N., 6
The Function of Reason (Whitehead), 8

Geist, 8, 23, 91–94, 134–135, 141, 214. *See also* Absolute Spirit, Spirit
Gilmour, John C., 248
God, 97–99, 109–117, 156, 163–165, 257–265, 274–277, 280–281, 285–286, 297–299, 302–307, 313–322
Goodman, Nelson, 240
Green, T. H., 26

Harris, Errol, 143, 147
Hartmann, Klaus, 142
Hartshorne, Prof. Charles, 6
Harvard University, 155
Hegel Societies, 6
Heidegger, Martin, 29
Heisenberg, Werner, 10
Henrich, Dieter, 121
History, 313–322
Hölderlin, Friedrich, 40, 239–240
Hume, David, 30, 32, 178

324 Index

Idealism, 4, 26–27, 29–38. *See also* Realism
An Inquiry Concerning the Principles of Natural Knowledge (Whitehead), 167

Jacobi, Friedrich, Heinrich
   Letters on Spinoza, 40
James, William
   Varieties of Religious Experience, 285
Jung, Walter, 142

Kambartel, Friedrich, 124
Kant, Immanuel, 23, 29–37, 39, 45, 65–66, 86–87, 126–127, 133, 178–180, 187–191, 223–225, 240, 294
   Critique of Pure Reason, 34
Kepler, Johann, 160
Kroner, Richard, 288, 290
Kuhn, Thomas, 18

Labarriere, Pierre-Jean, 112
Lauer, Quentin, 88
Lectures on Aesthetics (Hegel), 242
Lectures on the History of Philosophy (Hegel), 43
Lectures on the Philosophy of Religion (Hegel), 291, 296
Leibniz, Gottfried Wilhelm, Baron von, 30, 45–46, 170, 173
Lesser Logic (Hegel), 92
Locke, John, 178
Logic, Metaphysics and Philosophy of Nature (Hegel), 42
Lowe, Victor, 4
Lucas, George, 145

Marx, Karl, 29
Marxism, 3
Mathematics, 124–126, 134
Metaphysics, 63–69, 76, 109, 181–182, 272–273, 303–304
Merleau-Ponty, Maurice, 113
Mill, John Stuart, 223–225, 235
Modes of Thought (Whitehead), 167

Moore, G. E., 4
Morality, 219–236

Narrative. *See* Story
Nature, 26–27, 156–66, 178–182
Nature of Life (Whitehead), 167
Naturphilosophie (Hegel), 8, 155
Negativity, 19–20
Negation, 208–214
Neoplatonism, 167–181
Newton, Sir Isaac, 46, 160

Ontology, 69–75, 133–147
Organic wholes, 61–63, 194. *See also* Organism
The Organisation of Thought (Whitehead), 125
Organism, 135. *See also* Organic wholes

Parmentier, Alix, 6
Peirce, Charles, 100, 240
Phenomenology of Spirit (Hegel), 42, 62, 110, 186–203, 232
Philosophy of History (Hegel), 93, 242, 313, 315
Philosophy of Subjective Spirit (Hegel), 242
Plato, 30, 39, 156, 179, 221–223, 230, 240
   Republic, 223
Platonism, Hegelian, 157–159
Plotinus, 168
Popper, Karl, 5
Prigogine, Ilya, 10
Principles of Natural Knowledge (Whitehead), 155
Process and Reality (Whitehead), 4, 19, 21, 26, 29, 31, 46, 47, 62, 64–65, 80, 111, 121, 135, 155, 167, 171, 173, 207, 213, 229, 303, 305
Process philosophy, 18, 61–62, 74

Realism, 26–27, 33–36
Reality, 49, 193–198

Reason, 221–222, 231, 234
Religion, 5, 110–117, 285–307
Religion in the Making (Whitehead), 285, 298, 305
Rorty, Richard, 10
Royce, Josiah, 26
Russell, Bertrand, 4, 26

Schaper, Eva, 246–247
Schelling, Friedrich Wilhelm Joseph, 31, 40–41, 187–191, 239–240
Science, 110–117
Science and the Modern World (Whitehead), 21, 80–81, 116, 167, 172, 298
Science of Logic (Hegel), 43, 62, 73, 193, 290
Sherburne, Donald W., 246–248
Skepticism, 34–35
Smith, John, 136, 147
Spinoza, Benedict de, 20, 24, 39–50, 133, 142, 208–211
  philosophy of One Substance, 39–41, 44–45, 209–211
Spirit, 243, 314–319. *See also* Absolute Spirit, *Geist*

The Spirit of Christianity and its Fate (Hegel), 288
Stace, Walter
  Philosophy of Hegel, 88
Story, 268–281
Superject, 48
Symbolism: Its Meaning and Effect (Whitehead), 244
Symbols, aesthetic, 239–252
Systematic philosophy, 101–104

Taylor, Charles, 6, 17, 247–248
Teleological scheme, 61–63, 78
Theism, classical, 257–265
Theology. *See* Religion
Time theory, 67–68, 73–74, 79
Tolstoy, Leo, 240
Totality, 86–104

Universal theory, 121–130

Vlastos, Gregory, 3, 141–142

Wallace, William, 145–146
Wiehl, Reiner, 6, 124
Wordsworth, William, 239
Wyman, Mary, 239

www.ingramcontent.com/pod-product-compliance
Ingram Content Group UK Ltd.
Pitfield, Milton Keynes, MK11 3LW, UK
UKHW041915140426
52171PUK00013B/170